the secret peace

Exposing the Positive Trend of World Events

Jesse Richards

Book & Ladder Press

New York

BOOK & LADDER PRESS
346 E. 19th st. 2C
New York, New York 10003
www.bookandladder.com

ISBN 978-0-9843695-0-8

FIRST EDITION
2009913496

Every reasonable attempt has been made to identify owners of copyright.
Errors or omissions will be corrected in future editions.

Printed in the United States of America.
This book is printed on acid-free paper.

CONTENTS

LIST OF FIGURES

for Rachel, my source of peace

"I believe, sincerely,
as soon as people want peace ... they will have it.
The only trouble is, they're not aware that they can get it."

—John Lennon

INTRODUCTION

Getting Better All the Time

In 1206, the year Genghis Khan united the Mongol and Turkic tribes of Central Asia to form the Mongol Empire, he lived in a *yurt*, a portable circular tent. At night, the yurt was very dark and cold. Fire had to be used judiciously, and was not very effective at providing either light or heat. Although Genghis Khan was used to the smell of unbathed warriors and horses, the stench would most likely have made us nauseous.

For all his power, Genghis Khan did not have indoor plumbing. He had to wait for the right season to eat certain foods, and he had a smaller menu selection than we have available in restaurants today. When his sons traveled to distant countries for a battle campaign, he was unable to communicate with them for months. Violence flourished among the tribes of the Old World both before and after Genghis Khan united them. No slight went unavenged by a family or tribe. Genghis Khan's tribesmen didn't know how to weave cloth, cast metal, or bake bread. Instead, they took what they needed from their conquered neighbors.[1]

Eight hundred years later, Tom Robinson, 48 years old, teaches accounting classes about financial statement analysis and valuation. Robinson is an associate professor of accounting at the University of Miami, and he also writes a blog of investment and accounting-related news. Robinson is blessed to live in a developed country at the beginning of the twenty-first century. Like most people, he probably takes a lot of modern conveniences for granted: refrigeration, vaccinations, air conditioning, education, and a lack of violence in his day-to-day life.

Genghis Khan, on the other hand, received no schooling and was captured and enslaved by a rival clan as a child, though he eventually escaped. He also killed his own older half-brother. In 1162, when he was born (with the much less fearful name Temüjin Borjigin), few civilizations had any knowledge of the world beyond their immediate neighbors. Few people in China knew Europe existed, and vice versa.[2] By the end of his life, Genghis Khan ruled over more than twice as much land as any man in history and did so ferociously. As a result of warfare and conquest, the Mongols ended up fostering communication and knowledge between the lands they conquered. Genghis Khan presided over a multicultural society that de-emphasized ethnicity and, to some extent, fostered religious tolerance.[3] Nevertheless, the world of the thirteenth century was indescribably brutal.

Nearly a millennium later sits Robinson, the accounting professor. A moderate Republican, Robinson has been married to his wife Linda for 25 years, though they have no children. Genghis Khan had four sons with his primary wife, Borte, and most likely hundreds of other offspring. Robinson has a bachelor's degree in economics from the University of Pennsylvania and a master's degree and doctorate from Case Western Reserve University. He's a certified public accountant, a certified financial planner, and a chartered financial analyst.[4] But are those titles a match for the Lord of the Steppes, Father of the Yuan Dynasty, the khagan of his time, Genghis Khan?

"I'm not sure we have too many similarities," understates Robinson. "I obviously haven't conquered any countries, and though I've headed up accounting groups, I've done nothing as big as Genghis Khan."[5]

It's safe to say that none of Genghis Khan's descendants killed as many people as he did. But how many of Genghis's millions of descendents alive today have killed even a single man? In his day, everyone was familiar with bloodshed. Not only that, but people around the world were so malnourished that they were shorter, unhealthily thin, and had low resistance to disease. Today, even factoring in the scourge of poverty and AIDS, the world's average life expectancy is 64 years for men and 68 years for women.[6] Those ages were ancient by the standards of the Mongol Empire, when a life expectancy of 30 years was generous. That number was partially due to the more than 25 percent of babies that died in their first year of life—an expected number for most places in the world until about a century ago.[7] The ancient Mongols' literacy rate was essentially zero, while today the world's average is a surprising 77 percent for women and 87 percent for men.[8]

Even the most cynical among us would have to admit that we've come a long way in eight centuries. But just how far? Enough to shock Genghis Khan? I imagine he would be mortified to discover that his legacy is ... investment-blogging economist Tom Robinson. Yes, Robinson is the first man outside of Asia to trace his ancestry back to the great Genghis Khan. He could be Genghis Khan's great-grandson, some 40 generations removed. "I think I do have a certain number of administrative skills," Robinson explained, though he noted, "I haven't done any conquering, per se."[9] The two of them are such polar opposites you might envision them starring as roommates on a TV sitcom or maybe as mismatched partners in a buddy-cop movie, with Robinson teaching the Great Khan how to use "per se" in a sentence.

I think Robinson's story is an ideal metaphor for the concept of an evolving society in which history moves from violence to peace, from ignorance to education, from exclusion to equality. Despite all of Genghis Khan's belligerent power, who among us would choose to take his place, rather than live with the improved health, education, and conveniences of domestic modern life? Would you rather sleep on the ground in a *yurt* with no indoor plumbing or in a soft bed with fresh food, cold drinks, and a television nearby?

The story of Genghis Khan and his mild-mannered descendent demonstrates the hidden diversity, and thus unity, of us all. How much conflict might be averted if more people were to uncover a mixed cultural ancestry? Genghis Khan and Tom Robinson can help us visualize the calming influence of centuries of progress. Their story shows that human nature is not intrinsically aggressive, but that violence used to be only a necessity for survival. The accomplishments of the Mongols and other ancient cultures are seeds bearing fruit today. We have reached a time when aggression no longer needs to be a defining trait of humanity—a time of peace. If we want it.

Pessimism is easy to come by in these times. But positive stories litter the pages of our news daily. These snippets of information lie buried behind the blaring headlines of war and poverty. They are clues pointing toward a grand secret: we, as a global culture, are moving in a discernible direction—a positive direction. World events are not random, and eventual world peace is not just possible but probable. The world is in better shape than we think, and peace is on its way. But the inevitability of peace is only half the good news. The other half of the secret is that for much of the world, peace is already here.

By any standards of history, the majority of our civilization glows with peace. We've come a long way in just a millennium. Seeds to our partly-peaceful world were dropped into the furrows of many past centuries. The bulk of our progress, however, was realized in the twentieth century. The process of advancing world peace really started to emerge after World War I, encouraged by Woodrow Wilson's Fourteen Points and the League of Nations, the first attempt at a global body designed to avert wars. Global peace and unity seemed gone for good during World War II, but received a surprising boost at its end with the writing of the Universal Declaration of Human Rights and the founding of the United Nations in 1945. The third massive push toward global unity occurred with the dissolution of the Soviet Union and the emancipation of Eastern Europe in 1991. The past two decades have been marked by many formerly underdeveloped or war-torn countries clamoring for democracy and equal participation in the world economy. We haven't seen the "End of History," as Francis Fukuyama put it; we still have a long way to go.[10] But the world is now on an irreversible track to peace. Seeds that took centuries to take root are finally sprouting all at once—today.

This overarching trend toward peace would seem obvious to people of Genghis Khan's time if they were to hop into time machines and vacation in our world. To them, present conditions would look shockingly peaceful. At least if they were to land in any developed country, they would stop dead in their tracks, mouths agape, seeing a society more at peace than they could have imagined.

Just consider food, for example. When it comes to food, the developed world is a veritable utopia. My grandmother lived in London until she married my grandfather, a U.S. serviceman, during his tour in Europe in World War II. When she went food shopping for the first time upon moving to the United States, she walked into the local grocery store and was shocked. Aisles of food stretched as far as her eyes could see. After living through the horror and short-ages of the London Blitz, she cried when she saw so much food on our shelves. (Imagine if she had seen our "world-class" supermarkets now, over 60 years later!) Surely, this is how most people throughout human history, slaves to drudg-ery and eking a living off the land, would feel in the same situation. Without diminishing the plight of the millions of people still starving in developing countries, it's remarkable that today a huge swath of the world's population is able to eat whatever kind of food they want, at any time.

Recently, in *The Progress Paradox,* Gregg Easterbrook reported that life in America is getting better for nearly everyone, despite people's perennial com-plaints.[11] But even with today's roller-coaster economic news, it's not difficult to see that most Americans are still well-off by the standards of history. The bigger news is what's going on in the rest of the world. Vast swaths of our world have already reached a relative peace. Many developed countries—Australia, Canada, Japan, and European countries, for example—are doing better than the United States in categories such as healthcare and decreasing crime. The rest of the world—the developing world of Africa, Asia, and the Americas—is growing toward peace as well, through fits and starts, but at a remarkable pace. Most amazingly, China and India, which together hold half the world's people, have lifted millions of their citizens out of the worst poverty.[12]

Let's step back and look at the big picture of what we have accomplished. Each of the following achievements was inconceivable to our ancestors 200 years ago. Most were unthinkable 100 years ago, and some, such as the fall of communism, would have seemed preposterous even 30 years ago.

1. We have near-eradicated some of the worst plagues in human history: smallpox, leprosy, polio. We now have vaccines, treatments, and cures for

hundreds of other diseases and illnesses. Every day, child mortality rates get a little lower and the average life expectancy gets a little higher.

2. Slavery and child labor, though still dire issues, are illegal in every country and universally condemned. Child labor has plummeted worldwide in recent decades.

3. Having once been the system of government for 36 nations, communism completely collapsed in Europe and has declined globally as an influential political theory. North Korea and Cuba remain holdouts, but the more common brand of communism that remains, in China, Vietnam, and Laos, would be barely recognizable to Stalin or Mao because it is so liberalized.

4. Though far from perfect, the equality of women and men is established as the de facto standard in every arena in every developed country: business, society, education, the arts, government. While some parts of the world are far from these goals, barely a handful of countries do not at least pay lip service to gender equality. In some countries, women make up half of the parliament, half of the workforce, and over half of the college graduates.[13]

5. Inter-state conflicts between major global powers remain incredibly unlikely, thanks to both nuclear détente and interconnected world trade.

6. We have seen the collapse of the Austro-Hungarian Empire, the Ottoman Empire, the colonial empires of Britain, France, Spain, Holland, and Belgium, the Napoleonic Empire, Hitler's Reich, and the Soviet Union.[14] The age of empires and colonialism has ended, and self-determination in forming independent countries is a right achieved, to varying degrees, by most people on Earth.

7. The majority of the world's countries have some form of democracy, even if it is limited. The remaining true monarchs and dictators can be counted on two hands: Togo, North Korea, Burma, Sudan, Turkmenistan, Zimbabwe, Belarus, and Cuba, to name some. Even countries such as Iran and Saudi Arabia claim democratic trappings, even if these are so far laughable.

8. Basic education and literacy have spread faster than ever expected. The total world literacy rate rose from 63 percent in 1970 to 83 percent in 2005.[15]

9. Technology has brought us all closer together, especially in the fields of transportation and communication. With these innovations, world trade has become increasingly interdependent and dynamic. With the Internet, communication and the arts are reaching heights of creativity and individual empowerment never before seen in history.

10. Not everyone has to be a farmer today. This might seem obvious, but remember that before the twentieth century, the vast majority of humanity labored in the fields. In America today, only three percent of our population is employed in agriculture.[16] Thomas Jefferson envisioned the ideal American citizen as a "gentleman farmer," but centuries of agricultural advancements allow us to specialize in a million other jobs that are less physically punishing and better-suited to our individuality.

11. The world has drastically reduced its poverty rate, especially in the last few decades, with India, China, and other Asian nations pulling themselves out of poverty at lightning speed. In 1820, less than five percent of the world's population was in their own time period's middle class. Today, 50 percent of the world is—even with a population seven times larger.[17]

12. Finally, an accomplishment that we have taken a little more for granted in the last decade is the fact that we haven't blown up the world in a nuclear holocaust. For a while during the Cold War, no one thought the human race would make it to the twenty-first century. While nuclear terrorism remains a threat, the chances of an all-out nuclear war are slim.

The 12 achievements above are some of the biggest triumphs of humanity's recent past, but what we are accomplishing today may well dwarf them. The items above aren't secrets, but that's the problem: they're so obvious we take them for granted. It's easy to get caught up in daily minutiae and forget these big-picture accomplishments. But realizing the positive direction in which society is flowing places everything we do in a brighter context. To say the world is approaching peace is not to encourage us to rest on our laurels. Rather, my hope is that by seeing how much humanity has accomplished, we can be inspired to achieve even more. A global peace is almost upon us—we just need a final effort to reach out and grab it. By studying these under-the-radar trends, and why they are happening, we can discover how to help speed up the process. The areas of the world that have reached relative peace can learn how to spread it. By pointing out the positive interconnectedness of seemingly disparate world events, we can see the bigger picture of the world's increasing unity, and help guide it along the path to peace.

PART ONE

The Reasons

1

HOPE

Why We Are Pessimists

W hat if I were to tell you that there was a news story so big and so implausible that no one could see it? What if your morning newspaper skipped it, the evening news missed it, and your afternoon Internet surfing didn't unearth it? Most importantly, what if this story held one of the best-kept secrets in history?

What's your reaction to that scenario? If you are an optimist, you may assume that the story is going to be exciting and feel as if you can't wait to hear the good news. But some people are more skeptical. You might find the concept intriguing and want to hear more, yet have your doubts. Or, if you tend to be cynical, you'll most likely dismiss it. How could that big a story exist and remain hidden? If the story is real, how terrible could that news be? Probably something akin to global warming or the health risks of trans fats; better not to even know.

The concept of the secret peace is of a global civilization progressing from ignorance and violence to a world of peace—and that many parts of the world already enjoy a relative peace. I've heard lots of reactions to this big, "implausible" story, and most of them are skeptical. If you're an optimist, like I am, you've probably lost arguments to glass-half-empty friends and sarcastic coworkers. Hardened cynics picture optimists as clueless fools running blissfully through fields of daisies, wearing John Lennon glasses and waiting for it to rain Skittles. And maybe they're right … maybe being confident about the future is unrealistic. After all, you don't have any concrete reason for being an optimist, do you? This is particularly true if you're an American—because right now, a record 81 percent of Americans say the nation is headed "on the wrong track."[1] As I write this, the country is in a recession, swine flu may become pandemic, and the consequences of global warming are looming. The price of oil is roller-coaster unpredictable, and so is the price of food, worldwide. Our armed forces are still mired down in Afghanistan and Iraq. It's pretty clear that everything's in dire straits. "You only have to open the newspaper to see that," as they say.

So, let's open the newspaper right now. Let's call their bluff and find out if the leading headlines are as negative as everyone assumes. I don't have a newspaper handy, so let's just launch CNN.com and see what the lead article is today: "Elephant Dies at Los Angeles Zoo," followed by the report, "Gita, 48, was found sitting down when keepers went to her yard Saturday morning. …"[2]

OK, that news flash is kind of negative but it doesn't really prove my point. I think we can do better. This time let's check out the *New York Times* online. There we arrive at the headline "Hamas Fires Rockets into Israel, Ending 16-Month Truce." This is followed by the report, "Hamas fired the rockets after seven Palestinians were killed on a Gaza beach by errant Israeli shell. …"[3]

Ah, yes: Israel/Palestine. The perennial argument-stopper. "When there's peace in the Middle East" has become the current equivalent of "When pigs fly." So, we've found what we expected to: terrible news. We should note that while the news may be overwhelmingly negative, the media does seem to be peppered with daily feel-good stories to keep readers or viewers from growing entirely despondent. Television news particularly excels at this. "Sure, there's a war in Sri Lanka, but look! A puppy just saved a parakeet from a burning house! And then the parakeet flew back in and saved the kitten!" or "Never mind that he should be busy governing, let's watch the mayor as he reads to Mrs. Richards's fifth grade class!" But no one is really fooled by these half-hearted concessions to cheerfulness. The bad news drones on.

Bombarded by negative news coverage, we become disillusioned and believe the world is getting worse. Our generation seems just as unhappy, just as afraid, just as pessimistic as our parents or grandparents during the Great Depression—if not more so. At least they could slow down and savor their bad news. Since change—in communications, technology, politics, fashion, health—builds on itself, everything happens exponentially faster and faster now. It's easy to feel overwhelmed. As a result, we develop a negative mindset and consequently begin to perceive even more bad news, creating a self-fulfilling feedback loop. Our brains are wired to worry, because it's a useful survival skill. Ironically, worrying and focusing on negative issues provides very effective motivation for us to try to improve our lives, a positive effect. But, that positive effect doesn't reach our frazzled minds, flooded with depressing news.

But what if all the news is *wrong*? Okay, "wrong" is too strong a word. I'm not referring to the truthfulness of individual stories; they are for the most part factual. Mass media is not inherently as corrupt or manipulative or biased as politicians would have you believe. Instead, maybe the overall tone is erroneous. The unstated message of the news media seems to be, "The world is a random place. Evil things happen when you least expect them. And they keep happening, over and over. History repeats itself. Yesterday we showed you a bus crash, a spelling bee champ, and an attack on our troops in Afghanistan. Today we'll show you a car crash, a Little League winner, and an attack on our troops in Iraq. We're filling you with this information, but we all know it doesn't add up to anything meaningful."

SENSATIONALISM AND BIAS IN THE MEDIA

The idea to write this book first occurred to me years ago, when I realized that the doomsday tone of news coverage had no exact correlation with the overall state of the world. On any given day, a billion events happen and the media can only pick a few to report on. The TV networks and the press aim to make money, so naturally when there is a decision over what to air, they err on the side of sensationalism. Why not report on something that exploded, collided, or screamed? News reporters know that sensational subject matter is much more exciting for us to watch, and so we'll buy their newspapers or tune in to see their broadcast. For example, in 2005, with all the terrible news about Hurricane Katrina, some items were exaggerated. There were many reports of savagery and murder, but authorities later found that during the week of the hurricane the city of New Orleans had only four homicides—the same as in a regular week.[4]

Does this mean Hurricane Katrina's destruction of New Orleans wasn't a terrible event? No, of course not. Terrible things happen in the world, and it's the media's job to report on alarming news. But good things happen, too, and it's much harder to pick out positive trends, which tend to be slower and less dramatic. So the mass media, especially television, ends up presenting a narrow perspective of the state of the world.

Most media bias is unintentional—though not to hear conservatives and liberals tell it. The former TV journalist Bernard Goldberg ratcheted up the debate in 2002 when he wrote *Bias*, which claimed to expose how the liberal media distorts the news.[5] Not to be outdone, Eric Alterman countered with *What Liberal Media?* which rebuked Goldberg's claims and showed how the media might actually be conservatively biased.[6] What's the truth? Both journalists and their bosses are under a lot of pressure to be "unbiased," and so, at least when reporting actual events and facts, bias is not much of a problem. Opinion pieces are another story; and the television stations and newspapers that are directly partisan often make no attempt to hide it. But regardless, the worst problems with the media are not ideological, they're sensational. The media relies on sensationalism—playing upon shock and fear in order to sell papers and rope in readers, viewers, and listeners. The term "yellow journalism" was coined in 1897 to describe the unprofessional media practices of the time. Since then, the media has used exciting, exaggerated news to rake in profits. Boring but important stories, usually wide and complicated in scope, are bypassed in favor of "sexy" news. This is the reason why I felt there was a need for this book, and the reason the secret peace remains a secret.

Beside showing ideological and sensationalist bias, sometimes journalists just plain screw up. They're only human, and often they are rushed by deadlines. Sometimes journalists are not trained in the subject they're covering, so they don't know what questions to ask and don't scrutinize congratulatory press releases. Real scientific findings are often couched in caveats and explanations of the perfectly controlled circumstances in which experiments took place, but these can be ignored in favor of a general summary of the findings. Insignificant and unreliable reports such as those sharing preliminary scientific data are often overemphasized. Statistics are taken out of context, usually to overstate disparity and embroider drama (I've made sure the charts in this book show zero as the baseline.) The media heightens public fears of sharks and other improbable fatal absurdities, when thousands more people die in common car accidents. It's the journalist's responsibility to be accurate, but it's easy to see how mistakes and exaggerations can occur.

"Psycho-Facts," a term coined by *Newsweek* and *Washington Post* columnist Robert J. Samuelson, refers to stories repeated so often they become common knowledge regardless of their veracity. "Truthiness" is satirical television commentator Stephen Colbert's way to refer to the same phenomenon: a sense of knowing something is right with your gut, even if, inconveniently, it might not actually be correct.[7] Truthy tales can take on a monstrous life of their own and become incredibly difficult to disprove, particularly if they're around for a long time. For example, Betsy Ross didn't sew the first American flag, and most people living in the time of Columbus actually *did* already believe the earth was round, just much smaller.[8]

Here's a psycho-fact I just discovered: Tom Robinson and Genghis Khan, our perfect peace odd couple, might not be related. I wrote that segment in the introduction when I first found the story. I figured sources like the *Miami Herald* and the *London Times* would be accurate. And they usually are. But in this case, it turns out that while the first company to analyze Robinson's DNA found evidence that led back to Genghis Khan, when Robinson later went for a second opinion, another company found conflicting evidence. The end result? It's frustratingly inconclusive. Journalists jumped on Tom's story because it was such a perfect, and amusing, metaphor—but its retraction wasn't nearly as interesting. The follow-up was buried as insignificant news in the papers that even mentioned it. It's not as much fun to read a small, confusing, weeks-later scientific caveat blurb. If I hadn't been fact-checking, I wouldn't have spotted it. Nevertheless, I still think Tom and Genghis serve as an ideal metaphor; since Genghis does have thousands of descendants, I'm sure there are other accountants we can assume are in Tom's alleged situation. And it certainly illustrates what types of articles the media spotlights and what qualifying facts can be thrown by the wayside in the process.[9]

Nevertheless, despite the inaccuracies, there is some good news about media bias. One, the news is much less biased than it used to be. During the first few centuries of their existence, American newspapers were blatantly partisan. One-sided political reporting and libel filled the broadsheets, while the lifestyle, crime, and accident reporting that we are so familiar with today were rare.[10] Two—and we will explore this more in the chapter on technology—with a new world now of online bloggers watching their every move, large media outlets are unable to get away with errors because their facts are constantly being checked by readers and watchdog groups. Three, those same online developments are offering more diversity in the field of journalism. Newshounds are not limited to their hometown newspaper or the network stations in their area—the whole world is now available.

DELUDING OURSELVES INTO PESSIMISM

We ourselves are often guilty of making the same mistakes that journalists make: self-delusion. The way our brains work can deceive us into seeing patterns in mere coincidence and believing things we want to be true. When you run into someone you know on the street, it's easy to think of it as fate, due to the very small chance of encountering that particular person. But there is a much larger chance of bumping into *anyone* we know. If it had been some other acquaintance, we would have attributed it to fate as well. Or think about common optical illusions; they're good visual examples of the assumptions our brains can make. And most games of chance and gambling depend on our inability to conceive of incredibly small chances of winning. Streaks and lucky hands have been proven to be imaginary. Worse yet, we can barely even trust our own memories. Harvard professor Daniel L. Schacter attributes the following factors to faulty memory in his book *Seven Sins of Memory*: transience (forgetting over time), absentmindedness, blocking, misattribution (accidental mixing of memories), suggestibility, bias, and persistence (certain memories take precedence, like traumatic ones). Since our memories can be faulty, it's a good thing we are now in a world where people can easily corroborate their stories, and record their memories with handy camera phones.[11]

The "common knowledge" accumulated over a lifetime of sensationalized media stories, urban legends, mistaken statistics, and panicky rumors make it very hard to accept the reality of world peace. Our narrow worldview doesn't help either; we tend to focus on whatever story is making the headlines this week, if not *today*. Not only that, but we naturally are obsessed with how our own country is doing, knowing little of other countries' current events. If something bad happens in America, this week, we feel awful. If something good happens, it may not be reported, and we're more preoccupied with the riveting bad news anyway. For something to be reported from across the world, it has to be *really* bad, so we build up a subconscious picture of the rest of the world descending to hell. Africa conjures images of emaciated children stalked by vultures, not of mobile phones and fast economic growth. Both reflect real aspects of Africa today, but we visualize one more than the other.

Global awareness in general can make us cynical, because the scale of our problems has grown. How can we be optimistic when faced with global warming, or worldwide economic meltdown? Like the federal deficit, our minds can't comprehend issues that large. Of course, if we're ever going to solve those problems, we need to understand them rather than stick our heads in the sand.

It's easy for us to look at global crises and see a long-term trend of the world getting worse. Conjuring a worldview of civilization getting better is more difficult, and it's partly because of moral relativism. It's comforting that tolerance has increased so that people have a better understanding and acceptance of cultures foreign to their own. But, when carried too far, it makes us reluctant to judge other societies—current or historical. If things are getting better worldwide, we're forced to accept that things were worse in the past—placing judgments on past cultures. Extrapolating from there, once we realize that some parts of the world are closer to peace than others, it's clear that some countries are "ahead" of the others on a timeline of progress, and thus maybe "better." Our good-naturedness can make us hesitant to admit this potential ethnocentrism and racism. But it's possible to marry the thoughts that cultures may not be intrinsically better than one another but have just done better, through hard work and various historical accidents.

Another way that relative viewpoints come into play is with definitions. A lot of strife among talking heads in the media could be resolved today if they sat down like a pair of law firms and agreed on terminology. Just look at the loaded terms, "pro-life" and "pro-choice"; using the words "anti-life" or "anti-choice" for the opposite sides is a surefire way to rile people up, to say the least. This relates to the secret peace because people can argue the relative positive or negative strength of a trend and never reach agreement, even if talking about verified facts. Sometimes this confusion is intentional misdirection, other times it's unplanned.

For example, take the word "peace" itself. What does peace mean to you? Maybe it conjures dreams of peace and quiet, sleeping on a hammock strung between Caribbean palm trees. That's a vision of personal peace. To me, personal peace is reading on a park bench or drawing sketches of old buildings. Peace can also suggest spending time with your family, or practicing your religious beliefs. Maybe it means meditating on a mountaintop in Tibet, stringing that hammock between snowy pines instead of palms.

"World peace" seems a lot more elusive than personal peace. It is hard to define because it implies something more than just an end to war. The concept of world peace has mystical, poetic connotations of a time when everyone will live in universal love and brotherhood. It's easy for people to scoff at the concept of world peace approaching because they can define the term however they like. When some peace standards are met, they may still not live up to one's ultimate vision. When 99 percent of the world is at peace, can we officially say we have "world peace"? World peace seems impossible and unattainable, conveying feelings of hopelessness when we try to envision its practicality. But that wasn't always the case. Many philosophers have proposed versions of a utopia, from Plato to Sir Thomas More, who coined the word in his novel *Utopia* about an ideal, imaginary country of the same name. For them, utopia was never just a "pie in the sky." Those authors hoped that at least parts of their visions might one day be implemented. Their precedent was the simple fact that many people believed humankind had a united destiny, a peaceful one.

Not today. As of this writing, 81 percent of Americans are pessimistic about the state of the country. But ask them about their own lives, and you get a different answer. When asked about their jobs, schools, finances, and communities, people tell pollsters the situation is pretty good. In fact, a "world happiness survey" recently revealed that the world on the whole is much happier than it used to be. Happiness increased from 1981 to today in 40 of the 52 countries surveyed. Denmark is the world's happiest nation (and Zimbabwe its least.) And the U.S.? Even in this current economic downturn, we ranked a respectable 16th.[12] Who better to judge the state of the world than its citizens themselves, looking directly at their local level, rather than the news pundits?

Retreating from the media's and politicians' gloom-and-doom focus on negative details reveals large trends that are hard to discern but which come together to paint a vivid picture of our secret story of progress and peace. Newspaperman Ben Hecht said it best, "Trying to determine what is going on in the world by reading newspapers is like trying to tell the time by watching the second hand of the clock."[13] We are used to looking at issues in a reductionist way, breaking them down into smaller parts for study. Our short-term preoccupations often eclipse our long-term focus. Pulling back to contemplate the big picture goes against our instincts. But a lot of data does exist, and once you've spotted some of the trends, more jump out at you. The positive trends are hidden, but they can be found—a forest hidden among the trees. The media's focus on short-term, sensational stories, and our own tendency to make mistakes, are the two largest factors contributing to society's pessimism. But there are more. The positive message of the secret peace can be easily missed among a lot of false information.

The Many Ways We're Mistaken

Have you ever opened your inbox and received an email like this? "A nine-year-old girl, Penny Brown, has been missing now for two weeks. It is still not too late. If anyone anywhere sees anything, please contact Penny's mother at zico-zico@hotmail.com. It only takes two seconds to pass this message along. If it was your child, you would want all the help you could get. Please, all prayers are appreciated! Thank you so much for your kindness and help!"

Of course, Penny isn't really missing; she never even existed. That fraudulent email had already been making the rounds for six years before it got to me. Whenever I receive a forwarded e-mail like this one, I immediately visit Snopes.com. This urban legends reference center Web site lists hundreds of articles and myths and investigates each one's veracity. As for Penny's story, several clues tipped Snopes off. First, "Penny Brown" is an implausibly cute name. (To me, it evokes Inspector Gadget's niece Penny, with a dash of Charlie Brown thrown in.) Combined with the adorable photo that accompanied the e-mail, which bears an uncanny resemblance to a young Melissa Gilbert from *Little House on the Prairie*, Penny's cuteness is shamelessly meant to evoke sympathy. Second, notices about real missing children always include basic details such as the child's city, what she was wearing when last seen, her birth date, the phone number of the local police, and specific information about when the child went missing. "Two weeks ago" is completely pointless information in a medium in which messages can sit unread for months. Third, several other e-mails have made the rounds on the Internet with suspiciously similar wording but different names and equally cute photos.[14]

I'm happy we live in a world where I can disprove Penny's story with a click of the mouse. Years ago, there was no way to debunk myths that quickly, which is why we're still hearing people say "Chewing gum stays in your stomach for seven years" or "You'll get cramps if you go swimming right after you eat" or "We only use 10 percent of our brains"— all false.[15] But today, the speed at which information can be disseminated—for constructive purposes such as debunking a myth, or for nefarious purposes such as falsely playing upon people's sympathies—is part of the growth of individual knowledge. With newfound knowledge comes each person's responsibility to discern truth for themselves.

Receiving Penny's story in your inbox, and buying into it, even for a subconscious second, perpetuates a mood of fear and a foreshadowing of society's collapse. Penny's story is easy to believe because we all have a template in our head of how common kidnappings are today. (For while the email only says that she is "missing," our minds tend to jump to the worst-case scenario.) Never mind that abductions are incredibly rare, and on the decline.[16] There are many of these incorrect ideas and distorted truths percolating in society. Most of those mistruths are negative; so each feeds into an overall depressing mood that runs counter to the reality of the secret peace. When it comes to being deceived into pessimism, the mass media is the main culprit, as we've seen. A close runner-up is the tendency for our brains to often backfire with fear and assumptions. But there are other sources of falsely pessimistic information as well. Take a look at Figure 1:

FIGURE 1: THE TYPES OF FALSE INFORMATION

malicious
DISINFORMATION

Government propaganda
Marketing
Media Bias
Pseudoscience scams
Pseudoscience beliefs
Media sensationalism
Self-delusion

MISINFORMATION
accidental

The chart shows the wide range of false information we encounter every day. There are two categories of deception: disinformation and misinformation. Disinformation is worse because it refers to intentional lies, while misinformation deals only with mistakes, rumors, and ignorance. Disinformation includes government propaganda, marketing, and pseudoscience. Misinformation covers some other pseudosciences, plus media sensationalism and self-delusion. Since our main deceivers are media sensationalism and self-delusion, this means many more untruths are misinformation: accidental rather than malicious. Nevertheless, there are, so to speak, a few black-hat-wearing mustachioed super-villains out there trying to outwit you. Despite our big brains and fancy new technology, deception can be equally sophisticated, and we all get caught unawares now and then. We've already looked at problems with both the media and ourselves, but let's briefly examine the other techniques in turn, from the insidious to the benign.

CROP CIRCLES AND
POISONED HALLOWEEN CANDY

Government propaganda may be the worst kind of false information since it represents an effort to manipulate us to help wage war, make money, or consolidate power. It's a complete betrayal of the public trust. As the mass of people have gained more political power, governments have had a greater need to control public opinion. Before democracy, rulers had much more leeway to simply force citizens to do things. Now they have to convince them through propaganda. A new line of thought emerged alongside democracy, a horrifying funhouse mirror of Enlightenment logic stating that if society was to be ordered with reason, then the public had to be controlled. As Josef Goebbels, Nazi Germany's minister of propaganda, said, "It is the absolute right of the state to supervise the formation of public opinion."[17] He also believed that "the truth is the greatest enemy of the State."[18] The proliferation of propaganda today reveals that this view is still sometimes held by those in power, even if subconsciously.

But there is a bright side to propaganda: It's much harder to get away with in a democracy. The ruler of Turkmenistan—who seemed, until his death in 2006, to be vying with Kim Jong-il of North Korea for the title of worst dictator on Earth—wrote his country's school textbooks and filled them with whatever he wanted.[19] (Let's just say they were slightly biased in his favor.) In democracies, disinformation has to be more subtle. This makes it harder to track down, but at least there is a lot less of it. Say what you will about our beleaguered public school system, but at least President Bush didn't personally write the biology textbook, or Clinton the pamphlets on sexual education.

But is propaganda even necessary? George Orwell's dystopian novel 1984 took the horrors of the twentieth century and extrapolated them into a future in which individual thought is dead. Orwell made the assumption that in order to suppress reading, language, and thought, you need a harsh, tyrannical government. While this is true in the few remaining pure totalitarian societies, the larger danger in most of the world is misleading *ourselves*. Distracted by advertising and entertainment, it's tempting to lose motivation to educate ourselves. Apathy becomes the biggest danger. The most effective propaganda becomes sleight-of-hand: not so much telling direct lies about an issue, but directing our attention to minutia that distract us from larger, relevant topics.

With less outright propaganda today, our free time can be consumed with another type of disinformation: marketing. It may be hard to believe, especially when you are so frequently accosted by Internet pop-up ads and TV commercials, but marketing is more benign than propaganda. This is a good thing, because there is far more of it. Even though marketing sometimes uses the same tactics—if not outright lies, at least distortion of the truth—the purpose is less sinister. Marketers just want to sell you stuff. Yes, this is pretty bad, especially if it is marketing for cigarettes or greasy food, but the marketers are not trying to convince you to go to war or rescind any civil liberties.

In late 1993, a group called Mothers Opposing Pollution (MOP) appeared in Australia as a nationwide grassroots organization dedicated to the welfare and rights of Australian women. MOP, represented by a spokeswoman named Alana Maloney, waged a campaign against plastic milk bottles, citing studies of detrimental environmental and health effects due to storage of milk in plastic.

The group went so far as to claim that milk that came in contact with plastic might be carcinogenic. However, several suspicious clues started to turn up. MOP's addresses turned out to be various P.O. boxes, and there were no records of anyone by the name of Alana Maloney ever existing. In 1995, investigations by an Australian newspaper finally uncovered that Maloney was really Janet Rundle, head of a public relations company called J. R. and Associates. Rundle appears to have fabricated MOP for her client, the Association of Liquidpaperboard Carton Manufacturers—who make *paper* milk cartons. After that exposé, MOP unsurprisingly disappeared.[20]

This story is striking not just because of its hilarious acronym, but because it challenges many of our subconscious assumptions about business, marketing, and the media. It raises the fundamental question, "Whom can I trust?" As an optimist, I still answer, "Most people." In the book *Nonzero*, Robert Wright explains that it is in everyone's best interest to enter into honest deals because they have the best chance of succeeding, especially in societies with a healthy rule of law.[21] Do people cheat? Do companies and governments lie? Yes, but we each have hundreds of interactions with others every day, and the vast majority of those interactions are sincere. More importantly, the work of those who are trying to deceive us is getting harder every day, thanks to our access to information. That is why the story above and the examples cited here are so complex and subtle. Simple "snake oil" schemes don't work on us nearly as well anymore. Now, at least, we read the metaphorical bottle's nutrition facts before we buy any snake oil.

Propaganda is rarely justifiable, but honest marketing is an integral part of our capitalist system. In theory, it's supposed to inform people of products that are right for them. The problems crop up when it's not honest. The tale of MOP is a perfect example of one of the newest, most insidious techniques: the third-party tactic. This relies upon "experts" who are not credible—maybe they have credentials in the wrong field, misrepresent statistics, represent a fringe minority view posing as the majority, are merely celebrities with no expertise, or are even completely made up.[22] The marketers are often blatantly fibbing, but there are some gray areas. The experts might be honest, but their message is distorted. Similarly, products and their advertisements are sometimes presented in misleading ways. Bottled water, for example, is often for all intents and purposes ordinary tap water. Aquafina and other leading brands contain the tiny disclaimer, "public water source" on their labels.[23]

This brings us to areas in which it's not as clear who is lying and who is merely misguided, such as with pseudoscience. The catchall term "pseudoscience" covers a wide range of spurious beliefs and superstitions. When I was a kid, one topic of fascination for me was supernatural unsolved mysteries. I would go to the children's side of the public library and read about ghosts, UFOs, Atlantis, dowsing, the Loch Ness Monster, the Yeti and his pal Bigfoot, auras, crystals, haunted houses, Nostradamus's prophecies, and my personal favorite, spontaneous human combustion. But as I expanded into the grown-up side of the library, it turned out that there was no clear evidence for a single one of the beliefs that so fascinated me. I began to lose faith that any of them might be true. And what clinched it for me was a book I read years later, Carl Sagan's *The Demon-Haunted World*.

Pseudosciences are considered such because they use the trappings of science to appear scientific when in fact their claims are simply unfalsifiable. Their supporters explain away any contradictions or absence of evidence. For example, because there is no evidence for UFOs, there *must be* a government cover-up. Pseudosciences are really traditional superstitions that have adjusted to a new science-centered world by adopting the trappings of science as part of their mythology. As science disproves superstitions and old wives' tales, people can feel their traditional beliefs float away, too. The famous twentieth-century ennui—the vague sense of modern emptiness that Franz Kafka, Edward Hopper, and Jean-Paul Sartre each conveyed so expertly—can drive many people to search for new meaning in their lives. Pseudosciences often fill that need. Pseudosciences can encompass both disinformation and misinformation, since some are intentional scams (disinformation) while others are just rumors or misguided hopes (misinformation).

Let's look at two examples of pseudoscience, one related to the wider UFO phenomenon and the other a common urban legend. First, have you ever seen photographs of crop circles, the complex, giant circular patterns in wheat fields or corn fields that appear magically overnight and bewilder everyone?

Sorry to break it to you, but unlike many other pseudosciences, which stink of hoaxes but whose perpetrators elude detection, this one has been figured out. Two chaps in Southampton, Britain, started it: Doug Bower and Dave Chorley. They were artists who were inspired to play a prank on UFO buffs. Boy, did it work. Crop circles became a global phenomenon for decades. The two friends finally got tired and announced to the media in 1991 that they had been the ones making crop patterns in Britain for 15 years. They showed everyone how they did it, and made some examples. Did you hear about that? Probably not, because the media paid scant attention. Instead, the legend survives. Since Bower and Chorley stopped production, there have been fewer crop circles, but many copycats continue to create slightly less inspired versions. Scientists have investigated the circles, books of crop circle photos have been published, and countless online discussions offer them as proof of extraterrestrial visitation. Meanwhile, two ordinary blokes were probably flabbergasted at the gullibility of the world.[24]

In the realm of pseudoscience, intentional scams thrive (think of Whoopi Goldberg holding a faux séance in the movie *Ghost*), but misguided beliefs, myths, rumors, and lack of critical thought are even more common. This is the purview of misinformation. There is another pseudoscientific urban legend, one that only rears its ugly head for a single day each year—Halloween. We've all heard stories of despicable neighbors tampering with trick-or-treat candy. These sickos might add some cyanide, or razor blades, or needles. Well, this is just about as plausible as using Hershey's Kisses to hide a candlestick, a lead pipe, a revolver, or a wrench. In 50 years of records (and this legend is at least that old), there are only three cases of children dying related to candy that has been tampered with. One involved a child finding his uncle's heroin and his parents concocting the candy story as a cover-up. Another was an intentional poisoning by a boy's own demented father, and the third was a girl with a heart condition who had a seizure while trick-or-treating. There was also one incident in which some children got Snickers bars filled with marijuana. It turns out that a postal worker gave out Halloween candy that he had stolen from the dead letter office but hadn't sampled himself. The original senders, attempting to smuggle the drugs hidden in candy, lost their stash when they used insufficient postage![25]

Debunking urban legends reinforces a future of peace. Society is much better than it may seem because a lot of the scary things in our lives are blown out of proportion—or simply aren't true at all. You might say, "That sounds right, but I'm going to check my kid's candy just to be safe. What's the harm in that? Better safe than sorry." Ah, but it does cause harm: we distrust our neighbors more; we discourage kids from trick-or-treating; we waste time checking the candy; many hospitals offer X-ray services on Halloween, at a major expense that has to get passed along to someone; and worst of all, we scare our kids. It's the same thing as with our friend Penny. Does it cause any harm to send along her e-mail appeal, just in case? I think so. I don't believe that ignorance is bliss. In most cases we see that knowing the truth makes everyone happier and safer. Plus, we would be better served by focusing on real threats. We need to debunk pseudosciences and help make a distinction between scams and reputable (honest and safe) religion, ethics, and philosophy.

Now, if a theory is brand-new, like in 1970 when physicists came up with string theory, strong evidence might not abound yet, so we should still keep an open mind. But when a concept such as ghosts has been haunting our minds for millennia, the absence of evidence to prove their existence is notable. How, after thousands of years, can ghosts be floating around if no audio recording or reliable photograph exists, and no case study has survived rigorous scientific examination? Unfortunately, because of how science functions, we can never *entirely* disprove the existence of ghosts. So if you're a true believer, don't fret, you can always drink your Ecto Cooler and hang on to that millionth of a percent chance.[26]

Many people are reluctant to criticize pseudoscientific beliefs for fear of insulting others' personal religious beliefs. But religious claims that address the physical world are fair game for examining with scientific evidence. In fact, by eliminating the most fringe beliefs, as well as any harmful predators, debunking pseudoscience can help more traditional religions. And the cooler heads resulting from critical thinking can help alleviate religious strife. The Buddha, on his deathbed, emphasized critical thinking and individual responsibility thus: "Do not accept what you hear by report, do not accept tradition, do not accept a statement because it is found in your books ... Be ye lamps unto yourselves."[27]

THINKING CRITICALLY

The essence of the Buddha's sentiment is the concept of critical thinking. The term "critical thinking" can refer to many different techniques, but I define it as the combination of independent thought and scientific principles. Carl Sagan succinctly described critical scientific thinking as "the means to construct, and to understand, a reasoned argument and—especially important—to recognize a fallacious or fraudulent argument."[28] Combine this with individualized thinking—that is, questioning accepted knowledge and authority, being creative, and acting independently of outside pressure—and you have a potent tool. This method of thinking has gestated for centuries as humanity slowly absorbed its lessons. Now critical thinking subtly permeates our everyday lives in ways unimagined by our ancestors. We use critical thinking to decide what kind of peanut butter to buy from 30 brands on a supermarket shelf. We use it to see through the act of a sleazy salesman, to decide not to forward Penny's chain e-mail to our friends, to mistrust the government, and to scoff at the media. We use critical thinking to decide which books to read. (Thank you for choosing this one.) I am using critical thinking right now to decide how best to explain critical thinking.

Simple decisions you and I make every day would have been incomprehensible hundreds of years ago. As technology expands, as ideas multiply, as the economy grows, and as the population increases, we have millions more choices available to us than anyone who's lived before. With increased complexity come larger, more intricate problems than humanity has ever faced. And we cannot avoid facing them, especially because we all have the responsibility as citizens of a democratic society to participate in running the place. As Thomas Jefferson cautioned, "If a nation expects to be ignorant and free in a state of civilization, it expects what never was and never will be."[29] Our brains need to meet the challenge.

With all the propaganda, marketing, pseudoscience, media bias, and self-delusion clouding our minds, are we even learning anything? Yes. We are not all suckers who fall for Internet scams, UFO sightings, and wild marketing claims. Investigating disinformation and misinformation forces us to learn and adapt for the sake of our own sanity. The new availability of information, from the Internet and other sources, gives us incredible opportunities to educate ourselves—opportunities that are increasingly being harnessed. We are learning critical thinking. Albert Einstein once said, "The significant problems we face cannot be solved at the same level of thinking we were at when we created them."[30] With each new sphere of problems, humanity has expanded its collective brainpower to come up with technological and social solutions. Yet, tackling each set of problems has introduced new ones. The newest problems are only conquerable by an educated and united humanity. After centuries of experience, the world's citizens are confronted with their biggest problems yet—global warming, nuclear terrorism, eradicating poverty, and more. Hopefully everything we've been through has tested and trained us for our current challenges.

Critical thinking is essential to discern the trends of the secret peace. How do you use it? Take any issue in the news today, any event reported, tense situation talked about, furious controversy debated, law passed, or factoid mentioned. Then look at several sources. It doesn't have to take a long time—often, going to Wikipedia can lead you off to several other news sites referencing the item. Look, too, at the various sides of the debate. Then, the key step often underreported in the media: Look at the larger context. Examine history—you don't have to go back a thousand years, but situations today are the result of events in the past and the state of the society in which they occur. Put statistics in context; if the news reports a mugging, take a look at the number of muggings over a year, and then compare that to other years, before you get worried. Once you start keeping your eyes open, secret peace trends and tidbits will start jumping out at you. Let's look at a huge, important example.

Don't Be Depressed

We need look no further than our headlines today to see a compelling reason to doubt secret peace trends. To paraphrase the media: "There's a giant recession! It's the worst economic crisis since the Great Depression! The whole world economy collapsed!" With news like this, how can I say everything's fine?

First of all, everything's not fine. You're right, there is a giant recession. It *is* the worst economic crisis since the Great Depression. The secret peace does not imply that everything's going great—just that it's better than it used to be, and it will get better still. I started writing this book before the financial problems at the end of 2008. Some of my friends worried that the bad news invalidated the argument for peace. But I'm glad the crisis happened, as it's a good chance to explain that secret peace trends persevere even in times of trouble, and that things are not as bad as they seem. Using critical thinking, we can blow up people's exaggerations and find a more reasonable position—not a *falsely* optimistic view, but a more balanced one.

The media is justified—obligated, in fact—to cover all the news about the economic crisis, the recession, the stock market collapse, and the unemployment statistics. But one area that is not justified is the fear-mongering tactic of comparing the current crisis to the Great Depression. There are two relevant things to keep in mind about the Great Depression and New Deal here. 1) The reasons for the Depression seem frighteningly similar to some of the reasons for the current economic crisis. That scared me, but then I realized that 2) the reaction, response and consequences are totally different. Here are 10 reasons (counting up to the most important) why the current crisis, as bad as it is, can't hold a candle to the Great Depression.

10. **Information flow:** During the Great Depression, investors rarely had accurate and timely information about companies. The government didn't even have an accurate estimate of GDP. Today, of course, we're swimming in data.

9. **Two-income families:** Women work now. If a husband loses his job, the family still has an income. Not so in the 1930s, before women began entering the workforce in WWII.

8. **Diversification of labor:** When 30 percent of the country is employed in agriculture, and there is a Dust Bowl (partly because of poor agricultural practices), lots of people are out of work. Comparatively, today only three percent of the nation is employed as farmers. In general, if any single industry crashes, it affects a smaller number of people today. The

unemployment rate in the U.S. at the time of this writing has hit 10 percent, yet this is still lower than many countries have during good times. At the height of the Depression, U.S. unemployment was at least a whopping 25 percent.[31]

7. **Global cooperation:** In particular, the economic integration of Europe through the EU enables a high level of coordinated action. EU membership "binds national politicians into a set of essentially liberal, free-trading, internationalist standards," as the *Economist* puts it. Not so much cooperation in the 1930s, to say the least. For example, the international response to the collapse of the financial firm Lehman Brothers in 2008 (the trigger of our crisis) was much faster and more effective than the response to the analogous event of 1931, the collapse of the big Austrian bank Creditanstalt.[32]

6. **Activity:** World governments' willingness to act has been impressive so far. Even if they make mistakes, they're working on it. Compare this to Hoover, who took public pride in not doing anything: the markets will take care of themselves, after all.[33]

5. **"Stuff":** Even with a recent bump in food prices, commodities are a lot cheaper now than then. We also have a lot more infrastructure, such as our highway system, and people just have a lot more "stuff" too. The average middle-age man in the 1920s could afford just six outfits, and ate a lot fewer calories a day (this sounds like a good thing, but it wasn't.) We have refrigerators, microwaves, and air conditioners. Health care expenses will be one of the major pains that people feel during a recession today, but the quality of health care during the Great Depression was laughable even for the rich.[34]

4. **The East:** Other emerging economies, particularly China and India, spread the problem thinner. The US generates a smaller percentage of world GDP now. While our growth slowed from three percent to slightly less than zero (hence a recession), China and India saw GDP rise by about

six percent even in the first quarter of 2009. And the government of China has shown remarkable initiative in addressing the economic crisis so far.[35]

3. **Experience:** We've got 75 years of learning from other financial crises. We've been here before. We've had 10 recessions since WWII, and we've always pulled out of them. The average length of those recessions, in fact, is only 10 months—as opposed to an average of 20 months apiece for the 22 recessions before that war. In 1873, in fact, there was a depression that lasted over five years, even longer than the Great Depression.[36]

2. **Social security:** Roosevelt was smarter than us. We were stupid enough to repeat another financial mess. But he—and various other presidents and parliaments and elected leaders around the world over the years—figured that might happen. The New Deal put programs in place not only to mitigate the Depression, but to prevent future ones. We've got the FDIC, Social Security, food stamps, Medicaid, and unemployment insurance, just to name the big ones that come to mind. There are downsides to these programs—they cost money, of course. But paying into a system during boom times to help out during lean times is a pretty obvious concept. Imagine living in a world without any of that support.

1. **It's over?** Technically, we're already pulling out of the recession. In America, GDP is expected to have stopped shrinking by the time you read this. The stock market has made back some of its losses, in its fastest rebound since 1975. At least, that's what indicated by the news of the last few months as I write this.[37]

Who knows, more negative economic indicators might re-emerge in the coming months, and unemployment might continue to rise. A recovery may be a long haul. But keep in mind, when we do pull out of our economic slump, businesses will emerge leaner and stronger than before. Inefficiencies, unethical practices, and bad management will be exposed. The financial sector will return to a more reasonable percentage of total corporate profits. A recession doesn't mean our economy has stopped; Americans started 530,000 businesses *a month* in 2008, despite the recession. And studies have shown that businesses started in bad times are more likely to succeed.[38]

A snapshot of the state of the world at any given time—its wars and poverty, economic crises and environmental damage—will always be a natural argument against the concept of the secret peace. If the book had been published in 1982, or 2001, you could have looked at the weak economy and made the same argument. However, if you had been economically pessimistic in 1988, or 2000, or 2005, it might have been laughable, so obvious was inevitable economic growth. The point is, history is cyclical, but like the stock market, each cycle ends a little higher than the last one did. So that even with dips and peaks, the overall trend still goes up. Although it understandably can be small consolation to the many people hurting here and now, the trick is to step back and keep the big picture in mind. This is something that the media, in its rush for immediate relevancy and novelty, does very poorly.

Take all that false information out there, and throw in our own ability to deceive ourselves, and the natural outcome is the common knowledge that our future is bleak. Because outdated institutions and ideas are disintegrating at the same time that new structures are being built, it is often easier to see the destruction than the creation. So we have to build a pretty strong case to illustrate an increasing peace. It is always a dangerous idea to try to predict the future. Many have tried and failed. No one can say that the world's last war will end on a Wednesday or that all Sudanese children will be plump and healthy by next year. We can only look at overall trends and extrapolate from them. But as physicist and futurist Freeman Dyson said, "The purpose of thinking about the future is not to predict it but to raise people's hopes." Maybe those raised hopes can then generate a positive feedback loop to help our future even more.[39]

The optimistic theory of global progress presented here took me decades to construct. It's one that I believe in wholeheartedly, but I hope you don't feel the same way—yet. There is plenty of evidence to review before making your decision. My goal is to show you enough compelling clues that you can weigh the theory's merits for yourself and come to your own conclusion. In researching, whenever possible I tried to use widely available newspapers, magazines, web sites, and popular books to gather most of the evidence, rather than academic tomes. I want to prove that the information is out there, and that it's not hard to find if you are willing to spend the time to dig between the lines of the media's most commonly reported stories. I quote liberally from many excellent books and periodicals, and my aim is to take their pointed insights and weave them together into a larger tapestry. This positive framework can help us understand current events, new technology, and critical social trends. If you're perennially pessimistic, I hope *The Secret Peace* will be a shock to your system. And if you're one of us chipper and cheery folks, I hope the information provided here will give you some good, hard facts to back up an argument in favor of world optimism.

The quest to find the secret peace runs through the world's newspapers, TV shows, water cooler talk, and Web sites. In the next chapters, we will explore a positive outlook for our global future by first examining *why* the secret peace is happening, and then looking at the surprising evidence for peace. We'll look at the **History** of utopian thought and then go in-depth at the three forces driving today's peace: **Thought**, **Technology**, and **Unity**. Then we'll look at evidence in the realms of **Equality**, **Peace**, **Democracy**, **Economics**, **Health**, and the **Environment**. In these intertwined areas, we will search for similarities rather than differences, large ideas rather than singular incidents, and humanity's achievements rather than disillusioning setbacks. Our lifetimes will see the fastest changes the world has ever witnessed. Behind the scenes, the majority of civilization's tumultuous changes are boldly leading us on the path to peace—the fulfillment of the dreams of generations.

HISTORY

Utopian Theories

For the sake of argument, let's give optimism the benefit of the doubt. Say the world *is* advancing toward peace, and that humanity's on the right track. So the question becomes, why? Is it luck? Is it fate? Is it a coincidence—among millions of random events, is it just that more of them happen to be constructive than harmful? Or are all the items tied together—by big themes that quietly instigate change? And if so ... what are they?

Throughout history, the idea of peace has been developed and debated by the world's religious teachers, philosophers, creators, and scientists. Humanity has always been inspired by the dream of a future world peace. By first examining the history of these ideas, we can evaluate which theory, if any, explains what might be driving history. Some of the ideas seem at odds with each other, but upon closer examination they're more complementary than you might suspect.

IMAGINING THE KINGDOM OF GOD ON EARTH

For most of human history, all theories about the future were intimately tied to religious beliefs. Most religions feature ideas about the origin of the universe, the promise of individual salvation, and prophecies that promise a time of world peace when a corrupt humanity will return to righteous values. A prophecy theme eerily common to nearly all religions revolves around a decline in righteousness, which is to be followed by the return of a founding prophet, who will usher in a utopia. For example, Hindus await the end of the *Kali Yuga* – the age of darkness and destruction—and the start of a Golden Age. This will be marked by the coming of the *Kalki Avatar*, the tenth and final incarnation of Vishnu, who will bring a return to righteousness.[1] Buddhists await the coming of the fifth Buddha. Zoroastrians expect that a *Saoshyant* will arrive to pass final judgment on humanity and secure harmony in the world. In Taoism, it is thought that in the future a cataclysm will result from accumulated evil, which will be followed by the appearance of a savior, who will usher in an era of peace and prosperity.[2]

Some religious traditions focus more on individual development than on societal reform, mapping the stages of life and spiritual awareness along which we can travel. The belief in reincarnation is central to the theology of Hinduism, for example. Some Hindus believe that the self passes through 8,400,000 lives even before being born as a human.[3] Advancement in reincarnation is based on a system of karma—the cosmic principle of reaping what you sow. Buddhists, on the other hand, emphasize the individual's journey to a state of perfect enlightenment free of suffering. You could loosely interpret the Buddhist journey as mirroring that of society.

Buddhists believe in world-systems that advance and decline in cycles lasting billions of years. Virtuous people lengthen the cycle of an advanced civilization, while the unrighteous hasten its decline and inspire a faster world "reboot." In this scenario, however, human actions do not influence the world as prominently as they are thought to in other religions; the universe does not necessarily center around us.[4]

Of the philosophies to come out of East Asia, Confucianism offers the most suggestions about how to reach a peaceful society. The Confucian program for transformation begins with an orderly, educated self as the path to an orderly society.[5] Confucian commandments guided Chinese society for millennia. Meanwhile, by the fifth century BCE when Confucianism arose, the Jews in the Middle East had already formulated precise laws to govern their society and had a vision of events in their future. Like the laws of Confucianism, the Jewish laws only applied to their own people and were not necessarily intended to be extrapolated for the entire world. Indeed, no culture until perhaps the Romans or the Mongols had any concept of the scope of the world itself anyway.

The Hebrew Bible gives us what is perhaps the most oft-repeated quote about a promised peace, from the prophet Isaiah: "He shall judge between the nations, and shall arbitrate for many peoples; they shall beat their swords into plowshares, and their spears into pruning hooks; nation shall not lift up sword against nation, neither shall they learn war any more."[6]

Jews believe that the Lord promised the return of the prophet Elijah, who would herald a Messiah to deliver them from their oppressors, unite the world under one God, and usher in peace.[7] Some Jews believe that doing good deeds (mitzvahs) will speed this process. Today, Reform Jews believe that their religion can be progressive, changing to fit the times as better values are introduced. At the same time, many Jews—particularly Orthodox Jews and Zionists—see the founding of the state of Israel as the beginning of the fulfillment of events surrounding the coming of the Messiah.[8]

The ancient Greeks devised the idea of *logos* (reason, word, or purpose) as the driving force of history. Later, the philosopher Philo Judaeus of Alexandria, a Hellenized Jew, took the idea of logos and added God to it. Philo thought that this rational principle immanent in the world was a part of God's transcendent mind. The concept of logos also appears in Christian scripture and parallels several concepts found in other world religions.[9]

Christians trust that the Messiah prophesied in the Hebrew Bible already arrived two thousand years ago in the person of Jesus Christ. They believe Christ will return in the future to judge humanity and then establish a kingdom of peace (there's our common theme again). Christian thought emphasizes eschatology—the branch of theology that concerns itself with the end of history and the destiny of mankind—more than any other religion does. There are dozens of conflicting theories, many derived from clues in the book of Revelation, the final book of the New Testament. Interpretations range from literal to symbolic, some predicting a terrible tribulation and rule of the Antichrist before Christ returns, while others believe that Christianity will increasingly spread peacefully until culminating in Christ's return.[10] Unfortunately, a small number of Christians extrapolate End Times theories into hope for the world to get worse so the end times will come sooner. Subconsciously, this concept can encourage believers to see the world as more terrible than it really is, and take away any motivation to struggle for improvement.

For the most part, Muslims accept what Jews and Christians believe about a line of prophets bearing communication from God. The Qur'an mentions 25 prophets by name, some from the Bible, including Jesus.[11] Islam's uniqueness stems from the addition of the Prophet Muhammad and his status as the final Messenger from God. Muslims also await a Day of Judgment that will lead to a worldwide resurrection and then a world of peace. Many Shiite Muslims believe that the *Mahdi*, the lost twelfth Imam, will emerge from hiding to defeat evil and return Islam to its original purity.[12] The unity of humanity, a commonly accepted aspect of world peace, is of primary importance in Islam. The term *tawhid* (literally, unification) refers to the unity of religion and people centered around one God.[13]

A religion that started in the nineteenth century, the Bahá'í Faith, incorporates many beliefs from Islam. This religion started in a Muslim society, but while Muslims believe Muhammad is the final prophet, Bahá'ís believe that God will always send prophets. Bahá'ís believe each successive prophet of the world's religions has brought unique information to guide humanity along the path of an ever-advancing civilization.

Bahá'ís believe in a "Lesser Peace" and a "Most Great Peace." The Lesser Peace refers to the process already happening today, gradually leading to a basic end to war and violence. It's not a perfect process; it happens in fits and starts. People can work together as a global society and see peace sooner, or we can continue humanity's history of violence, making it a much slower process.

Bahá'ís feel that though it might take centuries, eventually Earth will inevitably enter the Most Great Peace. Bahá'ís define that ideal as a spiritually awakened globe with each individual having the freedom and means to reach his or her own potential. So the positive world trends identified in this book, from a Bahá'í perspective, are signs of the Lesser Peace.

As we see from the above examples, the majority of the world's religions provide similar scenarios of a future peace for humankind. One difference with the Bahá'í Faith is that, unlike some older religious traditions, it emphasizes the necessity of harmonizing religion with logic and science. This was timely, because just as the Bahá'í Faith was being born in Persia, Europe and America were eschewing traditional beliefs and coming up with new explanations for history. Theories arose based on culture, science, technology, and evolution. The debate over whether these new ideas are contradictory or complementary to religious beliefs continues today.

The Rise and Fall of "Progress"

After the European Enlightenment and the emergence of modern science, philosophers diverged from religious tradition and increasingly saw the world's purpose as directionless, and humanity as alone. Scholars discovered physical laws of the universe guiding cause and effect, and moved further away from any metaphysical or spiritual explanation of human history. It seemed that science, with its newfound ability to explain *how* the world works, dismissed the need to discover *why* it works.

Still, humanity remained ever curious about its origins and destiny, and so beliefs diverged into three general corridors. First, the majority of the world still believed there to be a religious purpose to history. Whether due to the gods, or fate, or a single God, they felt there was a plan for a future peace for humanity—the Kingdom of God on Earth. Secondly, some people embraced secularism and combined scientific beliefs with their hope for a perfect future world. They came up with new, non-religious theories to explain the unfolding direction of history. These science-based views posited an ordered and nonchalantly benign universe. To different people, this concept of "progress" encompassed varying degrees of secularism and religiosity, but all its supporters believed that humanity was doing a great job and would have everything about the world figured out any day now.

A third group took the non-religious theories even farther. By eliminating the concept of God, people were able to keep extrapolating and deduced that there must be absolutely no guiding purpose to the universe. From the long perspective of history, this sense of a directionless world with no guiding hand was a brand-new concept. It fully emerged only in the late nineteenth and early twentieth centuries. While some of the people who accepted the logic of a directionless world continued to lead happy and ethical lives, others became increasingly cynical.

The most cynical theorists held a concept of human nature as greedy, violent, and self-centered. Paraphrasing Thomas Hobbes, they believed that people were inherently nasty, brutish, and animalistic. While most people's beliefs were not this extreme, they certainly didn't think there was a goal or direction toward which humanity was moving. For them, this pessimistic view seemed the only rational conclusion to draw after history's wars and horrors, which looked too pervasive to lend credence to a positive future. The idea seemed well-founded. Scientifically, it made sense to trust only what you could verify, and there was certainly plenty of evidence to make the case for a doomed humanity, adrift from morality and with only a veneer of pointless "progress." So progress fell out of fashion among intellectuals in the West. But not everyone was convinced.

New Philosophies Explain History

In the first decades of the nineteenth century, Georg Wilhelm Friedrich Hegel proposed a new philosophy of history. He explained that, "The history of the world is none other than the progress of the consciousness of freedom."[14] He saw humanity's ultimate goal—world peace, if you will—as both freedom and the attainment of total knowledge. He deduced that critical thought propelled humanity forward through the development of the world's mind, a sort of collective spirit and culture.[15] This is reminiscent of Philo's *logos*.

Hegel was religious and felt that spirituality, particularly his belief in Lutheranism, was a necessary element along with reason. In his *Philosophy of History*, a flaw in Hegel's argument comes at the end when he chooses his own society as the consummation of history, a Rational State.[16] From our point of view, that seems a little shortsighted. But wait, there's more: Hegel reasoned that, since the culmination of absolute knowledge was complete self-awareness, by figuring this out he had personally attained the final goal of all humanity right there and then! If you ever feel guilty about your lack of modesty, remember Hegel.[17]

Due in large part to his influence on Karl Marx, Hegel is considered one of the world's most influential philosophers. Marx agreed that history has a purpose, and he described humanity's quest to reach our full potential. But then Marx infused Hegel's ideas of history with his own concept of an ongoing battle of the classes—poor laborers struggling against rich capitalists. (Marx was destitute his whole life and always had to borrow money from Friedrich Engels. Maybe if someone had bought his books he wouldn't have been so hard on capitalism.) Marx thought religion a fake idol, a distraction from the plight of the poor, and Marx's biggest split from Hegel was in rejecting his religious ideals.

Marx said that humanity would reach utopia only when the working class rose up and overthrew the capitalists—violently, if necessary. So, followers worldwide took him up on his idea, with disastrous results. During the twentieth century, governments founded on Marx's ideas turned out to be stifling, nepotistic, oppressive and violent. Though he imagined a coherent vision of a path for history, and though he had a positive end in mind, when tested on the world stage Marx's ideas failed. European communism died due to several reasons, the fundamental failure of a centralized economy primary among them. Ironically, Hegel's ideal concept, freedom, contributed to communism's downfall as well, due to Mikhail Gorbachev's policies of openness, *Glasnost*, which awakened his people's latent desires for freedom.[18]

Immanuel Kant was a contemporary of Hegel's who developed his own concept of progress. Kant wrote two essays that dealt with his theory, "Perpetual Peace" and "Idea for a Universal History." You can pretty much tell where he's going with those essays from the titles. Kant thought that, "Perpetual peace is guaranteed by no less an authority than Nature herself." He spoke of a "continued process of enlightenment" and envisioned a world federation of states and the abolition of armies of war. He saw in his time glimmering signs of world unity, increased trade, and universal freedom, and detected a hidden pattern created by Providence. It's funny that today's hidden peace trends are practically jumping out in front of us when compared to the scant clues available in Kant's time.[19]

Hegel and Kant's philosophies were unnecessarily complex and metaphysical for many people who believed in progress. A simpler case was put forth by scholars that technological progress alone is what drives humanity's history. This looks painfully obvious at first glance. Each radical invention has spurred humanity to grow by leaps and bounds. Consider the inventions of fire, the wheel, agriculture, the telegraph, the light bulb, the train, the car. Technological creativity spurs progress. The necessities of war have led to innovations such as the longbow, the spur, the tank, and the atom bomb—and medical necessity has led to the development of penicillin, contraceptives, X-rays, and gene therapy. But this technological determinism, as it is called, can't solely explain the social, moral, artistic, and philosophical advancements in human history. Scientific innovations build on themselves, but they also draw from humanity's ongoing cultural evolution and knowledge. Cultural ideas often shape the context and direction in which science chooses to develop.

Technology is important, but it is not the only force propelling history. If it were, humanity would have just as much of a chance for a future with the dark underbelly of science, such as nuclear weapons, eugenics, and man-made diseases, as it does with its achievements. As Neil Postman feared in *Technopoly*, "Something has happened in America [with technology] that is strange and dangerous, and there is only a dull and even a stupid awareness of what it is."[20] Fortunately, Postman's technological pessimism is contradicted by the facts of the countless positive scientific trends in the areas of health, communication, travel, energy, and more—which we'll be examining in detail soon.

Running parallel to technological theories of progress are biological theories of evolution. Since the publication of Charles Darwin's *On the Origin of Species* in

1859, evolution has fed many controversies. Darwin claimed that all life evolved through natural selection, the survival of individuals with favorable traits in a species, resulting in a gradual change in a species' population. Since this usually, though not necessarily, leads to more complex creatures, laymen reasoned that life gets "better" with time. While this is true in a way, if the idea is extrapolated further you could believe that it applies within the human population as well. So "survival of the fittest," a non-scientific term, became the slogan of the Social Darwinists. They believed that some cultures were more highly evolved than others, which led to ideas for eugenics and the subjugation of those not "fit" enough, such as the poor and minority groups.[21] Thankfully Social Darwinism has fallen out of favor. And while it seems logical to consider evolution a component of progress, biological evolution is too slow to affect human history. To see significant effects, we would have to wait several millennia. Perhaps unknown advances in genetic engineering might change this, but for all intents and purposes, on our time scale Homo sapiens have finished evolving.

Finished evolving physically, at least. The mid-twentieth century French Jesuit scholar Pierre Teilhard de Chardin wrote that the human race has an evolving consciousness, leading toward greater complexity and eventually the Omega Point—essentially, God. He was a proponent of orthogenesis, the belief that evolution is leading in a straight line toward a goal, due to some driving force. Teilhard's beliefs represent a fascinating bridge between secular, scientific theories and Christian theology.[22]

A decade ago, Robert Wright, the author of the fascinating book *Nonzero*, cooked up a melting pot of a theory combining technological progress, evolution, anthropological evidence, and social theories. He came up with a more holistic scientific rationale for a positive direction for history. Wright posits that humanity's social urges and needs compel us to interact more positively than negatively.[23] According to *Nonzero*, progress is a result of our anthropological survival instinct to have positive interactions with others. Over time, positive effects from non-zero-sum interactions build on each other and create more sophisticated civilizations. Wright describes human history as improving through a process of social or cultural evolution similar in some ways to Hegel's ideas. Though we're reluctant to pass criticism on any society, past or present, the fact remains that we do live in a measurably better world than that of the Mongols, the Romans, and the early Americans.

Wright's theory shares a lot of similarities with Teilhard's, but without the religious element. But this doesn't mean it's incompatible with religion; none of the ideas listed above are. Some of them work best when coupled with a belief in the inherent goodness of humanity. This goodness could be due to the existence of a benevolent God, or evolutionary necessity, or just millions of peoples' practical sense. We've taken a look at the views of religions and philosophers, a technological theory, a biological theory, and an anthropological theory. Which of these seemingly disparate hypotheses is correct?

It's likely that many of the theories listed above are at least partially correct. They aren't mutually exclusive, and all offer pieces of the puzzle. But if we dig deeper, we see that human destiny, religious prophecy, evolution, anthropology, positive social interactions, technology, and the march of progress are all different ways of looking at the same positive trends.

There are three positive forces that intertwine so closely, and are so equally indispensable to the process of peace, that it is mighty challenging to pull them apart. But by identifying and clarifying these three forces, we can absorb lessons needed to push them along faster. They are not new; but they are newly accelerating. Their impact grows more significant every day.

The first, and most essential, is the snowballing accrual of knowledge. Over the centuries, information has become increasingly easy to store and access, so that humanity rarely has to re-learn the same thing twice. Simply put, we're learning from our mistakes. In the past, even if this knowledge was considerable, it was only available to a small elite, a coterie of clergy, scholars and kings. No longer. This is the second force, the democratization of power to the world's mass of individuals. These newly-educated individuals don't just sit in caves reading books by themselves, however. Instead, they are increasingly connecting in revolutionary ways. The third force—our realization of the unity of the human race—pushes our worldview to expand past narrow circles of family or tribe to embrace our whole diverse world. By working together, people gain even more democratic power, and build up even more knowledge, and then share it with the world. This positive feedback loop unites the three forces together until more and more kernels of progress accumulate. It's no wonder peace is breaking out all over. Let's take a chapter for each of these three forces and find out what's really happening.

3

THOUGHT

Snowballing Knowledge

Do you remember using the encyclopedia? I remember crafting a report on wombats in elementary school using my parents' encyclopedia set. It was easy to look up wombats in the thick *W* volume, which gave me a few nuggets of information for the report. The book even had a nice photo of a wombat (a fuzzy Australian marsupial that looks like a cross between a pig and a bear). The picture was perfect for copying onto green construction paper with magic marker to make my report cover.

The encyclopedia worked well for that three-page report when I was nine, but my wombat research sources were pretty limited. Not so today. With a click onto Wikipedia, I can find the same information I saw in the encyclopedia plus an impressive number of other wombat facts:

- I can look at a list of recommended books about wombats and purchase them from Amazon.com. One is called *How to Attract the Wombat*.

- I can see dozens, nay hundreds, of wombat photos. They're adorable.

- I can discover that wombats are a recurring motif in the webcomic *Penny Arcade* —and then link to read episodes of the comic.

- I can visit "Russell's Burrow," the home page of a wombat named Russell that was rescued and released back into the bush. (He claims to have constructed the Web site himself, but I have my suspicions.)

- I can learn the wombat's scientific classification and click on each level to see related animals.

- I can study the exploits of Graham Eadie, affectionately known as "Wombat," one of the greatest rugby players of the 1970s.

- I can discover that an annual "wombats cabaret" at the University of Otago, New Zealand, included a skit titled "Beverly Wombats 90210." [1]

And so forth. With the Internet, a near-infinite amount of information is at our fingertips. It's a cliché, and we have all been reading about it for the past decade, but the Internet has completely changed the way we think about and experience information. It's worth pausing to contemplate how difficult it was to learn about wombats just two decades ago. Today, anyone who has access to the Internet can access any wombat factoid instantly. The digital equivalent of all the millions of books, photos, maps and documents that reside in the Library of Congress is now created online every 15 minutes. [2] If the easy spread of information is helping propel the secret peace, it's clear the world is in for a lot more good news. But the Internet is only one of the most recent developments in a long chain of innovations over the centuries. Each step of this progress increases our capacity for generating new knowledge and sharing it with others.

The Compounding Interest
of Information

Are you wiser now than you were 10 years ago? How about 20 years ago? It's not often that someone would say they grew less intelligent, made rasher decisions, or got more naïve with age. Kids in school grow smarter as they advance through grades, with each year's knowledge building on the previous years'. Every tidbit we learn makes it possible for us to learn more. After we graduate, we pick up job skills as we enter the working world, and accrue skills with each new task and job. Constantly accumulating knowledge increases your value and is why (assuming you haven't drastically switched careers) you're probably making more money now than you did years ago.

Just as individuals grow wiser with age, so does the human race as a whole. That's because, as a culture, we learn new things every day, but never unlearn anything. So all the knowledge piles up on itself, constantly increasing. This snowballing knowledge is the first of the three major forces pushing us toward world peace. Money serves as a good metaphor for this process. Just as compound interest means that a little money in the bank will earn a little interest, and eventually snowball into more and more, so does information build on itself. But if money were just stuffed under your mattress it wouldn't earn interest. It earns interest because the bank is using the money in productive ways, investing it. Likewise with knowledge. It doesn't create itself, but is generated as people take existing information, question it, contemplate it, and combine it into new ideas. In addition, even though it may not seem so sometimes, we are always learning from our mistakes. Simply put, history does *not* repeat itself. Motifs repeat, but not the exact details of an event. Then if you examine the repeating theme, you're likely to see that it improved a little bit the second time around.

As economist Steven Landsburg describes, "The reason you are wealthier than your grandparents, and the reason your grandchildren will be wealthier than you, is that each generation free-rides on the inventiveness of its ancestors."[3] Our relatively peaceful, prosperous world is able to exist because the generations before us invented certain things and thought of certain ideas. And just as in school, each new idea makes the next idea easier to come by.

This, in fact, is one of the defining traits of human beings—animals can only pass information (behaviors, really) to future generations via their genes. Landsburg goes on to say that, "The engine of prosperity is technological progress, and the engine of technological progress is people. Ideas come from people. The more people, the more ideas. The more ideas, the more we prosper."[4]

This jibes with several of the theories we looked at in the last chapter. Like Robert Wright's ideas, passing down knowledge is non-zero sum; the information-conveyer doesn't lose his knowledge, he multiples it. This theory also sounds like technological determinism—the idea that technology alone drives history.[5] But while science and technology are big components of the knowledge being passed down, they're not the only things "knowledge" or "information" can refer to. Knowledge passes from person to person, and from generation to generation, in the form of the arts, culture, sports, professional skills and crafts, ethics, and philosophical ideas. It's passed down by governments, too: legally, we are constantly creating and refining laws that are based on precedents. It's easy to see technology build on itself—as new and faster computers keep coming out, for example—but artists, writers, and musicians are creating more diverse, complex, and robust works, too, because they have generations of masterpieces to learn from and be inspired by. Just like scientists, they are always exploring new fields and new ideas.[6]

When ideas are passed as information, they are sometimes known by their trendier name, "memes." A meme is merely a kernel of information, an idea that spreads from one mind to another. Some examples are catchy tunes, belief systems, fashions, proper cell-phone-in-the-movie-theater etiquette, or a YouTube video of an awesome guitar player rocking out to Pachelbel's Canon.[7] I'm spreading memes with this book; all books do. I'm taking existing ideas, mashing them together into new ideas, and attempting to spread them to, well, you.

The creation of memes is a perfectly natural process; ideas evolve and change through a process of natural selection much like that of biological evolution. Not all ideas are brilliant, but eventually mediocre ideas are discarded in favor of catchier, smarter, better memes.[8] Like the philosopher Arthur Schopenhauer said, "All truth passes through three stages. First, it is ridiculed.

Second, it is violently opposed. Third, it is accepted as being self-evident."⁹ And what memes are spreading? Those that encourage the secret peace, of course.

All of the concepts in this book—democracy, equality, new technologies—are memes. They would not be growing in practice if they were not becoming increasingly popular in principle. Many of these ideas are becoming universal. And even where they are not yet put into practice, they're percolating subconsciously. That's why a single event can "suddenly" set off a revolutionary change, like the fall of the Berlin Wall. Today, thanks to democracy and to the Internet, people are free to argue and share their opinions across the globe. As ideas are shared more and more widely, people are weaving them together and thinking more quickly and creatively. And wider access to diverse opinions is making narrow-mindedness less and less acceptable.

There are so many people on Earth now, and so much information, that it doesn't take much from each of us to push progress along. I found a good parallel in a business article by James Surowiecki about Toyota's success. Toyota defines innovation "as an incremental process, in which the goal is not to make huge, sudden leaps but, rather, to make things better on a daily basis. (The principle is often known by its Japanese name, *kaizen* – continuous improvement.)"¹⁰

Because of the ability to store information and share it with others, we can try small changes to our tasks and ideas, and remember what works and what doesn't. Sure, there are sometimes dramatic events or inventions that pop up and cause a huge change, but it turns out these innovations are often built on previous work that was just under the radar. They didn't just come out of nowhere. There are also often missteps backwards, when bad ideas are momentarily popular, but the good outweighs the bad as time goes by. An important aspect of this idea generation is how widespread the improvements are among people, as Surowiecki describes: "And so it rejects the idea that innovation is the province of an elect few; instead, it's taken to be an everyday task for which everyone is responsible. ... Toyota implements a million new ideas a year, and most of them come from ordinary workers."¹¹

Take the same principles and spread them out among the world's people, and we see civilization improving daily. The vast majority of people are daily trying to make things better for themselves and their families. (Or, they can be lazy and do nothing; but the number of people actively trying to make things *worse* is very small.) Many errors are made, and big mistakes can push many people back at once, but adding together all that effort means history has no choice but to improve.

A CENTURIES-LONG CURRICULUM

Progress has been snowballing for hundreds of years, but it's really picked up speed in the last few decades. And in the twenty-first century, it's skyrocketed, thanks to the new public availability of information. Here's an example. I recently read a book about Leo Tolstoy's religious views. He was a student of the world's religions and dug up information about as many of them as he could. Yet, even though Tolstoy was one of the most famous and beloved people in the world by the end of his life (he died in 1910), he had trouble obtaining books he wished to read, especially translations.[12]

A century later, the difference in the general availability of books could not be more striking. I can order virtually any book ever written from Amazon.com, and I don't even need to do that if the information I need can be found through a simple Google search. A bibliophile like Tolstoy would have shrieked for joy if he had been able to wander into the four-story Barnes & Noble down the street from me. Then he might have sat down in its café and ordered a latté while choosing between translations (or strolled to the fiction section and looked at the dozens of editions of his own books.) It's amazing how quickly we have grown to take this remarkable progress for granted. And there are a lot of new twists you might not have heard about, such as the "Espresso Book Machine," which was briefly featured in the New York Public Library and might be coming to a library, café, airport or bookstore near you. I walked over to the library and took a look at the copier-sized machine, which can print a single copy of *any* book, from a digital file, in about four minutes.[13] "In stock" is becoming a completely moot point. Furthermore, we have the advent of Amazon's Kindle and other electronic book readers, which avoids the hassle of printing the book completely. Kindles can download books you order in an instant, prompting Amazon's CEO Jeff Bezos to flaunt the humble end goal of "every book ever printed, in any language, all available in less than 60 seconds." If you simply want to read at your computer, even more is available. The World Digital Library also recently launched; it's an electronic resource designed to offer the totality of human knowledge (in seven languages). Any country or library can contribute to its database. Of course, this is practically moot, as the Internet itself remains an ever-expanding repository of the world's wisdom.[14]

Tolstoy lived to be eighty-two, but that was unusual back then. Today, with our average life span nearly that long, the amount of knowledge that individuals can soak up in their lifetime is vastly augmented. This is only rivaled by the amount of information we can each now generate ourselves. It's estimated that almost one zettabyte of unique information will be generated in 2009. If you've never heard of a zettabyte (or an exabyte or yottabyte), trust me, it's a lot. It is more than humanity created in all the years leading up to the twenty-first century, *put together*. In fact, it's estimated that a stack of this past week's *New York Times*, piling up in your garage, contains more information than a person was likely to come across in their lifetime in the eighteenth century. The amount of new technical information alone doubles every two years.[15] Combine this growing knowledge with the current ease of storing information—we have evolved from clay tablets, to stone, to animal skins, to papyrus, to paper, to bound books, to computer punch cards, to disks, to web servers, and on and on—and it becomes much easier to pass knowledge on to coworkers, other countries, and our descendants. All of that accumulated knowledge empowers anyone who encounters it—not least of all the millions of scientists, writers, philosophers, inventors, and artists who are daily adding to our giant global database of wisdom. This constant refinement is described by Amazon's Bezos: "information perfection is on the rise."[16]

While the vast amounts of knowledge newly available can feel overwhelming, rest assured that we are smart enough to process it all. By all measures, we are much smarter than our ancestors. It's not that our brains have physically evolved to some superior state in only a few thousand years, although better nutrition surely helps our brains as much as it helps our bodies. Rather, our collective knowledge, education, and the thinking tools available make us better equipped to make complex decisions wisely.

For example, think about how there are now at least 600,000 words in the English language. This is five times as many words as Shakespeare had available in the sixteenth century. More words don't just make us more verbose. They make more creative, complex and sophisticated ideas possible—the opposite of Orwell's 1984 world, in which language was limited as a way to stifle independent thought. We also have tools like the vast resources of the Internet. We each have a finite amount of knowledge we can learn in a day, but in a way this is actually expanding, thanks to better technological filters and our own expanded capability to find what we want. So the data we take in daily is increasingly relevant and meaningful to each of us. In 2006, there were 2.7 billion Google searches every month. Sounds impressive, but wait—by 2009, it was 9.4 billion a month. That's 350 percent growth in three years. A lot of that is to find the best shopping and nudity, sure, but a lot of it is people looking for information. To whom were these questions posed before Internet search engines popped up? Most likely, no one; a large percentage must have simply gone unanswered. I would not have delved further with my wombat report in the past if it was too much effort (to drive to the library, for example). I just would have stopped at a certain point of limited knowledge.[17]

Our growth in knowledge is remarkable, considering it has only been 100 years since formal education first became available to significant numbers of people. Until relatively recently basic education was a luxury. Why did this change come about? Thanks to industrialization, the need for purely physical labor—such as farming—changed to a need for skilled labor. This led to an economic need to educate the masses, at least at minimal levels. The United States was at the forefront of this trend. At the time of its founding, the U.S. most likely had the highest literacy rate in the world; for instance, Massachusetts had public schools as early as 1635.[18]

Eventually, industrialized societies kept evolving until, during the twentieth century, they replaced a large part of their labor force with workers who needed to perform highly skilled tasks. Today, with the world's most advanced countries shifting from manufacturing to service-based economies, the labor demand has changed to a need for even more highly-skilled labor. Simultaneously, computerization has increased our productivity and taken over menial tasks. This leads to a need for advanced education and a way to foster the skills computers can't yet duplicate: creativity and innovation, social skills and management. On an individual level, people must keep educating themselves to get better jobs, which is challenging, but enables society to keep pushing forward. And the rise of literacy empowers people to want more voice, more democracy, and more education, leading to an upward spiral of continuous improvement.

The spread of education in America skyrocketed in just a few decades. In 1960, only 41 percent of adults had graduated from high school, and only eight percent had college degrees. By 1998, those numbers had jumped to 82 percent and 24 percent respectively.[19] Today a majority of countries are extremely literate, with a literacy rate of 99 percent in many Western countries. Earlier, I mentioned the astounding fact that the world's total average literacy rate shot up from 63 percent in 1970 to 83 percent today. One of the UN Millennium Development Goals is to reach full primary schooling by 2015; 46 countries have already achieved the goal, and many more are on track to hit the deadline. The literacy rate is now nearly 100 percent for people ages 15 to 24 in East Asia, Europe, Central Asia, Latin America, and the Caribbean.[20]

The *Economist* describes that newspapers are booming in newly-developing countries. "The demand for news tends to go up as people enter the workforce, earn more money, invest it and begin to feel that they have more of a stake in their society. Literacy rates also rise in tandem with wealth. For the newly literate, flipping through a newspaper in public is a potent and satisfying symbol of achievement."[21] A large portion of that gain in literacy is a result of women around the globe finally becoming educated. Once fully realized, the empowerment of half of the world's citizens will have dramatic effects—which will multiply over the years, since women are more likely than men to bestow their knowledge to the next generation. We'll find out more when we look at gender equality in more detail later on.

Our progress in education is impressive. But the United States, for one, could be doing better. Our children attend fewer days of school a year than other children worldwide. They're also in school for fewer hours each day, adding up to 32 hours a week. Compare this to, say, 44 hours in Belgium or 60 in Sweden. Likewise they only do an hour of homework a night, a shocking figure to schoolchildren in East Asia. Worse still, the long summer vacation causes "summer learning loss." Kids have to relearn a lot of information come each September—a fact my mother, a public schoolteacher for the past 30 years, fervently wishes there was a way to correct.[22]

But even with these problems, the good progress far outweighs the bad setbacks. Consider this surprising proof: a phenomenon called the Flynn Effect shows that over the past few decades there has been a steady increase in average IQ scores in the developed world. IQs have been rising at three points per decade for a long time, and this small increase adds up over time. As author Steven Johnson explains, "Imagine ... a person who tests in the top 10 percent of the United States in 1920 time-travels 80 years into the future and takes the test again. Thanks to the Flynn Effect, he would be in the bottom third for IQ scores today. Yesterday's brainiac is today's simpleton."[23] The gene pool is unable to change that quickly, and cultural biases in the test are ruled out since the whole population is being examined each time. So it must be education and our cultural environment that are making us smarter.

CULTURE KEEPS GETTING SMARTER

To hear a lot of people tell it, American culture is dumbed-down and simple, and getting more so by the minute. We're stuck with violent video games, reality TV, and brain-dead summer blockbuster movies. But this common assumption is simply not true. Believe it or not, today we're experiencing perhaps the richest renaissance of art and culture in history.

You might ask: how I can suggest that today is a new Renaissance when we can compare Homer's *Odyssey* to Homer Simpson, Haydn or Mozart to Hannah Montana, Puck from *A Midsummer Night's Dream* to Puck from *The Real World*? Well, it's not fair to compare today's worst entertainment, such as the MTV reality series *My Super Sweet 16* or the movie *Ace Ventura Jr.*, to yesterday's best, like Shakespeare. That's comparing apples to oranges. (Although, even *Comedy of Errors* has flatulence jokes.) There was always plenty of low-quality fare published, produced and painted in the past. We just don't remember it, since it's only the crème de la crème that survives and gets taught in school. In 500 years no one will remember *Transformers 2: Revenge of the Fallen*, either. (Hopefully.)

Steven Johnson, author of *Everything Bad Is Good for You*, posits that today's popular culture—especially television and video games—is improving in quality and is actually making us smarter. Neuroscience now shows that the brain's primary desire is not to avoid doing work, but to seek out new experiences and challenges. Knowing this, it isn't surprising that we seek out demanding entertainment.[24] The increasing sophistication of television, movies, video games, and other media is a plausible contributor to the Flynn Effect of continuously-increasing IQs.

TV shows and films have increased in complexity in several ways. They now feature more plotlines and subplots woven together through multiple episodes. They move faster. They present more sophisticated social networks because they showcase a lot more characters.[25] They just plain require more of your attention. Even the so-called "passive" mediums are a lot less so today. Several forces are contributing to this: new technologies give rise to new forms of entertainment, the Internet fosters a new sense of community, viewers often find themselves bonding over favorite movies and shows, the market rewards more intelligent products, and our brains demand new experiences.[26]

Television is a surprising example of increased complexity in the media. As Johnson describes, even old shows that were considered complex for their time—such as *Dallas*, *Hill Street Blues*, and *All in the Family*—have relatively simple plots and one-note characters. Compare them to a 1997 *Seinfeld* episode called "The Betrayal," which organized its scenes in reverse chronological order, with the last scene showing first and the first scene last. The punch lines followed the setups, until all was revealed at the end (er, beginning). *Buffy the Vampire Slayer* featured an episode that had no dialogue (nominated for an Emmy), another that had no soundtrack, and another that mimicked a Broadway musical. Larry David and the other actors on *Curb Your Enthusiasm* creatively improvise their lines for every episode of their show.

TV today consistently features shows with intricate mysteries, season-long arcs, multifaceted characters, historical accuracy, and incredibly fast-paced writing. Shows such as *Six Feet Under*, *The Wire*, *The West Wing*, *The*

Sopranos, ER, Veronica Mars, Arrested Development, and *The Office* are each more complex than anything aired before 1990. These are now called "long-form television" due to ongoing storylines that make it incredibly hard to jump in mid-season. Nowadays, the excruciatingly mystifying drama *Lost* has layers of fake Web sites devoted to it; created by the show's makers, the sites are peppered with clues to the show's enigmas. As Adam Rogers writes in the *New York Times,* "The most popular TV shows [today] look like elaborate role-playing games: intricate, hidden-clue-laden science fiction stories connected to impossibly mathematical games that live both online and in the real world."[27]

And then there is *The Simpsons,* arguably the densest, wittiest show in history, now passing the 20-year mark. As the *Economist* describes, "*The Simpsons* is not just the most successful cartoon on American television, but also a brilliant satire on American religion, society and politics."[28] *The Simpsons* 1995 Halloween episode, as one great example of complexity, referenced 15 movies, not to mention dozens of other pop culture references, gags, puns, and in-jokes. In that episode, Homer accidentally breaks through the wall of the third dimension and appears fully rounded (more so than usual) in our world. Compare this level of sophistication to *The Simpsons'* prehistoric predecessor, the simplistic *Flintstones.* Now, you may happen to prefer *The Flintstones* to *The Simpsons,* that's personal taste, but it would be impossible to argue that *The Flintstones* was more intelligent or sophisticated. Yes, there were quality programs in the past (*M*A*S*H* always comes up due to its innovative dark comedy and social relevance), but even as the total number of shows aired today has skyrocketed, their sophistication has increased across the board.[29] Ben Silverman, co-chairman of NBC Entertainment, explains it simply: "The audience is growing up now."[30]

In film, there is a new mini-genre of mind-benders: intentionally complex and unconventional movies that are so hard to figure out that you just *have* to watch them more than once. Think of *Mulholland Drive, Memento, The Matrix, Pulp Fiction, Run Lola Run, Primer,* or any Charlie Kaufman movie, like *Being John Malkovich, Adaptation,* or *Eternal Sunshine of the Spotless Mind.* Each of these movies presents weird mysteries, out-of-order scenes, subtle symbolism, multiple narrators or perspectives, or bizarre twist endings. Even children's films are much more dense and interesting. Johnson compares 1942's *Bambi* to 1964's

Mary Poppins and then to 2002's *Finding Nemo*.[31] Watch all three of these films with your kids chronologically to clearly see how the complexity of characters, subplots, and jokes has increased over time. Add 2008's *WALL-E* to it, too. Or take 2008's *The Dark Knight*. I was surprised to see so many children in the audience for this Batman movie, not because of violence or scariness, but because I couldn't believe they could follow the incredibly layered plot, let alone its dark philosophical themes and moral quandaries. That's not the Batman we saw on movie screens in 1989, or on TV in 1969, let alone the straightforward, crudely-drawn comics of 1939. (Though this transformation mirrors the trend of growing sophistication and quality in comic books and graphic novels, as well.)

The increased complexity of television and film is market-driven. Until the advent of the VCR, if you wanted to see a TV show, you had no choice but to watch it whenever it was shown. If you missed it, you missed it. Then came the VCR, then cable channels with a vastly expanded catalog of shows, then the repetition of shows in syndication, satellite TV, DVDs collecting seasons of shows, followed by TiVo and digital video recorders. Johnson describes, "These proliferating new recording technologies are often described as technologies of convenience: you watch what you want to watch, when you want to watch it." They are yet another example of increasing individual power due to the ability to personally access better-stored information. With these new technologies, television studios realized their most successful shows—the shows people would want to purchase season-DVDs of or watch again in syndication—are shows that are enjoyable upon repeated viewings. These shows need to be more complex in content. And, it turns out, the more complex and fast-paced shows are often the most popular.[32]

NOTHING'S THE MATTER WITH KIDS TODAY

Johnson's book focuses in large part on video games, the most dramatic examples of his idea. Video games are much more intelligent forms of entertainment than anything children have had access to in the past. Because the plot structures of modern video games are based on the concept of decision-making (unlike the plot structure of other forms of entertainment), video games are essentially critical thinking in entertainment form. As you play, the games respond by growing in complexity. They are organized to test the player's problem-solving skills. Easy video games are pointless; in fact, many of today's games are mind-bogglingly difficult.

Are video games less imaginative than previous forms of play? Maybe *Pac-Man* was, but twenty-first century games, such as *The Sims*, which simulates ordinary situations, or *Spore*, which lets you evolve your own animals, give you open-ended online worlds to explore. Children have always thrived on self-conceived imaginative play, with no prompts needed. I don't want to disparage that necessary form of learning; that kind of open-ended exploration is still available to kids, it's just that now we've loaded it with a lot more options. Think about how kids used to play a century ago: perhaps they had a few books, they played with some simple toys, and they improvised sports like stickball and kick the can. The rest of their time was spent with household chores (or worse, real child labor).[33] What isn't more creative than that? When I was young, a new toy brand called Discovery Toys was created, and my mother became a sales representative. The toys and books were fun (we had tons around the house), but their emphasis was on education. They were based on child development studies that revealed exactly what was best suited to help kids grow smart and healthy at every age. Today it's not unusual for toys to be engineered with education in mind. Some toys have become customized, such as the one-of-a-kind teddy bears that you create step-by-step at Build-a-Bear Workshop; Nintendogs, an addictive video game of personal pets; or Webkinz, stuffed animals that have simultaneous doppelgangers on their web site. Of course, kids still love running around, but now their interests are more diverse. Children today are technological gurus, with their video games, instant messaging, cell phones, e-mail, and online talkbacks about favorite television shows and sports teams.

To some people, these kids seem more impatient, shameless, narcissistic, shut-in, rude, distracted, and less well-read than earlier generations (i.e. the generation of the accuser, of course.) Mark Bauerlein puts it in absurdly alarmist terms in a 2008 book: *The Dumbest Generation: How the Digital Age Stupefies Young Americans and Jeopardizes Our Future (Or, Don't Trust Anyone under 30.)*

Maybe Bauerlein doesn't know any real children, because the ones I've met astonish me. I dare you to try to decipher the complexity of a Pokemon or Yu-Gi-Oh! card game, for example. And my co-worker's daughter writes a fantastic blog, in which she creates art projects and then gives you step-by-step instructions, often telling hilarious stories along the way. *She's eight.* She's writing and illustrating entire stories, while developing the skills of writing for an audience. That's pretty impressive.

When a National Endowment of the Arts report lamenting the diminishing role of voluntary reading among teenagers doesn't take into account the average 16 hours a week each teen spends reading and writing online, maybe fears about the dumbing-down of the next generation are overblown. Today's kids are choosing to read and write for fun; it's a regular part of their social lives, and we should applaud that. A far-reaching study of college students over the past decade found that they write far more than any generation before them, and 38 percent of it is not for school. Before the Internet, most Americans didn't write *anything* recreationally. The study also looked at papers by first-year students and didn't find a single example of "text-speak," just plain-old English. Perhaps fewer kids today can name North America's largest lake or tell you who William Rehnquist is, but the justification for having to memorize information like that is questionable when you can always instantly look it up. Today's technological developments lead to children who are more skilled at problem-solving than rote memorization, and thus better prepared for today's world. Another study, conducted over 20 years by researcher Dan Tapscott, found that today's youth are smarter, more tolerant of diversity, more happy with their family life, and care strongly about justice and actively trying to improve society.[34]

As the kids of today get older, they might be in the middle of a revolution making us smarter still: drugs known as cognition enhancers that improve memory, concentration, and learning. Scientists are currently working on more than 600 drugs for neurological disorders such as Alzheimer's, attention-deficit disorder, and schizophrenia. The *Economist* reports, "Mind-expansion may soon, therefore, become big business. Even though the drugs have been developed to treat disease, it will be hard to prevent their use by the healthy. Nor, if they are without bad side-effects, is there much reason to." While the idea of these mind-enhancing drugs might sound frightening, making people smarter can only help solve the world's problems faster. The key is to make sure any drugs released are non-addictive, safe, and equitably available.[35]

New ways to augment our intelligence shouldn't be scary. After all, we've been doing it for centuries: our technological leaps are nothing if not ways to make us collectively smarter. Written language, the printing press, the telegraph, the calculator—these can be seen as ways we enhanced our natural biological memory ability. All save us time, effectively making us think faster, and free up our thinking for the real important challenges. As our education has progressed, so has our technology, so that we're evolving symbiotically. "Personalized education" is growing, in which teachers can use computers to tailor lessons to individual students, rather than forcing a one-size-fits-all method of learning onto everyone. And the Internet is enabling everyone's intelligence to augment everyone else's. When you post your thoughts online, it's like I have direct access to your brain and all its experience and wisdom. A natural downside to that is information overload. But the real trouble isn't that we have too much information, it's that our tools to process and filter it haven't caught up yet. When they do, our knowledge will advance even faster.[36]

I THINK, THEREFORE I AM

The ability of each of us to work to make ourselves smarter is evidence of the increasing power that is passing from tiny elite groups to the masses of humanity. The rise of individual power is another unifying theme linking all of the world's positive historical trends in the last half-millennium. The increasing power and freedom of all individuals is in itself a result of the ever-growing dissemination of information—both from the invention of the printing press and new ideas that developed during the Renaissance. When people get more freedom, more political voice, more ability to express themselves, and more education, these combine with the increasing availability of information to create a self-reinforcing cycle that is leading to a more just society. Frederick Douglass wisely noted that "to make a contented slave, it is necessary to make a thoughtless one.

It is necessary to darken his moral and mental vision, and, as far as possible, to annihilate the power of reason."[37] This is why totalitarian societies penalize and discourage true education. Knowledge is subversive. The spread of education encourages the spread of democracy, freedom, and peace. Education also tends to increase tolerance, which promotes equality and reduces conflict.

The ongoing spread of information from a select elite to the masses has kept the wheels of progress spinning during the last few centuries. And it is continuing at an even faster rate today. Look at MIT's OpenCourseWare, for example: all of MIT's courses are available online, for free, right now. You can even download them to your iPod, as their tagline boasts: "From lectures to documentaries to museum tours, iTunes U lets you learn anything, anytime, anyplace." The information on the Internet in general is democratizing, and OpenCourseWare is a supreme example of data that used to be available only to an elite few, now reaching a huge audience. Cognitive psychologist Roger Schank describes this as the end of the commoditization of knowledge. Looking at it this way, the past consisted of two eras: a first phase of rulers and religious figures having exclusive access to scrolls, tablets, and hand-copied books; and a second phase that "is the era we have lived in ever since the invention of the book. ... In this era, knowledge is [still] a commodity, owned and guarded by the knowledge elite and doled out by them in various forms that they control, like books, newspapers, television, and schools." This second era is ending today.[38]

Such shifts are possible because of fundamental changes in human thought that originated in Europe's Renaissance, and which have fueled the other advancements we have made in the 600 years since. Without expanding our minds, it never would have occurred to us to embark on all the economic, scientific, medical, and political quests of the last five centuries. So it's important to examine how human internal thought has changed before studying the effects of those changes in today's external world.

The Renaissance, and the Enlightenment which it eventually led to, are steps along a path that enhanced humanity's ability to master our universe through reason.[39] The Enlightenment, a cultural movement of the eighteenth century, was the period in which the trend of social and technological progress took off and started to engulf the globe. One of the most striking developments of the Enlightenment is the acceleration of science. But science was percolating centuries earlier during the Renaissance, too (and in Islamic cultures before that). In fact, Renaissance means "rebirth" since it was a return of motifs from classical Greece: reason, math, philosophy, and curiosity about the world. The very idea of relying on evidence and reason, rather than faith, gave power to the world's people, as Clay Shirky explains: "The idea of evidence is consistently radical: Take nothing on faith; no authority is infallible; if you figure out a good way to test something, you can contradict hallowed figures with impunity."[40] Reason and science expand the mind and allow all sorts of new insights.

Let's examine Leonardo da Vinci as a perfect example of the ideals of the period, the quintessential Renaissance Man. On one of his 14 thousand notebook pages, in his trademark mirror-image cursive, he wrote, "The earth is not in the center of the circle of the sun, nor in the center of the universe." That was 40 years before Copernicus made the same realization. Observing gravity's effects 200 years before Sir Isaac Newton, Leonardo noticed that because "every substance presses downward, and cannot be upheld perpetually, the whole earth must be spherical." And four centuries before Charles Darwin, Leonardo placed humans in the same category as apes and wrote, "Man does not vary from animals except in what is accidental." Leonardo was the first person to draw up plans for a bicycle, helicopter, submarine, armored tank, snorkel, machine gun, gear shift, crane, and locks for a canal system. His extendable ladder design is still used by firefighters. He invented the parachute and amazingly deduced the only proportions that work, even though he couldn't test them, since planes weren't invented! In art, he revolutionized perspective by painting light and shadow more effectively, and invented the cross-section. He even drew ideas for a robot.[41]

Leonardo had the advantage of being arguably the greatest genius to ever live, but his curiosity, and appreciation for art and science, became common. As educated men grew more interested in thinking for themselves, they also grew more fascinated by the world around them and became increasingly inspired to learn everything about the natural order. In order to compete in business, art, and warfare, people had to think more creatively. Thus was the

Enlightenment launched. The principles of science exploded out into the world even faster with Johannes Gutenberg's invention of the movable type printing press in 1447.[42] Suddenly, information could be more easily stored and shared, and discoveries could disseminate more quickly.

Science as a method of thinking drastically changed the way we understand the world. There was a slow realization that knowledge is something to create, rather than preserve: humanity's best work now lay in the future, not the past of the "wise ancients."[43] Several scientific principles were revolutionary in their time, but now we take them for granted. Logic itself, as a general set of principles to help us think correctly, is so fundamental to us now that we forget it had to be created. Two powerful components of logic are deduction, reasoning with certainty, and induction, making educated guesses. The burden of proof puts the obligation to prove something on the person disputing existing knowledge. And science understands that authorities have no special control of information; they are not inherently trustworthy over anyone else. Similarly, objectivity reminds us that even our own opinions might be biased, an important ego-check. Lastly, the most fundamental principle is the scientific method—the tried and true process of observing things, coming up with explanations, testing them, and scrapping the bad ones.

In a fascinating synergy to our central concept of a peacefully globalizing planet, science thrives on sharing knowledge. Science knows no borders, and with mathematics and specialized notations in specific fields, science can even transcend language. Furthermore, scientific information builds on itself more obviously and even faster than other types of information. Once someone learns, invents, or discovers something, it is not long before it becomes public knowledge, and it can then never be "un-known." So there are rarely backward steps in science; it is always increasing its scope. In fact, a critical part of science is its capability, eagerness even, to prove itself wrong, a feature that was woefully missing from older thought systems.

Combining radical notions like logic, burden of proof, objectivity, and the scientific method was so successful that we can see how scientific thinking spread so quickly. Science led not just to physical improvements in technology, but to a belief system based on the tenets of the Enlightenment that also formed the basis of American democracy. Historian Clinton Rossiter remarks, "[Benjamin] Franklin was one of a number of forward-thinking colonists who recognized the kinship of scientific method and democratic procedure. Free inquiry, free exchange of information, optimism, self-criticism, pragmatism, objectivity—all these ingredients of the coming republic were already active in the republic of science that flourished in the eighteenth century."[44]

The development of science runs parallel to the rise of independent thinking. Before the Renaissance, the notion of the "individual"—that is, the idea that each of us is unique and thus inherently valuable—was scarcely emphasized. After all, how could you think of yourself proudly when your life was identical to everyone else's? Maybe a few miles away, up on a hill, there lived a wealthy landowner, but everyone you saw when you looked around was a peasant like yourself. You woke up, stretched, probably skipped breakfast since there wasn't much food to go around, put on the same clothes you wore yesterday, and walked outside to toil in your field every day for the rest of your life.

This daily toil may be an exaggeration, but not by much. This point hit home for me when I took art history courses in college. We studied the art made during Europe's Middle Ages (the term "Dark Ages" is passé now, to make sure we don't offend any long-dead peasants). All of the art depicts the Virgin Mary or the crucifixion of Christ. Much of the work is beautiful, until you look at more and more of it: nearly every painting looks identical no matter who the artist was. Truth be told, we don't know who many of the artists were, since the painters did not sign their work. Individualism and point of view were irrelevant, or worse, sacrilegious, taking away from the religious importance of a piece. Although there are notable exceptions, most of the pre-modern world treated art the same way. Egypt is the best example—the beautiful hieroglyphs and wall artwork carved by Egyptian sculptors look eerily identical, even over a 3,000-year period!

In the fourteenth century, however, something started to change in Italy. Early Renaissance figures such as the Italian poets Dante and Petrarch started working on more ambitious projects and received renown for their efforts. Petrarch posited of history as a series of artistic and social advances (sound familiar?), an idea shifting emphasis from religion to humanity.[45]

Florence and other Italian cities became hotbeds of economic activity that gave rise to a new merchant class. Many of these merchants earned their wealth rather than inherited it. This class was made up of neither destitute peasants nor spoiled rulers and became a real middle class—a collection of self-supporting individuals rather than a nameless population of serfs. What really kicked things off was all the money that started to accumulate and circulate. With this extra capital, the wealthy in Florence became the first "patrons of the arts" and funded grand art projects. Unfortunately, this patronage exposed the flip side of individualism—vanity—since patrons often competed for prestige. But without that funding, Michelangelo, Raphael, and Leonardo would not have been able to devote much time to their work. Luckily they had enough time to become masters—and to become famous. Suddenly, they were individuals, and believe me, they signed their work!

Several new ideas were now in the air. "Celebrities" now existed, and the most accomplished creators were in high demand. Europe also saw meritocratic ideas spread, in which people were praised and honored for their personal achievements and hard work. In addition, philosophy started to branch out into new realms, starting with Descartes, who kicked off the modern period. His famous *cogito ergo sum*, "I think, therefore I am," is as individualistic as you can get. A few centuries earlier he would have been more likely to come up with "God thinks, therefore I am … even though I'm not worthy." But his famous principle instead means that the only thing he can be absolutely certain about is that he's a thinking being, and that means an individual.[46]

Follow this thread of individuality to today and what do you have? A world community of self-empowered individuals slowly discovering that they can no longer rely on the bonds of tradition, the rigid laws of the clergy, or the arbitrary whims of kings. Today, individuals must think for themselves. Of course, that's not as easy as it sounds. It can create chaos and fear as the populace adjusts to its newfound responsibility. But as civilizations and generations have come out of darkness and into personal knowledge, they have realized that much more is possible when everyone is able to act independently. And this individual power isn't necessarily selfish; even group cooperation is transformed with independent thought, since everyone's actions are voluntary and committed.

The transmission of knowledge has accelerated because there is a much larger base of people passing information down. Once the province of a small elite, every educated and moderately well-off person now has the capability to absorb, create, store, and transmit vast amounts of information. This democratization of power—of knowledge, the true power of the world, spreading out to everyone—is our second force pushing towards peace. And far-reaching new participatory technology is powering that trend.

TECHNOLOGY

Audience Participation

Today we see a radically increasing amount of information being passed down, and realize that it's pushing the development of the secret peace. But if the small coterie of clergy or philosophers who had access to knowledge in centuries past were passing information solely amongst themselves, we wouldn't see the progress we're seeing today. Luckily, knowledge isn't just accumulating, it's spreading. It's reaching more and more people.

If knowledge is power, then today power is shifting from the bourgeoisie to the proletariat—as if in a calmer, behind-the-scenes version of a communist revolution. However, since knowledge is non-zero sum, it's being shared rather than violently wrested from existing hands. Even more importantly, this is a democratic revolution, the polar opposite of a top-down controlled system such as in old communist Russia. In fact, as we'll see in the trends we examine in this book, most significant positive changes throughout history have been from the people: bottom-up, not top-down.

Our history books focus on the names and dates of famous leaders and dramatic battles. And don't get me wrong, those things matter. But the books often scrimp on the quiet trends—those that bubble under the surface until one day people look up and realize the world has changed. This still happens with the media today. All of our front-page articles focus on Congress and the President, while many other important developments are happening in the background. Looking at it this way, the seeming stalemate of negative back-and-forth between political parties (in America especially, but also elsewhere) might be occupied with certain issues that are not even necessarily the most important ones. This contributes to our perception of all change being top-down, which is an illusion.

Governments, laws, politicians, wars, and big significant events do drive a lot of change, of course. But many significant shifts in our culture would have happened even without those headline-drawing catalysts. Smart politicians get on the bandwagon of an issue *after* it's already been percolating in the zeitgeist for awhile. They may seem to be pushing for radical new progress, but if the public is not already primed for change, their efforts will have little effect. Democratic governments can rarely force major changes upon a populace that doesn't want them; at least, not without them eventually getting overturned from public pressure. In fact, by definition, they're not supposed to—for better or for worse. Examples include Prohibition in the 1920s, and gay marriage today. Despite the right or wrong of either issue, legislation is not going to sway public opinion if a majority of people do not already share some support of the issue. Later, if those views become accepted by a larger majority of citizens, laws will pass more smoothly. (Although, naturally there will always remain some opponents to the idea.)

Sometimes, a government can speed up the acceptance of an idea by slowly introducing small changes, such as with smoking. Rather than ban smoking outright, governments at the *local* level passed increasingly strict laws, and over a period of many decades. Banning smoking in restaurants is not single-handedly inspiring millions of people around the world to quit smoking. No, education is doing that, as the public has become aware of smoking's health dangers. There is now more subtle peer pressure in society *not* to smoke than to smoke. Laws revealing smoking's effects were essential. Bans and other ordinances merely helped nurture the natural trend and nudge people further.

As another example of how grassroots public opinion is more critical than top-down decisions, take a look at Abraham Lincoln. Is it possible to believe that we would still have slavery today if he were never President? Lincoln deserves a lot of credit for "freeing the slaves," but remembering him as the sole instigator of that grand change insults the memories of the thousands of abolitionists that worked for decades to steer public opinion and raise awareness of the plight of America's slaves. Many vested interests had a stake in the existing system, but much of the public was already firmly on the side of freedom. Lincoln happened to be the right President at the right time, a time when the common view of the issue had shifted enough to support his efforts.

Just as with technical, scientific discoveries, a lot of changes are in the "ether," merely waiting for the right people to tip them over into reality. If those people miss the ball, someone else comes along a few years later. In general, secret peace trends are inevitable. Only the speed of their implementation is up to us. Often, these people are not world leaders, but small, committed grassroots individuals or groups. As the anthropologist Margaret Mead famously said, "Never doubt that a small group of thoughtful, committed citizens can change the world. Indeed, it is the only thing that ever has."[1]

Grassroots movements took off during the twentieth century, and knowledge began its democratic spread with the advent of public education, as we've seen. But in terms of democratizing power, it's almost as if the world was simply holding its breath waiting for the advent of the true game-changer: the Internet. Our second powerful force pushing towards peace is the democratization of knowledge and power, and its key instigator is our new information technology. This is the skyrocketing productivity from computers, the convenient access of mobile phones, and most of all, the Internet. The number of Internet users around the world exceeded one and a half billion in 2009.[2] Several of the changes we will examine in this book are slow processes. Not so for technology, and computers and communication technology have developed the fastest of all. In addition, computers act as a positive feedback loop advancing information to help speed along all of the world's other encouraging developments.

Decades ago, the fledgling Internet's use was limited to the military, a few scholars, techie folks, and scientists. There was a real cultural breakthrough once the general public gained access to the web to search for information and add its own. Visiting Google today, I can look up anything I need to know instantly. (In the past few years, we're suddenly able to do all that on our mobile phones, too.) Google's innovation was a web searching algorithm that factored in a site's popularity based on how many other sites link to it. We've examined how new information being developed and spread leads to the secret peace. But if that information were not easily accessible, if it were just generated and stored away in a dusty warehouse, its usefulness would be incredibly limited. We need technologies that enable us to sort through all the data—which are improving all the time. This is how software and design pioneer Kai Krause describes today's innovations:

> To get to research done anywhere, by anyone; to share findings and writings; duplicate them instantly, store them and save them; catalog them and index them, searchable among billions, in seconds! To have your own copy of the books, your own *Britannica*—how blissful that would have made Jules Verne, with his 20,000 wooden boxes of index-card snippets, or any of the other polymaths, like Athanasius Kircher, or T.H. Huxley, or Newton, or Leibniz. To have your own diviner of answers to any question, finder of any fact, in minutes or even seconds, an advisor like no Sun King or emperor, kaiser or pharaoh, could ever buy with all the gold in his empire. That's Google, now, in a smartphone, in the pockets of teenagers.[3]

COMMUNICATION: CAN YOU HEAR ME NOW?

In addition to being a storehouse of information, a window to new kinds of commerce, and a tool to transform the way we work, the Internet is the most efficient communication tool ever created. Any advance in communication technology helps people connect, and the Internet helps people discuss similar interests, coordinate nonviolent actions, join NGOs, attend support groups, sign online petitions, and participate in online learning. For example, in 2006 Alabama started a radical program called ACCESS, which uses the Internet and videoconferencing to connect rural students to particular teachers, vastly expanding the range of courses available to everyone.[4] Similarly, my mother tutors English as a foreign language online to students half a globe away. Communication technology is helping change the way we identify ourselves and the groups we associate with. By making it easy for collectives to form across national boundaries, we can organize around shared interests and principles. Grouping Internet users into multiple networks is another trend fostering a sense of global citizenship, one which we'll look at in more detail later.

One of the most obvious ways of connecting people, Internet dating, has completely taken off. Among my friends—young, Internet-savvy, and living in urban areas—online dating is the norm. It has made flirting and meeting potential dates more effective and more convenient for busy lives, not to mention safer, since with the right site, you can learn about and vet someone before seeing them in person. By 2006, one in eight couples married in the U.S. had met online—including myself and my wife.[5]

As a tool for fostering communication, e-mail represents a huge step in our technological evolution. Like many technological developments of recent years—answering machines, voicemail, caller ID, VCRs, syndicated TV shows, and TiVo—e-mail lets you control the timing of tasks in your life, since e-mail can be answered at your leisure. Granted, spam is a problem, but not an insurmountable one. The percent of email that is spam peaked in 1994 at over 90 percent, but it has been declining since then.[6] Filtering technology has advanced enough since that time to block much spam, and new anti-spam laws are being put in place as well.

E-mail practically crawls compared to newer developments such as instant messaging, text messaging, and writing directly on the Web. Droves of young people are adopting these new means of communication as naturally as an older generation did the telephone. And speaking of phones, the Internet is not the only new tool facilitating tighter bonds of communication. Cell phones are ubiquitous, and despite their downside—like the eardrum-piercing ring tone of "You Spin Me Round (Like a Record)" I heard on the subway platform yesterday—they surpass land phone lines in convenience, safety, and cost. The number of land lines in the United States has been declining since 2001, and estimates of 2009 show that 37 percent of Americans use their wireless phone as their primary phone.[7] As the *Economist* points out, "When it comes to bridging the 'digital divide' between the rich and poor, the mobile phone, not the personal computer, has the most potential."[8] This is because phones are increasingly being used *as* computers, and it's likely that in the future, more computer users and Internet surfers will use phones than actual desktop or laptop computers.

The number of mobile phone subscribers worldwide surpassed 4 billion in 2008—that's almost two-thirds of the world's population. China is the country with the most subscribers, constituting 19 percent of the world's total; 29 percent of the Internet users in China use their phones to get online. Developing countries, particularly in Africa, are advancing in phone use—leapfrogging over traditional land-line use to cell phones. Roughly four in ten Africans now own a mobile phone.[9] Since cell phones require so little infrastructure, they are a much cheaper technology and are far better for the environment. In this way, the cell phone is increasingly helping to empower the world's masses.

A London Business School study found that in a developing country, "a rise of ten mobile phones per 100 people boosts national GDP growth by 0.6 percentage points."[10] Among the world's very poorest, phones can be shared by an entire village. Phones let farmers check market prices, help people find jobs, and boost entrepreneurship. The Grameen Bank, an innovator of microfinance, has provided loans to 195,000 Bangladeshis to purchase cell phones and then sell their airtime minutes to locals who need to make phone calls to distant family members or business contacts. In other countries, such as South Africa, banks link ATM cards to prepaid phone accounts, providing secure banking services to people who have never had access to those services before.[11] While the cost of cell phones can still be prohibitive, companies are working to bring those costs down and reach vast new markets. One of the challenges of providing cell phones in the developing world is the increasing demand for additional features: because the phones are so expensive, consumers want their money's worth.

We have e-mail, cell phones, text messaging—what else do we need? Well, now the Holy Grail of communication technology is on the horizon: a universal translator. This is something humanity has dreamed of for centuries, ever since multiple languages were inflicted upon humankind as punishment for building the Tower of Babel. Douglas Adams, in the sci-fi novel *The Hitchhiker's Guide to the Galaxy*, imagined people using a tiny alien goldfish, stuck in the ear of its host, that took anything spoken and translated it into their brain. Researchers are on the cusp of making a similar, though non-goldfish-based, technology available today.

In 2003, in the early days of the war in Iraq, U.S. soldiers were given devices that stored Arabic phrases and recognized some English phrases as well. When a soldier spoke into the device using a common phrase such as "Where is the restroom?" or "Which way did Saddam go?" the device spoke the same phrase in Arabic—but could not translate back, so locals were only able to gesture in response. Researchers realized that storing common phrases was inadequate and that programming vocabulary and rules of grammar into a computer would allow greater versatility. Even so, there were too many exceptions to the rules. In response, researchers came up with "statistical machine translation" software. By entering long texts already translated correctly, like English and Russian versions of *War and Peace*, the software learns how to translate between two different languages statistically. And the software keeps improving.

What can language technology do for us in the future? It would facilitate real-time automatic dubbing, which would allow us to watch any foreign film or TV show and have it translated as we watch. We could finally share the profound magic of, say, *Perfect Strangers*, with everyone around the globe. Search engines could expand to let us search documents in every language. Some scientists are excited about the possibility of using such technology to translate dolphin speech. But even more exciting and lofty is the goal of incorporating the software into phone lines so that callers would be understood by the speakers of any language, anywhere.[12]

EVERYONE WANTS A BLOG!

These advancements remind us of the lack of means of communication that predominated throughout most of history. Even the mass media of the twentieth century—print, TV, movies, radio—allowed only a few select people to communicate to the rest of humanity. Until recently, the masses couldn't communicate a response. The Internet is changing that, and we are seeing people migrate to more participatory forms of entertainment and news. Media mogul Rupert Murdoch describes the phenomenon:

> Those of us in so-called old media have also learned the hard way what this new meaning of networking spells for our business. Media companies don't control the conversation anymore ... Options abound. Fans of small niches can now find new content they could never before. Going elsewhere for news and entertainment is easier and cheaper than ever. And people's expectations of media have undergone a revolution. They are no longer content to be a passive audience; they insist on being participants, on creating their own material and finding others who will want to read, listen and watch.[13]

With an increase in access to various modes of communication, companies are struggling over how best to advertise.[14] Particularly with the invention of Google's Ad-Words, this is theoretically good news for consumers, since new ads can now target us so well that we may actually appreciate the advertising. Viewing a commercial for Polident may be a waste of time for a youngster, but it's money well spent on the AARP Web site. With Ad-Words, and the web site Craigslist, printed classified ads are declining fast and driving the decline of newspapers. So, many pundits are worried that the fourth estate might be crumbling. As the *Economist* puts it, "At their best, newspapers hold governments and companies to account."[15] Today many newspapers are folding, but all is not lost. On this issue the Internet gives us more cause to celebrate than to worry, thanks to blogs.

Blogs are informal personal online journals, either written or video, up-dated frequently. Operating independently, bloggers have no editors or con-straints. Millions of blogs exist today, and while some are created by high-school girls squealing at their friends, thousands of blogs are politically and socially relevant. Besides serving as personal journals, blogs exist as advice col-umns, fan analyses of TV shows, political debate, technology reviews, financial columns, and poetry. Whatever you can think of, someone is probably blogging about it, right now.

Journalism blogs can provide a source of information outside the struc-ture of traditional media. *Foreign Policy* magazine describes blogs as a "Fifth Estate" keeping watch over the mainstream media of corporate newspapers and TV news. In this way, individuals on the Internet can be seen as a perfect reverse Big Brother, always with an eye on the government.[16] Gone are the days of trusting one large media source for accurate news coverage. (Most small cit-ies and towns have only one or two local newspapers, and for decades all TV news was only on the three networks.) You can still get news from those larger sources, but with blogs you can also double-check facts and learn additional perspectives on a story. In this role, blogs act as a citizens' brigade of amateur journalists, photographers, memoirists, critics, and commentators. Bloggers can also report on the hyper-local news of a small town or even a neighborhood. The door to the incestuous world of professional editors and reporters has now been flung open so that everyone can participate.[17] Sabeer Bhatia, who launched a company called BlogEverywhere.com, hopes that "journalism won't be a ser-mon anymore, it will be a conversation."[18]

With a wide variety of topics and interests, blogs might help increase the public's engagement with contemporary issues. After all, a recent poll revealed that Americans and Europeans trust the opinions of "average people" more than they do experts.[19] Bloggers and their readers (by adding comments to blog posts) act as "the man on the street," providing eyewitness accounts of events as they happen. Blogging is particularly good at catching errors made by the mainstream media and calling attention to suspicious items the media misses, sometimes blowing open overlooked incidents into necessary scandals. They also have the potential to greatly benefit scientific advancement. Science blogs and related sites allow collaboration and discussion to happen much faster than the traditional published journals, and with a greater audience. Today, many more academic articles are jointly authored than in the past.[20]

For the consumer, separating the wheat from the chaff of all these blogs can be daunting. Finding trustworthy sources can be difficult, but at least you can sample a variety of sources and judge for yourself. Technological answers to the problem of blog credibility are quickly emerging—improved search engines, an increased emphasis on credentials and experience, portals that pull the best from several blogs, rankings based on popularity and readership, and recommendations via links from other well-respected blogs. Internet-wide credibility rating systems, based on either vetted credentials or user input, would help even more. But the fact remains that we must become more aware of each author's reliability and learn to prioritize what we read. Blogs and other diverse sources of information underscore the need for critical thinking.

If you had mentioned to your ninth-grade English teacher that in a few decades, millions of people would be writing every day and loving it, she might have scoffed in disbelief. The blogosphere (yes, that's a word) helps society learn, helps the mainstream media get its facts straight, and helps keep tabs on injustice in the world—all for free. Many bloggers are experts in their fields and are able to provide in-depth expertise on topics in which mainstream journalists have no expertise. Millions of people are now reporting on events just because they love writing about their favorite topics, interests, and avocations. Blogging reinforces the trend toward increased individual participation in society, but it is only one aspect of how the Web is facilitating this democratic growth.

PARTICIPATORY DEMOCRACY

Democracy needs informed debate in order to function. Traditional media used to be the only large forum for this debate, but input from citizens was limited to newspaper letters to the editor, call-in radio shows, and watching broadcasts of Senate hearings and town council meetings on public television. The Internet provides a true democratic forum, demonstrating yet again how all of the trends we have discussed influence one another. Blogs greatly increase the transparency essential for democracy.

Fact-checking and monitoring of government activities is a common pastime of bloggers. In 1984, Orwell shows us an oppressive state that built its mystique by constantly revising historical documents to make itself look infallible. With the creation of photo-editing software and the relative ease of changing electronic documents, it's easy to fear that this future is upon us. But with the Internet, the opposite is true. The government has less of a monopoly on information. If it tries to censor documents, you can be sure that the originals will be found and then posted on some blogger's site. A good example was a recent photo of an Iranian missile launch. It turns out that the Iranian government (presumably) had Photoshopped in an extra missile, apparently to cover up one that had failed. The fake photo appeared in several newspapers, but it was only a day before the jig was up. False information is easy to spread, but even easier to discredit.[21]

In countries where autocratic governments attempt to silence subversive newspapers, blogs can provide an outlet for escaping censorship, expressing political opposition, and discussing taboo topics. Bloggers are blossoming in Egypt and Iraq, for example, and Iran has so many bloggers that Farsi is now the fourth most common language among blogs.[22] Worldwide, many bloggers are increasingly linked as a like-minded community and can often work together to publicize issues such as Sudan's crisis in Darfur. As countries such as China and Belarus crack down on bloggers, the blogging community works together to outsmart them, in a deadly ongoing game of cat-and-mouse.[23]

Other web tools are chipping away at the world's autocracies as well. Satellite TV in the Arab world (and Iran) has exposed millions of people to a wider world of news and debate. Mobile phones and social networking sites are inspiring innovative new global activism. The Internet is being used to organize underground groups, teach forbidden information, and alert Western media to human rights abuses. Underground opposition youth movements in Cairo are using Facebook to organize, support each other, and spontaneously get together—working towards the goal of undermining Egypt's repressive regime. Egyptian columnist Mona Eltahawy explains:

> ... the needs of the masses have sparked a wave of un-
> precedented activism among young Egyptians. ... Generation
> Facebook might not be able to change their regimes today, but
> in building communities and support groups online, they are
> creating the much-needed middle ground that countries like
> Egypt desperately require.[24]

Twitter (a site we'll examine in more detail shortly) was famously used to coordinate the efforts of Iranian protesters after the disputed 2009 election in that country. Iranian citizens were able to get around Iran's Internet blocks by using Twitter on their mobile phones. The messages they sent rallied public support for their cause around the world.[25]

Using mobile phones, election monitors in fledgling democracies are now able to coordinate their result numbers and call them in to radio stations before corrupt governments get the opportunity to distort them. This has helped make elections cleaner in countries like Ghana and Kenya. "Smart mobs"—group gatherings inspired at the spur of the moment and coordinated via cell phone calls or text messages—are often used as untraceable forms of protest. These were particularly effective in toppling President Estrada of the Philippines in 2001, and text messaging was key to rallying youth in South Korea's 2002 elections.[26] For the Chinese community, text messaging is often a safer mode of communication than the Internet, and its popularity is spreading faster than the authorities can squelch it. Just as citizens can use text messaging and cell phones to report human rights abuses as they happen, they can also use cell phone cameras and video to record things visually as well. The musician Peter Gabriel founded the human rights group *Witness*, which distributes video cameras to developing countries so that they can report abuse and injustice.[27]

The more technology spreads to the developing world, the more exposure to ideals of democracy and freedom its citizens receive. As a result of this exposure, those citizens can then use that technology to spread information, educate themselves, and organize protests against autocratic rulers. The rulers know this; that's why 45 countries still restrict Internet access in some way, even though it's increasingly difficult to do. Monitoring the connections of millions of Internet users is daunting even for the determined Chinese government.[28] UK Prime Minister Gordon Brown described the new status quo well when he said, "[The new] flow of information means that foreign policy can never be the same again ... foreign policy can no longer be the province of just a few elites."[29]

Citizens in already-democratic countries are on the cusp of a revolution in tools to engage their governments, as well. The election of Barack Obama marked a sea change in how candidates can engage and include their supporters—using the Internet to collect millions of small donations rather than a few large ones, discovering the more active supporters and training them in leadership roles, and helping supporters organize local house parties and get-out-the-vote canvassing. Obama also used online polls to help determine which issues most concerned his future constituents. His embrace of new technology mirrors both Howard Dean and Ron Paul, two presidential candidates who used online organizing tools such as Meetup to gather significant support in 2004 and 2008, respectively. Candidates like these proved that you do not necessarily need the full support of your party's political machine to enter a race—if you take advantage of new technology. In any case, complete control of every candidate's campaign and message is now out of their hands, and must be shared with their grassroots supporters. And with Obama, for the first time a candidate transferred over his grassroots base after the election, continuing the engagement with his constituents.[30]

The Internet doesn't just help elections. It enables better government-to-citizen information sharing, and direct citizen-to-government feedback and participation. Tim O'Reilly, coiner of the phrase "Web 2.0," is now pushing for what he calls "Gov 2.0," the next evolution of participatory government. The old model of government maintained the implicit assumption that ordinary citizens are well-informed enough to vote for candidates, but that's it—they aren't smart enough to make policy decisions, due to a lack of expertise. So participation was limited to voting, and perhaps local-level discussions. But by concentrating decision-making, governments make single points of failure, which are more prone to occasional catastrophic results.

With today's people-networking technology, government can take a different role. It can become a platform—a shell upon which citizens build useful tools. The government, rather than simply helping us, can also enable us to help ourselves. The government can articulate priorities and goals, provide needed information, and offer incentives, and then step back and let citizens form a response. New tools allow two opportunities for the public to get involved: greater deliberation, and greater collaboration. The new realization is that citizens *are* experts, in lots of different fields, and their opinions are essential for problem-solving. The digital collaboration of the public and private sector can help us solve problems that neither government nor the free market can solve on their own.[31]

It's an inherent good to enable more citizens to participate in the act of governing, but these new innovations also hold the promise to actually make government more creative, efficient, and effective. Transparency and accountability are essential for democracy, and now citizens can find tons of information online about their elected officials, like their voting records, sources of funding, and speeches. Sites for this include Congresspedia, an open wiki, and Open Secrets, which tracks lobbyist payments. Since a 2006 law (sponsored by then-Senator Obama), states are starting to put financial records online: contracts and awards, and lists of spending. So far, more than 20 states have put up web portals where people can see exactly where their tax dollars are going. Similarly, the federal government launched *recovery.gov* as a way to make economic indicators more transparent and accessible. The District of Columbia requires all government agencies to provide feeds of data available from a central web site. It then launched a contest to see who (whether a citizen, company, or other organization) could develop the best software applications from the data. In fact, many people are making "apps" (programs that take advantage of other programs or data) using newly-available government data, often using geolocation information to create informative maps and guides. GPS satellites, after all, were originally developed by the government—and now can benefit everyone. In fact, we're right on the cutting edge of a wave of innovation around location-centered "augmented reality," layering data on top of the real world. Using sensors on smart phones, you'll be able to find out information about whatever the phone is pointed at or takes a photo of. A company called CitySourced invented an iPhone app that lets you easily report any civil issue to your local government: take a photo of graffiti or a pothole and it knows where you are and automatically sends off a report.[32]

The U.S. Patent Office took a direct approach to harnessing citizens and opened up its process to any helpful laymen. Using social networking tools, it now uses a volunteer network of scientists and experts to help do patent research and participate in decision-making.[33] Many fields are diffusing their power from a small elite of experts to a wider base of amateurs (and even more experts). Blogs are transforming the field of journalism, and online self-publishing is ripping apart the publishing industry. Armchair astronomers are increasingly making significant discoveries. Physician assistants are taking on more of the responsibilities that doctors don't have time for. More legal issues are being settled out of court, sometimes with volunteer mediators. Volunteer organizations and community groups, easily formed online, are stepping up for more responsibilities as well.

Michael Wesch, a professor at Kansas State University, points out that technology used to engage citizens refutes both Orwell's and Huxley's dystopian predictions. Unlike in 1984, power is becoming less concentrated, and also more authentic; unlike Brave New World, citizens are participating and becoming engaged rather than enjoying mindless distraction. All of these technological developments merge into a single theme: giving people greater control over their own lives—including power over their own information, their own government, their own health, their own job, their own environment, their own creativity and self-expression. And when used correctly, the new technology elevates both the individual and groups at the same time.[34] It is the responsibility of humanity to harness this newfound capability and use it for everyone's benefit to keep pushing toward the secret peace.

Without that responsibility in place, the Internet can be abused, just as with any technology. According to the FBI, $183 million was lost online to auction fraud, extortion, debt consolidation schemes, and identity theft in 2005 alone. Viruses and hackers continue to plague systems. Fifty percent of U.S. male college students gamble online at least once a month, and some of them are becoming addicts. Over 200 new pornography sites go live daily.[35] Information overload can easily occur as a result of the dramatic increase in the amount of information available. Even those of us innocently surfing for information about wombats can waste precious hours of our lives away through distractions. We have to filter the information effectively or we can be overwhelmed by stress and indecision, throwing our hands up in despair. With too much faith in technology, we risk concocting what author Neil Postman calls a technopoly, in which we lose sight of what the goal of the technology was in the first place.[36] To keep in control of our creations, it will be necessary to stay grounded.

Besides fraud and spam, privacy issues are at the forefront of many software and Internet developments. Some search engines and portals keep records of everything you have searched. They keep these records private and don't associate them directly with your name, but this is still unnerving, especially considering that in 2006, AOL accidentally released the search records of 657,000 of its users.[37] It's essential to remain vigilant and not let large privacy decisions be made without consumer input. But this is understandably difficult when Internet ideas advance faster than the average consumer can keep track of them. The sites discussed in this chapter are still out of reach for the millions of people who do not yet have broadband connections, let alone Internet access at all. Since the newest Web sites feature so many videos and photos, they require a broadband infrastructure, which is ubiquitous in South Korea, Hong Kong, and Japan, with the United States and Europe catching up, but is not yet found in many other regions. Social networking in China, for example, is booming but many sites are painfully slow to use.[38] This demonstrates the biggest Internet caveat of all: like many of the new technologies in health, energy, and communications, the Internet remains dominated by the United States and the rest of the developed world. As science-fiction writer William Gibson famously put it: the future is already here—it's just unevenly distributed.[39] Now we need to share our technology so others get a chance to participate in the global conversation, too.

BECOMING YOUR OWN MEANS OF PRODUCTION

Participatory democracy and a global conversation are possible due to the Internet's most radical innovation: the social revolution of users creating information, not just reading it. This symmetrical participation means anyone has the power to express himself. This is participatory media, and online it's known as Web 2.0—an overly trendy term, but one that is still useful. Millions of people are now eagerly sharing videos, photos, music, memoirs, conversations, jokes, lists—you name it.

Think about the power the printing press had in Gutenberg's day, or in Ben Franklin's day, or in the days of the Watergate scandal. Now, millions of people have tiny printing presses sitting on their desks. (In the future, we may even be able to "print" in 3-D, with many increasingly-inexpensive "3-D printers" now available. Dr. Neil Gershenfeld of MIT has even created a small, low-cost "personal fabricator" that can create a wide array of materials: circuit boards, antennas, jewelry, car parts, and agricultural tools. It is already being used in a few villages in the developing world to great success.[40]) But much more importantly, we also have the ability to publish to the Internet and to our blogs.

Thanks to technology, people can gain easier access to creative tools offline, produce better work, and then share it online. The *Economist* explains, "The tools of media production—computers, desktop printers, video cameras— are now so widely and cheaply available that a generation of young people are becoming amateur journalists, commentators, film-makers and musicians in their spare time."[41] A 2005 survey found that 57 percent of American teenagers create some sort of content for the Internet, whether it be a diary, photo gallery, video . . . or whatever.[42] Today every person can be her own printing press, music studio, newspaper, and online salesperson. Marx would be shocked to learn that the means of production are quickly passing into the hands of the people without any need for violent revolution or state control. The increasing size and richness of a creative culture is giving everyone more choices, and the new tools of the Internet are helping us tap into this culture. By guiding us with smart information, the Internet empowers consumers to escape the homogeneity of mass markets.[43] As people discover unique media, their own creative efforts are further inspired and they in turn contribute to the creative culture of the Internet in even more integrated ways. The cycle is moving so rapidly that few people are able to keep up with all the new participatory media Web sites and innovations.

"Participatory media" is a suitably descriptive phrase, but not nearly catchy enough, and "Web 2.0" is pretty vague. A more apt phrase is the "living web." As *Wired* explains it, "What these sites have in common is a tendency to treat the Web less like a TV channel or magazine, which convey information, and more like an operating system or computer, which generate it. Except that this computer gets its processing power from the humans plugged into it."[44] Here are ten of the largest and most groundbreaking sites that have created new living web concepts.

- *Facebook* didn't invent the concept of connecting to friends through a social network; sites like MySpace, Friendster and Classmates has already done that. But Facebook added at least two big innovations to the "social graph" (the term they use): a dynamic news feed of everything your friends are up to, and the ability for companies to make apps that piggyback onto Facebook. These apps, or widgets, are another exciting Web 2.0 development. Meetup, for example, built a Facebook widget that is a small box on your Facebook page that updates with information about your Meetup Groups.

- *Meetup* itself is a living web site, populated by millions of users who use the site to organize into groups that meet offline about their interests, whether they be saving the world or letting their toddlers play together. Like social network profiles, people populate Meetup with photos, videos, and information—but about their groups, not just themselves.

- *YouTube*'s innovation is not just showing videos online, but showing *our* videos. Tens of thousands of new video clips are uploaded by YouTubians every day. Simple webcams now allow people to record themselves easily, pouring their hearts out to anyone. The proliferation of these grippingly solipsistic ongoing self-documentaries has produced a vast culture with its own popular dramas and stars. More meaty videos can spread, too, such as snippets of Katie Couric's interviews with vice presidential nominee Sarah Palin.

- *Flickr* is a photo-sharing Web site that lets you store and share digital photos, and tag them with descriptive words or phrases. Then users can search Flickr for whatever tag words they like. So strange combinations and associations of photos pop up, connecting seemingly disparate threads of users, and making searching and sorting incredibly robust.

- *Delicious* performs a similar function for bookmarks, the Web browser lists of favorite sites. Normally stored on one computer, this site stores them online instead, each tagged with a few words. This is the new concept of the "cloud," in which more and more of our data is stored online, accessible from any computer or mobile device, rather than stuck in a single concrete spot on our personal computers. Delicious shows how many other users have also tagged the same bookmarked site, revealing an ongoing Internet popularity contest. As with Flickr, you can search for whatever tags you like. Tagging is becoming one of the most useful ways to organize information on the Web—a personal touch rather than an automatic process.

- *Wikipedia* now has 12 times as many entries as the print version of the Encyclopædia Britannica. Its radical innovation is the ability for anyone—not only professional writers and editors—to edit any encyclopedia entry or contribute a new one. The satirical magazine *The Onion* wrote a fake Fourth of July article titled "Wikipedia Celebrates 750 Years of American Independence," which gives you a good idea of people's assumptions about pranksters and idiots writing entries. But with a critical mass of users, and some rules in place, a society of trust has built up in which mistakes are quickly ferreted out. Wikipedia is also useful because every interesting word in a given entry has a link; in "Wombats are native to Australia and have been known to attack humans much in the manner of soccer hooligans," *Australia, humans,* and *soccer hooligans* link to their own entries, giving us another way to search and learn. The *Economist* says, "Wikipedia's promise is nothing less than the liberation of human knowledge—both by incorporating all of it through the collaborative process, and by freely sharing it with everybody who has access to the Internet."[45]

- *Mercora* is a social music network that allows you to become a radio DJ. You can program a "radio station" using your own music, which other Mercora listeners can then tune into. This concept is similar to podcasting, another recent development (the term is an amalgam of iPod and broadcasting). With podcasting, people download radio shows (often user-generated), music, or videos and load them onto their iPod to listen to whenever they want. And you can set it to automatically download the newest podcasts from that publisher—a podcast feed. This is yet another way to give people more freedom, to avoid standard radio and its commercials. It lowers the cost of producing content since you don't need a radio station to pump out a podcast, just a Web site and a microphone.

- *Prosper* allows you to take out a loan, which other users then compete to fund. You can join forces with other borrowers to get better credit ratings, too. So if Mercora lets you become your own radio station, Prosper lets you become your own bank.[46] Similarly, *Donorschoose.org* brings an end to the days of wondering how your charitable contributions are being spent. The site lets teachers, especially in underprivileged school districts, pitch ideas for classroom projects and what materials they need. Then donors can pick out projects, even choosing to fund portions of various projects. The donors are often notified later about how the projects went, with adorable student thank-yous scrawled in crayon.

- *Second Life* is a groundbreaking idea that could have far-reaching effects. Second Life is not a Web site; it's software on your computer, but it connects to other users over the Internet. It is a *metaverse*—a 3-D-looking world in which residents can become anyone and do anything they want. It's akin to online role-playing games such as *World of Warcraft*, but it's not a game, and it doesn't have the limitations of a Dungeons-and-Dragonsy theme. Some people visit the Second Life world to have fun—to fly around, make virtual platypuses, meet faraway friends, fight samurais, or create flowers. Many people are using it for more serious purposes too—to hold press conferences and book launches, to form cancer support groups, to rehearse responses to earthquakes. The BBC has an island on which it holds music festivals. Second Life is well set up for long-distance learning as well. It also has economic repercussions—you can create anything you want in Second Life, but you can also buy cool things other people have crafted, which often translates into *real money*. The Second Life hype is dying down now as people realize the limitations of meeting virtually and remember the necessity of interacting face-to-face. But Second Life still promises creative new uses of which we've only scratched the surface.[47]

- *Twitter* has recently burst on the scene, with the media constantly bombarding us to pay attention to this hot new thing. Surprisingly, it's worth it. Twitter lets people announce short messages (tweets) to a group of followers. It seems completely inane and solipsistic (and indeed, can be) until you brainstorm a little bit about its near-infinite possibilities. Like blogs, Twitter gives us news from our peers, rather than filtered through media outlets—but it does it in real time, instantly tapping the world's zeitgeist at any moment. Twitter further democratizes the world, by de-mocratizing *the conversation*. Instead of big businesses, or politicians, or celebrities talking to their audience in one direction, we can talk back. When I met Jack Dorsey, co-founder of Twitter, he emphasized his love of this aspect of the service: opening up politics and companies and allowing a lot more transparency. Indeed, anything that helps spread information among people, and in a democratized way, helps push us toward the secret peace. So when used to its fullest, Twitter could become the perfect secret peace tool. Rather than just using Twitter to update your friends on what shoes you're wearing today, savvy users increasingly use Twitter to post links to photos, articles, and videos, or alert people to other conversations. Your Twitter feed thus becomes a personalized news service of things you're interested in. With new search tools, you can find out what people worldwide are saying about any topic, and participate as an equal in that conversation. Those new search tools are one of the many things developed by Twitter's users, which is another of its revolutionary innovations. Twit-ter itself is a simple program, but by letting other developers build on its platform, in an even more robust way than Facebook does, they've expanded its uses a thousandfold. Steven Johnson, in *Time*, explains that it's "like inventing a toaster oven and then looking around a year later and seeing that your customers have of their own accord figured out a way to turn it into a microwave."[48] This concept is also behind the success of Apple's iPhone, since thousands of companies and independent developers have created apps that perform different useful tasks and games on the phone. In this way, even the features of a software product are democratized.

What do all those sites have in common? Four developments are the backbone of Web 2.0. The most important is user-generated content, as we've seen. A second is mass collaboration, as exemplified by Wikipedia. One aspect of this is called crowdsourcing, in which companies use large groups of amateurs to do for free what one professional used to do in the past. A third development is widgets and feeds, such as what Facebook uses. Widgets could be a Yahoo box on your desktop that updates the weather or a YouTube video embedded into your web site. Widgets are easy to use and bring information to you rather than making you troll the Web. The era of widgets puts pressure on companies to open up their web site code for other people to use to make their own widgets: collaborative crowdware, if you will. As another example, I have a restaurant widget on my own web site that shows an interactive map of the Lower East Side. Google Maps powers the map, but I've used their code to add pushpins to every restaurant location I like. The ability for a visitor to my web site to interact with this map—zooming in, clicking on restaurants to see their names—is due to the fourth Web 2.0 development: moving software online. New web technology allows programmers to make pages with things to move and buttons to push, pages that behave more like other software than static pages of information. Using this "cloud-based" software is easier in some ways, especially since it allows for more collaboration.

The Internet changes so quickly that by the time you read this, any one of the companies I mentioned here may have crashed and burned, and any of them may be even more popular. They are simply examples of the trends we're discussing—the ability of the Internet to both inspire personal expression and connect people socially. *Newsweek* describes it well:

Less than a decade ago, when we were first getting used to the idea of an Internet, people described the act of going online as venturing into some foreign realm called cyberspace. But that metaphor no longer applies. MySpace, Flickr and the [others] aren't places to go, but things to do, ways to express yourself, means to connect with others and extend your own horizons. Cyberspace was somewhere else. The Web is where we live.[49]

THE PERFECTLY EFFICIENT MARKET

Participatory, collaborative, interactive web sites are also transforming how we deal with money—buying, selling, trading, consuming and shopping. With the advent of the Internet, commerce is reaching its ideal ability to flow without restriction—a perfect global market. We increasingly buy things online, but it affects our offline purchasing as well. You can place an order at BestBuy.com and then pick up the item at the store if you can't wait for delivery. Or you could test out the digital cameras in the store, remember the model you liked, and then return home to purchase it at a cheaper price online. Three out of four Americans start their new car shopping online and then take their newfound encyclopedic knowledge down the street to the dealer, already knowing what price to expect.[50] Price transparency on the Internet allows consumers to compare prices across hundreds of sites and then pick the least expensive item in the best quality from a seller they trust. With the Internet, uninformed consumers are a thing of the past—thanks not only to manufacturers but also to millions of customer reviews, comments, and diatribes. User-rating sites are now booming, allowing people to be easy informed about choosing dinner (Yelp.com), a workplace (Glassdoor.com), a trip (TripAdvisor.com), a college course (RateMyProfessors.com), lawyers (Avvo.com), and doctors (lots of sites.) In 2007, about one-third of all American Internet users rated something online.[51] Originally, enabling this required a new type of thinking, as Amazon's CEO Jeff Bezos describes:

In the very earliest days (I'm taking you back to 1995), when we started posting customer reviews, a customer might trash a book and the publisher wouldn't like it. I would get letters from publishers saying, "Why do you allow negative reviews on your website? Why don't you just show the positive reviews?" One letter in particular said, "Maybe you don't understand your business. You make money when you *sell* things." But I thought to myself, We don't make money when we sell things; we make money when we help customers make purchase decisions.[52]

Competition is fierce on the Web, and online companies have had to raise their service to higher levels than the typical service provided in a "brick and mortar" store. Amazon.com lets you search inside a book, almost as if you were flipping through its pages in a bookshop. The Land's End site lets you order custom-made clothes by answering simple questions about your body type. (It automatically adjusts for the fact that people understate their dimensions.)[53] Travel makes up a huge portion of online spending, as consumers play the role of travel agent, booking their own flight plans and travel itineraries. Similarly, hotels and car rental agencies are deriving most of their bookings from the Web. Then there is online banking, online dating, online movie tickets, and 99¢ music downloads. The Web, along with the advent of the personal computer and mobile phone, is the new best friend of entrepreneurship, drastically shrinking the cost of launching one's own business. New technology makes entrepreneurship easier than ever before in history; average people now have the access that only conglomerates could have achieved in the past. There are now three-quarters of a million people making their living selling merchandise on eBay alone.[54]

eBay allows users to auction products to the highest bidder. "Making inefficient markets efficient" is how the management at eBay explains its function.[55] You can sell your old comic books, vintage clothes, body armor, cars, caskets, used toothbrushes, whatever. Pierre Omidyar, eBay's creator, believes that the site's success is linked to a broader social good connecting strangers from across the country and across the globe. When he described eBay to early investors, he heard, "That'll never work! It's impossible! You can't trust anybody—you're going to get ripped off!" But he believes eBay has taught "more than two hundred million people that they can trust a complete stranger. People have learned that, in general, people are basically good. And we've demonstrated that."[56]

Amazon and eBay are both taking advantage of a catchy business concept, the long tail. In many businesses, particularly related to entertainment, the bulk of revenues were always generated from only a few "hit" products. Shelf space in stores is limited, and companies are limited by marketing budgets, which means they focus on promoting only a certain number of titles, so a great deal of effort goes into finding (or manufacturing) the next big hit. The long tail theory refers to a shift away from "hits" as businesses realize that in addition to selling many copies of a few titles, they can use the Internet to sell a few copies each of many different titles. The Internet has infinite shelf space, and can refer people to obscure products they might not find out about any other way (such as Amazon's "Customers who bought this item also bought ...") Many Web sites also let people create their own recommendation lists to point people to indie bands, books with small print runs, and old movies. So an infinite variety of products are available, and filters help consumers make smart choices about them.

FIGURE 2: THE LONG TAIL:
NUMBER OF BOOKS SOLD (APPROXIMATE)

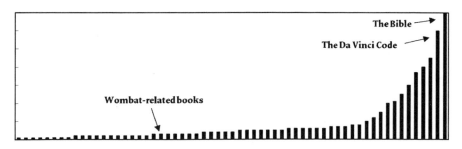

The phrase "long tail" comes from statistical charts such as the one in Figure 2. Each bar represents how many copies of a certain book were sold. (But imagine the "tail" on the left-hand side extending far off the chart.) It is most cost-effective for a company to stumble on a hit, such as *The Da Vinci Code*, and sell millions of copies. But if a company were to sell a few copies each of all the other books on the left side of the chart, it could make just as much profit.

The long tail expands niche markets and offers the possibility of a lot of obscure but high-quality music and books finally getting their due. There will always be top sellers, but with wider selection available, theoretically top sellers will be successful because they are genuinely good, not just popular. Two of the most successful long tail adopters are Netflix, which lets you rent movies from their web site to receive in the mail, and iTunes, which lets users download songs for only a dollar apiece. Even obscure songs and movies have a few enthusiasts who are now being well-served. Long tail proponents stress that everyone will be happier if they are able to find products perfectly suited to their tastes. It also increases overall demand as people are able to access more products that they like and find "perfect" things they never knew existed before. Also, the far end of the tail will always consist of amateurs offering their creations for free. Even farther than that will be products customized for you alone—such as designing your own shoes on Nike.com or putting your family's photo on a T-shirt on Cafepress.com.[57]

E-commerce is extremely successful at selling physical products, but it excels at offering services as well. Health care, travel, marketing, gym memberships, dry cleaning, Web site creation—all are intangible services, and we're spending more of our money on them every year. In 1959, Americans spent about 40 percent of their income on services; by 2000, that amount rose to 58 percent.[58] As physical goods become plentiful and cheaper, we can move beyond basic necessities and spend more money on services. This increased demand for services is affecting jobs in the developed world, and technology is speeding the demand. In *An Army of Davids*, author Glenn Reynolds explains that as more of our economy becomes based on services, people gain more freedom in their careers. The economies of scale that created huge office buildings and factories for producing mass-manufactured goods are no longer as necessary as they used to be. With more efficiency and specialization, individuals can work more independently.

This new trend in professional independence is what author Dan Pink calls a "Free Agent Nation," and it has many benefits.[59] It means that people don't have to work in company locations anymore, and it also means that they no longer need to work directly for one particular company anymore—that is, they can be hired as part-time freelancers. The ability to work from home is tempting to many people, and it is closely related to the idea that when parents work from home they are able to devote more time to their children because of flexible work schedules. Technology contributes to this trend by enabling careers that revolve around computer work—especially aesthetic-related careers such as any form of writing, art, or design. More people have opportunity to use their talent and skills to become entrepreneurs, like all those people making a living by selling products on eBay. Or like my friend Rich, who with a few friends started the Fulcrum Gallery, an e-commerce site that sells posters and prints. The Fulcrum Gallery spun out of some other projects the group worked on at home and in their spare time, and it is now an enormously successful company.

Rich worked at home for a while, but eventually ended up working in an office again. Companies will probably always prefer that most employees remain in the office, for many good reasons, but those who want to work remotely should be able to find a job suited for them, too. Today you can carry every essential office tool—computer, phone, red stapler—with you and work wherever you like. The Rolodex that used to sit on the desk is now a list of contacts in your cell phone. Elaborate presentations that used to require an easel and giant foam boards can now be shown on a portable projector hooked up to a laptop computer. Huge Wi-Fi access areas now cover major cities, as wireless Internet hot spots set up by both businesses and municipal governments overlap.

The downside to employment freedom is employment insecurity. Gone are the days of a guaranteed job for life. And in the U.S., access to health insurance is a growing concern as well. But without a 9-5 job, workers are free to have simultaneous diverse careers, like writing a book. Multiple revenue streams are always a good hedge against the risk of bad times. And a new Freelancers Union, one that represents the needs and concerns of America's growing independent workforce, has popped up, following radically different rules than traditional unions. Traditional unions have been declining drastically for decades in the United States due to an increased need for flexibility from both companies and their workers. But this new union has had increasing success offering health insurance and other benefits to workers without full-time employment.[60] The recent changes in employment and the quick rise of independent employees are still in an early stage of development; a great deal of effort will need to be made to balance them out to take advantage of the best opportunities without leaving too many people floundering in the new business environment.

Because of our global economy's shift to services and our increasing specialization, combined with the wealth and disposable income available to many of us in developed countries, citizens have a wide range of skills and knowledge. Offering these talents to everyone via the Internet grants society a vast resource. Web sites such as Wikipedia and the others listed above gather people together, harnessing their collective intelligence. Author James Surowiecki coined the phrase, "the wisdom of crowds." His book of the same name reveals many instances in which the average answer of a group is more accurate than that of an expert. Smart crowds need adequate information to make good decisions, and everyone must think independently rather than following a primary decision maker. If those conditions are met, crowds are brainiacs—as evidenced most clearly in markets and democracies. Surowiecki also uses his theory to argue that companies should decentralize decision-making.[61] Essentially, we are using networks of technology to form better networks of humanity—and those networks, as a unifying force, will bring us closer to peace.

We still need a new outlook, though, to handle the increasing power of those networks: a fundamental shift in the way we see ourselves and our world. Fortunately, that is emerging, too. We've looked at people getting more knowledge and spreading that knowledge (our first force pushing toward peace), and gaining the democratic, self-motivating power to use that knowledge themselves and with others (our second force). Now let's see what happens when people enlarge their outlook and get connected *globally*.

UNITY

Global Awareness

The first photo most people ever saw of our planet was taken on Christmas Eve, 1968. As Al Gore explains in his environmental documentary, *An Inconvenient Truth*, the image known as *Earth Rise* immediately exploded into the consciousness of mankind. Within two years, the modern environmental movement had been born, and the first Earth Day was held. Seeing the photo the day after it was taken, poet and writer Archibald MacLeish wrote, "To see the Earth as it truly is, small and blue and beautiful in that eternal silence where it floats, is to see ourselves as riders on the Earth together, brothers on that bright loveliness in the eternal cold—brothers who know now that they are truly brothers." There is another earth photo, a striking shot of clouds wrapping around a glowing Southern Hemisphere, taken in 1972. It is now the most published photograph in history.[1]

If the photos of Earth helped launch the environmental movement, it's environmental issues that have helped shape our image of the earth. In the past three decades, a new perspective on the Earth as a single interdependent system has emerged in the minds of humanity. The word "ecosystem" is now in our lexicon, whereas in centuries past people had no idea how much diverse parts of the environment impacted each other. They didn't realize that introducing all the birds mentioned by Shakespeare into Central Park would create a North American plague of European Starlings, or that discovering the island of Mauritius could lead to the extinction of the Dodo in only a few decades.[2] But today we're more savvy. Science has incontrovertibly shown us the unity of the world on a physical, natural level. According to Arthur Dahl, the environmental movement has grown out of a broader understanding of our shared ecosystem. In fact, "The slogan of the first world environmental conference in 1972 was 'Only One Earth.'"[3]

The world certainly feels smaller than it used to, and what is slowly forming behind the scenes is a sense of shared humanity and global awareness. This is the last of our three powerful forces ushering in the secret peace. Our new outlook entails widening our circle of concern to a higher level than in the past. We necessarily prioritize our own self-interest and survival and extend that to the welfare of our families. We then concern ourselves with networks of friends and coworkers, radiating our allegiances out to our neighborhood, our local community, our city, our region or state, and often our ethnicity and a powerful national pride. But one more layer of goodwill is needed: a sense of world citizenship. As former UN Secretary-General U Thant described:

> The sense of belonging to the human community must now be added to, and become dominant over, other allegiances. Man now has not only the possibility but the necessity for recognizing and for demonstrating his essential unity. This has always been the vision of the great religious teachers, philosophers, sages, and wise men of the past. Today, it is a basic requirement for progress.[4]

The printing press was the first catalyst for a global culture. It allowed literacy to obtain a larger scale and spread, creating a new class of transnational intellectuals. These intellectuals, along with a merchant class, were the first people to systematically think globally, influencing ideas of global ethics

and international law.⁵ It's ironic that after developing a powerful individualism after the Renaissance, humanity is now embracing everyone's diversity,
and accepting a view of the planet as an integrated whole. Perhaps we needed
to understand our own unique abilities first, in order to then expand outward
and appreciate everyone else. These progressive steps echo levels of evolution,
leading to a stage in which it is finally possible to comprehend the entire planet's true diversity for the first time.⁶ This again reminds us of Robert Wright's
concept of *Nonzero,* a cultural evolution. Charles Darwin had similar thoughts.
He said, "As man advances in civilization, and small tribes are united in larger
communities, the simplest reason would tell each individual that he ought to
extend his social instincts and sympathies to all members of the same nation.
. . . This point being once reached, there is only an artificial barrier to prevent
his sympathies extending to the men of all nations and races."⁷ Public opinion
surveys reveal that this cosmopolitan attitude increases among younger generations. Recent polls reveal that the older the person, the narrower their sense
of identity; people born more recently are more likely to claim an identity at the
global level.⁸

Pressing global issues are also pushing us to think about the planet holis-
tically. In particular, the state of the environment is a problem so large in scope
that it's forcing us to think beyond borders. Such thorny issues as pollution,
resource shortages, refugees, disease, terrorism, and human trafficking also
all demand worldwide solutions. One reason such global problems now loom
large is that it's the first time in Earth's history that we are capable of understanding them at that level. We have solved many local and national problems,
and now we're ready to tackle larger issues. For an environmental example, the
United States and Canada worked together to successfully reduce the pollution
that causes acid rain in North America. This was an important success, but now
more countries must work together to combat global warming.

In order to resolve these global problems, international teamwork is
required in many formerly unrelated fields of work and research. As author
Foad Katirai writes, these fields range from "obtaining information about the
weather to updating knowledge on health and technology. Ensuring the safety
of air and sea transportation, overseeing the smooth operation of international

postal and telecommunication systems and coordinating diverse economies and markets are other examples."[9] The increasing collaboration and interchange between scientists, scholars, doctors, and other professionals allows knowledge, skills, and technology to quickly spread between disciplines and between nations. This shared knowledge gives students everywhere access to universal curricula, and scientists around the world access to new discoveries. As scientists think more globally, there is an increasing emphasis on interdisciplinary research. New hybrid fields are popping up, with names like sociobiology, evolutionary psychology, and behavioral economics. Areas of study that used to be seen as isolated and distinct now reflect the world's interconnectedness.[10]

With researchers collaborating and crossing disciplines, ideas and inventions are bound to be discovered faster. However, ideas are already much more easy to come by than we might think. As bestselling author Malcolm Gladwell has reported, the history of science is full of ideas that several people had at the same time. Have you heard of the inventor of the telephone, Elisha Gray? He filed notice with the Patent Office in Washington, D.C. on the same day as Alexander Graham Bell. Are you aware of Alfred Russel Wallace, who discovered evolution? Or that the Pythagorean theorem was known before Pythagoras? Sunspots were discovered in 1611 by Galileo in Italy—but also independently by other scientists in Germany, Holland, and England. Newton and Leibniz both discovered calculus, and as Jason Bardi writes in *The Calculus Wars*, "All the basic work was done—someone just needed to take the next step and put it together. ... If Newton and Leibniz had not discovered it, someone else would have." Decimal fractions, oxygen, color photography, logarithms, and many other ideas and inventions were each discovered by different people at the same time. Science historians call these "multiples."[11]

Multiples lend support to the idea of information driving progress; inventions don't spring fully-formed from the mind of an individual in an ivory tower, but are essentially floating in the air, in the world's zeitgeist, inevitable. Because any given discovery or advancement has, say, 90 percent of its structure already formed and available as information, it's only that 10 percent that needs to be invented. And there's a good chance that several people will simultaneously think of that 10 percent. As Gladwell puts it, "Ideas weren't precious. They were everywhere, which suggested that maybe the extraordinary process that we thought was necessary for invention—genius, obsession, serendipity, epiphany—wasn't necessary at all." He goes on to explain a new concept of genius, as first put forth in the 1960s by sociologist Robert K. Merton. "A scientific genius is not a person who does what no one else can do; he or she is someone who does what it takes many others to do. The genius is not a unique source of insight; he is merely an efficient source of insight." This doesn't hold true for artistic genius, however: 50 engineering students might have been able to work together to invent the telephone, but 50 literature students probably wouldn't be able to collaborate and come up with the equivalent of a Shakespearean comedy.[12]

Scientific ideas may be inevitable, but their pace isn't—without the dedicated work of the geniuses listed above, for example, those inventions would have taken a longer time to invent, with a greater number of people. Yet with many more educated people today, and greater access to information, more people are trying out more ideas. This speeds up advancement, because as Clay Shirky describes, "In a world where anyone can try anything, even the risky stuff can be tried eventually. If a large enough population of users is trying things, then the happy accidents have a much higher chance of being discovered."[13]

Inventions and ideas are most often conceived as solutions to problems. Their basic inevitability is good news for our new globalized concerns. The spread of world-sized challenges is just one of the factors leading to the new view of a single, unified world. A second major factor is the global economy. Since companies now stretch across continents, employees often have to communicate and coordinate with foreign coworkers. As more countries undergo industrial development, new markets emerge and nations trade more eagerly. This process is helped by the strategic emergence of international regions of free trade, notably the European Union (EU) and the North American Free Trade Agreement (NAFTA).[14]

A third reason behind the new unifying attitude of humanity is tourism. Despite a temporary setback following September 11, 2001, air travel has bounced back to exceed its previous levels as tourism continues to increase. Americans travel overseas 30 times more than they did a hundred years ago, even adjusting for population growth.[15] Air travel is no longer the domain of the very wealthy, especially since it's easy for anyone to compare prices and book flights online. Visiting foreign countries and being exposed to new cultures is one of the most effective ways for people to absorb a global outlook.

Going a step further, a fourth cause of this global outlook is immigration and the increasing diversity of the populations of countries. The borders of most countries are codifying into regions more sensitive to ethnic and religious groups, after being arbitrarily divided by colonial powers a century ago (remaining holdouts include Iraq, Afghanistan, and a still-split Korea). But rather than becoming protectionist and sheltered, the obvious benefits of peace and safety are making citizens more amenable to befriending their neighbors. For example, Germany united after the fall of the Berlin Wall and became more successful after the reunification of its peoples. And the states of the former Yugoslavia, after horrifically but perhaps necessarily separating, are now collaborating again in areas of trade and diplomacy.[16] Forcing integration and unification of cultures can be difficult, so ethnic groupings are a good temporary solution as the world gradually becomes more integrated. The largest country with a truly mixed ethnic culture is the United States, though getting there has been, and continues to be, a bumpy ride, to say the least. Other countries can look to the United States as an example as they slowly become more diverse. As individual countries become increasingly diversified, tolerance is promoted and people can learn about other cultures without leaving their own.

THE GLOBAL RENAISSANCE

A fifth factor incubating a concept of global unity is the creativity of the arts and entertainment. As entertainment (a type of accumulating cultural "information") becomes available globally thanks to international trade and the Internet, people are exposed to diverse cultures through other countries' creative exports. Television and the Internet are the most successful media spreading this diversity. In fact, the arts are now so globally intertwined that we can speak of a single shared, global creative culture. And that culture, as the evidence will display, has never been more imaginative, diverse, intelligent, and exciting.

At the beginning of the twentieth century, Picasso, Modigliani, and other artists were exposed to African masks in museums for the first time, and each incorporated that art style into their own work. This exposure greatly expanded the creative range of modern art. Today, with the world's art available to browse online, it doesn't take special traveling museum exhibitions for artists to gain exposure to new ideas. Software and design pioneer Kai Krause describes this from the perspective of history's great geniuses:

> To be able to see all the works of all the great artists and keep a copy to examine up close, at your leisure, in your own home. To listen to the music of any composer, new or old— what an absolute dream that would have been, for any and all of them! Imagine that you'd heard about that new Beethoven symphony: You would have had to physically travel to a performance somewhere, and even then you could have heard only that one performance, not any of the others, and you would likely forget the music, since you would hardly ever get a chance to hear it again, to build a long-term memory of it.[17]

Tons of diverse influences surround today's creators. Television shows, music, books, movies, and other art forms are now easily spread globally.

In the past few decades, opponents of globalization have argued that this sharing process is, in reality, a euphemism for exporting American culture and forcing the rest of the world to consume it. Perhaps such a lopsided economic reality did exist to some extent, but I think the balance has been shifting, not because of diminishing American output, but because of a rise in quality and quantity of media around the rest of the globe. Culturally unique and artistic cinema thrives in many countries, such as India and Iran, not just in Hollywood. The publishing industry in many countries is also booming. The output of other cultures keeps influencing our own—for example, Eastern European music, and Japanese video games, manga and anime (comic books and animation). With the Internet, independent creators from many countries can enter the market on a level playing field. Artists have access to everyone else's cultural output and can simultaneously share their own. In fact, countries such as Ireland, South Korea, and Japan often surpass the United States in adoption of new technologies.

The global culture has overlaid and mingled with our own local and national cultures, not replaced them. Despite the fears of a monolithic world culture, when has more diverse art and entertainment—books, film, visual art, music, theater—ever been available? The past decades have seen a creative Renaissance that continues to expand.

Here's another part of the reason for more creativity: employees are working fewer hours than they used to even a decade ago.[18] Today, a 42-hour workweek is the average in the United States. That means most Americans are putting in about an eight-hour workday, and the average workday is even shorter in most other developed countries. Back in the 1830s, groups went on strikes to lobby for *only* a ten-hour workday. Figure 3 shows the slow decrease in weekly wage-hours worked (i.e., not housework, though that has also declined). Due to the immense differences in the types of jobs performed by women over the decades (and lack of records measuring them), their statistics are not added into these numbers.[19]

FIGURE 3: AVERAGE AMERICAN MAN'S WORKWEEK, IN HOURS

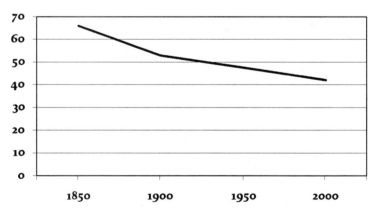

If we also factor in time saved from the decreasing burden of housework due to automation, the typical American gained the equivalent of seven weeks of vacation just since 1965. And Americans are workaholics compared to some European countries that hold four or five weeks of vacation a year to be standard issue. Our newfound perspective on leisure—that we are entitled to it, and lots of it—is enough to prompt the satirical newspaper *The Onion* to report, "180 Trillion Leisure Hours Lost to Work Last Year."[20] In 1930, the eminent economist John Maynard Keynes predicted that a hundred years hence, no one would need to work more than 15 hours a week, and humanity would be bored with too much leisure time.[21] He understood that whenever we do something, we can't help but get better at it, and thus our productivity is always increasing. He was on to something, but he didn't factor in the pace of innovation: our new inventions and ideas constantly beget more ideas (and more jobs), so we're going to keep ourselves busy for awhile yet. Nevertheless, due to the steady decline in workweek hours, as well as more years in retirement thanks to our longer lifespans, those of us who live in the developed world have a lot more time, energy, and disposable income to devote to art and entertainment, and we are creating and demanding new and unique forms of art.

In college, I was a fine arts major. In my art history studies I eventually reached the art of the mid-twentieth century. My friends and I hated a lot of what we saw from that period. Much of it was purely intellectual, focusing on tautological theories that you could only grasp by reading an artist's manifesto, not by looking at the piece of art. We sympathized with ordinary folks who go to a museum, see an all-red canvas or a video loop of a dog barking, and are bewildered. It was, I'm convinced, *intentionally* bewildering. Some of that art was very good, but a lot of it was boring.

Then we took a senior-level course that brought us to galleries in SoHo and Chelsea, and we could actually look at fresh contemporary art for ourselves. Much of the art we saw there was brilliant, colorful, energetic, fun, clear, and interesting. I realized that all the art being made today simply could not fit into the categories that art historians had designated in the past. Rather than feature one trend, all of the art styles ever created are now simultaneously in play in the fine art world.

As we learned in class, in the history of fine art generally only one or two major "movements" were popular at any one time. In the middle of the twentieth century, Abstract Expressionism was followed by Pop Art, which was followed by Minimalism, and so on. But today some artists are painting in an abstract expressionist style, some in a pop style, and some in a minimalist style.

Maybe some are even working in an expressionistic abstract pop minimalist style, silk-screening Marilyn Monroe's portrait onto a giant black cube and dripping paint on it. Everything is possible, and if it is possible, someone is doing it. Today, the only discernible industry-wide trend in art is diversity. The trend of single-trends seems officially dead in the art world. Snooty illuminati who once frowned on anything but the currently popular trend are now opening up to artists who would never have had their work shown at MoMA before. This development is true, too, for television, films, and especially popular music.

With the art world opening its mind to more diversity, previously-denigrated art forms are gaining more appreciation. The lines separating high and low culture have now completely blurred. Paul McCartney, on the eve of the release of the Beatles *Rock Band* video game, explained, "I've seen enough things that should never have become art become art that this looks like a prime candidate to me if ever there was one. Rock 'n' roll, or the Beatles, started as just sort of hillbilly music, just a passing phase, but now it's revered as an art form because so much has been done in it. Same with comics, and I think same with video games."[22] Art forms are mashing together into previously-undefined categories, which is how you can get books like *Pride and Prejudice and Zombies*; a graphic novel adaptation of Paul Auster's *City of Glass*; remixed pop songs endlessly layered over each other in the music of Girl Talk; and John Updike lending his voice to an episode of *The Simpsons*.

Increasingly creative forms of art are available because they are easier for artists to make, and easier for consumers to find. With new technology, music and movies can be made more cheaply and quickly than ever before. With the long tail of products, niche marketing is finally viable, so an Irish hip-hop reggae band can reach out on the Internet and find a market that might not have existed in their own hometown.[23] Say there are not enough people in the tiny hamlet of Hamletville (or wherever) to support their entire band. Well, there is plenty of demand if they can connect to the entire globe. It's much easier nowadays to find an audience for obscure interests and viewpoints. You don't have to be an "insider" in the creative community to have a voice. With more art available, and with online filters that lets people find the products they like the most, people seek out entertainment in their favorite niches. Consumers are happier with products that are customized for them, and they are eager to buy similar products. As a result, the mainstream is diversifying into many different paths and offerings. In fact, we are in the middle of an explosion of variety in all of the products and services available to us—from the 19,000 variations of Starbucks coffee to the millions of products on Amazon, Netflix, and iTunes.[24]

BUILDING INTERCONNECTED COMMUNITIES

New technology lets you be super creative without leaving your home. With this development, along with new entertainment media such as video games and on-demand TV and movies, which are seen as solitary activities, it's perhaps natural to expect a negative side effect today of increased isolation. Surprisingly, this has not been the case. Online activities are interactive and participatory in nature, and they are becoming increasingly cooperative all the time. The obvious benefit of the Internet is the ability to connect with millions of people across the globe. So, new networks and communities are forming of people who have never even seen each other. One prime example of this network are "massively multiplayer online role-playing games" such as *World of Warcraft*, which the *New York Times* called "the first truly global video-game hit since *Pac-Man*." The game allows users to create online identities and explore a world in which thousands of other gamers are simultaneously wandering around. They can fight each other or team up. Many users, especially in Asia, later meet up with their teammates and become good friends in "real life" too.[25]

World of Warcraft's popularity grew by word of mouth, like many trends and new ideas. Thanks to its online interface, it was able to spread extremely fast due to the lightning-quick capabilities of the Internet. Many other video games with similar immersive social features have followed. Another twist are the games *Guitar Hero* and *Rock Band*, which enable group participation in person—players sing and play instruments together as if they were in a band. No one could have guessed that video games would be a social medium, yet now over 11 million *Warcraft* subscribers worldwide, as well as millions of rock star wannabes, find that interactivity normal, and will expect it from their future games.[26]

FIGURE 4: HUMANITY'S SOCIAL STRUCTURE IN THE PAST

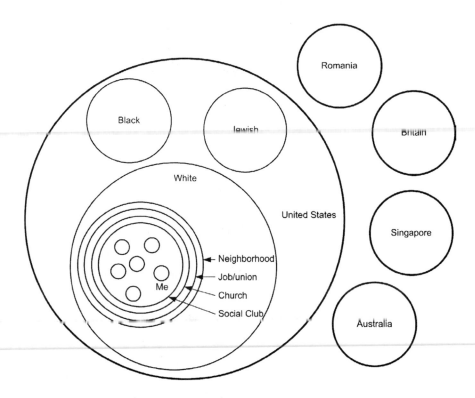

But the new worldwide interactions and friendships from the Internet need to be an additional level of association, not a replacement for local, face-to-face community. In 1995, an article (and later book) by Robert Putnam claimed more Americans were "bowling alone"—that is, they were participating in fewer group activities and organizations—which was undermining community life. On the other hand, in *Untruth*, Robert J. Samuelson makes the point that the decline in popularity of certain of the groups Putnam laments might actually be welcome, since they were sometimes discriminatory and often served mainly as diversions from a horrible factory workday. Putnam's book perhaps correctly described existing trends, but failed to see that these were about to be turned on their heads, as the Internet was just about to break into the mainstream. The Internet, ironically, is now the easiest way to find in-person groups.

FIGURE 5: HUMANITY'S SOCIAL STRUCTURE IN THE FUTURE

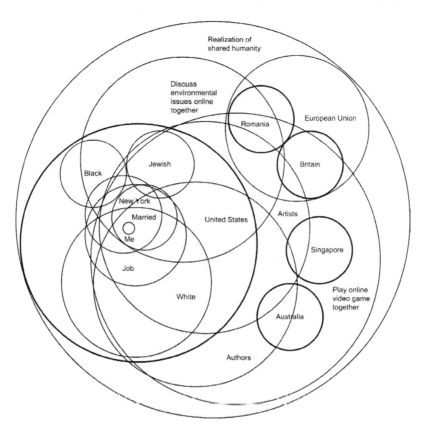

In the decade since Putnam wrote his famous article, the Internet has revolutionized local community. Today, people have more leisure time to devote to activities, and they have a much wider array of special interest groups, sports teams, classes, political causes, and social clubs to choose from.[27] The company I work for, Meetup, is a web site that helps people organize in groups online that then meet face-to-face. Meetup.com is home to thousands of political activists, museum-goers, business networkers, wine connoisseurs, dog owners, sports fans, movie aficionados, environmentalists, and tons of other groupings of friendly people meeting up in person with their neighbors. Meetup was founded as a response to Putnam's ideas, as a way to ensure that the Internet's potential is harnessed in the direction of personal human connections, not cold isolation.

One of the key benefits of the Meetup site is the ability to belong to more than one Meetup Group. This simple concept is fast becoming a new ultimate organizational structure for our time. In Figure 4, we can see a description of human identity structure as it existed until the past few decades. Of course, it's simplified and over-generalized, but the circles—each representing an identity, allegiance, or membership someone might have—rarely overlap. This represents the disunity of humanity; one held very close bonds to those inside his immediate circles, but had little interaction with those outside. Some of the circles were, for all intents and purposes, identical, which means that your neighbors all attended the same church with you, worked in the same factory as you, and belonged to the same social clubs you did. Someone from Romania, for example, or someone in your town but of a different race, had nothing in common with you. In this situation, it is easy to mistrust others, since you know little about them and have no personal connection.

In Figure 5, we see a generalized illustration of our social structure as it stands today and as it might move into the future. It outlines that people still have allegiances to their nation, locality, race and religion, of course. But most of us see ourselves as loyal to other groups as well. We are increasingly identifying ourselves with our interests, not the attributes defined by the chance of our birth. Today, as part of the ability to exercise individual power, the world's peoples can organize themselves any way they want.

For example, I am an American, a New Yorker, and a New Jerseyan, and I'm also an alumnus of Drew University, a donor to the International Rescue Committee, a member of Mensa, and a book lover. Though I'm not Jewish, I married a nice Jewish girl, overlapping our cultures. I see myself as an artist, a writer, an Internet developer, and specifically as a Product Manager for Meetup. I might meet a fellow New Yorker who disapproves of certain books I like, or I may meet a member of Mensa who dislikes artists—but most people today can tolerate these differences of opinion. With our circles of identity crossing all over the place, it's easier to relate to other people. After using Meetup, people are constantly sharing the experience of their surprise at the friendliness of everyone they met in person. It turns out that we don't have to be petrified of strangers; most people are good. We are now better able to see others as the diverse, dynamic individuals they are, which discourages polarized, black-and-white thinking. On the chart, you can see that the realization of our shared humanity has the power to encompass all our other groupings.

Generating war and conflict is dependent on shoehorning people into neat boxes, and we see tribal warlords and nationalist zealots demonizing their enemies by describing them via simple, unchanging categories. This should diminish, thankfully, since developing countries are now gaining broader access to the Internet as well. Their citizens are quickly gaining educational, business, and recreational networks that expand their horizons.[28] As *Nonzero*'s Robert Wright writes,

> Maybe this is the most ambitious realistic hope for the future expansion of amity—a world in which just about everyone holds allegiances to enough different groups, with enough different kinds of people, so that plain old-fashioned bigotry would entail discomfiting cognitive dissonance.[29]

The Internet and other improved communication technologies are enabling us to associate with whatever groups we like—they eliminate the handicap of distance, they make people with similar interests easier to find, and they allow better organization. By allowing looser connections among some groups, people can have more total group associations than in the past. Americans, in particular, have always formed small groups and associations, but in the past they were confined to a single locale. Organizations of global reach have existed for a long time, but without web technology they were usually top-down, not grassroots communities; it's hard to start something from the ground up in multiple places at the same time if you can't communicate instantly. The key is *self*-organization of the world's peoples, who can now form global networks of interests and activism much more easily. Technology guru Clay Shirky describes it simply:

> For the last hundred years the big organizational question has been whether any given task was best taken on by the state, directing the effort in a planned way, or by businesses competing in a market. This debate was based on the

universal and unspoken supposition that people couldn't simply self-assemble; the choice between markets and managed effort assumed that there was no third alternative. Now there is.[30]

The ability to get things done as a small group of people without a large hierarchical bureaucracy or even a profit motive is slowly transforming a lot of industries. As we discussed, certain capabilities, especially in information-driven industries such as journalism, are passing from professionals to the general public. New technologies are leading to an explosion of self-organized groups of people, whose number only promises to continue to grow.[31]

PROBLEM SOLVERS WORKING ALL THE TIME

This ability of people to organize in groups more easily is another new development helping us form an emergent global consciousness and sense of shared humanity. Throughout history, war has too often depended on demonizing the opposing side. The hatred that Nazis felt towards Jews and other minority groups launched the Holocaust. The disgust that Hutus felt for Tutsis inspired the Rwandan Genocide in 1994. Today, common sense tends to overrule this kind of large-scale racism, though sadly, still not always. But a sense of common humanity makes it harder for intolerant governments to manipulate their citizens into campaigns of hatred.

A global consciousness also helps increase our general knowledge as new discoveries float freely across borders, expands our markets as protectionism fades and the number of foreign exports is allowed to grow, and promotes economic development. Finally, a sense of global unity can inspire citizens of the developed world to feel responsibility for their brothers and sisters worldwide, and become more likely to reach out and try to help the rest of the world. Millions of people are already doing so, including some extraordinary individuals worthy of a closer look.

In recent years there has been an increase in non-profit organizations and charities, which now make up 11 percent of the American workforce. (Rough economic times provide an additional uptick of people wanting to help out, too.) Recent evidence even points to a need for do-goodery hard-wired into our brains: scientists have measured the many chemicals in our brain that infuse us with positive feedback when we help others. (MRI scans discovered that the same parts of our brain light up when we help and cooperate with other people as when we eat chocolate.)[32] Yet the vast majority of people throughout history held an outlook that was necessarily narrow. Everyone worked hard to help their own family and helped out their friends when they were needed. People were loyal to tribes, and then after the creation of the nation-state people started to support their nation, its ideals, and its efforts. It is only in the last century that some determined groups have been ambitious enough to look at the larger picture and try to help the world. Only within recent years have we obtained the data, technology, and global outlook required to determine the neediest areas of the world and effectively coordinate efforts to respond to them.

What's impressive today is the clout of celebrity advocates who are devoted to this push toward building a better world. For example, Bono, arguably the most famous rock star in the world, has devoted years to the cause of eradicating poverty by eliminating third world debt. Some people deride him and other cause-promoting celebrities as superficial and haughty. But Bono has helped to free up millions of dollars that developing countries can now use to help their citizens. Another example of a celebrity advocate is Angelina Jolie, who is the Goodwill Ambassador for the United Nations High Commission for Refugees (UNHCR).[33] This is a woman who can do anything she wants to do, including staying home with Brad Pitt. Instead, she has traveled to Sudan, Sierra Leone, and refugee camps in Pakistan, seeking to understand the plight of the world's refugees and lobby governments to help them. It takes a special type of person to say, "Wow, I'm rich! I'm famous! I'm beautiful! I can do whatever I want! I'll ... help refugees!"

Celebrities are not alone in taking up new causes. Experts, scientists, politicians, doctors, business leaders, and religious figures are increasingly working on new, focused ways to sort and solve the world's worst problems. Jeffrey Sachs is an economist who helped Bolivia, Poland, and other countries restore their economies to normalcy. Gradually learning more about poverty and development in each case, he shifted away from relying solely on economic policies and towards eradicating poverty through development. He is now Special Advisor to United Nations Secretary-General Ban Ki-moon and is pushing the world to meet the UN Millennium Development Goals, a sophisticated set of targets to reduce the world's poverty by half by 2015.[34] We'll look at his efforts in more detail in the chapter exploring economics.

One global problem solver has been outshining all the others. As the *Economist* put it, "Yes, Bill Gates really does think he can cure the world."[35] With the Bill and Melinda Gates Foundation, Gates has given *$28 billion* of his fortune to concentrate on helping global health. The Gates Foundation, by far the largest in the world, focuses on researching and delivering vaccines and treatments for diseases in the developing world: malaria, AIDS, tuberculosis, and others. The Gates Foundation is revolutionizing world charity due to Gates's concentration on efficiency and measurable results. The foundation is devising new ways to better distribute aid resources.

Gates brings this efficiency from his success at founding Microsoft, during which he quickly amassed the largest fortune on Earth. Originally loathe to spread his fortune, he preferred to concentrate on running his business. But his wife, his father, and his friends convinced him to become more involved in world charity and share the wealth. So he did what many philanthropists do as they start out, give to their alma maters or cultural institutions. Gates donated computers to poor libraries around the country (which raised accusations of his self-interest in spreading Microsoft products).[36] But he soon realized this was not where his effort was most needed. Throwing himself wholeheartedly into studying the problems of the developing world, and spending years traveling to underdeveloped countries with his wife and the Gates Foundation, he is now so dedicated to philanthropy that he stepped down as Microsoft's CEO to concentrate on his foundation work.[37] Due in part to his influence, more philanthropists are seeking measurable results from their charity work, just as they do in their fields of science and business.

The Gates Foundation, rather than starting from scratch and mirroring the bureaucracy found in some other charitable organizations, evaluates existing charities and scientific research and expands those that are the most successful. It also set up Grand Challenges in Global Health, a contest in which scientists compete for funding for long-shot technological ideas. Along with the X Prize Foundation, Grand Challenges is part of an intriguing trend to offer prizes to promote philanthropy. Gates admits he may be "overly optimistic," but he is shooting for finding cures for the 20 leading fatal diseases.[38] Gates is such an inspiration to others that he convinced investment guru Warren Buffett (the second-richest man on the planet) to give $31 billion, the bulk of his fortune, to the Gates Foundation as well. Buffett, like Gates, had been reluctant to donate large amounts of money, preferring to wait until his death to start another foundation. But he realized Bill and Melinda Gates would do a better job.[39]

Another noteworthy example of this smart thinking is the Copenhagen Consensus, in which a panel of the world's most distinguished economists, including Nobel laureates, were asked to split up a hypothetical $50 billion in the most efficient way to advance global welfare. The panel found that HIV/AIDS, malaria, micronutrients to prevent malnutrition, and free trade were the best areas to focus on in order to achieve the best results. Their detailed theories are already being deployed, as we will see when we look at global health in more detail later.[40]

What I find most incredible about the world's new crop of problem solvers is that every problem in the world has someone working on it. Name a cause, and you can find some grassroots club, government program, or nongovernmental organization (NGO) devoted to it. This greatly increases the chances of a breakthrough in one field, which can then spread to others. Because of the speed at which today's memes are spreading, those breakthroughs can immediately influence the rest of the world. Some organizations even focus solely on bringing others together in cooperation. In the past decade, 50-60 new groups called global public policy networks (GPPN) have emerged. The Worldwatch Institute reports that "These innovative groups bring various partners—governments, international organizations, the private sector, and NGOs—together under the umbrella of a cohesive working group to address shared international challenges." Since corporations are increasingly multinational, and the number of NGOs grew from 5,000 in 1975 to over 25,000 in 2000, this improved coordination is necessary.[41] These efforts reflect the growing consensus that global solutions are needed to address global problems.

In the past decade there have been a growing number of international conferences and meetings, many sponsored by the UN. The recent wave of major conferences began in 1990 but was unofficially inaugurated by the Rio Earth Summit in 1992, the largest environmental meeting ever held. International conferences allow representatives of governments, grassroots organizations, and NGOs to collaborate, share their successes, and foster an environment where they can embark on larger and more ambitious goals and solutions. While the conferences always run the risk of generating more rhetoric than action, their publicity helps spread the word about imperative global issues. As Angelina Jolie said, "If people are aware of the facts, I believe many will be driven to action."[42] There are already millions of individuals who are proving her right.

A GROWING GLOBAL ETHIC

The philanthropists mentioned above embody a global ethic, and we can look to their example. We need an agreed-upon broad ethical framework for all humanity in order to deal with problems that are universal in scope. The natural evolution of humanity's emerging global perspective is the implementation of global ethics. When any individual can conceivably have so much power that he can set off a bomb that kills thousands, then, as Spider-Man says, with great power comes great responsibility. The former secretary-general of the Parliamentarians for Global Action, Dr. Kennedy Graham, described a planetary interest that would give priority to the interests of humanity as a whole. He saw this as consisting of environmental stewardship combined with a concern for human needs and human rights.[43]

An important part of the theory of today's unfolding peace is the premise that world history is morally progressive. The world is not just improving in material goods, human knowledge, and capacity, but in morality as well. Ethics, laws and moral teachings are included in the types of information spreading throughout the world, and passed on by history. Just as we learn lessons from our moral lapses throughout our individual lives, so too does humanity learn from its much larger moral atrocities. As author Foad Katirai explains, "Included in this [global] consciousness is the growing awareness that the same basic elements of life are the common and rightful expectations of people everywhere. Besides enjoyment of the fundamental rights to life, liberty, freedom of worship and healthy natural and social environments, these expectations are assumed today to include enjoyment of the fruits of new technology ..."[44] A morally progressive history is the most secret part of a future peace, and one that is all too easy for many people to dismiss, even if they accept the facts of humanity advancing materially. It's a controversial stance, but the evidence bears it out.

The trick is to look at the long-term picture. Surely no one will argue that we're worse off morally than, say, sixteenth century Paris, when cat burning was a popular form of entertainment, even for kings and queens. Yes, that's exactly what it sounds like: hoisting a cat onto a stage and slowly lowering it into a fire. Or eighteenth century Britain, when people used to pay a penny to visit Bethlem Hospital ("Bedlam") and watch the lunatics have sex and get into fights. Visitors were allowed to bring long sticks to poke and enrage the patients. In 1814 alone, there were 96,000 of these visits.[45] Harvard psychologist Steven Pinker describes the trend best:

> Cruelty as popular entertainment, human sacrifice to indulge superstition, slavery as a labor-saving device, genocide for convenience, torture and mutilation as routine forms of punishment, execution for trivial crimes and misdemeanors, assassination as a means of political succession, pogroms as an outlet for frustration, and homicide as the major means of conflict resolution—all were unexceptional features of life for most of human history. Yet today they are statistically rare in the West, less common elsewhere than they used to be, ... and [when they do occur] these practices are, to varying degrees, hidden, illegal, condemned, or at the very least (as in the case of capital punishment) intensely controversial. In the past, they were no big deal.[46]

Conclusive evidence of a morally progressive history really begins to pick up speed with the Universal Declaration of Human Rights (UDHR), an amazing testament to universal tolerance and respect. Ratified by the General Assembly of the brand-new UN in 1948, the document lists rights that should be protected for all individuals. It stresses the rights to life, liberty, property, security, employment, religion, and expression. It describes the right to an education, the right to participate in a cultural life, and freedom from torture. Although it is not officially international law, the UDHR has served as a basis and inspiration for several documents that are now binding, both at the international and national level. While many dismissed the UDHR as mere rhetoric, several governments took the document very seriously indeed and set up offices to evaluate human rights cases. NGOs use the document as a reference for holding rights-abusing countries to account. Journalists found that they could measure a government's performance as compared to the UDHR. Individuals can use the document as a starting point to determine other rights, too. For example, Gates has said his dream is that his foundation will eventually "get rich-world health conditions to be a human right you take for granted."[47]

As long ago as 1795, Immanuel Kant already saw that "The peoples of the earth have thus entered in varying degrees into a universal community, and it has developed to the point where a violation of rights in *one* part of the world is felt *everywhere*. The idea of a cosmopolitan right is therefore not fantastic and over-strained; it is . . . a universal right of humanity."[48] Today, kicked off by the UDHR, the concept of human rights is leaping around the world as a lightning-fast meme. Most governments now recognize the value of basic human rights, humanitarian reasons are often cited as justification for intervention in the affairs of other states, and international treaties are suffused with human rights language.

The acknowledgment of those universal values is a necessary first step in order for them to be fully implemented, though some governments continue to push back against what they see as Western-imposed ideas. While the governments of, say, China or Russia might claim cultural relativism and oppose specific American or European plans, the broader values themselves continue to spread. Even authoritarian countries such as Belarus and Iran now feel compelled to pay lip service to democracy and human rights. Eventually, they will talk them up so much that their citizens will demand their governments' adherence to those universal values. Historian Howard Zinn says succinctly, "From now on all moral transgressions take the form of irony, because they are committed against officially proclaimed values. The job of citizens, in any society, is simply to point this out."[49]

The core of the UDHR and its global ethic is the simple concept of equality. After all, the axiom of all of the world's religions is a version of the Golden Rule: "Do unto others as you would have them do unto you." So, as we start examining evidence for the secret peace, with facts and figures that demonstrate the change wrought by the three major forces we've examined, we'll start with the realm of equality. Revolutionary developments in equal rights have occurred in the six decades since the birth of the prescient UDHR. Its drafters may have seemed like dreamers, but today an ever-growing segment of the world is realizing the single most important idea out of all the accumulating information swirling around us: that all people are created equal, and we all share the same earth.

PART TWO

The Evidence

EQUALITY

Achieving a Dream

On January 16, 2006, with foreign dignitaries such as Condoleezza Rice and Laura Bush in attendance, President Johnson was sworn in as the new leader of Liberia. Liberia has one of the bloodiest histories of the late twentieth century, and Johnson's relationship with the country is every bit as dramatic. Harvard-educated, Johnson was secretary of state of finance and then minister of finance in the'70s. A few years after the 1980 military coup that kicked off Liberia's troubles, Johnson was imprisoned for criticizing the military regime. Upon release, Johnson fled to Washington, D.C. and worked with the UN Development Program and the World Bank. Returning to Liberia in 1997, Johnson ran against the infamous Charles Taylor in the presidential election, lost by a landslide, and was charged with treason. But rebel groups forced Taylor to step down in 2003 and flee the country. Captured by the UN, Taylor is now on trial for 650 counts of war crimes and crimes against humanity. Meanwhile, Johnson, who had hung in there as Liberia struggled through the end of its civil war, ran for president again and won the 2005 election.[1]

The story of Chilean President Bachelet is filled with just as many impressive credentials (Bachelet speaks five languages, for example), and just as much conflict with a military government. Bachelet entered medical school in 1970, but when Chilean dictator Augusto Pinochet seized governmental power in a coup in 1973, he captured the Bachelet family because Bachelet's father Alberto had worked for the previous government. After months of excruciating torture, Alberto's heart gave out, and his family was exiled to Australia. Eventually, after being allowed back into Chile, Bachelet worked as a doctor, and also for an NGO that helped children with tortured or missing parents. In 1996, Bachelet earned a master's degree in military science, and began to work for the defense ministry, democracy having been restored to Chile when Pinochet was finally ousted. In 2000, Bachelet was appointed Minister of Health and then Minister of Defense two years later—an uncommon career path, to say the least. In late 2004, though initially reluctant, Bachelet was encouraged to run for the President's office. Bachelet was sworn in as President of Chile two weeks after Johnson became President of Liberia.[2]

Jamaican Prime Minister Simpson-Miller's story followed a less violent path. Born into rural poverty, Simpson-Miller has held an impressive potluck grab bag of political positions: Minister of Labour, Welfare and Sports (yes, they have a Sports Minister), then Minister of Labour and Welfare, then Minister of Labour, Social Security and Sports, and then Minister of Tourism and Sports. Simpson-Miller oversaw Jamaica's first foray into the World Cup, and helped restore the travel industry upon its decline after September 11, 2001. Simpson-Miller rose as an indomitable leader in the People's National Party and was elected Prime Minister in February 2006, vowing to fight corruption, to help the poor, and to ensure individual liberty.[3]

Why am I sharing these presidential biographies? What do all of these new world leaders have in common? They are all women.

That's right, I left out the leaders' first names and pronouns. Perhaps you already knew about these leaders, but there's a chance you jumped to a gender-biased assumption that they were men. Ellen Johnson-Sirleaf, Michelle Bachelet, and Portia Simpson-Miller are the leaders' full names. Together they demonstrate one of the points of this chapter: finally overcoming their historic lack of opportunity and recognition, women are steadily advancing in every walk of life, including serving as leaders of their countries. Indeed, for decades, the world has finally seen power slowly and subtly shifting from men to women.[4]

As of this writing, 17 heads of state out of 193 countries in the world are female, not counting three figurehead queens and the governors of some overseas territories.[5] President Johnson-Sirleaf is the first female elected head of state in Africa. The Chancellor of Germany, Prime Minister of South Korea, and presidents of India, Argentina, and Lithuania are all women, to name a few. I am willing to place a bet that the total number will be higher by the time you read this. There have been queens and female rulers throughout history, of course, but they have been few and far between. A stronger trend began 50 years ago and is reaching full steam now, as seen in Figure 6. It shows the number of female presidents and prime ministers since the end of World War II, when the arena was exclusive to men.[6]

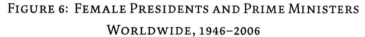

FIGURE 6: FEMALE PRESIDENTS AND PRIME MINISTERS
WORLDWIDE, 1946–2006

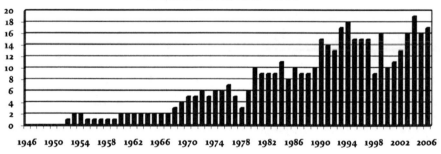

The news for women is even better in parliaments worldwide. Eighteen percent of world parliamentarians are now female. Not surprisingly, the countries with the highest percentages are the Nordic states—Sweden (with 47 percent), Finland, the Netherlands, Denmark, and Iceland. Costa Rica, Argentina, and New Zealand (the first county to allow women to vote) do pretty well, too. Spanish Prime Minister José Zapatero recently appointed the first Spanish Cabinet with a female majority – 9 out of 17 ministers, including the Minister of

Defense. That also includes the brand-new Equality Ministry, which will monitor women's status in Spain. Ironically, Iraq's and Afghanistan's new constitu-
tions mandate about 25 percent female legislatures, making them more inclusive than the United States, which has only 16 percent female representation in
Congress. Even Saudi Arabia, rightly infamous for its draconian treatment of
women, recently appointed its first female Cabinet minister. In all countries,
the percentage of women in power is usually even higher at local levels.[7]

Forbes ranks the 100 most powerful women in the world, and it is an impressive list. Just consider the top three in the article a few years ago: Angela
Merkel, the Chancellor of Germany; Condoleezza Rice, the U.S. Secretary of
State; and Wu Yi, the Vice Premier of China.[8] Those are important positions of
leadership in three of the most powerful countries in the world. This is likely to
keep increasing, and quickly. In fact, in 2006 Nancy Pelosi became the first female Speaker of the U.S. House of Representatives. Congress now has 90 wom-
en, a record.[9] And of course Sarah Palin received the second major U.S. party
Vice Presidential nomination (after only Geraldine Ferraro in 1984), in addition
to Hilary Clinton's recent campaign odyssey, both landing a woman tantaliz-
ingly close to the Presidency.

Representing slightly more than half of the world's population, the importance of women's fair representation in government is self-evident for
democratic reasons. But what will happen as more women gain seats of world
power? Will they have different priorities than men? Possibly. Across the world,
female leaders are typically perceived as more trustworthy and less corrupt
than men. Ellen Johnson-Sirleaf, for example, has been called the most honest
leader in Africa.[10] India has required female leaders in one-third of village coun-
cils since the mid-1990s, and an M.I.T. economist studying the results found
that the women on average did a better job in many ways. For example, women
constructed and maintained wells better, and took fewer bribes than men.[11]
Studies show that female leaders are more likely to invest in improving health,
education, infrastructure, and in reducing poverty, and they are less likely to
spend money on guns and tanks.[12] There are certainly exceptions—Margaret
Thatcher was nicknamed the "Iron Lady" because of her support for the military in her firm stance against the Soviet Union. It is a controversial issue, and

it's important not to stereotype, but some gender differences do seem to apply. This isn't to say that women should completely replace men in government and the workforce, of course. Rather, sharing power equally works best. As Professor of Political Science Valerie Hudson explains:

> Recent research has shown that when both males and females make decisions together, all participants are more satisfied with the outcome than when it is the product of all-male groups. Furthermore, researchers have found that mixed decision-making groups are less risk-acceptant than all-male groups, and that non-zero-sum outcomes are more likely. Additional studies have shown that levels of corruption in government are lower when more women are involved. Real gender equality, entailing a meaningful sharing of power within society, may thus be a prerequisite for optimal and rational policymaking, whether for households, countries, or the international community.[13]

Women in government also seem more likely to foster programs for women, and that's good news for several reasons. Elevating the status of women secretly feeds all the other trends toward peace. Promoting the equality of women offers the highest returns of any social investment. A report by the UN Population Fund showed that government spending on women's health (including birth control) has been responsible for up to one-third of the annual economic growth of many fast-growing places such as Brazil and much of East Asia. Since 1970, countries that have managed to reduce their birth rates have registered faster growth.[14] How do you reduce birth rates? One way is to educate women. According to the *Economist*, "Not only will educated women be more productive, but they will also bring up better educated and healthier children."[15] In addition, Isobel Coleman, Senior Fellow at the Council on Foreign Relations, explains: "Focusing on women is often the best way to reduce birth rates and child mortality; improve health, nutrition, and education; stem the spread of HIV/AIDS; build robust and self-sustaining community organizations; and encourage grassroots democracy."[16] Not bad.

The equality of women is at last a reality in many areas of daily life. Gender gaps in infant mortality rates, school enrollment, literacy levels, access to health care, and political participation have all narrowed steadily for decades.[17] Society is adjusting to these changes as women leap ahead in some areas and continue to lag behind in others. As former UN secretary-general Kofi Annan said, "At the World Summit, world leaders declared that 'progress for women is progress for all.' Let us ensure that half the world's population takes up its rightful place in the world's decision-making."[18]

LEARNING MORE, EARNING MORE

In at least one major way, Western women are now surpassing men: education. Women in developed countries get better grades in school than their male counterparts, and they are more likely to go to college. In the U.S., girls have now achieved exact parity with boys in math, even in high school, where the gap used to widen. Women have had a majority enrollment in U.S. college campuses for decades, and now a whopping 58 percent of U.S. college students are female. It is important to note that despite rumors of a "boy crisis," the status of boys has not really declined; they keep going to college in greater numbers. Girls have just drastically leapfrogged ahead of them. Several theories for this exist. Boys develop later socially and intellectually; a trend of anti-intellectualism can be found among boys, especially among minorities in America; crime and gangs offer less of a distraction for girls; and many technical jobs appealing to men do not require a degree. The *Economist* recently noted that, due in part to getting better grades and more degrees, "Women will thus be better equipped for the new jobs of the 21st century, in which brains count a lot more than brawn."[19]

Moving from education to the workforce, the oft-cited gender wage-gap continues to decrease. As seen in Figure 7, women made on average only 62 percent as much as men in 1975 but that number increased to 80 percent by 2004.[20] More surprisingly, the *New York Times* recently reported that young women's overall wages in New York City and other large cities have now substantially surpassed men's. Among full-time workers in their twenties, women in New

York made 117 percent of men's wages. Dallas has the biggest gap, with women making 120 percent of men's wages. Even among New Yorkers in their thirties, women and men's wages are now equal. Several explanations have been offered, mainly that women with college degrees are tending to move to more urban areas, and delaying the age at which they get married and have children. In jobs that were once considered male preserves, such as police officer and private investigator, young women and men now make the same wages. And in a growing number of careers women are now earning more than men: doctors, architects, lawyers, editors, reporters, and more.[21] In fact, women in the U.S. now make up nearly half of biological and medical scientists and almost three-quarters of health industry workers. President Obama explained that, "Women are just as likely to be the primary bread earner, if not more likely, than men are today."[22]

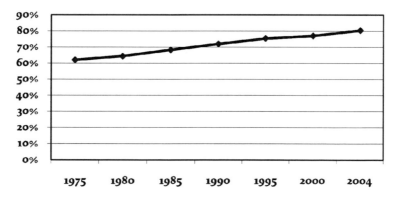

FIGURE 7: WOMEN'S WEEKLY EARNINGS,
AS PERCENTAGE OF MEN'S EARNINGS, 1975–2004

However, there are limits to closing the gap everywhere. Maternity leaves and the types of jobs taken—women tend not to take certain dangerous, high-paying jobs, and also pursue careers in the humanities more often than engineering or business—will continue to limit women's average salaries.[23] And in one major area, the gains are excruciatingly slow: women at the top of the corporate ladder in senior corporate jobs. The percentage of female top managers of Fortune 500 firms doubled in only seven years, from 8 percent in 1995 to 16 percent in 2002.[24] Yet despite the increase, this is woefully low. It's been shown that companies that actively promote women are more profitable; however, the evidence is inconclusive that this is a causal relationship.[25] The *Economist* reports that many companies are actively trying to address promoting women, and the newspaper recommends several methods to remedy the imbalance at the top levels of businesses. It suggests focusing on women when they return from long child-raising leaves and giving them most of their pre-leave salary along with some retraining. While on leave, women should keep in touch with their former employers and perhaps even work on part-time projects. Flex-time and telecommuting from home (and coffee shops) are options that could be the biggest help to mothers returning to the workforce.[26]

Is there any downside to promoting women's equality in the workforce? One popular theory suggests that women's participation in the workforce damages family ties—as in, they don't have as much time to spend raising their children. However, despite rumors of the collapse of the family, the average number of meals eaten together by parents and children has barely changed since the end of the nineteenth century. As Gregg Easterbrook points out, it's an urban legend that children are spending less time with their parents. "In 1924, only 60 percent of fathers spent at least one hour per day with their children, whereas today 83 percent do."[27] Based on these numbers, kids today have perhaps closer relationships with their parents than ever. In past centuries, the upper classes often felt hands-on child-rearing was beneath them and passed the tykes off to servants. And the rest of humanity needed their kids to work in the fields all day, which is true today in fewer and fewer places.

Even in the idealized America of the 1950s, most mothers spent less time with their children because they lacked many of our modern appliances and were too busy running their households. Compared to that scenario, today's families are close-knit and cozy. I suspect that the strength of families will continue to increase due to flexible working arrangements, for both mothers and fathers. Forty-five million Americans now do at least part of their job at home.[28] Personally, I've had jobs in the past in which I worked from home, just as efficiently in my cramped New York City apartment as in a cramped New York City office cubicle. And that's not to mention writing this book, which was done in my spare time. Even jobs that require in-house workers are granting more flex-ible time. If it can be argued that the only downside of women's gaining equal-ity in the work force is potentially less time devoted to raising children, then I think telecommuting technology will soon render that argument moot, as both men and women can flexibly split the time needed for child-rearing.

Here's another big improvement on the domestic front: as a result of women's advancing status, violence against women is declining worldwide. The *Economist* reports that in Britain, which parallels other developed countries, domestic violence has decreased by more than 50 percent in less than a decade, a stunning achievement.[29] In the U.S., domestic violence fell 21 percent in the 1990s, and rape is down an astonishing 72 percent since 1993. There are many contributing factors. A Clemson University study found that rape declined the most in states where Internet access expanded the fastest, suggesting that In-ternet pornography can be a less harmful outlet for potential predators.[30] In the developing world, as domestic violence is brought into the open, improve-ments in divorce rights, economic independence, and self-assurance all help to enable women to leave abusive situations. And remember, as with other secret peace trends, violence against women sometimes *appears* to be increasing be-cause we are finally reporting it more. Imagine how large the percentage drop would be if the numbers had been reported fully in the past.

Rania al-Baz is one moving example. At age 29, al-Baz was beaten by her husband in a gruesome incident. After a heated argument, he strangled her, threw her against a wall, and beat her until she passed out. When she awoke in the hospital, her prospects for recovery and safety were not as good as for American women because she lives in Saudi Arabia—arguably the worst coun-try in the world to be a woman. But al-Baz was luckier than most. She happens to be Saudi Arabia's most famous television personality, a newscaster. And be-cause she let someone snap a photo of her famous face, barely recognizable as she lay bleeding in her hospital bed, the incident became international news. Amidst that publicity, she decided to do the unthinkable and speak out against domestic violence and the inequity of Saudi laws affecting women. Al-Baz has now formed a group to combat the abuse of women in Saudi Arabia.[31]

UNVEILING WOMEN'S POTENTIAL

That brings us to an elephant in the room that we haven't discussed yet: the Muslim societies of the Middle East, Northern Africa, and Central Asia. The region is notorious for its ill treatment of women, and has seen the least recent improvement. This was one of the reasons that the United States offered for battling the repressive Taliban in Afghanistan (though its use as a rationale only seemed to gain prominence after the fact). And yet, while I hate to downplay the daily atrocities and indignities that do happen in these countries, there is a lot of good news on this front.

Take the headscarf, for example. Much news coverage was devoted to the liberation of Afghani women's attire, since they were forced to wear burkas under the Taliban. Many people might have gathered from the media that such fashion repression was rife in the Middle East. But only Saudi Arabia and Iran have laws requiring headscarves or veils; everywhere else the attire is popular but optional.[32]

I admit I was surprised to discover the significant advances of women in the Middle East. In its June 17, 2004, article entitled "Out of the Shadows, into the World," the Economist reports, "Female life expectancy is up from 52 years in 1970 to more than 70 today. The number of children borne by the average Arab woman has fallen in half in the past 20 years, to a level scarcely higher than world norms. . . . A generation ago, three-quarters of Arab women were married by the time they were 20. That proportion has dropped by half." Besides delaying marriage, women and men are circumventing laws about fraternizing with the opposite sex by dating online, and they are using mobile phones in increasing numbers.[33]

Though women are often still deprived of schooling because of traditions giving preference to males, there has been a lot of progress in education. Currently, 85 percent of Middle Eastern girls are enrolled in primary school.[34] Saudi girls were not allowed to go to school at all until 1964, but today 55 percent of the kingdom's university students are female. Jordan, one of the most liberal Middle Eastern states, has achieved the region's highest literacy rate, with equal literacy for both men and women.[35]

Women in the Middle East are gaining a foothold in the political arena as well. Women constitute 12 percent of members of Parliament in Syria, 11.5 percent in Tunisia, and 9.7 percent in Sudan.[36] These low percentages actually represent dramatic recent increases. Kuwait recently gave women the right to vote and run for elections, starting in 2007. This leaves only a handful of states in the world with elections in which women still cannot vote (Qatar, United Arab Emirates, Saudi Arabia, and Oman). Remember, it has been less than 100 years since women got the right to vote in our own country, and less in most other developed nations.[37]

The achievements of women in the Middle East parallel those of women in the rest of the world, though lagging behind by some years. According to the director of the Arab States Region of the UN Development Fund for Women, "The situation for Arab women has improved slightly in all spheres of public and private life. Women's access to education and health has increased considerably compared to past decades and their participation in the economy, environment and decision-making spheres is steadily growing."[38]

A CLEAR PATH TO ACCEPTANCE

The advancement of women is one of the most impressive achievements of the twentieth century. But within the other major realm of prejudice—race and ethnicity—the news is more mixed. The blockbuster headline, of course, is President Barack Obama. The historical precedent of his election has spurred Americans to report in polls that race relations have improved. In fact, more than two-thirds of African-Americans believe that Martin Luther King Jr.'s vision for race relations—laid out more than 45 years ago in his 1963 "I have a dream" speech—has been fulfilled.[39]

But worldwide, improvements in racism and ethnic conflicts are progressing at more varied paces. While we are still moving forward on most fronts, with racism and ethnic conflict we are progressing at a slower pace. Granted, there's a lot of astounding news: South Africa ousted apartheid. The Balkans are at relative peace. Germany is united. The Kurds are no longer subjugated by

Saddam Hussein. And the number of countries in the world with any institutionalized, legal form of discrimination is now miniscule. Underlying tensions between ethnic groups such as the Arabs and Persians, Turks and Kurds, and Chinese and Japanese may well continue for decades. But with the increasing global economic ties between these groups, many are unlikely to flare into conflict. Since fewer than 20 percent of the countries in the world are ethnically homogenous, it is in the best interest of governments to promote diversity within their own borders too.[40] Worldwide, countries eager to join the world community are ending their ethnic feuds in order to attract investors. More of the world's marginalized groups—including indigenous peoples re-embracing traditional cultures, languages, and beliefs—are demanding their rights from the majority, and succeeding.

Since I am an American, I'm going to talk about race issues in the United States, which have always been one of the country's most pressing problems. It's curious that when we talk about race relations in this country we usually refer to it as an issue primarily between blacks and whites, when Latinos just surpassed blacks as the largest minority, and of course there are many other ethnicities here as well. The U.S. population in 2050 is projected to be 50 percent white, 24 percent Latino, 13 percent black, and 9 percent Asian.[41] Keep this metaphor for the change in mind: from 2001 to 2004 white bread sales were down 12 percent while tortilla sales were up 18 percent.[42]

But there is a reason why the country still focuses on black-white relations. Most immigrants (including Latinos) have chosen to come to America and are therefore invested in the American Dream. Many of them aim to fit in, and they tend to succeed after only one or two generations. But the history of blacks in America is one of *involuntary* immigration. With many black Americans here because their ancestors arrived against their will as slaves, a contentious history with other groups is understandable. Another unique situation exists with American Indians, whose history of shameful mistreatment makes their situation different from that of other ethnic groups, as well.

A recent poll found that 65 percent of blacks and 72 percent of whites felt black-white relations were either "very good" or "somewhat good," numbers that have increased since Obama's election. However, a majority of both whites and blacks still prefer to live in voluntarily racially-segregated neighborhoods. One black man in three will see jail at some point in his life, two-thirds of black children are born out of wedlock, and African-Americans do not perform as well in school as whites and Asians.[43] Race issues, more than 30 years after the passing of the revolutionary Civil Rights and Voting Rights Acts, are in many ways still deplorable.

And yet, in a diversified community, every marginalized group goes through natural stages on its way to integration. Some groups are forced into an initial stage that may include the worst horrors of history, such as slavery and ethnic cleansing. Other groups, such as many immigrants, start at a second stage in which the focus tends to shift to government programs that encourage discrimination rather than violence. But independent isolated acts of violence often remain—think of America's lynchings decades ago, and racial supremacy groups such as the Ku Klux Klan. Third, laws are put in place to promote equality, while the children of immigrants benefit from their parents' gains and begin assimilating into the dominant culture. Eventually, they start joining the middle class. Fourth, a sense of tolerance grudgingly gains ground as the benefits of the new groups are seen. Overt racism becomes taboo. This is the current state of the black community in the United States today. The remaining problems might seem intractable, but the first step in creating a truly integrated society is to make expressions of racism socially unacceptable. Even hidden racism will eventually disappear with subsequent generations. We still have a long way to go before reaching the fifth and final stage of true acceptance, when racial issues practically evaporate. But this has been achieved by ethnic groups in America before: the Irish, Jews, Italians, etc.

One example of the process of acceptance is how Americans reacted after September 11, 2001. While there were some instances of discrimination toward members of the Muslim community, most Americans realized that the attacks were the work of a small minority. This reaction was mild compared to historical standards. The U.S. government did not lock up all Americans of Arab descent in internment camps as we did to Japanese Americans during World War II. There were no lynchings or public executions. Increased tolerance flows from our growing global perspective and then contributes back to it in a positive loop.

In the United States, African-Americans are successfully moving along the path of true integration, just like dozens of other immigrant groups. While it's certainly our duty to criticize the slow speed of this process, we must acknowledge the true achievements that have been made. Naturally, President Barack Obama is practically enough of a historic example to symbolically render most of the other data here redundant. But in the past few years, the United States has also seen two black secretaries of state. Ten percent of the House of Representatives are African-American, close to their proportion of the U.S. population. Black actors, athletes, and musicians in the U.S. rank among the people with the highest incomes worldwide. Due to a lack of educational resources and opportunities, blacks have historically tested lower than their white peers. But teaching reforms aimed specifically at black students seem to be bearing fruit.[44] The gap in reading scores between black and white nine-year-olds, for example, shrank from 44 points in 1971 to 26 points in 2004. When polled, large percentages of both blacks and whites say they have close friends of another ethnicity.[45]

More than 90 percent of voters say they'd be willing to support a black presidential candidate, as well as one who was female, Catholic, or Jewish. When voters were asked that same question in 1967, while 90 percent said they might support a Catholic (this was right after Kennedy), only 62 percent would support a Jewish candidate, 57 percent a female candidate, and 52 percent a black candidate. Going back to 1937, only 60 percent would support a Catholic, 45 percent a Jew, and 35 percent a woman. Back then, it didn't even occur to the pollsters to ask about a black candidate.[46]

While discrimination and racist views are on the decline in the United States, poverty is still holding blacks back. Race and poverty have always been inextricably linked. Only 13 percent of white children are raised in poverty, whereas a third of black children are.[47] Poverty is the reason why women have fared better in reaching equality than blacks. After all, blacks paralleled women in pushing towards equality in the last century, with the Civil Rights Movement and the Women's Movement. The two movements diverged because women are not a group that specifically has a history of poverty; since they share households with men, their poverty rates match that of the whole country.

The achievements of women have not been racially selective. Today black women are much more successful than black men; in fact, the median women's incomes are the same among whites and blacks.[48] In 1940, 58 percent of black women who worked were maids; today, only one percent are.[49] But black women are much less likely to be married, and with the legal and economic advantages of marriage, this hurts black poverty rates overall.[50]

In many places in the world, the worst remaining inequality is economic. At present, there are many legitimate concerns about the gap between the richest of the rich and the poorest of the poor. But the dichotomy between rich and poor has existed throughout history; it's not new. And much of the economic inequality in the United States is a result of the high numbers of immigrants who start out poor before gaining ground in subsequent generations. As we'll examine later, worldwide poverty is in the decline, thus decreasing economic inequality overall.[51]

LOVE CONQUERS ALL

America has always been a melting pot. In the past this term implied that immigrant communities should try to "blend in" and assimilate to the majority. Today, on the other hand, each ethnic and cultural group is learning how to live together without abandoning its own cultural ideas, practices, and traditions. The constant addition of new, diverse people is what keeps America's culture vibrant and strong. Well, there is a new element to the melting pot metaphor: mixing in not only whole cultures but individual relationships. On this issue, I have some experience. Like 40 percent of Americans, I've dated people of different races.[52] I dated a black woman for several years, for instance, and during that time I was prepared in the back of my mind to put up with some prejudice. But we didn't experience a single incident. Now, this was in Central New Jersey, a tolerant area, but I still thought we might get a few stares or comments. But, no. Since then, my interest was piqued about interracial dating and marriage; I realized America's tolerance in this area might be better than many people suspect.

FIGURE 8: PERCENTAGE OF WHITES AND BLACKS
APPROVING OF MIXED-RACE MARRIAGE

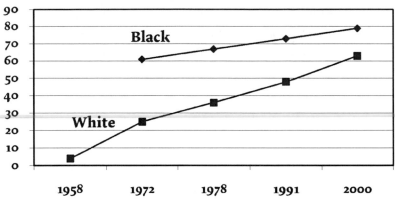

Figure 8 shows the results of a series of five polls taken over the years that asked, "Do you approve or disapprove of marriage between people of different races?"[53] It shows the percentage of blacks and whites who approved of mixed-race marriages.

As you can see from the chart, only four percent of white Americans approved of interracial marriage in 1958; 63 percent do today. That change in outlook reflects the reality of American life: there are now over 1.5 million mixed-race marriages, a number that is doubling roughly every decade. This represents quite a change from the past, particularly since 42 states had laws banning interracial marriage at one time or another. (The Supreme Court struck down those laws in 1967.) Randall Kennedy, author of *Interracial Intimacies,* puts it succinctly, "We talk about desegregation in the public sphere; here's desegregation in the most intimate sphere."[54]

Now that interracial dating and interracial marriage have become commonplace, what do we have? Multiracial kids. Thirty years ago, one in every 100 children in the United States was born of mixed race; the 2000 census tallied it as one in every 19.[55] There is perhaps no better symbol of our increasing diversity than the Census Bureau's long-overdue decision to let Americans check more than one box under "race" in the 2000 Census. Compare this to the 1790 census, in which slaves counted as only three-fifths of a person, and Indians weren't counted at all; or the 1890 census, when people of mixed race had to identify as "mulatto" (one-half black), "quadroon" (one-quarter), or "octoroon" (yes, one-eighth.) A study by the Population Research Center in Portland, Oregon, predicts that 37 percent of blacks living in the United States will claim mixed ancestry by 2100, as will over 40 percent of Asian Americans, and 70 percent of Latinos. Mexicans and other Latinos, by far the largest group immigrating to the United States, have a long history of cross-cultural interactions—perhaps since the history of Central and South America is a synthesis of indigenous peoples with the Spanish.[56]

While some of the stigma held by past generations toward those of mixed racial ancestry still lingers, there's now a certain exotic celebrity chic attributed to people with multicultural ancestry. Today, many celebrities are of mixed race, and that's part of their appeal: Tiger Woods, Halle Berry, Vin Diesel, Derek Jeter, Jessica Alba, Vanessa Hudgens ... not to mention Barack Obama. The trend of using multicultural models in marketing has also taken off in recent years, but it's not just a flash-in-the-pan event. "Today what's ethnically neutral, diverse or ambiguous has tremendous appeal," says one marketer. "Uniformity just isn't appealing anymore," says *Allure* magazine's editor in chief.[57]

For some, the trend toward diversity may not sound like good news—after all, there is a danger that our unique cultures and traditions may be lost in one big homogenous society. However, I doubt that will ever be a problem; multicultural families, even those with two different religious backgrounds, often manage to keep both traditions alive while enjoying the richness of both cultures. People today have much more diversity in their genes than they would like to admit, and so it is illogical to assume that further mixing up our genes will result in a society in which everyone looks identical. Rather, I think that visually, diversity will only increase as more combined ethnicities are added to the mix. At any rate, anthropologists, geneticists, philosophers, biologists, and sociologists have in recent decades condemned the notion of "race" itself as a human construct. People are interconnected genetically in such complex ways that choosing a single race to identify someone is practically arbitrary. Philosopher Naomi Zack points out that the only sane way to view race is as a continuum, a spectrum of diversity, not as a series of categorized buckets. Simply put, we are all part of the human race, and that's it.[58]

DIVERSITY DAY

Today diversity has become quite a buzzword in business and marketing. Is this a permanent trend or just a fad? Certainly, we can hope for a day when appreciation of diversity will be a natural occurrence and will not need to be stressed. In the meantime, it's pretty amazing to compare today's diversimania—diversity training seminars, diversity specialists, diversity mission statements, and diversity press releases—with the popular culture from past eras.[59] As superficial as some of that may seem, its message must be rubbing off on us. I can't imagine what must go through a racist's head when he flips through a magazine today, encountering hundreds of carefully diversified photos. (I used to design ad campaigns; believe me, everyone's demographic makeup is excruciatingly deliberated by a marketing team.)

Consider these random advertisements: "Be yourself. Race. Ethnicity. Religion. Nationality. Gender. In the end, there's just one variety of human being. The individual. All six billion of us. Be bullish. Merrill Lynch." Or, "Bringing together talent from all races, beliefs, ages, sexual orientation and disabilities is what makes us a leading innovator and the multi-billion-dollar powerhouse that we are today. Different is what spawns ideas. Different is what creates unique solutions. Different is what makes Xerox ... Xerox."[60] What's notable is not just that these two companies are embracing and celebrating diversity, but that by expressing that in advertisements, they are betting that diversity appeals to their audience, too.

As the U.S. economy moves from manufacturing to more abstract services, creativity is a key commodity. Diversity brings in creative ideas and different points of view. Many businesses are becoming motivated to appear diverse and accepting to other countries; you cannot be prejudiced against Egyptians and expect to open up a branch on the Nile. It also helps to have some employees who speak Egyptian Arabic. I like to think that the majority of companies stressing diversity mean what they say, and that as the message becomes more common, it seeps into our subconscious.

U.S. businesses have done such a good job of stressing diversity that the workplace has become one of the most integrated arenas of American life.

When asked about race relations at work, 90 percent of whites and 71 percent of blacks thought everything was "generally good."[61] The gap in perspectives is still apparent, but nevertheless the numbers are higher than ever. Many companies appreciate the value of diversity, especially diversity of backgrounds, experiences, and opinions. The *Economist* reports that "diverse groups are acknowledged to be better at spotting threats coming from unlikely directions."[62] And promoting equality is beneficial to the economy. Economist Joseph Stiglitz writes, "It is possible to promote equality and rapid growth at the same time; in fact, more egalitarian policies appear to help growth."[63]

The only institutions that might be surpassing corporate America in promoting diversity are our schools. America's university campuses are hotbeds of diversity—most universities now have diversity days, diversity events, diversity-themed courses and majors—you name it. Catching kids long before college, many schools and non-profit educational organizations are now promoting diversity to the elementary school set. The Southern Poverty Law Center has a project called Teaching Tolerance that gives teachers lesson plans and ideas on the subject of diversity.[64] I designed the web site for Kidsbridge Children's Museum, a nonprofit group in Trenton, New Jersey, that promotes diversity through character-building programs and events. They sponsor awards for children who have worked to promote diversity in their schools and communities.[65] Hundreds of similar resources are available on the Internet.

In addition to the growing acceptance that Americans of various races and ethnicities are experiencing, other minority groups are gaining ground in U.S. society as well. Although media coverage of the same-sex marriage debate can give an impression of limited progress, the LGBT community is actually experiencing increasing tolerance in the United States. For example, the percentage of Americans who think homosexuals should have equal employment rights increased steadily from 56 percent in 1977 to 89 percent in 2007. (And a bill protecting against discrimination in the workplace on the basis of sexual orientation was recently approved by Congress.) The number of Americans who think homosexuality should be considered an acceptable alternative lifestyle rose from 34 percent in 1982 to 57 percent today. Gallup polls on nearly every issue relating to the gay community follow the same trend.[66] Interestingly, as acceptance grows, gay neighborhoods in cities like San Francisco and New York are slowly dissolving as gay couples safely spread out into suburban and rural states.[67] Tolerance is expanding worldwide as well—even, for example, in China, where Shanghai now has a tentatively-thriving gay culture. And in Iceland, Johanna Sigurdardottir was just elected as the world's first openly gay prime minister.[68]

People with disabilities are experiencing greater integration and greater acceptance in society as well. In the United States, great changes have been made thanks to the Americans with Disabilities Act (ADA) of 1990, as well as follow-up laws. These basically guarantee rights similar to the 1964 Civil Rights Act, but for the disabled. Covered are such issues as fair housing, access to air travel and other public transportation, discrimination in the workplace, the accessibility of public spaces, and education.[69] Over 500 million people world-wide can be considered disabled in some way.[70]

The trajectory of tolerance for, or acceptance of, these groups mirrors that of many other minorities—though it does so at a different pace for each group. While racial and ethnic minorities, people with disabilities, and same-sex couples are making incredible gains toward equality, gains are also being made in an area where you might not expect it: between generations. Though it remains to be seen if this is a permanent trend, *New York Magazine* recently reported on how many of today's 30- and 40-somethings are acting as if they're still 22, by delaying marriage and children, choosing trendy music, and taking advantage of stay-at-home job flexibility, which promotes a college-like schedule and dress code.[71] This trend continues with the elderly, who are a fast-growing segment of Internet users, increasing their exposure to younger cultures. Why does this matter? Well, it helps to bridge the classic "generation gap," and anything that brings disparate groups closer together promotes unity, leading toward peace.

Today, entertainment is more often cross-generational, blurring the lines between kid culture and grownup culture. Take *Harry Potter* or the *Lord of the Rings* movies, and animated films marketed to kids but with plenty of sly, sophisticated jokes to reel in parents. The entertainment we assume is kids' fare can surprise us. The average age of a comic book reader in America today is not 12 years old, as it was in the 1950s, but 25.[72] And the average video game player is now an over-the-hill 33 years old.[73] With more video game manufacturers upping the difficulty of their games to keep up with their aging audience, the kids who do play need to make grown-up decisions in video games such as *The Sims, Age of Empires,* and *SimCity*. Kids are able to think more like adults with more sophisticated entertainment, while adults can learn new technology from their children and remember the importance of play and imagination.[74] In nearly every arena of equal rights, each generation tends to be more accepting of diversity than the last. So, if adults are "acting younger," perhaps inclusivity is something else they can also learn from kids.

Despite all of the good news about increasing acceptance of diversity of all kinds, there is some bad news. One of the only growing areas of enmity, particularly in America, is between political party zealots. The U.S. media consistently focuses on ideological differences between liberals and conservatives. As I have mentioned, this is an effective way to create conflict and stir up interest. It's easy to get sound bites from people who hold extreme, opposing views, and it makes for exciting news stories. The political parties themselves play to their extremist bases, particularly for fundraising. But all is not lost. The majority of the American public remains moderate. Many people are liberal about some issues and conservative about others, and are often more pragmatic than ideological. But you wouldn't know it from watching the pundits on TV. Unfortunately, one of the side effects of a representative democracy is that you have to pick the representative who best supports your views on issues—and with only two parties to choose from, there's not much chance that you will agree with a candidate on every single issue. A majority of Americans—58 percent—said that they would prefer for candidates in elections to run without party labels. And in six states so far, registered independents outnumber Democrats and Republicans.[75] The majority realizes that big-party politics is not the only option and that the political process could benefit from wider choices. It's not a new development for political extremists to antagonize each other, but politicians and the media have been particularly rancorous in the past decade.[76] In polls of how Americans self-describe their political views, more than a third call themselves moderate.[77] So it's important to keep in mind that the extremists hurling accusations at each other do not represent all Americans.

THE NEW RELIGIOUS MARKETPLACE

We have examined gender, race, age, sexual preference, people with disabilities and political differences, and we will be examining class issues in the chapter addressing economics. So that delivers us to our last sphere of equal rights: religious tolerance. The scientific view of progress, which this book is emphasizing in so many ways, turns out to be wrong so far on one point: the projected demise of religion. Secularism was inarguably ascendant for decades: in April 1966, *Time* ran the cover story, "Is God Dead?"[78] With the all-too visible effects of fundamentalist terrorists on the world stage, that story wouldn't fly today. Nevertheless, this non-religious trend can still be seen in Europe, and more surprisingly, in the United States as well. Europe is well-known as the poster child for advancing secularism, since the population has been attending church less and less frequently for decades.[79] And in America, a wide-ranging survey on religious beliefs found that the percentage of Americans claiming they had "no religion" had increased from 8.2 percent in 1990 to 15 percent in 2009. (Unsurprisingly, the Northeast is the least religious part of the country, with Vermont reporting 34 percent of its citizens citing no religion.)[80] However, this reflects more of a turning away from organized religion than personal beliefs, as we'll examine shortly; over 90 percent of Americans still believe in a God.[81]

The rest of the world seems to be in the middle of a religious boom. As Africa gains technology and becomes more accessible to the rest of the world, millions of new believers are embracing Christianity. And since the collapse of the Soviet Union, many other parts of the world are now open territory for proselytizing, such as Eastern Europe, Russia, and Central Asia. As China slowly modernizes, its communist leaders are relaxing the enforcement of its anti-religious maxims. The Bush Administration actively pushed for religious tolerance in China. Visiting Beijing, former President Bush gave a speech that was broadcast across China, stating, "Tens of millions of Chinese today are re-learning Buddhist, Taoist and local religious traditions, or practicing Christianity, Islam and other faiths." Soothing China's leaders, he added, "Regardless of where or how these believers worship, they are no threat to public order."[82]

Underground "house churches" are proliferating so quickly that neither the Chinese government nor Christians themselves can keep count.[83]

The world's religious believers are trending toward two camps: fundamentalism and tolerance. The first is directly detrimental to world peace, while the second is beneficial. Today's most challenging religious conflicts are not between different religions, but between intolerant people (whether religious or not) and the more tolerant (again, whether religious or not.) While the most obvious expression of religious intolerance is indeed fundamentalism, there can also be "secular fundamentalists"—as the worst extremes of historical Communism have shown.

Let's look at fundamentalism in more detail. By fundamentalist I'm not referring to all devout believers who are trying to closely follow the teachings of their faith. Rather, the best way to define fundamentalism is anyone who believes he has an exclusive path to truth and therefore has no tolerance for those who do not share his beliefs. Fundamentalism requires a reification of language and literal interpretation of scripture—super-literal. It has also been described as an "expectation of guaranteed outcome," since many fundamentalists believe that they know God's plan and are certain that they are destined for heaven. But this fixedness of destiny clashes with basic concepts of freedom and acceptance of others.[84] As much as fundamentalists like to think they are getting back to the roots (the "fundamentals") of their religion and returning to ancient traditions, the kind of extremism we see today is a relatively new phenomenon. It emerged in large part during the early twentieth century as a reaction to modernity and science encroaching on tradition.

It's important to note that of the millions of fundamentalists worldwide, whether Buddhist, Christian, Muslim, Sikh, or Jew, there are only a small percentage who negatively lash out at society—those so intolerant that they are willing to use violence to advance their cause. Some studies now show that a backlash is emerging against the most vicious forms of fundamentalism.[85] But world fundamentalism remains common news fodder, and the focus on terrorism has pushed Islamic fundamentalism into the spotlight for the past decade. So let's examine instead the parallel trend of religious tolerance, which the media typically neglects. It's a long-hidden movement that is helping to usher in world peace. Robert Wright, who I mentioned earlier as the author of *NonZero*, provides a lot of evidence that religion is "evolving" away from conflict in his book, *The Evolution of God*. He sees the world's major faiths as exhibiting long-term tendencies toward inclusiveness. This should lead to a decrease in fundamentalism, especially its most violent forms. [86]

I perceive an increase in religious tolerance manifesting itself in two ways. One is in the public sphere, where the most limited version of the word "tolerance" is truly in play: people "putting up with" other people's religions. In the West, religion is rarely discriminated against through laws or by the state. This was not the case a few centuries ago. Thanks to the American Bill of Rights (although Thomas Jefferson's Virginia Statute for Religious Freedom deserves an earlier credit), Americans are free to choose their own form of worship, or even not to worship at all. By personalizing religion, Jefferson separated church and state and started America down the path toward religious acceptance. This attitude has since been adopted throughout Europe and in other developed nations. As a result, there are very few theocracies left in the world, Iran being the most conspicuous.

In recent decades, both Christian evangelicals and fundamentalists have become increasingly involved in U.S. politics and have gotten a lot of press, culminating in the Bush Presidency. But in an interesting trend that Adam Smith first theorized about in the eighteenth century, the act of finding allies and building a coalition across many smaller Christian groups has served to necessarily moderate the movement. As Walter Russell Mead reports in *The Atlantic*, "the evangelical movement in the United States looks as if it is maturing. That means more social and political influence, not less, as the movement broadens, reaches into the elite, and develops messages with wider appeal. Yet it also means a more pluralistic and less strident movement, more apt to compromise and less likely or be held hostage by a single issue or a single party."[87]

Seventy-six percent of Americans feel that religious diversity is a "source of strength and vitality."[88] America has always been at the forefront of this inclusivist trend. Boston University Professor of Religion Stephen Prothero explains, "One of the key features of American denominations had long been their neighborliness: their willingness to see other denominations less as rivalrous sects (the European model) than as friendly competitors."[89] Even the Catholic Church, oft-cited for historical intolerance, is officially inclusivist. At the Second Vatican Council, the Church declared that salvation is possible for people outside the Church, as long as they "seek God with a sincere heart."[90] Seventy-nine percent of Americans share the belief that people of other religions can get into heaven, and even 57 percent of evangelical Christians agree that "many religions can lead to eternal life."[91] Professor of Religion Charles Kimball explains that, "Ecumenical and interfaith cooperation is happening today on all levels and among people in all religious traditions."[92] Interfaith groups are another example of religious inclusion. A high point of this interfaith spirit was the Millennium World Peace Summit of Religious and Spiritual Leaders held in August 2000. As noted by Jeffrey Huffines, "... some one thousand religious leaders representing every major religion gathered together for the first time at the UN to issue a declaration that called for peace, tolerance, equality, and religious freedom."[93] On a local level, young people are particularly interested in religious tolerance, and interfaith groups abound on college campuses and even in high schools.

An increase of tolerance in the public sphere is paralleled by the second trend of religious tolerance: the melding of our personal belief systems. In the West today, many people think about religion in a more fluid way than they did in the past. After all, once you admit that all religions deserve respect, it is much easier to appreciate their diversity. Then you may start to think, "Maybe they have something to offer. Maybe they are all partially correct." As we investigate other beliefs, we may pick out some that we like and combine them into our own syncretism. The days of rigid creeds and clearly-defined denominations are on the decline, especially within Christianity. Many Christians no longer identify themselves as Methodists or Lutherans or Baptists, but simply as "Christian" or "Evangelical." Even some churches, especially the newest "megachurches," don't play up their membership to a particular sect.

Today many Americans feel comfortable holding individual beliefs that differ from their church's teachings, and fully 44 percent have changed faiths since childhood.[94] Westerners are picking and choosing from a smorgasbord of religious ideas. Many Americans are coming up with general ethical and religious principles that are becoming increasingly universal, as opposed to focusing on restrictive dogma. A recent study, perhaps the most detailed ever done about religion in America, states that the current religious landscape "reflects the new challenges involved in trying to categorize religiosity in America, where people increasingly blend religions, church-shop and worship in independent communities. Classic labels such as mainline, evangelical and unaffiliated no longer have the same meaning."[95]

Along those lines, 79 percent of Americans describe themselves as "spiritual," while only 64 percent claim to be "religious." Weekly religious service attendance is down in America (and even lower in Europe), and yet 84 percent of Americans say that spirituality is important in their lives.[96] More and more people are seeing things they like in more than one religion. While you might remain a devotee of one faith, a few of your beliefs could be drawn from other sources. This pluralist outlook is explained in the Qur'an as the idea that God created humans different from one another so that they could learn from each other.[97]

This new form of religious belief naturally emphasizes a personal religious experience. Pentecostalism is a good example of this. Pentecostalism is arguably the fastest growing religion in the world, particularly in the Southern Hemisphere, and like other blended beliefs, it is Christian but not a rigid sect of Christianity. It's a broad way of thinking and a set of beliefs that you can even mix into other churches. It emphasizes a direct experience of God and a direct connection to the Holy Spirit (often outwardly expressed through speaking in tongues). Above all, it's an active form of religious expression, not a passive one: another aspect of the theme of the empowerment of the world's population.

In their push for diversity and inclusiveness, and with constant exposure to other cultures, many Americans are also mixing in Eastern religions. This current Western interest in Eastern religious thought started in the 1970s with the introduction of Buddhism and yoga to mainstream culture. (Yoga today is a $27 billion industry practiced by over 18 million Americans, and no longer necessarily tied to a religious component.)[98] Traditionally, Asian countries have had less difficulty with practicing multiple religions. Buddhism in particular mixed successfully with Shinto and Taoist cultures, and Hinduism has always been a diverse belief system. Drawing from these rich traditions, an astonishing 29 percent of Americans say they meditate every day.[99]

So religion maintains its prominence today, but it is a more tolerant form of religion, one less at odds with modernity. In fact, it is modern ideas—a belief in individual rights, gender equality, separating church and state, and the idea of a religious marketplace—that are facilitating religion's rise. Alan Wolfe, director of the Boisi Center for Religion and Public Life at Boston College, explains:

> Religious monopolies or near-monopolies, such as state-sponsored churches, generally throttle religious practice over time, especially as a country becomes wealthier ... Lacking any incentive to innovate, churches atrophy, and their congregations dwindle. But places with a free religious marketplace witness something very different: entrepreneurs of the spirit compete to save souls, honing their messages and modulating many of their beliefs so as to appeal to the consumer. With more options to choose from, more consumers find something they like, and the ranks of the religious grow.[100]

Wolfe's use of the word "consumer" highlights a concern about the new spiritual state of things. Is it too much of a "marketplace"? Are people spoiled by being able to just pick and choose whichever belief they like, discarding anything challenging or difficult to comprehend? It's a valid concern, but look at the historical alternatives: sticking with whatever religion you were born into, a matter of demographic chance, for its own sake rather than as a choice; hastily choosing a belief system because you don't like the one you were born into, but don't have that many other alternatives; or being coerced to join a religion by force. Compared to those, having access to all belief (or non-belief) systems and being able to think critically about which portions you believe in, is certainly preferable. This diverse way of thinking about religion thrives in America and is now starting to spread worldwide. Wolfe goes on to explain that:

> Those who worry about religious revivals in the world today usually post an either/or choice between religion and secularism. In reality, the two can work together. ... fanaticism

should not be confused with religious intensity. One can pray passionately to God and lead an otherwise balanced life. ... Religious peace will be the single most important consequence of the secular underpinning of today's religious growth.[101]

All of the new religious ideas share a common belief in universal brotherhood. They all want world peace. Many of these shared religious beliefs reflect the global outlook we've been discussing—seeing the world as an integrated whole, with a "We're all in this together" sense of global tolerance. Religions are perfectly poised to enshrine our new set of global ethics, since they already have a base of followers, laws, and legitimacy.[102] And equality must be the centerpiece of their ethical teachings. As pastor William Sloane Coffin said, "The challenge today is to seek a unity that celebrates diversity, to unite the particular with the universal. ... What is intolerable is for difference to become idolatrous. Human rights are more important than the politics of identity, and religious people should be notorious boundary crossers."[103]

The most famous religious boundary crosser was also at the forefront of this new trend of inclusion: Mohandas Gandhi. Gandhi invented his own personal religious belief system, drawing from various traditions and stitched them together into a cohesive set of beliefs. This was for his own personal relationship with God, a relationship he worked to refine throughout his life. The result was one of the most logical and inclusive religious worldviews in history.

Gandhi grew up in the diverse Hindu culture of nineteenth-century India, but he wasn't particularly religious. However, while studying in England to become a lawyer, he began examining Christianity and Buddhism and also delved more deeply into his native Hinduism. Gandhi saw religions as resources, and he saw spirituality as a way of life, not merely a set of beliefs. He kept refining his Hinduism and increasingly incorporated Christian ideas, particularly Christ's ideal of suffering love, which deeply influenced him. In fact, a small crucifix was the only decoration on the wall of his ashram. The two most important religious guides for Gandhi became the Bhagavad Gita and the Sermon on the Mount. Gandhi drew equally from Christian, Hindu, and Muslim teachings, as well as incorporating Jain and Buddhist teachings on nonviolence.

Gandhi's faith centered around a belief in God, but he disliked anthropomor-phizing God and came to feel that *satya* (ultimate reality or truth) was the only correct term to describe Him. He finally came to the conclusion that "Truth is God" and felt this to be one of his most important discoveries. According to Gandhi, there was one eternal religion that transcended all limited, organized religions, though they each demonstrated a different aspect of God. Since they were all true but different, it was impossible to judge and compare them, much as you can't "rank" Michelangelo's *David* over the *Mona Lisa*, or *Ulysses* over *Crime and Punishment*. He felt the proper attitude to have toward other religions was not just tolerance or respect but the stronger *sadbhava*, which embodies goodwill and spiritual humility.[104]

Gandhi expressed it this way: "I believe in the fundamental truth of all great religions of the world. I believe that all are God-given . . . if only we could all of us read the scriptures of different faiths from the standpoint of the fol-lowers of those faiths, we should find that they were at bottom all one and were all helpful to one another."[105] One of Gandhi's classic aphorisms perfectly em-bodies our age's burgeoning cooperation and appreciation of religion: "I do not want my house to be walled in on all sides and my windows to be stuffed. I want the cultures of all lands to be blown about my house as freely as possible."[106]

It is important to mention Gandhi in our discussion of equality because he is one of the most important figures in the history of equal rights. And after Gandhi employed his techniques of civil disobedience in India and South Af-rica, Martin Luther King, Jr. applied Gandhi's tactics and insights to the Ameri-can civil rights movement. Gandhi and King were prescient in their faith that nonviolence would win out over violence in the fight for equality. Gandhi lived until 1948, just long enough to see the end of humanity's worst war, which was inextricably bound up with racial hatred. But since then, the world's history of conflict, ethnic and otherwise, has been ebbing. Gandhi's philosophy of equal rights and nonviolence has been filling its place.

7

PEACE

War Is Over

A t the time of this writing, there are conflicts raging in Sudan, Uganda, and Somalia. In recent years, Israel waged attacks on Hamas in Gaza, and Georgia was invaded by a reassertive Russia. Pakistan, newly destabilized, remains in a cold war with India and is now fighting on its western border as well. The United States is swamped in parallel military quagmires in Iraq and Afghanistan. Thousands of people, both soldiers and civilians, have lost their lives as a result of these conflicts. So what possible good news could there be about war, that age-old scourge of humanity?

WHAT WAS IT GOOD FOR?

As it turns out, simply put, war is ending. The gradual decrease of the use of violence as a means for asserting influence is one of the most surprising positive trends today. More and more conflicts in the world are being solved nonviolently, and in recent years large nonviolence movements have had increasing opportunity to flourish. So when we sit down to read the newspaper, why does it still feel like the world is infested with war? War tends to be one of the most publicized news items, and when it's intensely covered—as it should be—it may seem like the whole world is fighting. This simply is not true. At all levels of society, from the international realm to the personal, violence is declining worldwide, and nonviolence is increasing as a problem-solving method.

Today, fewer people are dying from war-related incidents than they have at any other time since the 1920s. Take Afghanistan, for example: the longer the U.S. occupies the country, the more it is being compared to Vietnam. But 55,000 American soldiers lost their lives in Vietnam; after six years in Afghanistan, we've lost 850 soldiers (our allies have lost an additional 570.)[1] In fact, four times as many people die from car accidents as from combat worldwide.[2] The number of wars throughout the world has declined by 40 percent since the end of the Cold War, and the numbers keep on dropping. The year 2005 had the fewest international conflicts since 1976.[3] Even the United States' astronomical military spending, which totals more than most other countries' put together, while higher in absolute numbers is lower now as a percentage of the country's GDP. From almost 40 percent during World War II and above 10 percent during the Cold War, it's now less than five percent. War and genocide, when all added up, accounted for *less than three percent* of all deaths in the twentieth century. Anthropologists estimate that early human societies could attribute up to 25 percent of all their deaths to violence—showing that "human nature" can change.[4]

As conflicts have decreased, the number of anti-personnel land mines in use around the world has also plummeted—an important achievement since land mines are notorious for harming civilians long after wars have come to an end. More than 100 governments agreed to ban the use of land mines a mere eight years after the start of a citizen campaign advocating their elimination.[5] In addition, as wars decline, fewer people are forced to flee their homelands as international refugees. That number has drastically declined from a high of 17.8 million people worldwide in 1992 to about 8 million in 2005.[6]

In 2005 alone, 22 cease-fire agreements were signed. After the disastrous effects of the 2004 tsunami, the Indonesian government and rebels in its Aceh province reached a peace agreement and decided to work together on reconstruction rather than destruction. The last rebel weapons to be decommissioned in the Aceh province were destroyed in a public ceremony. Northern Ireland has eased into peace after a century of religious strife between its Catholic and Protestant communities. For that matter, the entirety of Europe is at peace for the first time in its history.

More and more conflicts around the world are finding political rather than violent solutions. Using broad criteria, researchers at the Heidelberg Institute for International Conflict Research in Germany counted 249 political conflicts worldwide in 2005 and found that the majority did not feature violent conflict. Twenty-four political conflicts were in a state of high violence, and 74 experienced occasional violence, but the remaining 151 were being handled nonviolently. An even simpler way of looking it examines military coups: in the '60s through '80s there were an average of 12 military coups (or attempted coups) a year. 1963 alone saw 25! But that started declining fast in the 1990s, and now there are only a few each year. In 2007 there was only one effort. Clearly, governments and their peoples have grown less tolerant of those who shoot their way into office, preferring instead to use the ballot box to choose their leaders.[7]

Though it may seem that our world is becoming increasingly violent, it is simply because our *awareness* of violence has grown, not the violence itself. In a provocative article, professor Michael Mandelbaum argued that major war is obsolete. It no longer serves its original purpose, whether it be to gain resources, conquer new land, take revenge, consolidate power, or take riches. War has become socially unacceptable for many reasons, all of which add up to give war rising costs and declining gains. Mandelbaum states, "While 100 years ago acts of war were considered legitimate, necessary, even heroic, war has now come to be widely regarded as something approaching a criminal enterprise."[8] For example, Ethiopia and Eritrea fought a war in 1998 that killed 70,000 people, yet they signed a peace agreement in 2000. Ethiopia's prime minister now says, "Theoretically there are two options: Fight it out or talk it out. Fighting is stupid."[9]

What caused this shift toward non-violent solutions? Seven contributing factors stand out:

1. The age of colonialism has ended. Most nations have already gained their independence, leaving only a few that are still fighting for it.

2. The Cold War has ended, ending U.S./Soviet proxy battles around the world.

3. The international community has developed a sophisticated system comprised of both diplomacy and UN peacekeeping to prevent war.

4. The public is gaining more influence on the world stage, and pressure internally from a country's own citizens and externally from the international community provide powerful incentives to avoid war.

5. Most countries are tempted by the promise of joining the world marketplace and have wisely decided that it's to their financial advantage to focus on development rather than war.

6. World borders are almost all codified, so fewer border disputes are taking place.

7. More people are realizing the repercussions of state failure in a smaller world—one in which everyone is a neighbor and weak states can incubate terrorism, disease, and pollution. With terrorism and trade disruption to contend with, many countries are eager to help rein in global conflicts.

These trends toward peace happened in major stages over the last 100 years. We can pinpoint three events that shaped these stages in the twentieth century: Woodrow Wilson's Fourteen Points, the founding of the UN, and the emancipation of Eastern Europe.

The first peace-inspiring event was World War I, or more specifically the ideas ignited by its horrors. In 1918 President Woodrow Wilson presented his "Fourteen Points," a blueprint for peace after the war, and changed the ideas that governed the world forever. Many of his innovations were soon to crash and burn, but it was their introduction that mattered. In fact, the proposal catapulted Wilson to international stardom near the end of World War I and gave him the moral high ground, which some say helped convince the Central Powers to surrender. As H. G. Wells wrote, "For a brief interval Wilson stood alone for mankind."[10]

It is a rare moment in history when someone can step outside his own vantage point and see the world in its entirety—both its injustices and the solutions needed to bring about change. Woodrow Wilson's fatal flaw was his attempt to transform the militaristic, divided, colonial powers into a peaceful community in one fell swoop. Wilson proposed nothing less than global free trade, world disarmament, and the right to self-determination for all of Europe's colonies. This was more ambitious than anything that had ever before been proposed.

But Wilson's most memorable point was the fourteenth: the establishment of a League of Nations. The League was established in 1919 as part of the Treaty of Versailles (one of the better parts of the treaty). Its purpose, as Wilson put it, was to establish "not a balance of power, but a community of power; not organized rivalries, but an organized common peace."[11] But the League of Nations was hindered from the start. Despite the fact that Woodrow Wilson initially inspired the idea, the U.S. Congress effectively blocked American involvement in the League of Nations. The League grew unpopular in America due to a reappearing isolationist sentiment after the war; the League's premise depended partly on America assuming a global leadership role. Due to a sense of revenge and a territory grab among the winning countries, Germany was not allowed to join, which fostered resentment among the Germans. Bickering among the League's members also thwarted progress.[12] Nevertheless, the genie was out of the bottle, and the ideas of democracy, peace, and international cooperation were spreading rapidly. But the nations of the world still needed to witness, for a second time, the increasingly destructive power of widespread war before they would be ready to try again.

In 1945, the end of World War II brought a renewed determination to save humanity from the continued scourge of war. The writing of the Declaration of Human Rights and the founding of the United Nations were watershed moments in the history of world peace. The ensuing decades saw colonialism end completely, partly because Europe was financially unable to support its colonies after being devastated in the war, and partly because the colonies demanded their independence. The bad news? The vast scale of the transition resulted in several military conflicts as the new countries struggled to their feet, especially in Africa. Furthermore, while the United States and the Soviet Union were locked in a Cold War nuclear stalemate that deterred them from ever attacking one another directly, they instead vied for influence over as many third world countries as possible. Many of the newly established countries were internally divided by factions, each seeking political power and each supporting conflicting alliances with the West, or Russia, or neither. So cold-war proxy battles became common as the two superpowers supported factions that were sympathetic to their own respective causes. Because of their bottomless pockets, the U.S. and Russia practically encouraged conflict, resulting in worst-case scenarios in Korea and Vietnam. Meanwhile, as we'll soon examine in detail, the UN was quietly working to keep the peace. It helped end many conflicts through diplomacy and peacekeeping. Its gradual improvement in efficacy is one of the major factors helping to maintain a secret peace today. The potential of the UN was slowly growing, and it would take one more pivotal event to lead to its recent successes.

The middle of the twentieth century was humanity's experiment with gazing over the brink of destruction. The world reached the edge of an abyss and realized that the only option was to pull back. Perhaps this moment of truth came with the Cuban Missile Crisis in 1962, when a tense U.S.-Russia standoff brought the world close to annihilation, but thankfully President Kennedy's and Premier Khrushchev's cooler heads prevailed.

The Cold War continued, but the Soviet Union had an unforeseen challenge: its citizens, who over the course of decades grew to realize the shortcomings of communism as an economic system and yearned for a taste of both capitalism and democracy. By 1991 the fall of the Soviet Union and the emancipation of Eastern Europe were complete. The newly liberated countries clamored for democracy and participation in the world economy. This third major event, after Woodrow Wilson's Fourteen Points and the founding of the UN, blew open the floodgates of peace. Jonathan Schell describes these three conflicts—World Wars I and II and the Cold War—as the civil war of the Western world. At stake was what form of government would rule: fascism, communism, or liberal democracy.[13] Luckily, democracy won. Since then, the trend of declining violence has been unstoppable.

In 2000, 150 world leaders gathered in New York for the Millennium Summit, by far the largest gathering of heads of state in history. The summit specialized in photo opportunities, but the group did recommit itself to strengthen peacekeeping and peacemaking and offered resounding support for the UN and its founding principles.[14] This historic gathering would have been nigh impossible during the decades of the Cold War. Today, the world that Wilson envisioned—one of self-determination, peace, and democracy—is largely a reality. It took decades, but Woodrow Wilson finally won.

ESTABLISHING THE RULES OF ENGAGEMENT

World-spanning laws of war were first negotiated extensively at two peace conferences at The Hague in the Netherlands in 1899 and 1907.[15] Treaties were established to mitigate new war technology—chemical warfare, hollow-point bullets, and bombing from the air via balloons. Since then, international humanitarian law has come a long way. Upon the signing of the UN Charter in 1945, wars of aggression became illegal. International law permits war under only a few circumstances: in self-defense, during a civil war, or when sanctioned by the United Nations Security Council to maintain international peace. International humanitarian law, as expressed primarily through the Geneva Conventions, can be summed up in a few principles:

- Persons not taking part in hostilities shall be treated well and protected.

- Captured combatants shall be treated humanely, without torture. They have the right to a normal judicial procedure.

- No unnecessary suffering shall be inflicted on the opponent.

- Civilian populations and property shall not be the target of attacks.[16]

If we want to act justly and follow the rules of the Geneva Conventions for behavior *during* war, what dictates whether or not we can go to war in the first place? The attempt to use universal values and justice to allow or to ban war in certain cases is called Just War Theory. In an ideal world, the one envisioned by Gandhi, Just War would be unnecessary because the world would agree that war can never be just. Just War Theory can also be abused by aggressive countries twisting the rules to justify any conflict. Nevertheless, for the time being, international law needs a set of criteria by which to determine when countries are behaving badly.

Just War Theory is a tradition that draws from Plato as well as from Christian theologians dating from Saint Augustine in the fourth century. Immanuel Kant devised a number of rules for judicious governances—no state can be traded or acquired by another, standing armies should gradually be abolished, and countries may not go into debt with military expenditures (a little hard for us to imagine).[17] Modern theories of Just War contain several useful guidelines to judge a war's moral validity:

- Only duly constituted public authorities may wage war. For example, in the United States, only Congress can declare war. Some countries argue that, based on the UN Charter, only the UN has the right to dictate when force can be used, and that individual countries are no longer permitted to make this decision alone.

- Force may only be used for the right intentions. Preventing genocide is a just intention, while trying to obtain more land is not.

- The probability of success must be high, so as not to embark on a futile cause.

- The amount of destruction and death must be outweighed by the good that could potentially be achieved.

- Force is a last resort, to be used only after diplomacy and other methods are exhausted.[18]

The international laws of war listed here are working remarkably well. Fewer countries are waging war against each other. However, war between countries, the problem the UN was originally created to prevent, is no longer the main instigator of world conflicts. Today, more battles are fought within countries, or by non-state actors (terrorists). Jonathan Schell, in his excellent book *The Unconquerable World*, categorizes all conflicts according to the motives and tactics used to conduct them. We will discuss four types of confrontation throughout this chapter: total war, people's war, terrorism, and nonviolence. These conflicts are listed in order of severity or, as I like to put it, the order in which you would least like to be caught in one. This order also corresponds to the historical age of the type of conflict, ranging from millennia-old total war to the newest forms of nonviolence. Due to the rise of individual power, conflicts are trending away from the most violent types and towards more peaceful solutions.

CHANGING TRADITIONS OF VIOLENCE

The most violent form of conflict is total war, also known as traditional war. This is our common vision of what war is, a situation in which giant armies line up against each other and shoot. Total war involves two or more governments fighting for their survival. World Wars I and II were the twin apexes of this horrible type of conflict, involving countless bombs, chemical weapons, air and sea battles, and millions dying in trenches. Since World War II, there have only been a few large total wars: the Iran-Iraq War and several wars in Israel, Yugoslavia, and Africa, to name some examples. At their worst, total wars are no-holds-barred and take-no-prisoners. The goal is to subdue the enemy using any means necessary, limited only by the technology available at the time. In previous centuries, almost all wars were fought as total wars, even though most would have been unrecognizably low-tech. In fact, while 100 million people died from war-related causes in the twentieth century (including disease and famine), anthropologist Lawrence Keeley notes that the total would have been 2 *billion* if our rates of violence were as high as the average primitive society.[19] Today total war is nearly extinct.

People's war, the second type of conflict, consists of a grassroots group fighting a government or another independent group, and is less extreme than total war. The power relationship is often lopsided, which means that the smaller side has to use innovative tactics such as guerilla warfare to succeed. While there are several instances of people's war taking place throughout history, the first notable example was the American Revolution, which ushered in people's war as an effective method of conflict. Though the colonists didn't know it, they were inventing a new style of fighting that would eventually replace total war. Two centuries later, the tables had turned, and America found itself enmeshed in the Vietnam War, in a similar position as the British 200 years earlier. This time the Vietnamese were playing the part of the guerrilla warriors. Although the motives and political situations underlying these two conflicts were very different, the approach to fighting in each is comparable.

While total war involves countries fighting for land, resources, or global influence, the proponents of people's war are usually fighting for political independence, power in government, or human rights. This may make the motives of people's war appear nobler than those of total war, though this is not necessarily the case. Current examples of people's war range from the extreme violence of the wars in Iraq and Afghanistan to the minor disturbance created by the Spanish freedom fighters in Basque Country and Catalonia. In Iraq, different warring sides (Sunnis vs. Shiites) can be seen as fighting a civil war that verges on total war, while the insurgents fighting the United States are using people's war tactics. Other examples of people's war include the Palestinian-Israeli conflict and the conflicts in Somalia, Colombia, and Aceh.

"WAR" ON TERROR

The third category of conflict is terrorism. Terrorism involves fewer people than total war or people's war. Small groups or even individuals acting alone can be terrorists. Rather than killing great numbers of people or destroying an army, terrorists defeat enemies by striking fear in their hearts. While people are often killed in the process, that is not usually the primary goal but rather a means of getting a certain reaction. The number of victims resulting from terrorism is tiny compared to the casualties of people's war or total war—although unlike the other two categories, terrorists often intentionally target civilians. Terrorism is most effective when its proponents harness technological weapons (though the Ku Klux Klan managed to spread plenty of terror using simple fire), and our biggest fear today is a terrorist gaining access to nuclear or biological weapons.

Participants in a people's war often realize that they can't win using a traditional army, and so they adopt guerilla warfare techniques. Similarly, terrorists are unable to make use of a traditional army *or* guerilla warfare techniques because they simply have too few members to fight the enemy directly. Instead, they use another effective method of warfare: creating isolated and often fatal incidents designed to seem more imposing than they really are, thereby creating "propaganda by their deeds." So, *by definition*, terrorism is not as much of a threat as we make it out to be. Terrorism seems worse than it is because our brains overestimate the risks we can picture dramatically—such as catching anthrax through the mail or a terrorist detonating a nuclear weapon—and ignore those we can't, such as heart disease and lung cancer. For all the fear that terrorism (intentionally) inspires, "for the vast majority of Americans, the chances of dying in a terrorist attack are close to zero. There's a higher probability that you'll die by falling off a ladder."[20]

While terrorism may not be as bad as we fear it to be, incidents of terrorism have come to the forefront in the past decade and are, of course, still happening worldwide. However, these incidents of terrorism have low casualty rates that replace the higher casualty rates of total wars and people's wars. While it may seem difficult, and even callous, to think constructively about the emergence of terrorism, it does show that people have learned to use less violent methods to accomplish their goals. Since the relative success of an act of terrorism depends on instilling fear in a community rather than on the actual number of people killed, it is less violent than other methods of warfare. The rise of terrorism shows that many large groups of people (governments, revolutionary groups, mainstream religions) no longer find violence tempting, and it is only a minority of individuals who are clinging to this terrible method. I see terrorism as a clumsy intermediate step for humanity before absolute nonviolence becomes widespread.

But even this clumsy step of violence is in retreat. Many agencies and organizations tracking terrorism report a significant rise in the past few years, and the media has reported this accordingly. But *Newsweek*'s Fareed Zakaria figured out the problem with those reports: they all count civilian deaths in Iraq as casualties of terrorism. This doesn't make sense: Iraq has clearly been at war, a people's war in which different groups are fighting the United States as well as each other. As disastrous as that conflict is, it doesn't mean civilian deaths are an act of terrorism. Excluding Iraq and Afghanistan, casualties from terrorism have dropped 40 percent since 2001 worldwide.[21]

Yes, the West seems to be winning the overall battle against terrorism. Al Qaeda is in a sorry state. "Most of [Al Qaeda's] leaders are now dead, captured, or in hiding; unable to travel, send money, or communicate with one another. All that's left is small, 'self-starter' terror cells with few resources and little expertise," *The Week* reports.[22] Al Qaeda is on its last legs in Iraq and Afghanistan, having been backed into a corner in the border regions of Pakistan, its one remaining stronghold. And we're getting more effective at fighting them there; rather than just throwing money at Pakistan (and watching them arm themselves against India instead), we're training local Pakistani troops directly. Overall, Al Qaeda has been unsuccessful at attacking Western targets since the bombings in London in 2005. To top it all off, FBI Director Robert Mueller recently told the U.S. Congress that there is almost no evidence of terror sleeper cells in the United States.[23]

Most importantly, support for suicide bombing and violence against civilians is declining across the Muslim world. For example, five years ago 74 percent of Lebanese citizens and 33 percent of Pakistanis approved of suicide attacks in certain situations. Today, those numbers dropped to 34 percent and nine percent respectively, depriving terrorists of the popular support they need. By January 2008, support for Osama bin Laden had plummeted to four percent in Pakistan's Northwest Frontier province, where Al Qaeda has bases. This sea change in opinion in the Muslim world is due to the large numbers of Muslim civilians killed by Al Qaeda itself in Iraq.[24] Al Qaeda suicide-bombed itself in the foot, invalidating bin Laden's professed "story arc" of America as the worst villain, occupier of Muslim soil. Harvard professor Noah Feldman puts it well:

Perhaps the greatest lesson is that despite the gift we gave bin Laden by becoming occupiers, he ultimately failed to convince the Muslim world to join him on one side of a global jihad. The reason the clash of civilizations never materialized was that at least one side didn't seem that interested in a fight—and it wasn't ours.[25]

This withdrawal of support is essential because the Middle East and other Islamic countries are the main source (and target) of terrorist attacks today. This was not always the case: in the 1970s Europe was the center of most terrorist incidents; in the 1980s Latin America had by far the most; and in the 1990s Africa and Asia were attacked more.[26] It's important to remember that global trends in terrorism remain in a state of flux; we need to harness that potential flexibility to keep pushing events in a more peaceful direction.

Since terrorism is a tactic, not an independent entity, the notion of a "war" against it is as nonsensical as the World War II allies declaring war on *Blitzkrieg* rather than on Germany.[27] The techniques and tactics of total war are not effective against terrorism, as the long struggle in Iraq has shown us. But the other approaches we are using are working. I've grouped the relatively nonviolent ways to combat terrorism into three categories. They should be used on principle because they are less violent (and thus have a smaller chance of hurting civilians), and in addition they have often been shown to be more effective.

The first method is to use cooperative law enforcement rather than overwhelming military force. Using military force to counter terrorism is like pouring gas on a raging fire. But many regular methods of catching international criminals can apply to terrorists. In fact, terrorist organizations are often tied into other criminal activities, so it might be useful to treat terrorism as only one facet of a wider attack on transnational criminal networks. A key aspect of law enforcement is its adherence to legal and moral constraints, giving it more validity in the eyes of a nation's allies and its own citizens. Cooperative law enforcement not only includes tracking down and capturing terrorists, but also working to withdraw funding of terrorist networks by freezing financial resources, denying them travel and safe haven, and taking measures to help prevent the arming of militants. Tremendous success has been achieved using some of these methods. An appropriate success story is New York City, where the NYPD counter-terrorism division is receiving acclaim for its innovative work. They have stationed people overseas to gather information, and an important achievement was turning the city's cultural diversity to their advantage, by building a team of more than 600 linguists fluent in 50 languages and dialects.[28]

Saudi Arabia is another example, surprisingly. Though late to the anti-terrorism biz (they only really got involved after their own cities were attacked), they have had success using creative public awareness campaigns. For example, television spots air testimonies from repentant jihadists and from scholars challenging the textual basis of jihadist beliefs, and moderate religious scholars are being hired to combat extremist ideas in online chat sites. In addition, captured terrorists receive religious counseling.[29] Globally, international cooperation has increased and is supported by a UN resolution passed after the 9/11 attacks. Much terrorist funding has been discovered, and much of it has been seized. Counterterrorism officials are attacking terrorist networks online, by planting bogus e-mail messages and Web site postings, to sow confusion and distrust among their supporters. American diplomats are also working behind the scenes to help promote the writings and speeches of Islamic clerics who renounce terrorist violence.[30] Treating the terrorists as criminals instead of warriors also helps to invalidate their cause. With cooperative law enforcement there is less of a chance of killing the terrorists; trying them in a court of law is not only the right thing to do, it is more humiliating to their cause than if they become "glorious martyrs."

The second way to combat terrorism without violence is through increased security. This one is not controversial; the world has been working hard to secure its borders for the last few years, the United States as much as anyone. Since 2001, tighter U.S. entry requirements, increased airport security, and other measures have no doubt made Americans feel safer. We've made significant progress on port security, and the Coast Guard's budget has grown much larger.[31] However, there is still a lot of work to be done in this area, as the 9/11 Commission's Report showed. Other nations are enhancing their border security dramatically. Britain and Israel, two countries that have lived with terrorism for decades, are known for effective security. Britain recently implemented a new biometric fingerprint program, by requiring fingerprints with all UK visas. Israel has been building its controversial West Bank security fence for years, a move potentially being echoed by Saudi Arabia as it plans to build a 550-mile long fence along its border with Iraq. These measures are part of the reason why terrorism is less common in the world's most developed, high-tech countries than elsewhere.[32]

The third nonviolent way to combat terrorism is far more ambitious and will take many years to achieve, but it is essential: addressing the root causes of terrorism. On the surface, there are two kinds of motivations for terrorism: political and extremist. Examples of political goals include creating a Palestinian state, releasing prisoners, or expelling U.S. troops from the Muslim holy lands in Saudi Arabia. Extremist goals include converting the entire world to Islam, killing infidels, or enforcing the strictest form of sharia law (Islamic law as dictated by the Qur'an). Political goals are possible to sate directly; when Palestine becomes a peaceful state, some terrorists will give up arms and be satisfied. Extremist goals, on the other hand, will never be achieved. These terrorists claim to be fighting for Palestine (for example), but would in reality keep on fighting even if every Palestinian were swimming in milk and honey. They exploit political excuses to justify their violence and gain support. Resolving the political and social issues of concern to terrorists will most likely put an end to political terrorism and at least take excuses away from extremist terrorists so they lose support, too.

There are many political and social injustices that will have to be addressed if we hope to ensure an end to terrorism. Getting devastated countries like Afghanistan, Iraq and Somalia back on their feet is essential for many reasons, not least to eliminate safe harbors for terrorists. Luckily, good news has been coming out of Iraq. The *Economist* writes, "By all the main measures—military, political and economic—Iraq is now improving, [though] from a dire base." In July 2009, U.S. troops successfully met a deadline to pull back from Iraqi cities. Optimism is popping up in the country, thanks to more ceasefires, fewer casualties, more political cooperation, and a bit of restored infrastructure, including a surge in cell phone usage. After many disastrous blunders surrounding the invasion, progress is finally being made out of a bad situation. In 2008, the Army drafted a new operations manual that elevates the mission of stabilizing war-torn nations, recognizing that this is of equal importance to winning battlefield conflicts. The manual states that "Winning battles and engagements is important but alone is not sufficient. Shaping the civil situation is just as important to success."[33]

As countries become lawful, terrorists are forced to flee to another for sanctuary until eventually they will be left with nowhere to go. Alleviating poverty and unemployment in Middle Eastern countries wouldn't affect many terrorists right away (most members of Al Qaeda, including the 9/11 hijackers, are not poor) but would be a worthy social goal in itself.[34] More important would be encouraging equality, religious tolerance, and critical thinking. After all, sub-Saharan Africa is much poorer than the Middle East, but its poverty does not inspire terrorism. The 9/11 Commission recommends increasing secular education in Muslim countries, as well as providing library, scholarship, and exchange programs. All of these efforts should aim to drive a wedge between terrorists and their potential sympathizers.[35] The vast majority of Islamic fundamentalists are not violent; but, like anyone, they can be tempted to become violent if they feel that their culture is under attack. Perhaps if they feel that they are living in a more just world, they will be less motivated to resort to terrorism. Without the excuse of oppression to fall back on, the remaining extremist terrorists will become ostracized in the Muslim world, losing their funding, their public support, their sympathetic havens, their claimed moral high ground—and their ability to recruit.

Studying history can help to reduce our fear of the future of terrorism. In the past, terrorism has occurred in waves, and each wave eventually dissipated. A major spasm of terrorist violence came to a head in the 1890s with the attacks of anarchists. They used dynamite as their early "weapon of mass destruction." In some ways, they were more effective than today's Islamic fundamentalist terrorists: they exploded more bombs (though their bombs were less destructive than today's), they had a wide geographic spread, and they successfully assassinated several heads of state, including U.S. President William McKinley. Ironically, the anarchists' goal—a free world without government—was the antithesis of what today's Muslim extremists want—a strict Muslim world in which all are compelled to follow sharia law. Yet the violent methods of both groups are similar and their beliefs equally passionate and intractable.[36] The anarchist movement eventually ended of its own accord, with the anarchists discrediting their own cause.[37] Likewise, it has been shown that "religious-nationalist fervor does not constantly burn with the same intensity," and the young (terrorists today are most often young adults) tend to mellow with age.[38]

The threat of terrorism will probably always exist; the realistic goal then becomes not to try to eradicate it, but to limit it as much as possible until it dissipates on its own. Framing the war on terrorism as an epic battle only fuels the terrorists' delusions of grandeur and their fantasies of martyrdom. Terrorists want to bait us into playing the aggressor—a role that fits the skewed story they present to the world. Atrocities committed by the West in the name of fighting terrorism, such as abuses at Abu Ghraib prison, only serve to push more moderates into the arms and recruitment tents of violent extremists.[39] As author Matt Armstrong observes, "Iraq has become a stage on which terrorists, insurgents, and Coalition forces compete for a global audience ... Today, bullets and bombs often have a much smaller impact than the propaganda opportunities they create."[40] By staying true to the principles of social justice and treating terrorism as the valid-but-not-all-consuming threat that it is, we can defeat it using relatively nonviolent means. By and large, the less violent tools we are using to fight terrorism are working, while the most violent ones are not. We can back this up with numbers: Rand Corporation analyst Seth Jones has found that 43 percent of terrorist groups end up denouncing violence and joining the political process, while another 40 percent are defeated by police and intelligence operations. Only seven percent end as a result of military force.[41]

Glenn L. Carle, a longtime CIA officer involved in fighting terrorism, calls the global threat of terrorism a myth and describes today's remaining jihadists as "small, lethal, disjointed, and miserable opponents ... small men and secondary threats whose shadows are made large by our fears."[42] Our resources devoted to terrorism should be reasonable: for example, with 1,800 FBI agents reassigned to anti-terrorism duties in the wake of 9/11, prosecutions of fraud against financial institutions dropped 48 percent. Perhaps if half those agents had kept their assignments, some looming signs of the financial crisis might have been noticed earlier.[43]

Today's remaining acts of terror are the isolated and diminishing death throes of the world's violent past. The future belongs to the fourth and final category of conflict style: nonviolence. Nonviolence can be used between two countries (like total war), between groups within countries (like people's war), or by small groups or individuals (like terrorism). It is quickly replacing the other three types of conflict.

TRUTH-FORCE: NONVIOLENCE BECOMES THE NORM

On September 11th, in the beginning days of a new century, an unprecedented event took place that changed the course of history for the nations of the world. In Johannesburg, South Africa, in the old Empire Theatre, a full house of Indian South Africans stood up and vowed to disobey their country's unjust racist laws. They took a solemn oath to do so without shedding a drop of their enemy's blood, though they were prepared to sacrifice their own, "to die but not to submit to the law." They agreed to voluntarily sacrifice and bring suffering upon themselves rather than let the state rob them of their basic human dignity. With that act, a diminutive 36-year-old Indian lawyer standing onstage created *satyagraha*, active nonviolence. His name was Mohandas Gandhi, and the date was September 11th, 1906.[44]

Gandhi crafted the word *satyagraha*, which refers to using peaceful resistance methods for political or social reform, to replace "nonviolence" and "passive resistance," terms that most practitioners don't like. Why? Because *nonviolence* is a negative word, defining itself as the opposite of violence, e.g., *not-violence*. In reality, nonviolence is the active, positive force, while violence should be described as its negative corollary. Nonviolence also carries the stigma of passivity, but according to Gandhi, it is the most active force in the world. Simply not being violent is not practicing true nonviolence—I am not emulating Gandhi just because I refrained from attacking any passersby today. Practicing nonviolence is difficult, certainly harder than practicing violence. As Martin Luther King, Jr. said, "Gandhi resisted evil with as much vigor and power as the violent resister, but he resisted with love instead of hate."[45] That is why Gandhi described satyagraha as *active* nonviolence. Satyagraha can be translated as "truth-force," although Gandhi also described it as "holding to truth," "pursuing truth," and "direct action for truth."[46] He defined the three core principles of satyagraha as truth and fairness, refusal to harm others, and the willingness for self-sacrifice. Throughout this chapter, I'll be using the terms "satyagraha" and "nonviolence" interchangeably.

Martin Luther King, Jr. described nonviolence as "the answer to the crucial political and moral question of our time—the need for man to overcome oppression and violence without resorting to violence and oppression."[47] When used correctly, nonviolence works as a powerful moral force that can help to transform societies. Gandhi identified the ways people can resolve conflict: rational debate, violence, and moral appeal. History shows that humanity often attempts to use rational conversation to sort out arguments and conflicts. But whenever that fails, we quickly resort to violence. Gandhi agreed that rational debate should be our first attempt to settle a conflict. But, unfortunately, reason does not always work. Often people's feelings and fears are so deeply ingrained that they cannot listen to reason. Gandhi felt that combining reason with a spiritual, moral appeal would work every time.

This moral appeal is the special power of satyagraha—it aims to change the oppressors' hearts so that they willingly change their policies. Changing policies through force or coercion only breeds long-term resentment. An act of nonviolence serves as an awakening to truth—a moment of moral epiphany in the hearts of those it targets. And when you boil it down, this moment of realization is always some aspect of "We are all equal." When nonviolence succeeds, it helps both the oppressed *and* the oppressor, which is why King stated that his goal was to save both blacks and whites from the effects of racism.

Gandhi found that violence sometimes works in the short term, but never in the long term. Sometimes violence quickly solves a problem, only to breed hatred that rears its head with more, and often greater, violence. On the other hand, nonviolence always wins out in the long term, and often brings short-term gains as well. And even in cases when nonviolence does not solve an immediate problem, it causes no harm and sows seeds of peace that are guaranteed to sprout later. As social critic Theodore Roszak wisely put it, "People try nonviolence for a week, and when it doesn't 'work' they go back to violence, which hasn't worked for centuries."[48] Gandhi learned that the anticipated end of any problem, and the means for achieving it, couldn't contradict each other. To build a permanently peaceful society, only peaceful methods are effective. (Gandhi said of Stalin in 1938, "He dreams of peace, and dreams he will wade to it through a sea of blood.")[49] The use of violence, no matter how lofty the motivation or end goal may be, cannot help but beget further violence. Only by nonviolent means can ultimate peace be reached.

Practitioners of nonviolence can be grouped into two categories: those who follow satyagraha because of its strategic efficacy, and those who cite a more spiritual and ethical inspiration. Gandhi was in a unique position to harness both paths. His inclusive religious views, which we examined last chapter, helped motivate him to harness nonviolence and enabled him to exploit its practical advantages. He saw it not only as the sole method that could ethically be used against the British, but also as the only path that would work.

To criticisms such as the inevitable, "Well, nonviolence didn't work against the Nazis," Gandhi may have responded that nonviolence wasn't *tried* against the Nazis—not true active nonviolence, and not of a force equal to the Nazis' might. To counter such a powerful movement, organized satyagraha efforts of thousands of civilians would have been needed and should have been started long before the 1939 outbreak of war. On modest scales, when nonviolence was tried against Nazi occupation, it often worked, as demonstrated, for example, in the mass noncooperation that took place in Denmark under German occupation.[50]

Gandhi can be considered a scientist who discovered the new field of satyagraha. As he fully admitted, he only scratched the surface of the techniques and power available. Methods of nonviolent action are incredibly diverse. Professor Gene Sharp, who is senior scholar of the Albert Einstein Institution for the study and use of strategic nonviolent action in conflicts throughout the world, categorized and described no fewer than 198 of them.[51] Sharp's first category, acts of protest and persuasion, are primarily symbolic and useful for conveying a message. These include speeches, marches and protests, mass petitions, banners, pamphlets, and media messages through newspapers, radio, television, and the Internet. Art and writing are important acts of satyagraha. Art is a medium that refuses to be caged, and artists and musicians are often the first to speak out against looming injustice. Journalists and photographers can have an even stronger influence on struggles of all types, since their medium can access millions of people quickly. If we look at the use of violence as a form of ignorance (its practitioners lack knowledge of a better method), then educating the public about satyagraha is an important step toward eradicating violence.

Sharp's second category of nonviolent action is social noncooperation, which includes student strikes, boycotting social clubs or sports, and social disobedience. Economic noncooperation describes boycotts and strikes: consumers' boycotts, workers' boycotts, general strikes, slowdown strikes, sympathy strikes, and so forth. Martin Luther King, Jr. often targeted businessmen rather than politicians; the Montgomery bus boycott was the most famous example. During the boycott, blacks refused to ride the city's buses for 381 days—which cost the bus company three thousand dollars a day and cost white-owned downtown businesses a pretty penny too.[52] Gandhi organized boycotts of schools, courts, government buildings, and imported goods such as cotton. Sharp's category of political noncooperation includes boycotting unfair elections and civil disobedience of unjust laws.

Other satyagraha actions can be very effective at the national level. In 2003, antiwarprotestorstriedsomethingnew:a"virtualmarch."Hundredsofthousands of people simultaneously sent antiwar e-mails, faxes, and phone calls, flooding the Senate and the White House with messages.[53] Local communities at the town, city, county, and state levels drafted antiwar resolutions, mostly fueled by economic concerns about the potential cost of war. A more drastic antiwar approach is the refusal of soldiers to serve in war. Soldiers can choose noncombatant or conscientious objector status, which is becoming increasingly acceptable. If they do accept a combat assignment, soldiers should have the right to know what it is they're fighting for, and whether it constitutes a just war.

At the national level, governments can practice economic noncooperation by imposing sanctions and trade embargos, and they can practice political non-cooperation by severing diplomatic relations with governments that maintain inhumane policies. Sharp also describes a category of nonviolent intervention in which practitioners of nonviolence interpose themselves directly to disrupt a community's normal affairs. Gandhi's fasts and hunger strikes are examples of this, as are sit-ins, teach-ins, ride-ins, and pray-ins.[54]

Martin Luther King, Jr. was inspired by Gandhi and built on his work to innovate new methods used in local campaigns. "The whole concept of satya-graha ... was profoundly significant to me. ... It was in this Gandhian emphasis on love and nonviolence that I discovered the method for social reform that I had been seeking for so many months."[55]

Satyagraha has a distinct process that releases the strength of its full impact:

1. The goal has to be precisely defined. A broad struggle for civil rights is hard to achieve all at once. But a struggle for equal rights on buses is an effective stepping stone.[56]

2. Each issue should be carefully researched, and attempts should be made to resolve the problem through dialogue. Action should be the last step, not the first.

3. A supportive group of advocates is essential; strength in numbers is a key concept for these efforts.

4. A nonviolent action tailored specifically for the group should be designed, one that everyone can participate in.

5. Using local connections in the community where the group already has credibility is most effective.

6. Throughout the campaign, it is important to remain nonviolent, even if provoked.

7. The nonviolent action must be proportionate to the violence or oppression it is fighting.

8. It is important not to harbor any animosity for the group's opponents, but to think of them as uninformed people whose minds need to be changed. This can be the most difficult step of all.

9. Use words, not just action. All participants should have the same message and should spread it to the media.

Gandhi was a master at getting media coverage. One of satyagraha's weaknesses is that it only works well under the light of public scrutiny. Luckily, public scrutiny is ubiquitous today. Getting media coverage is essential in swaying the opinions of third parties—gaining the support and sympathy of citizens, neighbors, and voters. It is often the pressure of these third parties, and not the pressure of the original proponents, that enacts change.[57]

Until Gandhi's efforts, nonviolence as a means for positive social change had been tried in only a few small, isolated incidents, and was rarely well organized. As King described, Gandhi lifted those efforts up to the national level and made nonviolence a powerful social force. Gandhi wrote that, "Nonviolence is not a programme of seizure of power. It is a programme of transformation of relationships, ending in a peaceful transfer of power."[58] And it works. Today, many countries are having peaceful revolutions rather than bloody ones. The greatest empire of the nineteenth century, the British Empire, was toppled in part by nonviolence. The world-spanning empire of the twentieth century, the Soviet Union, was obliterated nonviolently, too. During the 40 years of the cold war, who would have imagined that the Soviet Union could be brought to its knees without millions of deaths? Nonviolence as a political force has skyrocketed in use since the collapse of the Berlin Wall in 1989. As the *Economist* put it, "If outsiders make such a mess of getting rid of despots, why not encourage the locals to have a go?"[59] One thorough recent study showed that nonviolent action was decisive in 50 out of 67 transitions to freer regimes.[60]

There's a distinct pattern in nonviolent revolutions: they are either completely or mostly bloodless, and they usually involve demonstrations, strikes, and protests from thousands of citizens. Many of the leaders of these revolutions have studied the techniques of nonviolence, especially those employed by Gandhi, and many are excellent organizers. At the beginning of their efforts, violent reprisals from the state are common, but they often backfire, serving only to enrage the public. As Lech Walesa explained about striking against communist Poland, "At the moment when they hit us, I said this, 'Right at this moment, you have lost. We are winning. You have driven the last nails into your communist coffin.'" After a regime is deposed or abdicates control, there is often a transfer of power to the opposition leader, followed by democratic elections, which the already-popular opposition leaders usually win. When the masses are responsible for a government's transfer of power, the new rulers gain much more legitimacy in the eyes of their people.

Good examples abound, most with catchy, colorful tag names. The Prague Spring was a brief but inspirational 1968 uprising in Czechoslovakia against Soviet control; it was followed in 1989 by a nonviolent Velvet Revolution. The Polish Solidarity Movement started small with labor union strikes led by Lech Walesa, and took years of modest gains to eventually lead to a democratic Poland. Walesa described his nonviolent strategy against the Communists, "If they just open a small crack in these doors of freedom, I put my working-class boot in those doors, and they won't close them."

The Singing Revolution was a series of mass protests in Estonia, Latvia, and Lithuania. The two thousand demonstrations in Yugoslavia, supported by the youth movement *Otpor* (Resistance), led to the well-deserved downfall of Slobodan Milosevic. Otpor went on to inspire and train other youth movements in Eastern Europe. A largely nonviolent revolution in South Africa led to the release of Nelson Mandela from prison and the end of the racist apartheid system.

The 1974 Carnation Revolution in Portugal deposed one of the longest-running fascist regimes. Though it was a military coup and it took another two years before elections were held, there was no violence and large crowds turned out to wave carnations and stick them in soldiers' guns. The next year, neighboring Spain saw a fascist regime voluntarily yield to the peoples' demands and give power over to a democratic government without violence. The 2003 Rose Revolution in Georgia is perhaps the most famous of these nonviolent "color" revolutions. Without any weapons, and holding roses in their hands, opposition leader Mickheil Saakashvili and his supporters marched into the parliament building and forced the resignation of Georgia's corrupt regime. It was followed, with varied success, by an Orange Revolution in Ukraine, a Tulip Revolution in Kyrgyzstan, and a Cedar Revolution in Lebanon that forced Syrian troops out of power after 29 years of occupation.

The human-rights abusing regimes of Augusto Pinochet in Chile and Ferdinand Marcos in the Philippines were replaced nonviolently. Today, both the Irish Republican Army (IRA) in Northern Ireland and the Basques Homeland and Freedom (ETA) in Spain have finally renounced violence, drawing those conflicts to a close and passing opposition solely into the political realm. In all 17 of the examples cited here, we see nonviolence replacing existing or potentially violent conflicts—situations in which total war, people's war, or terrorism would have been used in the past. The evidence has other authoritarian countries running scared: China's chief press regulator recently admitted, "When I think of the color revolutions, I feel afraid."[61]

Satyagraha is being used to transcend conflict at the national level, but what about on a smaller scale? Since satyagraha is about transforming relationships, it also works well for groups operating at the local level. Many national movements started as small local organizations. Peace groups, religious groups, civic groups, and other community organizations help to spread the practice of nonviolence. The subtle but widespread concept that violence is not the best way to resolve personal conflicts is becoming ubiquitous.

For example, crime in many developed countries has been steadily decreasing. Crime rates started dropping in the 1990s and still show no signs of slowing, even during the recession: crime rates in most of America's cities fell in 2008 as well as the first half of 2009. Violent crime in U.S. schools fell by half from 1992 to 2002, dropping from 48 to 24 incidents per 100,000 students.[62] The juvenile crime rate overall dropped two-thirds from a peak in 1993.[63] This was during a video game boom, which suggests that the commonly believed link between violent media and real-life violence is imaginary. New York City had fewer than 500 homicides in 2007, the lowest level since the police began keeping track in 1963. Despite salacious news reports of muggings and random attacks, fewer than 20 percent of those homicides involved perpetrators who were strangers to their victims. In fact, New York City's violent crime rate has dropped almost *80 percent* since 1990. These results are likely due to an increase in the police force as well as new tactics that are consistently improved and refined—another example of the passing of knowledge contributing to progress. Some of those tactics are aimed at domestic violence: police visits to homes with histories of domestic abuse, as well a huge public awareness campaign about domestic violence.[64] These tactics are working, and nationwide, incidents of rape and domestic violence dropped precipitously from their highs in the 1980s. In fact, incidents of rape have dropped 72 percent and domestic violence 65 percent just since 1993.[65] As a corollary, in 2007 the U.S. divorce rate dropped to its lowest level since 1970, reflecting two trends: people marrying later and thus more carefully, and couples working harder to repair troubled marriages.[66]

The Southern Poverty Law Center reports that the number of paramilitary militia groups in the United States has declined significantly since the height of their prominence right after the Oklahoma City bombing in 1995. In 1996, there were 850 known antigovernment militias, and now there are roughly 150, thanks to the efforts of the police and the FBI.[67] Today only a third of American households even have guns, down from 57 percent in 1977.[68] In total, the number of violent crimes in the United States fell from some 1.8 million in 1995 to 1.37 million in 2004, a 25 percent decline.[69]

Nonviolent principles are increasingly gaining credence in all situations, at all levels. Nonpartisan mediation organizations such as the Centre for Humanitarian Dialogue, which helped Kofi Annan broker a peace deal that averted a civil war in Kenya, are increasingly useful. In fact, one study has shown that over the past 15 years, military victories have resolved only 7.5 percent of conflicts worldwide, while negotiations prevailed in 92 percent of cases. Negotiators are especially important in intrastate disputes, such as between warring political parties, or insurgents battling over resources with international companies.[70]

Negotiation is being harnessed at the local level, too. For the last ten years, my father has volunteered his spare time as a dispute resolution mediator for the Mercer County Court System in New Jersey. In the mediation process, judges hear disputes that typically involve matters such as noise complaints, harassment, trespassing, neighbor altercations, minor assault, property damage, and the like. After hearing a dispute, a judge may decide to assign it to a mediator. My father and other mediators are trained by the courts in the principles of legal mediation. The fundamentals of the process parallel those of nonviolent action: the parties reach an agreement based on their own terms. The mediator does not impose solutions, and when an agreement is reached the case is usually dismissed from the docket of the court. The parties feel better about the outcome because they arrived at a resolution themselves rather than having a court-imposed resolution. The process of mediation eases the burden on our justice system and lets citizens participate more fully—above and beyond basic jury duty. Lawsuits, too, are being resolved in a similar pattern and are increasingly being settled out of court to reduce the amount of time and money spent to reach resolution.

The trends of nonviolence and conflict resolution are also making a big impact on the younger generation, ensuring the trends' increasing popularity. One nonviolent trend is particularly relevant to the youngest of us: the decline in corporal punishment. Out of the world's 194 countries, 106 have banned physical punishment in schools, and 23 have banned it altogether—meaning it is illegal to strike your own children. Sweden was the first country to do so, in 1979. While the law was initially controversial, a public education campaign made smacking, and belief in its value, quickly decline. And that's a good thing, since lots of studies find a correlation between corporal punishment and aggressive, delinquent behavior later. In fact, a growing amount of scholarly evidence is showing that physical punishment is at best useless and at worst, harmful.[71]

Children are learning the principles of nonviolence in another creative way, too. Remember when we spoke before about how video games are actually good for you? Well, here's further evidence: video games that encourage the use of nonviolent tactics. I'm not referring to *Tetris* or *Solitaire* (and the exploding bombs of *Minesweeper* rule that one out completely), but games that teach players nonviolent tactics. The UN produced a wildly successful aid-relief game called *Food Force*; MTV made one called *Darfur Is Dying*; and a game called

PeaceMaker lets you try to make peace in the Middle East, allowing you to play as either Israel or Palestine. A game called *Pax Warrior*, in which you play the role of a UN commander during the Rwandan genocide, has been incorporated into the curriculum of thousands of schools.[72] In fact, many schools include peacemaking curriculums to discourage violence and bullying. Informing kids about the benefits of nonviolence is a trend that promises to continue as students grow older. Maybe today's children can help to remind adults of the opportunities for nonviolent solutions that are available. After all, those of us who live in democratic countries have the power to make our voices heard. We need to take advantage of this right, which millions of people have earned and millions more continue to fight for.

On February 15, 2003, a friend and I participated in the largest protest march in world history. Several hundred thousand marchers in New York City, along with millions of marchers in over 400 cities in 60 countries around the world, shouted their resistance to a U.S.-led invasion of Iraq.[73] While the protests were impressive, as we all know, they didn't work. Why did they fail? They were nonviolent, but unfortunately they fell short of achieving true satyagraha. For one, the protests were not truly united—though organized efficiently on the same day, there was not a coherent message of *why* the country should not go to war. My friend and I were surrounded by lots of nice folks, but I have yet to figure out how signs promoting legalization of marijuana or abortion rights relate to the Iraq War. Secondly, the protests did not affect the U.S. government in a practical, tangible way. There was no boycott, no economic slowdown. Thirdly, and most importantly, the protestors held no love for their "enemy." Most of the signs and speeches bashed the Bush administration harshly and offensively, leading to further polarization. Why would you want to listen to the opinions of someone who paints devil horns on a poster of you? Instead of listening, the government dug in their heels against the protestors, whom they may have rightly seen as their enemies.

But the protests were part of a larger landmark event. Rarely had the world participated in such a long and heated conversation about the benefits and detriments of war—indeed, a debate about the nature of war itself. And certainly never before had a vast majority taken the antiwar stance. I don't think it is going out on a limb to expect that, from now on, most wars undertaken in the world will be scrutinized as thoroughly as the war in Iraq. With that much public pressure, many governments, especially democratic ones, will buckle to public scrutiny and forgo their militant plans. As Eisenhower said, "I like to believe that people in the long run are going to do more to promote peace than our governments. Indeed, I think that people want peace so much that one of these days governments had better get out of the way and let them have it."[74]

Satyagraha has worked many times in the past, and social conditions are increasing the likelihood of its effectiveness today. Nonviolence is a strategy that everyone can use, whether rich or poor, woman or man, child or adult. It will always be more successful than violence, which can only be used by the physically aggressive and by military arms of states. Nonviolence can be seen as the ultimate humility, while violence is the ultimate hubris. Gandhi reasoned that the world was based on love, not violence, and he used simple logic: if human nature is violence-centered, we would have eradicated ourselves by now. At any given time—and increasingly so as world peace grows—the vast majority of families, communities, and nations are peaceful. Gandhi saw the past not as a narrative of the overwhelming violence of humanity, but as a record of interruptions in an otherwise peaceful history.[75]

The four types of conflicts we've just discussed are visualized in Figure 9, showing how they have changed over time. It is too difficult to assign numerical "weight" to a nonviolent revolution versus a violent one, or a large conflict versus a smaller one, so the chart is only a broad symbolic representation of the history of war. Total war has existed throughout history, but today it is almost obsolete—it reached its peak with the two world wars. The next type of conflict, the less-violent people's war, started on its global scale with the American Revolution and peaked a few decades ago when developing nations fought for independence. Terrorism, less violent still, is temporarily on the rise because of the decline of total war and people's war, but may have already hit its peak—time will tell. Nonviolence as a peaceful and effective method for implementing change on the national level was started by Gandhi in 1906. Today it is becoming more widely used than terrorism and is replacing both total war and people's war.

FIGURE 9: THE FOUR TYPES OF CONFLICT

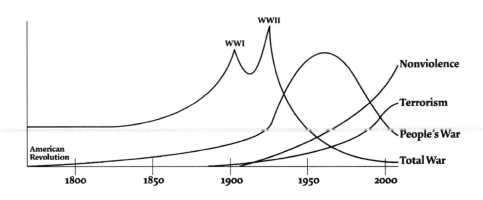

What about the Cold War? Which of the four types of conflict does it fall under? Cold wars can be seen as a form of total war because they involve large military buildups and conflicts between two opposing countries. Besides "The" Cold War, India and Pakistan have been in a tense cold war for 60 years, as have North and South Korea. Today, Iran can even be said to be in a minor cold war with the West, since it supports proxy wars through Hezbollah. While cold war precludes the use of direct violence due to the destruction that it would cause, this is not true nonviolence. The amount of fear and instability generated by nuclear weapons—as well as biological, chemical, and traditional weapons—keeps enemy countries effectively in a permanent state of war. Creating a world free of violence requires eliminating this ever-present Damocles's sword of possible annihilation.

HOW I STOPPED WORRYING
ABOUT THE BOMB

As long as we live in a world with even a single nuclear weapon, danger abounds. So why am I not losing sleep worrying about the threat of nuclear weapons? The total number of nuclear weapons in the world has been drastically reduced since the height of their buildup in 1985, when plutonium was practically available in every corner store. Look at Figure 10. (I've projected the figures out a few years based on international agreements that are currently in effect.)[76]

FIGURE 10: GLOBAL NUCLEAR WARHEADS, 1945–2012 (2009–2012 PROJECTED)

We're inundated with news coverage focused on the possibility that rogue nations or terrorists may have access to nuclear weapons (or some combination thereof: rogue nations may get them and then give them to terrorists.) However, while people may know that the United States and Russia have been reducing their nuclear arsenals, it is not common knowledge just how successful that effort has been. While nuclear terrorism is a very real danger, there are simply far fewer bombs around than there used to be. With the nuclear powers at relative peace after the Cold War, the world is left to worry about possible isolated or regional nuclear incidents, a severe threat to be sure, but not nearly as intimidating as a worldwide nuclear holocaust.

In addition to understanding the threat of nuclear weapons, we have come to realize the dangers of biological and chemical weapons, particularly after the 2001 mail-based anthrax attacks in the U.S. But luckily, the large-scale bioterror attacks people assumed were imminent have not materialized. We've learned that Iraq had no bioweapons program, Al Qaeda is far from having the capability for one, and even Russia shut theirs down in 1992. Before 2001, we were too complacent about bioterrorism, and now we're overly vigilant. This is a good thing, but thankfully the true chances of biological weapons attacks are much less than we had all once feared. Terrorist attacks using nuclear weapons are, unfortunately, at least a little bit more likely.[77]

The world has not greatly adjusted its nuclear weapons strategy since the end of the Cold War. Nuclear weapons were always dangerous, but now they are unnecessarily so. There are several issues that need to be addressed when it comes to an international approach toward nuclear disarmament. As the *Economist* explains, "These would need to include obligations not to develop, test or produce new weapons; a transitional moratorium on use; a timetable for dismantling weapons; an obligation on all states to prevent the transfer of nuclear skills and materials; and a program for converting or shutting down completely all weapons-related facilities."[78] While some of these measures are partly in effect, others still need to be implemented. In order of decreasing urgency but increasing controversy, the goals of a non-nuclear world consist of: (1) preventing terrorists from getting nuclear weapons, (2) preventing non-nuclear countries from becoming nuclear, (3) further reducing the world's current arsenal of nuclear weapons, and finally (4), eliminating all of the planet's nuclear weapons.

As a first step, let's start with the simplest goal: preventing terrorists from obtaining nuclear, biological, or chemical weapons. This measure is a relatively simple one because it is the least controversial; that is, every country agrees that we need to prevent nuclear or biological terrorism and chemical warfare. The most likely disaster scenario today is no longer a nuclear war but the detonation of a nuclear weapon or disease agent by a terrorist organization. Most nations agree on what steps to take to prevent this from happening. What stands in the way of carrying the steps out is prioritizing the steps and funding the efforts to implement them. You would think that getting funding would be easy. With all the money we're pouring into eliminating terrorism, it seems only natural that the number one anti-terrorism priority should be preventing nuclear, chemical, and biological terrorism. But there are a lot of different ideas about which is the best way to eliminate terrorism, and every idea is vying for attention and resources.

We already know the bad news about nuclear terrorism: Al Qaeda and other terrorist groups want nuclear weapons, and they are desperately trying to get them. Even if they are unable to buy nuclear weapons, it's feared that they could build their own bomb. But easier said than done. As Steve Chapman of the *Chicago Tribune* reports, "Terrorists would first have to steal about 100 pounds of bomb fuel from a government, and then transport the material hundreds of miles across borders without detection. Even if that were possible, building a bomb isn't something you can do in a garage or a cave; you need specialized, high-tech equipment, and people with training and skills. Any weapon would then have to be smuggled into the U.S. without detection—and without anyone in the expanding circle of conspirators screwing up."[79] Thankfully, no terrorists have managed to gain access to nuclear weapons or use biological or chemical weapons effectively. The largest example of terrorists using biological weapons was the 1995 sarin gas attack in Tokyo's subway, which caused 12 deaths, fewer than many attacks using conventional bombs.[80]

The hardest task with procuring nuclear weapons is getting the highly enriched uranium (HEU) to use in the bomb. So, the goal should be to secure as much of the world's bombs and HEU as possible. Since the U.S. supply is already safely tucked away, our focus should be to help Russia. Starting with Gorbachev's landmark efforts, Russia has already drastically reduced its nuclear arsenal, but it still has more nuclear weapons than it can afford to keep. Storing them safely and securing them properly is an expensive proposition, so the United States is working to bring Russian storage facilities up to safer standards with reinforced steel doors, secure fences, motion detectors, and more radiation detectors.[81] In fact, the United States has helped to secure over 75 percent of all Russian sites where weapons-grade nuclear material is stored.[82]

The U.S. Department of Energy is also working with Russia to gather up HEU that is being used in nuclear research centers in 40 different countries. More than 220 pounds of HEU has already been returned (that's a lot when it comes to HEU). Along with this broad cleanup of nuclear research centers, those governments are being encouraged to switch from HEU to low-enriched fuel. In Russia about half of the surplus HEU has already been blended down into safer fuel.[83] Most impressively, both Russia and the United States are in the process of destroying their *entire* stockpiles of chemical weapons.[84]

To discourage scientists from selling information about nuclear or chemical weaponry to terrorists or saboteurs, the U.S. is helping to pay for new civilian jobs for scientists who worked in Russia's nuclear and chemical weapons programs and now find themselves unemployed. The United States is also working to dismantle Russia's unused nuclear submarines. Although there is little chance that terrorists will do anything with these, some of the submarines are leaking nuclear waste into the Arctic. A final way to prevent against nuclear terrorism is securing borders and ports by installing radiation detectors. But this effort is still only in its fledgling stages.

Our second step toward nuclear disarmament is to prevent non-nuclear countries from getting nuclear weapons. This is somewhat less important than stopping terrorism, because terrorists with nuclear weapons are more likely to use them than governments. History has shown that most countries act rationally and prefer to use nuclear bombs as bargaining chips rather than as active weapons. After all, countries are vulnerable to retaliation; whereas nomadic terrorists are not (or simply don't care). Nevertheless, international tensions can often run high and the unthinkable explosion might happen, either as the result of a hastily made decision or a complete accident. So the fewer countries with nuclear weapons, the better.

The Nuclear Non-Proliferation Treaty (NPT) is the key to preventing non-nuclear countries from getting nuclear weapons. Under this landmark agreement, which went into effect in 1970 and which 189 nations have now signed, non-nuclear states have promised never to develop nuclear weapons. In exchange, the nuclear countries have promised to provide member nations with civilian nuclear power. Also, the nuclear countries agreed to disarm and reduce their arsenals and eventually eliminate them completely.[85]

There are only five official nuclear states, the members of the UN Security Council: China, Britain, France, the United States, and Russia. In addition, India, Pakistan and Israel also have nuclear weapons, although no one's supposed to know about Israel's. Even when you add the newest member of the nuclear club, North Korea (the only country ever to withdraw from the NPT), that still makes only nine nuclear states out of 193 total. And this is more than 60 years after the bomb was created.

New historical research confirms that it's much more difficult for countries to obtain nuclear weapons than you might infer from media reports. J. Robert Oppenheimer once said that nuclear bombs "are not too hard to make," but not all of us share his talents, and so thankfully history has proven him wrong. Thomas C. Reed, a former secretary of the Air Force, and Danny B. Stillman, former director of intelligence at Los Alamos, explain it well in a recent book about the history of nuclear proliferation. They write, "Since the birth of the nuclear age, no nation has developed a nuclear weapon on its own, although many claim otherwise." In other words, all nuclear weapons technology today is descended from the original Manhattan Project in the U.S., and every country that now has the bomb was either given the technology by another country or stole it via espionage. Russia was the first country to get the bomb after the U.S., thanks to its spies in the Manhattan Project. Moscow then freely shared their secrets with China. France shared secrets with Israel, Israel shared them with South Africa, China helped Pakistan, and a Pakistani scientist ended up selling secrets to North Korea, just to name a few links in the chain.[86]

In late 2007, North Korea had agreed to shut down all of its nuclear programs, in exchange for aid, oil, and potentially restored diplomatic relations with America. North Korea is notorious for reneging on its obligations, and indeed, it did. But the agreements it's maintained on-and-off over the years are a sign of its willingness to negotiate and cooperate, and of its susceptibility to basic carrot-and-stick diplomacy. In addition, the leaders of North and South Korea signed an eight-point peace pledge in October 2007, working towards a permanent peace and an end to hostilities between the two nations. Unfortunately, it looks as if Iran is likely to get the bomb as well, although most calculations estimate that to be a few years away. In fact, Mohamed ElBaradei, the former head of the International Atomic Energy Agency, called the threat of Iran getting the bomb anytime soon "hyped."[87] Making nations feel secure is an essential step to preventing nuclear proliferation; the Iranian regime's insecurity lies behind their desire for the bomb, not just a thirst for power or prestige. If Iran gets the bomb, that would bring the total to ten nuclear states. We now know that Iraq has no nuclear weapons program, and Libya just stopped theirs. Libya's story is heartening: after years of being a leading sponsor of terrorism, it recently gave up its nuclear program and pleaded to join the world of international cooperation, essentially renouncing its aggressive ways. Libya's dictator, Muammar al-Qaddafi, is now cooperating somewhat with the rest of the world, and Libya's nuclear program, at least, is no longer in operation.

It is hard to believe, but very few countries want nuclear weapons. In fact, fewer countries want nuclear weapons than at any point since World War II.[88] Most are too invested in participating in the world economy to want to jeopardize that status by creating a nuclear arsenal. To compare, dozens of countries in the 1950s and 1960s sought the bomb. Today, after Iran, the next most likely candidates to instigate nuclear development include Syria, Turkey, Egypt, Saudi Arabia and Algeria.[89] South Korea and Japan, too, may soon develop into nuclear states, their motivation being to counter North Korea. When the Soviet Union split up and Russia began consolidating the Soviet arsenal into Russia proper, Belarus, Kazakhstan, and Ukraine voluntarily turned over their arsenals. South Africa had a nuclear program but decided to abandon it, offering a perfect example of the nuclear inspection and dismantling process in operation. Several countries such as Argentina, Brazil, South Korea, Sweden, Australia, and Spain considered acquiring nuclear weapons but later abandoned the idea.[90] Many countries of the world have banded together to create "nuclear weapons free zones." These zones encompass all of Africa, South and Central America, Australia, and New Zealand.[91] While no one wants Iran, Syria, or other countries to get the bomb, even if they do start accumulating weapons the total number of nuclear states would still be small. If the current nuclear world plays its cards right, and upholds the promises of the NPT, the number of nuclear states will never grow substantially.

Accomplishing one of the most fundamental tenets of the NPT—reducing the world's current nuclear arsenal—is the third step toward disarmament. The primary focus is on the United States and Russia: together the two countries hold 95 percent of the world's nuclear weapons.[92] However, until the U.S. and Russia completely disarm, the rest of the world has an excuse to break the agreements stipulated in the NPT. After all, as long as they still have nuclear weapons, the United States and Russia are not keeping up their end of the bargain. Luckily, both countries have already drastically reduced their arsenals from Cold War heights (see Figure 10). Under a 2002 treaty, they both agreed to cut back their deployed warheads to between 1,700 to 2,200 each by the year 2012. In addition, President Obama is pushing harder and just signed another agreement with Russia to reduce arms to between 1,500 and 1,675 warheads. When this reduction is complete, the United States will have reduced its number of deployed strategic nuclear warheads by 80 percent since 1990.[93]

The trend of reducing nuclear arsenals brings us to the fourth and final step in this nuclear quest: eliminating all of the planet's nuclear weapons. Robert McNamara, U.S. Secretary of Defense during a large part of the Cold War, now feels that he would "characterize current U.S. nuclear weapons policy as immoral, illegal, militarily unnecessary, and dreadfully dangerous." He goes on to say that, "The risk of an accidental or inadvertent nuclear launch is unacceptably high." And he should know, since he was intimately involved in the 1962 Cuban Missile Crisis, the point at which we came closest to nuclear war. Nuclear weapons can never be used wisely, for to use them against another nuclear country means suicide for all involved. And to use them against a non-nuclear country, according to McNamara, would be "militarily unnecessary, morally repugnant, and politically indefensible."[94] There is no way to win.

In addition, since the remaining cold wars are now regional, nuclear fallout would directly hurt the countries deploying the bombs in the first place. For example, North Korea is too close to substantially bomb South Korea without bringing fallout on itself. During the Cold War, the U.S. and Russia lacked this extra deterrent. To absolutely prevent nuclear terrorism, total nuclear disarmament and enforcement is the only solution. As Kofi Annan said, "Ultimately, the only way to guarantee that they will never be used is for our world to be free of such weapons."[95]

Total nuclear disarmament is a lofty goal that is often derided as too idealistic. How would it be possible? Well, it's not easy, but it's doable if we advance in careful, progressive steps. America's inspiration would be essential, such as with a declaration that our current weapons have no purpose other than to deter others' use of nuclear weapons, and with a diplomatic effort to convince the world of the benefits of disarmament.[96] As the number of nuclear weapons decreases, inspections and effective verification will become more and more essential. A system will have to be devised to ensure that countries trust the inspections and thus trust their neighbors to remain nuclear-free. Also, ways are now being explored to ensure that countries can receive all the supplies of nuclear fuel they need for civilian reactors so that they won't have to enrich uranium themselves. One daunting but plausible theory is to transfer *all* the world's uranium enrichment and reprocessing to the International Atomic Energy Agency or a new global institution. Then countries couldn't hide burgeoning nuclear weapon programs behind the façade of civilian nuclear power production, as Iran is purportedly doing now.[97]

Nuclear weapons helped keep the peace during the Cold War, making total war too costly in terms of loss of life and destruction. But there are three reasons why deterrence would still be possible in a world without nuclear weapons. One, it is the scientific knowledge of how to create nuclear weapons that is dangerous. This knowledge will always exist, and if one country starts developing weapons, it would be with the understanding that other countries could also create bombs quickly and retaliate. Two, the world now is so integrated that economics and culture could replace nuclear weapons as a deterrent. It is too costly for countries with strong economic ties to go to war (such as the United States and China), and most countries increasingly have cultural ties as well—tourism between nations, large immigrant populations, and more. Three, it's possible that cool heads prevail more often than we give them credit. The fact that even totalitarian societies such as the Soviet Union and China never used their bombs indicates that world leaders are wisely reluctant to kill millions of people. Whether that is for moral reasons or simply to avoid the political "fallout" is debatable. Nations have their reputations to uphold in the international community. In wars with non-nuclear countries, neither the Soviet Union in Afghanistan, Israel in Lebanon, France in Algeria, nor the United States in Vietnam found nuclear weapons helpful.[98] As more countries come to their senses and realize the futility of owning nuclear weapons, the incentive to obtain them will continue to diminish. As a global ethical framework continues to evolve, nuclear weapons will soon become a political albatross. Significantly, Barack Obama has become the first U.S. president to explicitly agree with the goal of complete disarmament:

Some argue that the spread of these weapons cannot be checked—that we are destined to live in a world where more nations and more people possess the ultimate tools of destruction. This fatalism is a deadly adversary. For if we believe that the spread of nuclear weapons is inevitable, then we are admitting to ourselves that the use of nuclear weapons is inevitable ... So today, I state clearly and with conviction America's commitment to seek the peace and security of a world without nuclear weapons. I'm not naïve. This goal will not be reached quickly—perhaps not in my lifetime. It will take patience and persistence. But now we, too, must ignore the voices who tell us that the world cannot change.[99]

PEACEKEEPING: LOW-COST, BIG RETURNS

The fall of the Soviet Union inaugurated the likely end of the worst type of nuclear danger, but that wasn't all it inspired. Its demise let loose other forces that had been held at bay, such as the UN. Even though the UN's original mission was to prevent conflict, its first four decades were only intermittently successful. The United States and the Soviet Union kept a balance of power in the Security Council, rarely coming to a consensus and thus effectively tying the UN's hands. But even these early troubled cases allowed it to slowly create a knowledge base of institutions, rules, and processes that have improved every year. The international community now has a set of mechanisms specifically designed to overcome warfare.

International preventative diplomacy and peacekeeping are two of the main reasons why violent conflicts are declining. Countries continue to enter into conflicts, both internally and with their neighbors, but the world stands waiting to quickly quell the fire or, better yet, smother it before it starts. The UN is often maligned by its member nations for failing in large conflicts such as those in Rwanda, Sudan, Srebrenica, and Iraq. The organization—especially its bickering member nations—*should* be criticized for these failures. And yet, with little fanfare, the UN tirelessly fights in troubled spots around the world, achieving quiet victories in places such as Slovenia, East Timor, and El Salvador. There are now over 70,000 soldiers, 10,000 police, and thousands more civilians and volunteers deployed in 17 UN peace missions worldwide. And believe it or not, UN peace-building operations have a two-thirds success rate. Since 1945, the UN has negotiated 172 peaceful settlements of various conflicts. In 2005 alone, 22 cease-fire agreements or peace treaties were signed worldwide.[100] It's easy to be pessimistic about UN initiatives because we usually only hear about the ones that don't work—but many do work as planned.

UN peacekeepers perform a wide variety of functions—they create buffer zones, enforce cease-fires and peace agreements, support and train local militaries or civilian services, monitor elections, and provide social and economic development and rebuilding as conflicts wind down. Successes in peacemaking have been accumulating since 1991, and though we still have a lot to learn, the UN and many individual countries are now peacekeeping experts. Peacekeepers are getting more effective at working with local groups and NGOs, and each mission effectively assembles ad hoc coalitions of countries. Naturally, one of the only downsides of conducting so many peacekeeping missions is the cost, which hit a record $7 billion in 2007.[101] Yet this amount is only a fraction of what the United States has spent in Iraq, for example—an astounding $100 billion a year.[102] Dollar for dollar, peacekeeping missions are an excellent investment. And as developing nations grow economically, they will become increasingly capable of contributing money and personnel to peacekeeping efforts. There are already signs of this. For example, as Africa improves its economic situation, more countries in Africa will be able to contribute to African Union forces. Western countries now account for less than 10 percent of peacekeeping personnel, down from 45 percent in 1998.[103] Unfortunately, this is also a reflection of diminished contributions from the Western countries—for example, Rwanda now contributes more people than Russia.

Perpetually strapped for cash, the UN has learned how to squeeze out the best return on the dollars it spends. It found, for example, that peacekeeping is ineffective during the worst of the fighting. Rather, it works best before war breaks out, through diplomacy and attempts to reach agreements to avert conflict, and as fighting winds down, when a fragile peace begins to emerge and needs to be nurtured to avoid any slides back into chaos. The UN has also learned how to plan for reconstruction early so that it can quickly act once a conflict settles down, and it has also gotten better at judging the size of forces needed. For example, according to Jean-Marie Guéhenno, the under-secretary general for UN Peacekeeping, the "robust force in Liberia has enough military muscle to ensure that rebels won't overrun it, as they nearly did a much lighter force in Sierra Leone in 2000."[104] Today nearly every conflict in the world has a number of other countries working hard to keep the peace, and not only by sending peacekeeping troops. Efforts are needed on many fronts, and the nations of the world are stepping up to help.

Increasingly, help in conflict resolution is coming from non-state actors—not countries, but organizations and individuals. One example of learning from our mistakes, channeling past experience, and harnessing every available resource can be seen in the present-day activities of former IRA leaders. With the conflict in Northern Ireland over, the men who led the IRA are now advising on conflict resolution abroad. These ex-terrorists are helping to negotiate with terrorist groups such as the ETA in Spain, the Tamil Tigers in Sri Lanka, and Palestinian terrorists to convince them to abandon violence. Gerry Adams, the leader of Sinn Fein, flew to Tel Aviv to meet with the Palestinian president, Mahmoud Abbas. Describing suicide bombings as having "no legitimacy," Adams encouraged political battles as an alternative to armed action.[105]

At the other end of the spectrum, religious groups are another prime example of non-state actors. In countries where war has destroyed the government's effectiveness or legitimacy, religious groups remain one of the only sources of leadership for people. Religious groups and other NGOs can serve as truth tellers, lending a voice to the experience of injustice, providing impartial mediators between parties, and conveying the importance of conflict resolution, diversity, and other values. By harnessing a network of local parishes, mosques, temples, or local fellowship groups, religious organizations can provide the glue to help keep civil society together. Likewise, grassroots groups can harness widespread networks of volunteers, especially through coordination over the Internet. Reconciliation is one of the most important roles in peace building that religion can hope to play, and one for which it is perfectly suited. Religious groups have a unique authority to foster mutual forgiveness and start a healing process to build bridges between survivors. South Africa's Bishop Desmond Tutu epitomizes this important step toward peace. The Truth and Reconciliation Commission, of which he was the chairman, was set up to transition South Africa from its former apartheid government to democracy. Anyone who felt that he or she were a victim of persecution, and conversely, any perpetrators of violence seeking amnesty, could come forward and be heard before this court-like body. Testimonies were used to seek out the truth of past abuse and advance toward the nation's healing.[106]

Religious groups are an important force waging against war. But public pressure, the media, and governments themselves are also working on the problem. One example of a less violent approach that governments can use to fight aggressive countries is through sanctions, a potentially effective way to pressure despotic or violent regimes. Many sanctions are poorly or hastily planned; they can invert their original goal and end up hurting innocent citizens rather than a country's leaders or military. This is why Gandhi considered sanctions to be almost as violent as war itself.

The results of the economic sanctions taken against Iraq in 1990 after its invasion of Kuwait provide the best known example of the harm that sanctions can inflict. The good news was that the sanctions worked against Saddam Hussein to some extent, since he wasn't able to rebuild his military or gain weapons of mass destruction. The bad news was the harm the sanctions inflicted on the Iraqi public, resulting in scarcity of food and supplies. But other examples are more positive, such as the international sanctions from corporations and governments that helped end apartheid in South Africa. The world continues to learn from its mistakes and is implementing more targeted smart sanctions— arms embargoes and freezing of specific financial assets. Currently, UN sanctions remain in place against Afghanistan, Ivory Coast, Democratic Republic of the Congo, Iraq, Liberia, Rwanda, Sierra Leone, Somalia, and Sudan.[107]

The media also helps to stop violence. By shining a light onto human rights abuses, newspapers and television alert the public to atrocities overseas.

Governments also use the influence of the media, such as Radio Free Europe, which the Eisenhower administration started in the 1950s. This radio broadcast of pro-Western messages into the Eastern Bloc helped students and other reformers coalesce into organizations to protest Soviet domination. The program is now smaller but is targeting hot spots such as Kosovo and Iraq. Spreading pro-democracy and pro-peace information can inspire the public to rally against tyranny by making use of protests and other nonviolent actions. The work of ordinary citizen groups has been effective in banning land mines and raising public awareness about environmental causes, for example. And the UN also knows how to spread information to the public as a way to influence governments. The UN Human Rights Commission has focused world attention on cases of torture, disappearance, and arbitrary detention. Their efforts have pressured governments to improve their human rights records.[108] Likewise, NGOs often serve as extra eyes searching the world's dark corners for human rights abuses and war crimes, using their members at the grassroots level to help peace on the ground.

While we are on the subject of justice, I must digress from the international scale to discuss an issue in the United States. The U.S. prison system is one area in which positive trends are *not* prevailing. Crime in the United States has drastically declined in the past two decades, no doubt in part due to the sheer number of criminals incarcerated. But studies have shown that overcrowding and harsh conditions found in some prisons make criminals more likely to be repeat offenders. America has five percent of the world's population but holds 25 percent of the world's prisoners.[109] The crime rate might have decreased even further if the focus were on rehabilitating criminals, rather than merely punishing them. This is a point that Gandhi stressed repeatedly—that a prison system should dispense help, not punishment. Many prison education and psychological programs have seen their funding cut in recent years. The correctional system then becomes a revolving door for repeat offenders. Prisoners often experience extreme difficulties in securing jobs and living regular lives once they rejoin society. Some new programs are trying to address this, including a successful entrepreneurship course in Texas that teaches prisoners business skills.[110]

On the other hand, one major trend in the prison system is encouraging—the imminent demise of the death penalty, which very few countries in the world still administer. Twenty-five countries held executions in 2006, down from 40 ten years earlier. China (which has the most executions by far), Iran, Pakistan, Iraq, Sudan, and the United States account for nearly all the world's recent criminal executions. This is not a glamorous group for the United States to be associated with. Indeed, even China reformed its laws in late 2006, now requiring their highest court to approve each death sentence. This is expected to dramatically reduce their number of executions from today's count of about 1,500 a year. Activists in China pushed for this reform after the media revealed stories of innocents accidentally put to death.

Around the world, concerned citizens have pushed for the elimination of the death penalty in a majority of countries. In the United States, since 1999 the number of executions carried out has declined 46 percent and the number of death sentences imposed dropped two-thirds. New Jersey recently abolished capital punishment, the first state to do so in 40 years. But it looks like the question of the morality of state-inflicted death is not going to be what hammers the final nail into the death penalty's coffin. Rather than address the larger moral issue, the public is more often heard debating over how many innocents are put to death. (In the U.S. so far, more than 130 people sentenced to death have been exonerated.) This is an essential aspect that needs to be discussed, as are arguments that the system is discriminatory, and that it is too expensive to keep inmates on death row due to the lengthy appeal process. Indeed, the recent economic downturn has inspired eight states to propose eliminating the death penalty in order to cut costs. In addition, the death penalty does not seem to be as much of a deterrent to crime as its supporters insist; avid executors Texas and Oklahoma, for example, have higher crime rates than other states. And the most recent discussions have centered around semantic debates about what type of death is humane—whether being killed hurts. Even doctors are refusing to administer lethal injections based on the possibility of its inhumanity and violations of the Hippocratic Oath. However, all of these (legitimate) concerns skirt the larger ethical issue.[111]

The death penalty contributes to an environment of violence, sending a message that helps perpetuate a violent cycle for society. That we execute people less painfully than before is of minimal concern compared to the larger moral question of a society's right to condemn others to death. However, if these detail-oriented debates are what ends the death penalty, then so be it— and good riddance.

SECURING THE FUTURE OF CONFLICT

What is the future of war? Traditional total war is on the decline in most regions except perhaps for central Africa and central Asia. As the *New York Times* describes, "Entire regions that were strife-torn 20 or 30 years ago, including East and Southeast Asia, are largely peaceful today. North Africa is quiet; Latin America suffers from political instability but not warfare."[112] With the Yugoslav wars of 1991–2001, Europe may have seen its last large-scale war. Smaller wars of terrorism or proxy wars will continue in the Middle East. As for Africa, almost half of the world's peacekeeping missions are currently located there. They are paying off; in Darfur, for example, three years ago an estimated 6,000-10,000 people were dying monthly from violence, disease and hunger, while by 2008 the figure had dropped to 100-600 people a month.[113] Ivory Coast's civil war ended in March 2007, and thousands of citizens packed a stadium to watch the president light a bonfire of hundreds of weapons.[114]

Technology, as always, is also driving some future war trends. Quietly, three new changes have been unfolding that together may have the biggest technological impact on war since the atom bomb. One trend is the development of non-lethal weapons. These already exist, of course: many citizens use mace to protect themselves rather than carry a handgun, and some law enforcement districts use tasers. But now the U.S. military is developing non-lethal weapons for war: a futuristic "heat beam" that inflicts searing pain into a person's skin's nerve endings without actually burning the skin, and a "long-range acoustic device" that emits sound waves to cause terrible pain without damaging eardrums.[115] A second trend, as a corollary to these, is the simple increase in the ratio of injured soldiers to soldiers killed in battle. In Vietnam, three Americans were wounded for every one killed; in Iraq, it's at least 7 to 1. Thanks to Kevlar body armor and sophisticated mobile medical teams with full medical resources, injuries that were life-threatening in the past are now survivable.[116] A third trend is right out of science fiction: the Pentagon is building increasingly sophisticated robots to fight in war. Some types of robots already exist, but need direct control. New research is looking to give them increasing autonomy and decision-making skills. One benefit is to decrease the chance of killing civilians; with the proper set of logic rules, a robot could make battle decisions without the effects of stress or confusion.[117] These three trends are indicative of humanity's increasing unwillingness to lose lives to war.

As the occurrence of total war declines, the world's peacekeeping resources will be able to concentrate on the remaining isolated regions. But all of these peacekeeping efforts will require political unity, diplomatic stamina, and financial sacrifice. All peace efforts should be filtered through the UN to reinforce a sense of impartiality. If present trends hold, the future will see peacekeeping become more organized and efficient. Diverse and conflicting policies will coalesce into one framework the world can quickly use to diagnose a conflict area and prescribe an appropriate intervention strategy.

This holistic framework of unified policies is a concept called collective security. The idea has been germinating for a long time, harkening back at least to Immanuel Kant's vision of a civic union of republics that would keep perpetual peace in the world.[118] A tentative plan was first introduced in the League of Nations but was quickly squashed as unrealistic. The concept is simple: all the nations in the world agree to work together for peace. If one nation disobeys the law and makes war, the other nations unite to stop it. The world already has a form of implied collective security. The best example of its use was the first Iraq War in 1991. When Iraq invaded Kuwait, the UN gathered an ad hoc force to go in and kick Iraq out. Of course, the conflict was a lot more complicated than that, but it was the first large-scale implementation of collective security the world has ever seen.

Using collective security is a three-step process. The first step is for the nations of the world to decide on what is acceptable behavior for nations. There must be agreement on the rules, and in order to do that, the nations must agree on some common fundamental values on which the rules will be based. Some of these rules are already codified. Based on the UN Charter, wars of aggression are illegal. But as it stands today, the UN must laboriously decide each instance of aggression on a case by case basis. If rules of war and peace were more clearly defined, action could be taken faster because it would be clear when one of the rules was violated. That's the second step of collective security—deciding if a particular country has broken the rules. This must be done by a strict process that is fair and democratic. If it is found that the country is in violation of international law, the third step is to decide what action to take in response.[119]

To be truly effective, collective security needs to be strengthened. The development of the UN already constitutes significant progress in that direction. The League of Nations was only given the mandate for the first two steps of the process—agreeing on acceptable behavior and deciding if a particular country has broken the rules. The League was ineffectual on the third step, deciding how to deal with violations of international law, since it could not require nations to comply with its security decisions. The UN, however, can. The UN was founded to maintain "international peace and security, and to that end: to take effective collective measures for the prevention and removal of threats to the peace, and for the suppression of acts of aggression or other breaches of the peace."[120] Hence the UN can impose economic and military sanctions. The trick is supplying the necessary resources and political will to enforce them.

Another aspect of collective security is arms reduction—not just nuclear arms, but all weapons. There are precedents: the 1999 International Anti-Personnel Mine Ban Treaty was signed by 156 countries, though the U.S., China and Russia were all conspicuously absent. Nevertheless, as of the end of 2007, 42 million antipersonnel landmines have been destroyed; 81 countries are now completely clear of them.[121] The goal is for no single country to have large surpluses of arms, so that only when they are used together will they be particularly deadly. Since the UN does not have a standing peacekeeping army, it tends to temporarily delegate its powers to member states to carry out actions on its behalf, as it did when it gave the United States control over the military forces of the first Iraq War. If there were a small world police force and a permanent fund of financial resources, the UN could move faster and carry out more pre-emptive peacekeeping missions without having to drum up support each time. In such a scenario the democratic vote at the UN would consist solely of eval-uating whether or not a country has violated the law and would not include questions of what the laws are or how to drum up support and money to deal with those violations. An international poll by the Chicago Council on Global Affairs showed that 72 percent of Americans are in favor of allowing the UN to select, train and command a standing peacekeeping force. Twelve out of 14 other countries polled agreed, with an average 64 percent in support.[122]

An ideal step would be to split UN peacekeepers into two forces, one mili-tary and the other nonviolent, and deploy the appropriate teams according to each situation as it arises. Peace armies (Gandhi called them *Shanti Sena*) could be phased in with military UN peacekeeping teams to try out as many methods of conflict resolution as possible. UN peace armies have the advantage of be-ing less expensive to support because even though they must have extensive training, they require much less equipment. This is essential, since the world devotes over one trillion dollars a year to defense. With the decrease in total war and the end of the Cold War, this is less than the world's peak in 1987, but re-mains a tragedy since that money could be used for peacekeeping or any other number of health initiatives or education-related programs.[123] And as an added advantage of peacekeeping, multinational forces can sidestep a government's reluctance to let an armed force into their country as well as allay any fears of giving the UN too much consolidated military power.

While advancements are slowly taking place in the UN, the difficulty lies in generating the political will to give more power to the organization. Such a transfer of power would require that member states give up some of their sover-eignty, which is never easy to part with. Nevertheless, member states that think they have absolute sovereignty today are only fooling themselves. The number of international laws and regulations crisscrossing the world means that we already have the beginnings of an international governing system. And while that may sound scary to some, the key point is to make sure that the system is democratic. Because as history has shown us, democracy is what the people want.

DEMOCRACY

Federation of the World

The fall of the Berlin Wall in November 1989 caught everyone by surprise. Like the dozens of revolutions we discussed, the reunification of Germany was unexpectedly peaceful. A decades-long experiment in splitting a culture in half came to its logical conclusion. Author Andreas Ramos was in Berlin that night, and his riveting description has been reprinted in many history books:

> After a while, we walked to Potsdammer Platz. This used to be the center of Berlin. ... Now it was a large empty field, bisected by the wall. Nearby was the mound that was the remains of Hitler's bunker, from which he commanded Germany into total defeat. ... It was still very dark and cold at 5 a.m. Perhaps 7,000 people were pressed together, shouting, cheering, clapping. We pushed through the crowd. From the East German side we could hear the sound of heavy machines. With a giant drill, they were punching holes in the wall. Every

time a drill poked through, everyone cheered. ... Many were using hammers to chip away at the wall. There were countless holes. At one place, a crowd of East German soldiers looked through a narrow hole. We reached through and shook hands. ... Someone lent me a hammer and I knocked chunks of rubble from the wall, dropping several handfuls into my pocket. ...

There were fireworks, kites, flags and flags and flags, dogs, children. ... At the Berlin Wall itself, which is 3 meters high, people had climbed up and were sitting astride. The final slab was moved away. A stream of East Germans began to pour through. People applauded and slapped their backs. ... Packed in with thousands, I stood at the break in the wall. ... Looking around, I saw an indescribable joy in people's faces. It was the end of the government telling people what not to do, it was the end of the Wall, the war, the East, the West. ... Around me, people spoke German, French, Polish, Russian, every language. ... Near me, a knot of people cheered as the mayors of East Berlin and West Berlin met and shook hands. I stood with several East German guards, their rifles slung over their shoulders. I asked them if they had bullets in those things. They grinned and said no. From some houses, someone had set up loudspeakers and played Beethoven's ninth symphony: Alle Menschen werden Bruder. All people become brothers.[1]

The fall of the wall sounded the death knells for communism across Eastern Europe. Two years later, the Soviet Union, the last great empire on Earth, collapsed. With its demise, the epoch of overreaching nations systematically subjugating faraway peoples came to an end. Communism is dying as an ideology; since China, Vietnam, and Laos are increasingly market-oriented, only Cuba and North Korea remain explicitly communist states. Europe gave up on its centuries-long reign of global colonization. Today the sun *does* set on the British Empire. With Saudi Arabia as one of the most notable exceptions, most monarchies have been eliminated. The majority of monarchies that remain exist only as figureheads (e.g., Britain) and in small nation-states such as Tuvalu and Swaziland.

Despite all of these changes, the concept of absolute sovereignty lingers. Countries are reluctant to cede power to international treaties, and several assume a role as authoritarian as the Soviet Union once had, only over smaller areas. But that is changing, and fast. Nationalism and sovereignty are breaking down. Political scientist Samuel Huntington writes, "The nation-state is a rare and recent phenomenon in human affairs. ... the concept of the nation—an ethnic or cultural community—[became] linked to that of the state—a purely political organization. No reason exists in logic or experience, however, why sources of identity and authority should coincide, and through most of human history they have not."[2] For thousands of years, humanity's loyalties lay within tiny groups of family members, tribes, and small religious communities. Only after the onset of mass communication, with the invention of the printing press, could people living far apart unite around common languages and values. At that point, small communities developed more fully into countries, and a sense of national consciousness evolved. Patriotism for one's country represented a higher level of unity than humankind had ever achieved before. Patriotism began to take preference over other loyalties, however, gradually evolving into its extreme form, nationalism, in the nineteenth and early twentieth centuries. Though nationalism has caused a lot of problems—Fascism as the most extreme example—it can be seen as a dangerous yet necessary stage that humanity has to pass through as we advance from a family-centered life to a community-centered life to a world-aware existence characterized by a wider loyalty.

After a century defined by strict national sovereignty, the concept of the nation-state is becoming fuzzy again. National governments are going through the simultaneous processes of disintegration (think of breakaway states such as the Balkans and East Timor) and unification, as with the European Union. This is what political scientist Benjamin Barber calls "Jihad vs. McWorld." Because of their newfound democratic power, more people are demanding independence from large states. So the world is becoming more tribal and breaking into smaller groups, yet at the same time it's coming together through the spread of world trade and a developing global culture.[3]

The countries breaking apart are simply being pushed toward a peaceful equilibrium. This process has happened before, as Robert Wright points out in his book *Nonzero*. Nineteenth-century nationalism broke the Austrian Empire apart while joining Italy together. The printing press broke the Catholic Church's monopoly apart by enabling Protestantism to flourish in Europe while it strengthened Catholicism's international reach because it provided the ability to print and distribute consistent church teachings.[4] Countries are now settling into more cohesive groups linked by ethnicity or culture.

While the idea of forming nations on the basis of ethnic groups can seem like a form of segregation, it is at least self-segregation, and it does promote short-term peace. It's a much better solution than the way countries were divided before—through negotiations between European colonizers.[5] After they have restructured themselves and settled into relative peace, the countries can do a much better job of interacting with others on the world stage and becoming integrated again. In fact, the disintegration and codification of national boundaries is almost complete. As of 1998, 17 percent of the world's land boundaries were disputed. But these are slowly getting resolved, as the United Nations quietly brokers important accords, such as the recent agreement settling a long-running border dispute between Guatemala and Belize, or the resolution of issues over two islands claimed by both China and Russia. Indeed, instead of fighting over borders, countries are crossing them, such as with a new construction plan to build a 17-mile long bridge across the Red Sea from Yemen to Djibouti, connecting Africa and Asia. Also, in 2007, in two echoes of the demise of the Berlin Wall, a road opened linking the Greek and Turkish sides of the capitol city of Cyprus for the first time in 40 years, and a new train linking North and South Korea traveled across the demilitarized zone for the first time since 1953.[6]

There are only a few remaining areas that might restructure their boundaries in an attempt to become more independent—most notably Kurdistan, Kashmir, Chechnya and other south Russian enclaves, the Basque Country and Catalonia in Spain, and Aceh province. Maybe even Québec. Greenland recently gained more autonomous power from Denmark. There is a chance Belgium will be peacefully split into two nations someday soon. Kosovo has declared itself independent from Serbia, becoming the world's newest country, but that delineation still remains controversial. These are all tough decisions since many citizens of these territories feel conflicting loyalties to a larger country as well as to a smaller ethnic group. Conflicting loyalties continue to spur the change of group identities. Jonathan Schell describes the situation profoundly: "The eclipse of sovereign, coercive power and the rise in our time of divided, cooperative power in the domestic affairs of dozens of governments suggest that a similar eclipse in the international sphere is possible." Schell talks about nonviolence, and describes how the world's war system—which is now breaking down—depends on absolute sovereignty. When one country was fighting another, that country had to stay united and needed a strong, centralized authority. War encourages nationalist, state-centric thinking. Today, with fewer total wars, loyalties can be more fluid.

With the spread of democracy and citizen groups, states do not have the grip on power that they once did.[7] Our loyalties are being determined more by what we believe than by where we live. People are increasingly identifying themselves not as part of a single group such as "Brazilians" or "Belgians" but as members of several groups. Our identity is no longer necessarily imposed upon us by geography—at least, not completely. Rather, we can form our own unique identities. And when every person's identity is slightly different, strict segregation along national lines is more difficult to uphold. This subversion of nationalism is another way of describing the overlapping spheres of identity we saw diagrammed in the chapter about unity.

Following the trend of the dispersal of power, some regions in the world are trying out new forms of modified sovereignty. East Timor, a tiny group of islands with fewer than a million people, is now an independent country, but achieving independence was a multi-stepped process. The UN worked for years on negotiations between Timor and Indonesia after a quarter-century of violent occupation by the Indonesian government. In 1999 the Timorese voted for complete independence from Indonesia, leading to a brutal attack from Indonesia. A multinational force stepped in to quell the fighting, and a presidential election, which Indonesia honored, was held in 2002. But the newly renamed East Timor was not quite prepared to govern itself. Multinational experts and civil servants were called in and eventually phased out. Today East Timor still relies on international forces to help with its security while it slowly gets on its feet.

Montenegro (cinematic home of Casino Royale, James Bond's favorite gambling retreat) is another case of modified sovereignty, a sovereignty that has been earned each step of the way. Yugoslavia officially disbanded as an independent country in 2003, but Serbia and Montenegro were still connected under a loose agreement that was enacted to keep peace in the Balkans. Montenegro worked hard to meet conditions set by the international community and eventually earned a vote for independence. Montenegrins voted on June 3, 2006, and three weeks later, Montenegro became the 192nd member country of the UN.

Northern Ireland utilizes modified sovereignty, too. Long a contested and nebulously governed area, Northern Ireland signed the Good Friday Agreement in 1998. This agreement "dictates devolution of power from the parent state [Britain] to the province, which would progressively share and then assume power over time once certain conditions are met and once a majority of citizens consent."[8] According to the terms of the agreement, a referendum can be held in Northern Ireland every seven years to determine whether or not its citizens want to be independent, part of Ireland, or part of Britain. Power-sharing institutions that were in place were suspended in 2002, but autonomy returned and was expanded on May 8, 2007—a historic day, since the new government is headed jointly by Democratic Unionist Party leader Ian Paisley and Sinn Fein's Martin McGuiness, sworn enemies for decades. The BBC called it "a benchmark for improbability."[9]

The UN and international monitors helped in the cases of East Timor, Montenegro, and Northern Ireland. All three of these examples clearly demonstrate that "country" or "no-country" are not the only two options in creating viable and successful governments. Remaining aware of the various options for governance helps to further peace agreements, since conflicting parties are better able to reach compromise if they have the option of forming power-sharing governments. As absolute sovereignty dissolves, we realize that true sovereignty lies in empowering the people it serves. Former UN Secretary-General

Kofi Annan said, "State sovereignty, in its most basic sense, is being redefined—not least by the forces of globalization and international co-operation. States are now widely understood to be instruments at the service of their peoples, and not vice versa. At the same time individual sovereignty—by which I mean the fundamental freedom of each individual . . . has been enhanced by a renewed and spreading consciousness of individual rights. When we read the [UN] charter today, we are more than ever conscious that its aim is to protect individual human beings, not to protect those who abuse them."[10]

As the decades-long process of national disintegration draws to a close and conflicts over disputed territory are settled, the process of larger-scale integration is taking off. Sovereignty is not just changing from the bottom, with smaller regions gaining various degrees of independent government; it is also changing from the top. Countries are increasingly tied together through trade, defense, tourism, media, and technology. To facilitate this integration, nations have realized the benefits of working together, and some of these new partnerships are being codified officially. At the national level, governments have had to give up some of their sovereignty to their citizens for a variety of reasons—expectations of democracy, wishes for greater autonomy, and even the demands of nonpolitical organizations. It's a wonder that countries still exist at all.

A More Perfect Union

The idea of the nation-state may be weakening, but larger, unifying partnerships hold exciting promise. There is no greater example than the European Union, whose integration has been enormously successful. The two main benefits to European integration have been peace and trade. One of the initial goals of the European Community, as it was first called, was to get France and Germany to "play nice." The two countries had been fighting each other every few decades for a century, and everyone expected them to keep warring *ad infinitum*. However, thanks in part to the EU, Western Europe has been at peace since World War II. And as the European Union expanded eastward, so did peace. Today peace reigns in all of Europe. As Robert Wright puts it, "If 90, even 60, years ago, you had predicted that someday France and Germany would have the same currency, the reply would have been, 'Oh, really? Which nation will have conquered which?'"[11]

Forged in 1957, the European Coal and Steel Community was the first glimmer of the European Union (see Figure 11), and additional trade and monetary agreements brought about the unification of more nations. Soon agricultural and political pacts were added. Eventually, nearly all barriers to the flow of people, goods, and money evaporated. The presence of fewer obstacles helped everyone grow faster, and increased competition drove the cost of products down and their quality up. As a final step, 12 European Union countries adopted a single currency, the euro, and as a result the EU essentially became a giant free-trade mega zone.[12] Among the other most significant benefits to integration are the following:

- Since pollution easily crosses borders, the European Union made sure that environmental regulations do, too. Over 200 environmental measures have been put in place and have been incredibly successful in reducing pollution, including that which causes acid rain. It was particularly revolutionary to bring the despoiled Eastern European countries up to par in this regard, but it worked.[13]

- Like environmental policies, labor policies tend to focus on improving conditions in the states with the worst records so that they match the standards of those with the best. Enabling workers to take jobs in higher-paying countries is a win-win situation, since new jobs are created. A study found that when the new member states from Central Europe joined the EU in 2004, economic growth and employment increased not just in those countries but in the other EU countries as a result.[14]

- Crime tends to cross borders as technology advances, so the EU has closely integrated its intelligence and police forces. This is of great help in fighting all crime, including terrorism.

- The growing size of the European Union gives it more political clout in the world.

- The integration of militaries, while still quite weak, has strengthened the European Union's capability for peacekeeping missions.

- Passports are no longer needed when crossing state borders within the EU. In fact, with the recent completion of the High Speed One train between London and the Channel tunnel, you can zip from London to Paris in two hours and 15 minutes.[15]

- The European Union helped strengthen democratic institutions within new member countries such as Greece, Spain, and Portugal.

- Likewise, the countries that were formerly under the Soviet umbrella advanced to democracy and capitalism faster with the help of the EU. The nations that haven't joined yet are motivated to improve their policies so that they will be invited to join.

- Furthermore, the European Union is working to promote democracy and encourage growth in countries outside of its borders through trade and development aid, particularly in Eastern Europe and Africa.

When an impressive 10 countries signed pacts to join the European Union in 2003, a ceremony was held at the foot of the Acropolis in Athens. As the center of ancient Athenian democracy, the Acropolis symbolizes the democratic integration of the European Union.[16] Today the EU continues to expand, with Iceland setting its sights on membership. Bulgaria and Romania are the two newest members. As those former Warsaw Pact countries join, excited Bulgarian Prime Minister Sergei Stanislav stated, "This is the genuine and final fall of the Berlin Wall."[17]

The European Union is in a constant state of flux, and certainly many of its current institutions need to continue to be reformed. The EU must become more democratic and transparent if it wishes to entice its citizens to support it. But in general it's setting such a good example that other continents are starting to emulate it. The European Union has shown that a small group of developed, democratic countries can gradually spread their achievements to those around them.

Figure 11: Growth in membership of the European Union

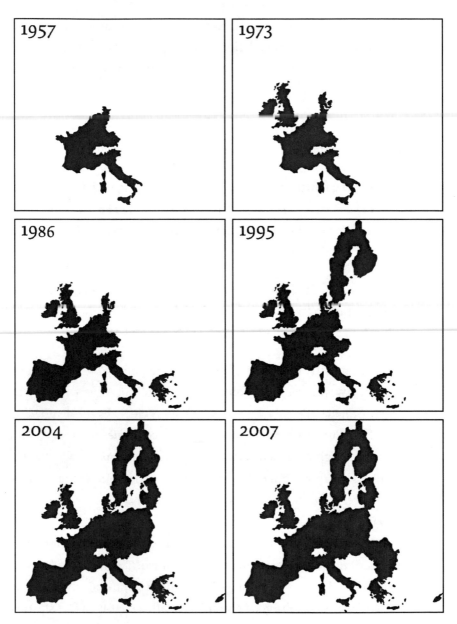

Other groups of nations are forming their organizations in the opposite direction; rather than gradually adding members, they are starting out as a unified coalition and trying to build everyone up at the same time. Time will tell if this method will work, but the concept of starting out with an organized plan seems logical.

The African Union is the best example of creating this type of coalition of unified nations. The predecessor to the African Union was the Organization of African Unity (OAU), which was founded as an intergovernmental organization in 1963 to promote unity and solidarity among African nations. Rather than organizing around economic issues, as Europe did in 1957, the OAU was organized from the start to handle many issues, particularly diplomacy and border disputes. In 2003, the OAU was replaced by the African Union, and the goals of the former organization were broadened to include an all-African parliament, a central bank, a court of justice, and a peacekeeping force.[18] Nearly all of Africa belongs to the African Union—at last count, 53 countries. The African Union's lofty official vision statement reveals what it aspires to accomplish:

> The AU is Africa's premier institution and principal organization for the promotion of accelerated socio-economic integration of the continent, which will lead to greater unity and solidarity between African countries and peoples. The AU is based on the common vision of a united and strong Africa and on the need to build a partnership between governments and all segments of civil society, in particular women, youth and the private sector, in order to strengthen solidarity and cohesion amongst the peoples of Africa. As a continental organization it focuses on the promotion of peace, security and stability on the continent as a prerequisite for the implementation of the development and integration agenda of the Union.[19]

And even more regions are attempting to create unity and solidarity among their constituent nations. The Union of South American Nations now loosely unites South America. Today it is essentially a huge free trade zone with little other integration. But its leaders have specifically expressed the goal of following the example of the European Union with a common currency, common passport, and common parliament.[20] They believe this can be accomplished by 2019.

France recently helped inaugurate the Union for the Mediterranean, which combines the EU states with the other countries that border that sea. The new group, among other things, seeks to solidify the increasing trade within the region. And the Association of South-East Asian Nations (ASEAN) aims to create a regional vision "encompassing the values of openness, freedom, diversity and cosmopolitanism." The 10 members recently took a big step by adopting a legally-binding charter.[21] In addition, many other loosely-integrated zones exist in other regions of the world. If current trends continue, these will continue to cohere into larger groups, sharing the benefits of democracy, trade, the free flow of information, and political unity among their peoples.

GLOBAL PROBLEMS
NEED GLOBAL SOLUTIONS

As the nations of the world struggle with how to share their sovereignty, problems are emerging that transcend sovereignty and borders altogether. Infectious diseases, climate change, water resources, terrorism, human trafficking, drug trafficking, refugees, fair and free-flowing trade—all of these issues stretch across borders. As the international community works to respond to these developments, the problems continue to slip through the loose treaties and voluntary agreements they set up. We have an integrated world, yet many international agreements, treaties, and policies were developed for short-term or limited use, and lack necessary sophistication. As agencies and organizations attempt to mete out responsibility, there is a basic problem of deciding who will assume responsibility for each issue. If jurisdictions overlap, are competing groups duplicating each other's efforts or even negating them? Ann Florini, author of *The Coming Democracy*, describes the issue thus:

There is an increasing disjunction between the (transnational) problems to be solved and the (mostly national) systems and procedures available to solve them. And to the extent that transnational and multinational systems are emerging. . . . these systems are not directly accountable to the people whose lives they affect. No constituency elects international organizations, multinational corporations, or nongovernmental activists. Moreover, those new systems are often organized as though the issues on the global agenda could be resolved separately.[22]

Florini proposes seven options for the future of world governance. In broad strokes, these are the options for the world's nations in the coming decades. One is to adjust polices to reflect a period before globalization, when countries were isolated from one another with no free trade to speak of. This protectionist and xenophobic tendency is consistently advocated by some politicians in every country. It might be a plausible scenario for the resource-rich United States, but most countries would not be able to survive. Poverty rates worldwide would skyrocket. And the irony is that such a period of impermeable borders has never truly existed; humankind has been trading and communicating across oceans and continents for many centuries.

A second option Florini proposes is to rely exclusively on the demands of the market to shape the future. However, this brings up the *collective action problem* because most people are tempted to coast on the contributions of others unless they are forced to pay for something (e.g., taxes). An exclusive market approach would also mean that public goods would be difficult to raise money for—why should I pay for someone else's roads or education? The market works in specific ways, not as a be-all end-all solution. A third potential path of governance is to rely on one country to take care of the rest—the umbrella of the United States, most likely. While the United States has played this role on many issues, it leaves other countries dependent on the whims of voters half a world away. Can developing nations depend on the United States to send aid and development packages when needed? American voters would naturally rather spend their money on issues closer to home. At any rate, there is only so much any one nation can do single-handedly.

A fourth option is simple coercion—each country forcing its citizens to obey a nationalized agenda. But the most coercive states, with little democratic input, do not perform well and do not foster economic growth—look at North Korea. A fifth option is simply to preserve the status quo. This leaves us reliant on treaties and voluntary cooperation, which may have worked in the past and might work for a time, but are bound to be more successful with some issues than with others and could disintegrate when any large, unforeseen problem comes up.

Throughout history, some people have argued for a single world-spanning government. This is the sixth option proposed by Florini. In the thirteenth century, Dante wrote, "Among all the things ordained for our happiness, the greatest is universal peace. ... To achieve this state of universal good, a single world government is necessary."[23] In the 1960s, the Catholic Church's groundbreaking Second Vatican Council advanced the proposal that "a universally recognized world authority should be established, possessing adequate power and authority to assure the protection and safety of all, guaranteeing justice and the observation of human rights."[24] In 1837 the famous British poet laureate Alfred Tennyson wrote "Locksley Hall," in which he envisioned war drums beating no longer thanks to the "Parliament of man, the Federation of the world."[25]

The concept of world government has an appealing logic. Even Albert Einstein proposed the idea as the only solution to tame nuclear weapons. As he put it, "There is only one path to peace and security: the path of supra-national organization."[26] It seems like a natural outgrowth of current trends, and its implementation seems temptingly efficient. In his book *Nonzero*, Robert Wright optimistically states, "In 1500 B.C., there were around 600,000 autonomous polities on the planet. Today, after many mergers and acquisitions, there are 193 autonomous polities. At this rate, the planet should have a single government any day now."[27]

Unfortunately, today a single world government is at best drastically premature. Skeptics are right to be scared of the potential for abuse. An autocracy, by definition, is unlimited power placed in the hands of a single person, so to avoid this fate, dispersing power among many people is necessary. As Gregory Dahl, author of *One World, One People*, explains, "A democratically constituted multi-institution government is generally regarded as the best defense against totalitarianism for any nation. Why should it not be for the world?"[28]

The dispersion of power in a new world government can be achieved through *federalism*—the seventh option proposed by Florini and our best hope for a peaceful world. An important early advocate of global federalism was Immanuel Kant, who argued that peace could be achieved if self-governing republics linked by commerce replaced monarchies. He explained that monarchs (or dictators) don't mind launching wars because they simply do not care about the welfare of their people, only their own. And war doesn't require sacrifice of their mansions and gold. The public is more reluctant to fight since they're the ones who have to do the fighting. Kant envisioned a "Federation of Free States" 150 years before the UN was launched. He noted that "A federation of this sort would not be the same thing as an international state," meaning that countries would still retain most of their independence.[29]

FEDERATION OF THE WORLD

The simplest definition of federalism is a unified organization that distributes control between local units and a central authority. It's one of the best ways to harness democracy. So federalism could refer to the United States' federal government and its 50 states, or it could refer to one of those states and the counties within it, or it could refer to the world's nations uniting under an overarching political organization. While the word "federalism" has political connotations—in the United States, "federalist" traditionally referred to people who supported a strong central government, but recently is associated with the opposite—for the purposes of this chapter I am using the term in its broadest sense to refer to any organization with a federalist structure, no matter how weak or strong.

If the goal of any governance is, as Florini describes, to solve "dilemmas of collective action in just and legitimate ways," then we can easily understand that different types of government are necessary to solve different collective issues.[30] Local governments know best how to handle local problems. National governments can best understand issues that stretch across an entire country. A federation integrates these different levels of government into one structure. The give and take between different levels of government is one of the longest-running stories of political theory, and since the end of World War II this debate has extended to the struggle between nationalism and internationalism.

Governance tends to expand to the size required to solve critical problems.[31] Integrated governance has often emerged in response to an external threat—such as the American colonies banding together to fight Britain, or the Allies and the United States working together to battle the Axis powers. Solving these needs, and planning to prevent their repetition in the future, led to larger organizations—in these examples, the United States, and the UN and NATO. Similarly, global federalism is the only solution to today's daunting world-spanning problems such as pollution, scarce resources, disease, and terrorism. Liberalizing trade, which we will examine soon, is also one of the many benefits of a more closely integrated world governance system. To advance peace, our goal should be a democratic global federation in which control is distributed between local units, such as individual nations, and a central authority. In many ways, the European Union is an excellent model to follow, although it still has no true military or right to levy taxes—key government rights. A global federation should grow like the federal government of the United States—slowly and with constant checks, balances, and debates. An essential way to make sure it builds smoothly is the principle of *subsidiarity*, which means to always err on the side of local institutions when distributing power. Power should only be granted to global institutions when dealing with global issues. Ideally, the government should be kept as close as possible to the people it serves.

To rein in the potential abuse of a global federated system, power needs to be dispersed to as many hands as possible. Democracy is a great way of fairly dispersing power because it is only through the democratic process that candidates compete for the votes of the people they serve. Despite its idealistic merits, a savvy politician could still get voted into office and then simply change the law to make sure he never steps down. The founders of the United States

understood the potential dangers of this system better than anyone. To minimize transgressions of absolute power, the founders of the United States also
decided to disperse power with competing branches of government. As a result,
they established our classic division of power between the executive, legisla-
tive, and judicial branches. The United States also harnessed the final fail-safe
of federalism by creating competing layers of government. Each state competes
with the federal government over jurisdiction, and local governments compete against both the state government and the federal government. Each level
has checks and balances among its branches, making absolute power almost
impossible for one group to grab.

The United States is the world's longest-running federated government,
and its federalist concepts have spread around the globe. The Articles of Con-
federation, ratified by the states in 1781, called for a union between the American colonies. How different would our history be if this temporary agreement
had not been replaced by a permanent constitution? What if the colonies had
banded together to free themselves from England's rule and then gone their
separate ways? Surely those states would not hold as much sway in the world
today as the United States does. One civil war would have been traded for several, if not dozens, of bloody skirmishes—with some even using twentieth-
century weapons. And without the liberalizing trade we now take for granted,
the overall wealth of the continent would be greatly diminished. In short, the
history of this country might have looked more like the history of European
nations and colonies, in which different sovereignties vied for resources and
power instead of working together for trade and security. (We should note that
Europe's colonialism of centuries past was *not* federalism, since the local units
had not voluntarily chosen to be part of the whole. Also, an empire retained
more total control than in a standard federation. So the state had no legitimacy
in the eyes of the native population.)

Here's a profound example of the benefit of federalist thinking. The U.S.'s
competing intelligence and military agencies' inability to share information
contributed to their missing the ball on September 11th, 2001. The United States'
belated response to the disaster of 9/11 was federalism of a sort, since it highlight-
ed the need for an efficient organization with someone at the top to integrate all

of the incoming information and devise a plan to foster the nation's safety and security. Out of this disaster was born the Department of Homeland Security, which is designed to integrate the different government agencies and enable them to work together more efficiently. While some people see the emergence of this Department as the consolidation of too much power, and its results so far have been mixed, keeping competing agencies uninformed and therefore ineffective is clearly not the best way to create a safe and secure community.

Coordinating efforts between countries at a larger international level is necessary for global security. One of the most important problems for the world to address is the possibility of state collapse. All democratic countries should be eager to prevent other nations from falling into anarchy, since local problems can easily spill over borders to become international issues. Solving the problem of state collapse creates a cyclical positive feedback loop:

- It is in the best interest of the world community to prevent state failure.

- Democracies are much less prone to state failure than are autocratic regimes.

- The probability of a country's becoming democratic rises with its per capita income level.[32]

- Raising the incomes of the world's poorest citizens requires a united global effort and international cooperation, as we will discuss shortly.

- As states learn how to successfully enforce the rule of law, grow their economies, and build a thriving civil society, they become better equipped to join the world community and contribute to helping other countries.

Inviting floundering states, weak states, and even strong autocratic states into the process of trying to solve problems like that of state collapse incentivizes them to democratize, reform, and modernize. Working together to solve issues like state collapse, terrorism, and environmental destruction knits the international order closer together. As countries share stakes in the same institutions and solutions, their vested interests make conflict less likely. International global political unity is beneficial—and can best be achieved through federalism.[33]

But surprisingly, the whole world is already federated in hundreds of different ways. Intertwined international agencies control many global laws and regulations. Over 300 international treaties have been enacted through the efforts of the UN alone. These cover a wide variety of topics from seabeds to outer space.[34] Worldwide, law enforcement and intelligence agencies compile and share information to prosecute international terrorists, drug traffickers, and perpetrators of other organized crimes. Aviation, postal services, time zones, currency exchange, the Geneva conventions and rules of war, phone service, work visas and passports, technology standards, the Internet ... the number of ways in which the world is already working together is near infinite.

Since the end of World War II, when the benefit of collaborating to prevent another war became apparent to millions, several intergovernmental agencies have been created. Many of these agencies fall under the auspices of the UN. We can all picture the representatives of the world's nations sitting in an auditorium, debating issues of trade, governance, and peace. But this was far from the reality of governance that took place throughout most of history. We take for granted that worldwide organizations exist, when in reality they are quite new. The success of these international agencies has fostered a growing sense of legitimacy and confidence in international law. In this respect, global governance can mirror the European Union, which in 1950 was envisioned thus: "Europe will not be made all at once, or according to a single, general plan. It will be built through concrete achievements, which first create a de facto solidarity."[35]

But there's a downside. Unfortunately, because it lacks an overarching plan to unify its efforts, the system is loose and ad hoc, making it difficult to enforce treaties, easy to find loopholes, and hypocritical and counterproductive when a country's new leaders reverse agreements their predecessors signed. Today our system can best be described as loose global governance, not yet global government or true federalism. We need to start expanding the scope of this governance to address current global concerns.

REFORMING THE UN

The most palpable model we have for global governance is the United Nations. We see the public face of the UN in the news during contentious debates over military actions. The overall message relayed by the media is that the organization is completely ineffectual and that there is nothing it can do to stop its members from bickering. If this is the model for global governance, we're in deep trouble. But if we look beyond the media spotlight, we can see that the UN has many different branches. Despite its problems, the UN's various aid agencies and peacekeeping forces work tirelessly behind the scenes on many fronts. They are responsible for many of the improvements in the world we've been discussing in the past few chapters.

As one of the delegates to the 1945 UN Drafting Conference said, "The planet has become a unitary system. It can no longer be managed piecemeal by nations acting unilaterally. Unless Earth's life support systems and human affairs are managed in the common interest, disaster is certain."[36] The founders of the UN hoped that by establishing international organizations and creating a global forum, a world order would spontaneously emerge. They were right, but world order has not been the sole focus of the UN, and today's world order is far from effective in many arenas.

The UN was basically designed for a single purpose: to prevent another war among the "Great Powers." To that goal, it has succeeded. It has also succeeded in creating an international forum and scuttling isolationist tendencies. But its founders did not foresee the preponderance of people's wars or the rise of modern terrorism. Nor did they anticipate new worldwide problems such as environmental degradation. Today, the UN needs to adopt an approach better suited to the times we live in, but its hands are tied. The UN was intentionally created with only limited power. The five permanent Security Council members (the P5) were reluctant to give up too much of their sovereignty. This unwillingness to judiciously distribute power among the worldwide community was a missed opportunity, but at the time it was still a much better choice than having the United States (or any of the other four nations) back out as the U.S. had with the League of Nations.

Today we have the opportunity to reform the UN. The most critical change that needs to occur is the elimination of the Security Council veto; with it, each of the P5 members can paralyze the entire organization on any issue. This has often resulted in a delayed response to conflicts (or a complete unwillingness to address atrocities, as with Rwanda), and the inherent unfairness undermines the legitimacy of the UN in the eyes of its other member countries. There are ways to slowly phase the veto out; one possibility would be to limit its application to certain areas or to restrict its use to a limited number of times per year. But eventually the Security Council veto has to go. The opportunity is ripe; in previous decades the United States and the Soviet Union constantly blocked each other, but now the veto is used less frequently. A second essential reformation of the UN is the enlargement of the permanent seats on the Security Council. The *Economist* explains:

> The Great Powers of 1945 are no longer the great powers of today. Questions have to be asked why Britain, with its 60 million inhabitants, should have a veto and not India with its more than one billion, or why Japan, the world's second biggest economy, does not have a veto, though France, with an economy less than half the size, does? Why doesn't a single Arab or Muslim country have a permanent seat? The system is manifestly unfair and a source of huge resentment in the third world.[37]

Of course, any of these suggested modifications to the UN would require the approval of the very five countries who stand to lose some of their power. But of the countries whose constituents are accustomed to democracy, an outcry of public opinion could pressure their governments to capitulate.

Another important reform for the UN would be financial. Since its various agencies and organizations are chronically underfunded, revenue streams other than member state dues should be examined, and higher penalties should be put in place for members that do not pay their dues. With more money, the UN could invest in exploratory teams and early warning systems to work preventatively, rather than trying to resolve conflicts after they occur.

THE PRESENCE OF JUSTICE:
THE INTERNATIONAL CRIMINAL COURT

One of the obstacles holding the UN back is its lack of enforcement power. Civilization depends on the basic concept that the rule of law must dominate over the rule of force. The rule of law is the keystone to pacifying the world's few remaining anarchic countries such as Iraq and Afghanistan. To this end, democratic institutions are important because they legitimize the rule of law; people who have had a hand in making the law are more willing to follow it. The UN's members are making laws, treaties, and recommendations, but what happens when member states don't obey them? Not much. Sometimes sanctions are imposed, but the UN has only limited military force. However, there is more that international agencies can do to promote the law and establish order.

Rev. Dr. Martin Luther King, Jr. wrote, "True peace is not merely the absence of tension, it is the presence of justice."[38] To reaffirm the rule of law and emphasize accountability after severe conflicts, it's essential that courts and tribunals try war criminals. Fact-finding missions are a useful strategy for bringing wider recognition to the suffering of victims and for creating a historical record of atrocities. Such a record and its ability to shame perpetrators can contribute to healing the wounds of conflict through reconciliation and closure—essential tasks to help the community achieve a sense of closure and settle back into a "normal" society.[39]

The benefits of prosecuting criminals at a supranational level are becoming increasingly apparent. War criminals can now be tried more effectively thanks to the advent of international tribunals. The first example of an international trial was the Nuremberg trials after World War II. Because wars have changed increasingly to target civilians, charges of genocide, crimes against humanity, and dramatic human rights abuses demand justice. But only with the tribunals in Rwanda and the Balkans in the 1990s did the tribunal concept take off. Sierra Leone became one of the most notable successes. In 2002 the UN Security Council and the government of Sierra Leone set up a special court to try war criminals from its recent bloody civil war. Scores of town meetings were held around the country to investigate crimes and inform the people about the court, and 12 people deemed partially responsible for the war were indicted. Among the 12 was the president of Liberia, Charles Taylor. Partly due to events set in motion by the indictment, he was forced to step down, his government held a democratic election, and Taylor is now behind bars facing trial.[40] Another special UN tribunal was also just set up to try surviving members of Cambodia's Khmer Rouge regime.[41]

In 2002, inspired by the successful outcome of special courts seeking justice for criminal behavior, 66 countries (not including the United States) ratified a Rome treaty to bring into effect the official International Criminal Court. The treaty was created in 1998, with officials believing it might take up to 20 years to ratify; it only took four. The International Criminal Court replaces the ad hoc tribunals and brings them under one jurisdiction. That jurisdiction only applies when countries are unwilling or unable to prosecute individuals accused of the worst war crimes—crimes that cross international borders or those too heinous for one country to handle. Cases can be referred by any signatory to the treaty or by the UN Security Council.[42] The flaws in the current international justice system are apparent—look at the slow speed of Slobodan Milosevic's trial—but these are early mistakes that will be straightened out with more experience. Saddam Hussein's trial went faster; even though it was not technically international, it had the same goal of prosecuting war crimes. The International Criminal Court offers a relatively new approach for quelling injustice and is therefore less honed in its experience and skill than peacekeeping and nonviolent revolutions as a resolution of conflict, but the court will surely develop in the future as it gains experience and legitimacy. The court is currently investigating cases in Uganda, the Democratic Republic of Congo, Central African Republic, and Darfur, Sudan. By seeking to indict Sudan's president, Omar al-Bashir, for genocide, the court has gone after a sitting head of state for the first time. And the number of ratifying countries has now expanded from 66 to 107. [43]

Angelina Jolie, as goodwill ambassador for the United Nations High Commissioner for Refugees, has seen the effects of the new court firsthand:

Make no mistake, the existence of these trials alone changes behavior. Seeing the indictment of Thomas Lubanga and the detention of Germain Katanga by the ICC brought to mind a trip I had taken to Congo five years ago. In the Ituri region, where Mr. Katanga's reign of terror had been most intense, our group attended a meeting of rebel leaders. They had gathered in a field to discuss the prospects for a peace agreement—which were not looking very good. The conversation turned hostile and the situation grew extremely tense. At that point, one of my colleagues asked for the name of one of the rebels, announcing, perhaps a bit recklessly, that he was going to pass it along to the ICC. It was remarkable: this rebel leader's whole posture changed from aggression to conciliation. The ICC had been around for only five months. It had tried no one. Yet its very existence was enough to intimidate a man who had been terrorizing the population for years.[44]

Universal jurisdiction is an additional supranational approach to resolving injustice. More than 100 countries now have some version of universal jurisdiction, which facilitates prosecution of war criminals by a country no matter where the crimes were committed. Spain's attempt to prosecute former Chilean dictator Augusto Pinochet for human rights abuses is a good example. While Pinochet's age and illness prevented him from standing trial, he spent the last decade of his life on the run from humiliating accusations—an ignoble end. If it becomes well-implemented, universal jurisdiction will serve as another example of a breakdown in the strict separation of national sovereignties.[45]

The International Criminal Court and universal jurisdiction examine corruption and abuse after they occur. But with the concept of sovereignty dissolving, we have increasing opportunity to stop abuse as soon as it happens. Rulers have a responsibility to nurture and protect their citizens. When they don't act in the best interests of their citizens, it is now possible for the world community to intervene on the people's behalf. Violating sovereignty is no longer a valid excuse to let major human rights abuses occur around the world.

As the *Economist* puts it, "So these are uncomfortable times for tyrants, past or present. They used to be able to escape justice through brutality at home, or if that failed, fleeing abroad. Now justice's arms are looking longer and more muscular." It added, "Many a highly placed thug, it is hoped, is beginning to sleep less easily at night."[46]

THE SPREAD OF STRONG DEMOCRACIES

The world defeated fascism in the 1940s, and communism in Eastern Europe fell in the 1990s. Both of those political models feature the same authoritarian tendencies at opposite ends of the political spectrum. Fundamentalism, another threatening movement of the far right, has now risen in power, most notably in Iran and the Middle East. But today's autocratic states, for all the misery they inflict, are pale imitations of the horrible regimes that used to exist. The few remaining authoritarian leaders fear the rumbling democratic aspirations of their people. They even pay lip service to democratic ideals for fear that their fed-up citizens may storm through the palace gates holding up flowers in some sort of Mauve or Begonia Revolution. Thomas Jefferson, in some of the most brilliant and oft-quoted words ever written, said:

> We hold these truths to be self-evident, that all men are created equal, that they are endowed by their Creator with certain unalienable Rights, that among these are Life, Liberty and the pursuit of Happiness. ... That whenever any Form of Government becomes destructive of these ends, it is the Right of the People to alter or to abolish it, and to institute new Government.[47]

Thus modern democracy was born. The American and French Revolutions showed the world that sovereignty ultimately rests in the hands of citizens, not monarchs—a sentiment echoed in the collapse of the Berlin Wall. Democracy means more than having elections. It means allowing change and creativity, as opposed to inflexibility; as Yale University Professor John Lewis Gaddis describes, "The totalitarian tyrannies of the twentieth century collapsed because their single solutions promised liberty but failed to provide it. Democracies survived and spread because they allowed experimenting with multiple solutions."[48] Democracy also means having media freedom, freedom of speech, and freedom of assembly. It includes mechanisms to hold the power of rulers in check and to remove them from power if abuse arises. So the basic functioning of democracy implies three essential rights: the inherent right of all citizens to voice their opinions, the right to elect their leaders, and the right to hold those leaders responsible for their actions.

Any global model of federalism must be democratic in nature. The current trend worldwide is toward a global appreciation of democratic ideals and principles. In 1971 there were only 30 electoral democracies in the world. In 1987 that number had grown to 66 electoral democracies, and by 2005 there were 122 (out of 193 countries). Put another way, in 1900 only 12.4 percent of the world's peoples enjoyed democracy, and even that was limited, and without universal suffrage. By 2005, 44 percent of the world had gained full democracy while another 18.6 percent lived under partial democracy.[49] For the first time in history, a majority of people live in countries governed by democratic ideals. Much of the remaining percentage of the world that is not "fully free" is at least "partly free," meaning that their democracies are not yet fully mature. Perhaps there is only one political party, or elections aren't yet fair, or the media is restricted. These are considered weaker democracies. For example, China, while authoritarian, has stronger democratic institutions than, say, North Korea does.

Let's take a look at Africa, where democracy is also quickly taking root. Today the continent embodies the exciting fits and starts of growing democracies. Since 1990, 42 of the 48 countries in sub-Saharan Africa have held multiparty elections deemed to be mostly fair. Many of these countries are marred by some corruption, and some fledgling democracies depend on the West for food and development aid even to cover the costs of basic government budgetary items, including the elections themselves. But as the *New York Times* states, "The development of flawed democracies is still considered progress to people carrying the physical and mental scars left by authoritarian regimes." Mr. Lamine Jusu Jarka, for example, was exhilarated to be voting in Sierra Leone, where, in 1999, his hands were cut off in a rebel attack. He voted by stamping the ballot sheet with an ink-stained toe, saying, "This morning, I am voting for the future."[50]

The rush to embrace democracy in the early 1990s was so dramatic that it has been called Africa's "second independence." We can see the results clearly. In the nineteenth century and all the way into World War II, Europe had divided Africa into colonies it controlled and often exploited. In 1936, for example, there were only four independent countries in Africa: South Africa and Southwest Africa (still under British control anyway), Egypt, and tiny Liberia. There were no democracies on the continent. After World War II, Africa violently shook off its colonial rulers (its "first independence") until every inch of the continent was part of an independent country. Of those new independent countries, most were multiparty democracies by 2002, as illustrated by the countries colored solid black in Figure 12.[51]

FIGURE 12: THE TREND TOWARD DEMOCRACY IN AFRICA

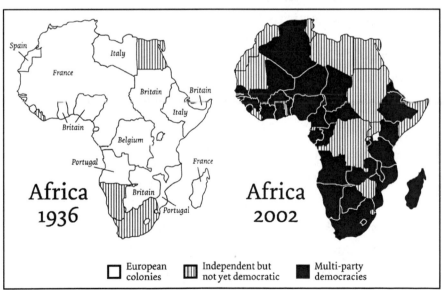

Fledgling democracies are sometimes worse than the autocrats they displace—more chaotic, certainly. The Russian people, for example, suffered through several impoverished and uncertain years of democracy and decided to retreat to the "safety" of a form of authoritarianism. But more and more countries that adopt democratic policies are sticking with it. It can take time to grow a democracy into what is known as a strong democracy. Strong democracies are particularly difficult to grow in poor countries just being introduced to the democratic process. They face daunting pressure to adopt Western-style democracy and to grow quickly so as to attract investment. This isn't quite fair, since democracy in the United States and Europe took centuries to evolve into the forms of governance we know today. Even though there isn't a country in the world that couldn't improve its democratic process in some way, there is still a cavernous gap between Sweden's type of democracy and Iran's. What makes some democracies stronger than others?

- An effective system of checks and balances is something that gets stronger with time, as precedents and traditions build up. Without checks in place, you could elect someone that then just stays in power. In a country with a strong functioning rule of law, everyone is held accountable for their sins, even (especially) the people in charge.

- Universal suffrage is a must for a strong democracy. This is one area in which most democracies are doing quite well. Only a handful of democracies still deny women the right to vote, and while there are subtle ways to discriminate against voters by race, this is rarely institutionalized. The United States demonstrates the trend of equal voting rights: originally, only white male landowners could vote, then in 1856 all white males were granted the right to vote. In 1870, blacks and other minorities were included. Fifty years later women were finally given the vote, and as of 1971, 18-20-year-olds can vote, too. (Incidentally, the first women's suffrage in the United States was granted accidentally in New Jersey in 1776. The word "people" had been entered in the lawbooks instead of "men." But the law was rescinded in 1807.)[52]

- Multiple political parties are also necessary for the establishment of strong democracies. The existence of multiple political parties helps to create balance, minimizing the possibility of one party's overwhelmingly dominating the political stage. The United States lacks diversity in this area, since it has only two significant parties. Most European countries have more.

- The less corruption and backroom lobbying taking place among politicians, the stronger the democracy.

- Many government jobs in democratic countries are appointed—necessary since voters can't vote on every single employee of the government. But for the most part, the more elected officials a country has, the broader its democracy. This is even evident on a large scale: for example, members of the EU's European Parliament are directly elected by European citizens.

- Another feature of a strong democracy is the use of referenda in which citizens vote directly on issues and bills rather than voting for representatives. This is often used in Switzerland, and in the United States at the state and local levels, notably California. There's a radical movement in California right now called Repair California, that looks to use ballot initiatives to completely overhaul California's government (which can use all the help it can get.) Repair California hopes to get an initiative on the ballot soon that would allow a constitutional convention to be called. That convention, attended by randomly chosen citizens who were given time and resources to research all the issues, would propose a new structure of government for California that the citizens could then vote up or down in a later ballot initiative.[53]

  A similar concept of truly direct democracy first existed in Athens, a city small enough to have direct citizen involvement. On a larger scale, it's difficult to pull off, since it slows down the government and requires a well-educated populace. (People tend to want to pass every spending measure, yet they want lower taxes, which doesn't always add up.) But thanks to communication technology such as the Internet, the effective use of referenda has much more potential as an effective democratic tool.

- Democratic elections typically fall within a wide range of effectiveness, from completely fair to just for show. Proportional representation is more fair than "First past the post" elections, meaning it's better for people to get a share of power based on how many votes they receive than to have a single winner-takes-all no matter how thin his margin. To be more effective, the United States should move toward a system of proportional representation and eliminate the electoral college system, which allows someone with fewer total votes to become President, as George W. Bush in 2000 and Benjamin Harrison in 1888 both did.

- A "clean election" system allows candidates who receive a certain number of small, qualifying contributions to get public financing for their campaigns, provided that the candidate does not take private donations. Such systems provide a fixed amount of financing from the government, but if a rival outspends them, the government will match a higher figure. With no private donors to cater to, clean elections offer fewer opportunities for corruption and for favors after a win. The effect is to encourage candidates to lobby all citizens equally rather than focus on rich donors, making each vote as important as any other. Many states have passed initiatives in this direction, especially Maine and Arizona.

- Equal air time on TV and radio for all candidates is good for democracy as well. Because the current U.S. system is based on paid commercials, those who can afford to pay the most get the most advertising time. The idea of equal air time goes along with public financing of elections.

- Fair, nonpartisan election officials and administrators are also necessary.[54]

All of the above democratic ideas are on the rise worldwide. Hardly a day passes without some nugget of news about increasing democracy in a far-flung country. In the summer of 2008 alone, there are at least five examples. The Himalayan kingdom of Bhutan had a century of royal rule, but they just held elections for the first time. Their King, Jigme Singye Wangchuck, voluntarily abdicated and declared the country a constitutional monarchy, with a popularly elected parliament. Most Bhutanese like their king, but he simply explained that no nation should be in the hands of one person, and that the changeover should happen while the country is peaceful. The tiny island nation of Tonga is having a similar experience, with their king due to forfeit most of his powers to Parliament by 2010. Turkmenistan's infamous dictator, Saparmurat Niyazov, died in 2007 and the new ruler has been slowly but surely dismantling the cult of personality around the former ruler. A giant, rotating, gold-plated statue of Niyazov has been removed from the capital, the names of the months have been restored after Niyazov named them after himself and his mother, Internet access is increasingly allowed, and the ban on car radios might even be lifted (Niyazov banned them because they annoyed him.)

Even Cuba, long held tightly in the hands of Fidel Castro, has been slowly allowing freedoms under their new ruler, Fidel's brother Raúl. "Socialism means social justice and equality, but equality of rights, of opportunities, not of income," he announced in 2008, dramatically reversing his brother's philosophy. Ordinary Cubans can now own mobile phones, televisions, and computers for the first time, and farmers can decide for themselves what to plant. Lastly, the 2008 Summer Olympics spotlighted China's worst anti-democratic impulses, such as its stifling of dissent, but a recent *New York Times* headline reported that "Despite flaws, rights in China have expanded." China is a significantly more open place than it was a generation ago, with its citizens able to choose where to live, own some property, travel abroad, and gain access to technology.[55]

TRANSPARENCY IS THE KEY

New ideas keep popping up to make elections fairer and to facilitate interaction between citizens and their governments. Above all, to make democracies strong, the electoral process and all elected officials must display honest and transparent practices to their citizens. Facilitating universal voting rights, ensuring that elections are fair, and running multiple political parties in every election—these are the crux of democracy. But there is no point in having elections if the voters don't know how they'll be represented once their candidates are elected. That's why shared information is essential to democracy. Voters need to learn about who it is they are electing and what those representatives will be voting for on their behalf. And that leads into the second part of the democratic process: the ability to hold leaders accountable. To do so requires a free flow of information as well.

The key to global democracy and increasing federalist integration is transparency. Transparency is the core of Florini's argument for democracy and global problem-solving. Transparency refers to the free flow of information—the opposite of secrecy. It means deliberately revealing your actions, decision-making process, opinions, and policies so that others can evaluate them. If citizens and the press get all the knowledge they need, they can make informed decisions at the voting booths and corruption can be brought to light. The principal-agent problem will always exist: citizens (principals) elect representatives (agents) to work for them—passing laws, enforcing laws, making decisions, all the things that governments do. But citizens need to be able to ensure that their agents are working with the people's best interests at heart. And we cannot forget that the world's peoples are the true principals for intergovernmental organizations like the UN, too. Overall, transparency can be a huge advantage that democracies hold over less-free governments. Autocracies have a top-down, closed structure that hinders the free flow of information, and in fact, often intentionally distorts it. There is censorship and no open debates about policies. Since the free flow of knowledge, compounding on itself, is what drives the secret peace, it's easy to see that autocracies are inherently limited in how far they can advance.[56]

Thanks to technology, transparency is improving quickly in both the government and business arenas. It is harder for governments to get away with human rights abuses when their actions can be documented by any citizen with firsthand accounts and photographs which can be posted online for all the world to see. For example, Amnesty International has a Crisis Prevention and Response Center that uses satellite photos to compare before-and-after images of villages in Darfur that have been attacked and burned, which contradict the official Sudanese government's stories.[57] China was recently shocked to discover that its secret Communist Party buildings are viewable on Google Earth's satellite map, accessible to anyone who is online. Much to the dismay of China's leaders, transparency is the obvious foil to a 1984-style government. In George

Orwell's dystopian novel 1984, citizens were unable to investigate the truth for themselves—they only knew what the government told them, and they even believed Big Brother if he claimed two plus two was five. In the novel, the government didn't have any transparency whatsoever; it was a perfectly opaque system. Today that is much more difficult to achieve.

The popularity of transparency is increasing faster than true reforms are being implemented, but reforms are on the rise nonetheless. Nobel Prize-winning economist Joseph Stiglitz, who emphasizes the role of transparency in international economic institutions, says:

> Secrecy also undermines democracy. There can be democratic accountability only if those to whom these public institutions are supposed to be accountable are well informed about what they are doing—including what choices they confronted and how those decisions were made. ... Modern democracies have come to recognize the citizens' basic *right to know*, implemented through laws such as America's Freedom of Information Act.[58]

A few decades ago, only the United States and a few other countries (mostly in Scandinavia) had laws like the Freedom of Information Act. But by the year 2000, over 40 countries had freedom of information provisions in place or under debate. Many of these new laws are not robust or well-implemented, but public access to information is improving.[59] As Jefferson said, an educated public is essential to democracy—and the public has the right to information that used to be hidden.

While democracies should always err on the side of transparency, there are a few obvious exceptions—for example, certain aspects of military operations and undercover police work need to be kept secret for obvious reasons. But it should be up to the public to decide what specific areas of information should be kept under wraps, rather than let the government keep every fact they don't like hidden away in filing cabinets. Surprisingly, as Florini writes, "The norm of transparency has spread widely in a field where it seems most unlikely: military security. The world's major military powers, and many of the minor ones, have enmeshed themselves in a web of agreements to disclose an astonishing level of details about their military capabilities and practices."[60] This includes inspections to ensure adherence to chemical, biological and nuclear weapons treaties. Governments as well as corporations are finding that a high level of transparency is becoming necessary to attract foreign investment.

Florini writes, "Corporations that refuse to disclose detailed information about their labor practices find that secrecy leads to a presumption of guilt in the court of public opinion."[61] Countries now pour out information on their own Web sites as well as to the press, both domestically and internationally. They are voluntarily starting to sign the UN's Global Compact Agreement, which holds them accountable to nine principles of operation in the fields of labor, human rights, and the environment. The companies act in the belief that the UN's stamp of approval will enhance their public standing. Other types of certification are popping up as well, all to reassure consumers and investors that they are making sound choices. Certification should continue to grow in many other fields as a guide for people to sort through the sea of new information floating around.

Even simply releasing information about an organization's operations, without any specific standards to meet, can be helpful to the communities it serves. Several countries grade companies on environmental standards. For example, the United States requires companies to report emissions to the Environmental Protection Agency and then compiles that information into a list that is made available to the public. The United Kingdom also releases lists of chemicals given off by companies, and Indonesia has begun its own system of grading companies. The desire to move up on the lists and avoid negative publicity has successfully encouraged businesses to clean up their acts. Some CEOs are increasingly implementing transparent business practices. By encouraging employees and consumers to freely comment on their businesses online, they become working partners with their customers.[62] Consumer groups and international organizations also post many informal evaluations online. Ideally, transparency is enacted voluntarily, although this is often not the case. Increasing accountability goes beyond punishing people after the fact, by providing motivation to prevent abuses before they take place: with the threat of exposure hanging over them, elected officials and corporations often rein in their own exploitative plans.

A free flow of information will engage more citizens as they see how issues might personally affect them. Only an eagerly participating and well-informed electorate can make true democracy work. With a larger electorate, a greater diversity of perspectives will be able to join in on the discussion of any issue. And with broader participation, laws and policies will have greater legitimacy, increasing their effectiveness as people become more willing to follow rules they feel are fair.

THE RISING POWER OF NON-STATE ACTORS

Through the process of democracy, power is spreading away from governments and into the open arms of individuals. We can accidentally abuse that power if we don't have sufficient knowledge of the potential repercussions of our actions. As ordinary people gain power, we are quickly and eagerly arranging ourselves into new, unique, creative, multiple groups, called non-state actors. All those groups need to be informed, and all deserve a voice: ways to make their views officially heard, and representation in decision-making. Consent to be governed must now come from an ever-widening circle of people affected by those in power. These new groups, in their turn, must also become transparent and cooperate civilly.

Non-state actors are simply anyone who's not part of a government: experts and scientists, the media, corporations, intergovernmental organizations (IGOs) like the UN and NATO, religious groups, universities, charities and foundations, entertainers, even Internet groups. Terrorists are also considered non-state actors. The fastest growing groups are nongovernmental organizations (NGOs). NGO is a broad term that generally refers to groups of concerned citizens lobbying for a social or political cause, such as environmental groups. One of the largest NGOs is the International Red Cross (and Red Crescent, which serves Muslim countries). The concerned citizens who work and volunteer for these groups add them to their identities in the style of the circular charts we looked at earlier in the book. So someone can simultaneously hold allegiance to a nation while advocating for global issues that cross national borders, and work with a network of people spread across several countries. NGOs allow citizens to be involved in global policies that affect not just their own nations, but everyone worldwide. The political scientist Samuel Huntington writes, "Global politics is, in a sense, coming to have the pluralism and diversity typical of politics in democratic countries."[63]

Connecting with other citizens is something that happens naturally. The term "social capital" refers to the levels of trust and goodwill within a society. It is the glue that holds society together—the informal part, outside of laws and police enforcement. When you trust your neighbor to return the snowblower he borrowed, when you join a church group or become a Little League soccer coach, when you wait in line politely at the bank, social capital is at play. This is the natural partner of democracy. The two reinforce each other. The informal level of trust we build with our neighbors carries over to the formal standards we expect from our politicians. Without this casual form of organization, voters would not be able to share views to educate each other, nor would they be able to team up to push for certain changes from the government. Social capital is what Meetup works to build, by gathering people together and reminding us how easy it is to work with, learn from, and hang out with our neighbors.

The United States has particularly strong social capital. Our country has always been known for an extraordinary number of organizations, clubs, charities, sports, after-school activities, political activists, and religious groups. Today, many of these groups are no longer content to work at the local level, but strive to influence events nationally and internationally. They need a voice to do so. NGOs are incredibly successful at harnessing the grassroots skills of their members and have triumphed in securing seats at the table of world affairs for millions of concerned citizens. They effectively build social systems by focusing on local initiatives and taking advantage of the expertise and diligence of their members. Because there are so many NGOs and they each address specific causes, they can bring new issues to light and force them into the public consciousness and mainstream press. With NGOs working in these ways, political abuses or looming social problems are less likely to slip under the radar.

One drawback to the growth of NGOs is the lunatic fringe—an effort must be made to verify the credentials of organizations and their leaders. And of course only NGOs with relevant agendas should participate in certain venues—environmental groups should not lead an international conference on fighting terrorism, for example. While civil society is becoming increasingly successful at making itself heard, it still needs a forum to participate in environmental and labor treaties, in trade deals, at the UN, and in any decision that drastically affects a group's members.

International corporations are also becoming increasingly powerful, and their power must be balanced. They should have direct representation at international forums to offset behind-the-scene government lobbying. Companies need to be transparent, and NGOs should be able to rein them in if their decisions affect underrepresented peoples of the world. In the corporate realm, almost unanimously, companies have very idealistic mission statements (Google's is, "Don't be evil"), and while some are very broad and filled with rhetoric, after years of reiteration, employees start to want to follow them. Companies already have some accountability to their consumers, but consumers can tolerate a lot of abuse before complaining. Consumer pressure is only effective in certain circumstances—branded companies like Starbucks and Nike are especially vulnerable, since their reputations with customers are very closely connected to their profit margins.[64] Public companies are beholden to their shareholders and boards of directors, but again, transparency is necessary for this to be useful as a check. One reassuring trend is social investing—choosing a portfolio based on company practices, such as a company's record of low environmental impact.

Non-state actors have a lot to offer. Diverse viewpoints provide a wider range of suggestions, with a much greater chance of finding an ideal solution. Technical experts in every arena should be on hand to correct mistakes and misperceptions by politicians and inexperienced debaters. For maximum transparency, all governance meetings could be broadcast live on TV or online. Then Internet bloggers could give real-time commentary, translations, and synopses. Many NGOs see themselves as battling against corporations and/or governments. But we all live in the same world; we all have a vested interest in peace. With increased participation, NGO members could feel less disenfran-chised and could begin to view themselves as working *with* governments and corporations rather than against them.[65]

The issues of increased transparency and the participation of non-state actors often arise in relation to the world's leading economic organizations—the International Monetary Fund (IMF), the World Trade Organization (WTO), and the World Bank. Like the UN, these organizations are three times removed from the individual at the grassroots. we elect government representatives, who then choose economists and diplomats, who then meet with these three IGOs to make decisions. The secrecy of these groups has infuriated concerned citi-zens, sparking protests at every WTO and IMF meeting. Florini writes, "Achiev-ing the degree of transparency needed for informed widespread participation in the debate over economic globalization will be no easy task, but it is clearly possible. And it is essential. Secretive decisions by small groups of elites cannot and should not continue."[66] Once these organizations are reformed to be more democratic, they could be powerful tools for humanity's next great challenge: eliminating poverty.

ECONOMICS

Ending Poverty Forever

The remarkable reduction of the world's extreme poverty is one of the most dramatic—and surprising—trends leading toward peace. There is a proven path out of poverty, and two examples illustrate it perfectly. Korea and Vietnam share the dubious distinction of being the targets of the United States' worst military conflicts since World War II. Though Korea and Vietnam are more than two thousand miles apart and have very different cultures, parts of their recent histories are strikingly similar. After World War II, both countries remained occupied against their wills. Then, around the same time, they each became embroiled in conflicts that were simultaneously civil wars and proxy battles between the United States and the Soviet Union. Korea and Vietnam each supported Communist forces in their northern halves supported intermittently by Communist Russia or Communist China. They each had southern forces supported by the United States and its allies, who were attempting to block the spread of Communism. Both wars were waged as opposing sides vied for control of the country's central parallel. Although each country began its conflict under very different circumstances, each ended a vast war—Korea in 1953 and Vietnam in 1975—with hundreds of thousands of casualties, an impoverished citizenry, and a devastated countryside.

Here their histories diverge. North Korea's Communist forces were unable to conquer the southern half of the country and were only able to maintain control of the northern half of the peninsula. North Korea became isolated, and for 50 years it carried out a countrywide experiment in pure communism and totalitarianism. Today North Korea faces economic collapse and is more cut off from global civilization than perhaps any other nation. Its people exist in a semifeudal society: hungry, destitute, and scared of being shipped off to labor camps for any dissent. In fact, one in 40 North Korean citizens have spent time in the gulag. Every year many North Koreans risk death as they attempt to escape by crossing the heavily armed border. In the 1990s, a massive famine due to the regime's neglect killed between 600,000 and one million people, and food shortages remain chronic. Only top-level Communist Party bosses enjoy luxuries like cars and foreign food. What little wealth their leader Kim Jong-il amasses gets diverted into outdated military forces and giant, solipsistic statues. Fifty years ago, South Korea was less developed than the industrial Northern part of the peninsula. But today, if you look at satellite shots of the earth at night, North Korea remains dark next to the shining electric wealth of South Korea (which has the highest penetration of broadband Internet on Earth), Japan, China, and much of the rest of the globe. At $1,118, or about $3 a day, North Koreans have a GDP per person that is 20 times lower than South Koreans. North Korea remains a pariah, and its desperate attempt to horde nuclear weapons reveals its weakness: it has no other power or influence in the world beyond its military threats. It relies on energy from China and aid from South Korea. In terms of its economy, the health of its citizens, and its reputation in the world, North Korea is one of the most failed states in modern history.[1]

In contrast to the situation in North Korea, North Vietnam's communist forces seized control of the entire country. Vietnam united under communism, and the United States, having suffered a terrible loss, expected the worst. Vietnam seemed destined to follow in North Korea's footsteps. True to form,

Vietnam played the role of a strict communist state for a decade. But then something strange started happening. In the mid-1980s, facing potential famine, the Vietnamese government had a change of heart. It started enacting market reforms under a policy called *doi moi* (renovation). It abandoned its attempt to collectivize industry and agriculture, and slowly began to allow free-market enterprise. Foreign firms were invited into the country to open new factories and provide employment. Private ownership became acceptable. The changes didn't translate into political freedoms; they focused only on the economy. Nevertheless, the people of Vietnam saw their standard of living start to improve. Life expectancy went up, and infant mortality rates went down. The number of Vietnamese living in extreme poverty dropped from 50 percent in 1990 to a scant 10 percent in 2003. The United States restored trade relations with Vietnam in 1994, and in 2006 removed it from a blacklist of countries that suppressed religious freedom. Today Vietnam is engaged with the world community, participating in international law and encouraging tourism, and has a relatively free press. To complete the metamorphosis, Vietnam's leaders recently unveiled a plan to establish the country as a fully modern, high-tech nation by 2020.[2]

Every day, totalitarian isolationist North Korea is looking more like an anachronistic aberration. Meanwhile, different versions of Vietnam's success story are manifesting all over the world.

THE DECLINE OF EXTREME POVERTY

Gross world product (GWP), the sum of all finished goods and services made everywhere, has been climbing at an average three to four percent for 30 years. It reached an astonishing $59.6 trillion in 2005.[3] The first few years of the twenty-first century have seen the fastest growth in world income in recorded history, even after taking into account the latest stock market and housing woes.[4] The creation of amazing wealth in the past two centuries, particularly during the last half-century, is one of the strongest trends toward peace. As shown in Figure 13, this amazing trend can be summed up in five words: World poverty is declining—fast.[5]

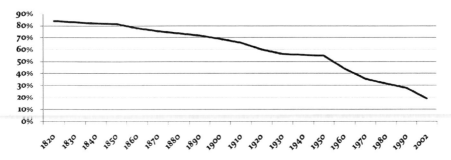

FIGURE 13: PERCENTAGE OF WORLD POPULATION
IN EXTREME POVERTY, 1820–2002

For thousands of years, until as recently as the eighteenth century, practically all of humanity lived equally in poverty. For example, Japan and Africa had the same small gross domestic product (GDP) per capita, meaning their economic output and standard of living were comparable. Western Europe had a higher percentage of its citizens in extreme poverty during the Industrial Revolution than Africa does today. Every impoverished region today—Bangladesh, Niger, North Korea, you name it—has less extreme poverty now than it did in 1800. This was just over 200 years ago, a virtual blink in the vast span of human history.[6] Even if we fast-forward to the middle of the twentieth century, half of the world's population still lived in extreme poverty, as we can see in the chart above.

As of 2004, the latest date for which figures are available, only one-sixth of the global population still lives in extreme poverty.[7] Some studies provide even more optimistic figures than that. The estimates are controversial, but the conflict is over the rate at which poverty is being reduced, not whether it is being reduced. No significant studies claim that global poverty levels are on the rise over the long-term.[8] Declining poverty levels are even more striking when you consider that the world's population ballooned during the past two centuries. Though the percentage of people in poverty declined, the actual number of people in poverty always grew a bit—resulting in discouraging statistics. But that trend changed around 1980, when the absolute number of people in poverty started declining, too. While 1.9 billion people were extremely poor in 1980, 1.7 billion were in the same position in 1990, and by 2004, the figures dropped to less than 1 billion people. While this is still an appalling number, the decline is remarkable.[9]

It is important to note that when I refer to poverty here, I'm talking about *real* poverty, what economists define as extreme poverty. This is not forced-to-work-for-minimum-wage poverty, trailer-park poverty, or even shack-in-deep-Appalachia poverty. I don't mean to belittle the struggles of those who work for minimum wage or live in substandard housing, but the majority of the poor in the developed world are considered poor based on their low income relative to the high standard of living in their countries. While they may struggle to make ends meet, most poor citizens still have access to food, clothing, shelter, electricity, and at least one car. In comparison to the extreme poor of Africa or India, they live comfortably. For example, the rapper Jay-Z was deeply moved by trips to Africa:

> I come from the Marcy projects, in Brooklyn, which is considered a tough place to grow up, but [visiting Africa showed me] how good we have it. The rappers who say, "We're from the 'hood," take it from me, you're not from the 'hood. You haven't seen people with no access to water. It really puts things in perspective.[10]

And Jay-Z isn't even taking into account that just by growing up in America, there is the slim-but-real opportunity to strike it rich no matter how poor you are. He grew up in the Marcy projects, but now takes home $25 million a year.

World-renowned celebrity economist Jeffrey Sachs has dedicated his recent efforts to stopping the scourge of extreme poverty. In his book *The End of Poverty*, he describes the extreme poor:

> They are chronically hungry, unable to access health care, lack the amenities of safe drinking water and sanitation, cannot afford education for some or all of the children, and perhaps lack rudimentary shelter—a roof to keep the rain out of the hut, a chimney to remove the smoke from the cook stove—and basic articles of clothing, such as shoes. ... Extreme poverty occurs only in developing countries.[11]

THE HISTORY OF WEALTH-CREATION

In the back of our minds we are all aware that much of the world is dying of hunger and disease. We may wonder, if the global economy is zipping along so well, why does poverty still exist? If every region of the world shared the same high levels of extreme poverty in 1800, why did the economies of some countries skyrocket to today's level of wealth while other economies grew very slowly? Hundreds of years ago, available resources and geography were most critical for economic success. For example, Britain had both a good location and lots of resources; being an island, it was well protected. America had access to a whole continent of resources—endless miles of timber, coal, water, and buffalo. Meanwhile, the places now known as Mongolia, Afghanistan, and Sudan, for example, were isolated and relatively barren.

Along with resources, the exchange of ideas encouraged economic growth. Limited democracy, the rule of law, free trade, education, and the benefits of equality helped some places grow faster than others. Once those ideas started fostering advanced technology, it was all over for global economic equality. Europe created an economic feedback loop enabling it to grow through technology, science, education, and improved governance. During a dark period with tendrils stretching all the way to World War II, colonial Europe also used those gains to exploit other peoples—building even more wealth for itself. By the twentieth century, Europe had grown so powerful that not even two world wars could permanently set it back. Meanwhile, Africa and other regions of the world became mired in conflict, debt, lack of resources, and disease. The world seemed destined to remain divided until recent trends started working their magic.

If we examine economic patterns over the past two centuries, we can see regions pulling themselves out of poverty, starting in Europe and then spreading out to the rest of the world. Wholesale reductions in poverty originated in Britain and Northern Europe, when the Industrial Revolution took off in the mid-eighteenth century. By 1825 in Britain, for the first time ever, the added value of a country's industry outpaced that of its agriculture.

Technology, development, and capital soon spread throughout France, Germany, Scandinavia, and other parts of Europe—and then traveled further, improving the United States and then other British colonies such as Canada, Australia, New Zealand, and some of the Caribbean. All of these places became known as "the West."[12]

Small economic gains can quickly compound into significant progress. The Industrial Revolution kicked off an economic growth rate in the West of three-quarters of a percent a year, which was large compared to generations of essentially zero growth. By the beginning of the twentieth century, per capita incomes were growing at 1.5 percent per year, and since 1960 they've been growing at about 2.3 percent. Economist Steven Landsburg cleverly describes this growth in today's terms:

> If you're a middle-class American earning $50,000 a year, and you expect your children, twenty-five years from now, to occupy that same modest rung on the economic ladder, then with a 2.3 percent growth rate, they'll be earning the inflation-adjusted equivalent of $89,000 per year. *Their* children, another twenty-five years down the line, will earn $158,000 a year. And if that 2.3 percent growth rate continues, then in fewer than four hundred years, your descendants will earn about $1 million *per day*—a little less than Bill Gates's current income, but at least in the ballpark. I want to make clear that these are not some future inflation-ravaged dollars we're talking about; they're the equivalent of a million of *today's* dollars. If it strikes you as implausible that we could ever generate that kind of wealth, keep in mind that this is a conservative extrapolation of a centuries-old trend. It assumes today's 2.3 percent growth will continue unchanged, whereas in fact, growth has been accelerating ...[13]

This growth trend started in the West but soon kicked in elsewhere. Japan embarked on a plan to technologically match the West and became the only non-Western country to industrialize before the twentieth century. But wealth creation soon spread to small East Asian former colonies such as Taiwan, Hong Kong, and Singapore. Modern economic development reached Russia, Ireland, Central and Eastern Europe, and some remaining parts of Western Europe in the early twentieth century. A few tiny Persian Gulf states like Dubai struck it rich once oil became a precious commodity. South Korea benefited from investment from the United States after the Korean War, as did Israel, and a rebuilt Europe.

The twentieth century also saw countries that built some wealth but continued to struggle to spread it to poorer portions of their populations, such as Latin America and South America, South Africa, Turkey, Egypt, Jordan, Saudi Arabia, and Iran. Even as the countries listed above work to build greater wealth, new areas are booming economically: China and the rest of East Asia, Southeast Asia, the rest of the former Soviet states, Mexico, and India. Eventually, there will be economic hope for even the poorest parts of the globe: Central Asia (the "Stans") and Pakistan; the rest of South Asia (Bangladesh, Cambodia and others), West Africa; the isolated states of North Korea and Burma; Afghanistan and Iraq; sub-Saharan Africa and the anarchic Horn of Africa.

If you can visualize a map, the global trend toward decreased poverty levels is much like waves radiating out from wealthier countries to other regions of the world. There will always be exceptions to this wealth distribution, of course: regions with few natural resources, or obstinate autocratic governments like North Korea. But soon poverty will shrink its dominion and hold sway over only the most intractably lawless parts of the world such as Somalia, Sudan, and Afghanistan. Then, with laser-like focus, we can work to eliminate extreme poverty there, too.

Can the entirety of humanity progress from dirt-poor to iPod-rich in 300 years? It's estimated that if current trends continue, the income of the median person on Earth will more than double over the next 25 years.[14] This extrapolated trend is based on the successes many parts of the world have already had in eliminating poverty. Our challenge and responsibility is to help this trend spread to the remaining pockets of impoverishment even more quickly. The proven way to do this is to foster globalization.

GLOBALIZATION, OR, THANK GOODNESS
AFGHANISTAN HAS A SUBWAY®

Most of the world has learned that wealth does not necessarily come from physical power—the size of a country's territory or its military might. Economist
Martin Wolf, author of *Why Globalization Works*, calls those beliefs, "The great
collectivist delusion of the late nineteenth and first half of the twentieth centuries."[15] Belgium is a fraction of Russia's size, but it has a higher standard of
living. Nigeria has lots of oil, but it also has terrible poverty. Germany lost all
the land it conquered in World War II, yet in the peace that followed the war it
became wealthier than it was before. China has the world's largest population
and one of its largest armies, yet tiny Hong Kong is much richer per person. It is
not only power that builds wealth, but also natural resources, policy decisions,
trade initiatives, and a good work ethic.

After World War II, the world evolved on three economic paths. The "first
world" promoted democracy, liberalized their markets, and prospered through
globalization. First world countries signed the General Agreement on Tariffs
and Trade in 1947, which kicked off a new era of free trade. The "second world,"
communist countries, centralized their economies, refused to embrace private
enterprise, and refrained from trading with the first world. The "third world"
consisted of the other countries that did not fit into the first two categories.
While the third world tried very different methods of government, from military juntas to democracies, a common theme was isolationism. These nations
avoided communism and were hesitant to trust the first world, and with good
reason—many first world nations had recently been their colonial masters. As
a result, many of these third world countries closed their borders and tried to
be self-sufficient.[16]

Two decades after the fall of the Berlin Wall, we can see the long-term results of these three different approaches: the countries that embraced globalization profited the most. The communist economies of the second world and
the isolationist trends of the third world both failed. Today, most of these countries are embracing the global perspective of the first world, though at different
speeds and with different methods. Wolf sums this up:

> What the successful countries all share is a move to-
> wards the market economy, one in which private property
> rights, free enterprise and competition increasingly took
> the place of state ownership, planning and protection. They
> chose, however haltingly, the path of economic liberalization
> and international integration. This is the heart of the matter.
> All else is commentary.[17]

What do we mean by "globalization"? It's a word that could be used to de-scribe many of the trends discussed in this book; most of them represent vari-ous aspects of globalization. But the term "globalization" most often refers to an increasingly interdependent world economy. Thanks to globalization, capi-tal (money in investments), jobs, goods, and services are now reaping the ben-efits of worldwide accessibility. The common refrain that there are McDonalds in Paris used to be a cliché of globalization, but now it's a gross understatement. Today, you can travel to war-torn Afghanistan, and sure enough, 30 miles north of Kabul there is a Subway restaurant. The car you drive, the cell phone you (prob-ably shouldn't) talk on while you drive, the handheld game system your daugh-ter plays with in the back seat—all of them have parts manufactured in differ-ent countries which are then assembled somewhere else. If you wanted to, you could transfer your life savings from your local bank to one in India, to Uruguay, to Qatar, and then back again. Even more than jobs or products, the fluid trans-fer of funds across borders is one of the most dramatic effects of globalization.[18]

In the book *Globalization and Its Discontents*, economist Joseph Stiglitz writes that globalization is powered by the "enormous reduction of costs of transportation and communication, and the breaking down of artificial barri-ers to the flows of goods, services, capital, knowledge, and (to a lesser extent) people across borders."[19] One of those artificial barriers is the hundreds of currencies in use throughout the world that constantly have to be traded and exchanged, slowing down the rate of business. So one result of globalization is the convergence of currencies. Of course, the euro has been extraordinarily successful in the European Union—after less than a decade, 15 countries now use it. But did you know other regions of the world are also thinking about consolidating their currencies? One region already has: 14 countries in Western and Central Africa use the CFA Franc as their currency. It was invented after World War II, and more and more African countries have adopted it over time. Today, over 100 million people share the currency. South America has plans for a single currency as well, as part of their unification mentioned earlier. Bahrain, Kuwait, Oman, Qatar, Saudi Arabia, and the United Arab Emirates formed an organization in 1981 called the Gulf Cooperation Council, which cooperates on security matters and is considering a common currency, too. Central America recently pledged to create a common currency and shared passports among their citizens. A section of East Africa, independent of the African Union, is also looking towards a common currency.[20] It is likely that many regions will increasingly see their economies and currencies tied together more closely, further reducing barriers to trade.

Globalization tends to make products cheaper and increase productivity and economic efficiency by fostering competition. It creates new jobs and expands economies, building free enterprise. With new jobs, new businesses, and access to new markets, the growth rate of freshly globalizing economies is often incredibly high. Productivity speeds up that cycle, too: for every hour that someone works, his or her output has increased enormously due to efficiency, shared knowledge, and advanced communication. In the United States, productivity has increased almost three percent per year in the first years of the twenty-first century, which is more than double the annual rate over the previous 25 years.[21]

One essential key to globalization is advancing technology, which spurs productivity, enhances the economy, allows greater specialization of labor, and calls for more specific needs to be met—needs that different countries can naturally step in to fill. Common sense dictates that since there is a limit to how far the costs of transport and travel can be reduced, there will always be a finite limit to globalization. After all, Bangladesh cannot ship sandwiches to fill up your neighborhood deli's display cases every morning. Nevertheless, if current trends continue, we can look forward to even more globalization than we're seeing today.

In just a few decades, computers and communication technology have revolutionized business and culture and lie behind much of globalization's power. Computers have introduced more efficient communication, and improved organization and productivity by automating many processes. The Internet facilitates more efficient financial markets, allows investors instant access to opportunities around the world, and reduces the cost of market entry for new businesses. Amazingly, as new technology improves, its costs continue to decline. For example, a three-minute call from New York to London cost about $250 in 1930, but now the same call costs only a few cents. Making that same call over the Internet reduces the price to almost nothing.[22] As soon as new technologies develop, they spread around the world, giving other willing countries access to the best of everything.

THE DEVELOPING WORLD CLOSES THE GAP

Developing countries (sometimes called emerging economies) such as China, Vietnam, and India, have been embracing globalization like crazy. Despite the fact that they are starting with fewer resources than the West, they're growing at a much faster rate. The simplest way to put it is that they are catching up with the Western world. For example, particularly since the turn of the twenty-first century, companies' initial public offerings have increasingly appeared on worldwide stock exchanges, not just on Wall Street.[23] The emerging world now accounts for over half of global economic output—which is as it should be, since the emerging world also contains over half the world's population and over half the world's land.[24] This means that the rich countries no longer control the majority of the world's economy.

For developing countries, globalization is not a rigid step-by-step process. In fact, as Stiglitz writes, the countries that have benefited the most from globalization are those that have taken charge of their own destiny and implemented changes in the order and speed best suited for them.[25] Globalization's benefits can easily be seen in China, the world's biggest poverty-reducing success story. China's success is Vietnam's achievement writ dramatically larger. A half-century ago, Mao Zedong's disastrous economic plan known as the Great Leap Forward inadvertently caused the deaths of tens of millions of Chinese in the worst famine in human history.[26] Even by 1981, 64 percent of the population still lived on an income of less than a dollar a day.[27] The contrast with today could hardly be more striking. China started opening up to globalization in 1978, once its leadership changed. Beginning with reforms to the agricultural industry, China saw wealth start building up quickly. The government allowed its citizens to work where they wanted, and it liberalized trade so its citizens could make labor-intensive goods that other countries could buy. Since it started with little corporate infrastructure, China was able to quickly adopt the newest Western technology.

While there is still much disparity between China's rural west and urban east, from 1990 to 1999 the country reduced its poverty level from 33 percent of the population to 18 percent. Given China's population (the world's largest), that works out to some 150 million people pulled out of poverty in only nine years. Never before has the standard of living for so many people risen so quickly. China even joined the World Trade Organization (WTO) in 2002 and recently further liberalized its property rights laws—which seems pretty remarkable for an ostensibly communist country.[28] Since 2008, China accounts for more than 10 percent of world trade, up from only four percent in 2000.[29]

Many other countries have begun to enjoy the benefits of globalization too. Other parts of East Asia followed a similar path to China's, reducing the overall poverty in that region from 24 percent to 10.6 percent.[30] Even after suffering an economic crisis in 1997, East Asia rebounded much faster than anyone expected. India was a little slower than China to fully join the global economy, but it is now growing just as quickly. Not every country follows the same path to globalization; India focused on more advanced industries than China, exporting IT services to the developed world. With the advent of technology, customer service, tech support, and computer-related work can now be exported from other countries. The result is that India's number of extreme poor plummeted from 250 million people in 1978 to only 30 million in 2006, even while the population grew.[31] India also just expanded an ambitious plan to hire millions of its poorest citizens as laborers in their own communities—a kind of localized "New Deal" for India. There is also evidence that India's economic liberalization is doing what government mandates so far have not finished—destroying the caste system. The Dalits, once considered untouchable, are pulling themselves out of poverty, as well as gaining education. As a result, they're less likely to be employed in traditional caste jobs and are also enjoying more social status and perks once denied to them.[32]

All told, the middle class is expanding worldwide. To look at the widest possible picture, less than five percent of the world's population in 1820 was in the "middle class" of their time. By 2006, that proportion had reached 50 percent—and with a population seven times larger![33] A new Goldman Sachs study reveals that 70 million people around the world enter the middle class every year—households with annual incomes between $6,000 and $30,000. For example, Latin America, an area infamous for extremes of wealth and poverty, has recently had enormous success expanding its middle class. This is particularly noticeable in Chile, Brazil, and Mexico; Mexico's poverty fell from 37 percent of the population to 14 percent in the decade leading up to 2006. Chile's dropped from about 24 percent to 13 percent. This is creating a much larger consumer market, and sales of products such as cars and computers are booming. As the *Economist* reports, "A new middle class ... is emerging almost overnight across Brazil and much of Latin America. Tens of millions of such people are the main beneficiaries of the region's hard-won economic stability and recent economic growth. Having left poverty behind, their incipient prosperity is driving the rapid growth of a mass consumer market in a region long notorious for the searing contrast between a small privileged elite and a poor majority."[34]

Even poverty-stricken Africa is finally reaping the benefits of globalization. As the last frontier market, as some call it, Africa has seen foreign investment and loans rise from $11 billion in 2000 to $53 billion in 2007. Aid is no longer Africa's main source of foreign income. What's been reassuring Western investors—and recently, many Chinese investors—is improved financial management as well as somewhat less corruption, thanks to spreading democracy. Average inflation is down to 10 percent from 60 percent just a decade ago. (Zimbabwe remains an unfortunate exception.) The proportion of very poor Africans fell from 47 percent in 1990 to 41 percent in 2004—not as dramatic as China, but still notable. Mali's extreme poor fell from 75 percent of its population to half that. Small countries such as Togo and Gabon are aggressively following the path of industrialization that Taiwan, South Korea, Hong Kong, and Singapore successfully took in the 1980s, but even faster. Rather than Asian tigers, they're being called lion cubs. All over Africa, infrastructure is improving, especially in education and health. Industrialization is pushing people to the cities, the same kind of urbanization that has worked well elsewhere. Fully one-third of all Africans, about 300 million people, are now estimated to be middle-income consumers.[35]

It is important to note that the economic gains of the developing world do not come at the expense of developed countries. While globalization may change the West, on the whole, globalization is not an either-or, win-or-lose scenario. When done well, everybody benefits. For instance, U.S. exports are increasing nearly 20 percent a year, helping to ease the recession woes of other sectors. It's also reassuring that the emerging nations are not rallying around any one cultural theme or a single monolithic supranational identity; this is not a new rising Communist Block, but an enriching mix of very different nations.

Economic integration means that growth rates around the world are more synchronized than ever, with the fastest-growing countries helping the slower countries speed up their development.[36] Increasingly, Asia, not the United States, is driving global demand. The economies of many Asian countries are growing because of their success in exporting to developed countries. But Asia is importing products, too. As it successfully generates wealth, a middle class is growing, and many people are reaching the stage where they can start buying products that are not necessities. This helped make the impact of the 2008 recession on China much milder than it might have been, and it is pulling out of it sooner than the U.S. Some parts of China and India now look like an episode of *Supermarket Sweep*, as new consumers pack into malls and splurge on mobile phones. The United States' share of world imports fell from 21 percent in 2001 to 16 percent in 2006. Though emerging countries' economies can be volatile, with a more even distribution of wealth the world is less vulnerable to any single country's problems.[37] The world's economy is finally becoming balanced to match its actual population distribution, and this helps to promote equality.

OTHER BENEFITS TO GLOBALIZATION

Growing market economies have other ancillary benefits. Nations that are both prosperous and have democratic outlets are much kinder to the environment. The Soviet Union was responsible for huge environmental catastrophes, including the draining of the Aral Sea.[38] After Russian communism fell, Western Europeans were surprised to find out just how much pollution was hovering over their Eastern neighbors. With no competition within the Soviet Bloc, there was no drive for the government to use resources efficiently. With no democratic accountability to their people, there was no public pressure to encourage sound environmental practices.

Another benefit to globalization is the reduction in child labor, as parents become more prosperous and move away from agrarian work. In 1980, an average of 23 percent of 10-14-year-old children in developing countries were working. By 2000, that number had dropped in half, to 12 percent. In China alone, those 20 years saw a drop from 30 percent of children laboring to a mere eight percent.[39] Remember, going back a century ago—let alone longer ago than that—many countries had a majority of their children out working in the fields.

Globalization also helps reduce the number of global conflicts. Columnist and globalization optimist Thomas Friedman coined the "Golden Arches Theory of Conflict Resolution"—a clever way to describe the economic disincentive for war. Friedman realized that no two countries that hosted McDonald's restaurants had ever gone to war with each other. Once a country had a successful economy and middle class large enough to support fast food restaurants, its citizens were more inclined to make money and eat burgers than go to war. At the national level, the leaders of these McCountries realized that fighting other developed countries only severs trade between them, which in turn hurts everyone. The eighteenth century French philosopher Montesquieu came up with this theory first. He called the world of international trade a Grand Republic whose reciprocally dependent merchant countries would only destroy themselves if they attempted to resolve conflict through acts of warfare.[40] Same idea, fewer Chicken McNuggets.

Trade is often the primary incentive to join international agreements and common treaties, which naturally fosters cooperation and peace in other fields. Kant saw that, "The spirit of commerce, which is incompatible with war, sooner or later gains the upper hand in every state . . . states see themselves forced, without any moral urge, to promote honorable peace." For example, in order to attract investment, China has improved its human rights record to some extent, and India has downplayed its war with Pakistan. Sachs agrees with Kant's basic philosophy of commerce improving international relations when he points out, "The findings of the CIA Task Force on State Failure [show] that open economies are less likely to fall into state failure than are closed economies."[41]

Though the process is a slow one, influencing an authoritarian country through trade and culture turns out to be a more thorough way to destroy regimes than through military force. As we discussed earlier in the chapter, communism in Vietnam lost its primary foothold when the country embraced globalization, even if the government still considers itself to be aligned with Communist principles. Dictators realize the potential effects of globalization, which is why Kim Jong-il keeps North Korea sequestered. He dreads that if his people knew what they were missing, they would boot him out, or leave the country if they could.

A Trampoline in Every Driveway

Another benefit to globalization is its potential to eventually eradicate extremes of wealth and poverty. But it's easy to find reports to the contrary, that globalization is in fact increasing inequality. So what's the deal? Economic inequality is a *cause de jour* of the press, and seems to be increasing around the globe. We see TV reports of Africans in abject poverty, yet *MTV Cribs* shows us the latest rapper's bling-filled indoor pool. Since the United States contains many of the world's wealthiest citizens, economic inequality here is particularly conspicuous. It's true that income inequality is rising in the United States, and has been since the 1980s. The same is true in other rich countries: while inequality has dropped in some, such as Spain and France, it has risen in more, adding up to an overall seven percent increase in inequality in the past 20 years (based on income levels). This means workers at the bottom of the pay scale have seen their wages fall relative to people at the top of the pay scale. If we compare the incomes of the top and bottom fifths of American households today, we see a disheartening ratio of 15 to 1, meaning the top 20 percent earned 15 times more than the bottom 20 percent. Even within the top 10 percent, the top one percent have left everyone else far behind. (Although this has evened out a bit in the most recent recession. The richest 10 percent of Americans own 85 percent of all stocks, ensuring that market crashes affect them disproportionately.)[42]

Regardless of the "official" measure of inequality, as W. Michael Cox and Richard Alm of the Federal Reserve Bank of Dallas explain, income statistics "don't tell the whole story of Americans' living standards," and in fact are a pretty poor measurement of how well people are doing. Measuring household consumption gives us a better picture, and it shows that the poor have been catching up to the rich. This is because the types of things rich people buy more of—services and luxury goods—increase in price much faster than the types of things poorer people buy more of—"non-durables" like food, clothing, foot-wear, toiletries, etc. In fact, some of those non-durable items are actually still coming down in price, thanks to low-cost imports from China. (Unfortunately, this also means that any rises in food and oil prices, such as in early 2008, hurt the poor more than the rich. But those increases did not come close to revers-ing the trend of the previous decades.) For example, the price of the cheapest refrigerator ($350 at IKEA) keeps falling as the price of the most expensive re-frigerator (the SubZero PRO 48, $11,000) keeps rising—and the poor get more value compared to the rich. Because honestly, there just isn't that much differ-ence between fridges in the big scheme of things. That cheap fridge is probably better than the fanciest fridge from 20 years ago.

So, if we compare consumption, the difference between the top fifth and bottom fifth of American households is no longer 15 to 1, but 4 to 1. Taking it further, since rich households have more people than poor households (3.1 vs. 1.7), consumption per person shows the difference between the top fifth and bottom fifth falling to 2.1 to 1.[43] And falling inequality is also reflected in wealthy countries' responses (including the U.S.) to surveys of "life satisfaction": the difference in satisfaction between the rich and poor has been falling, suggesting that the quality of life is becoming more equal, not less. Likewise for declining inequality in things like height, life expectancy, and leisure time.[44]

Furthermore, if we look at economic inequality between countries, and take population sizes into account, the trend is even more prominent. Because China and India contain many of the world's poorest people, their superfast growth rate means that, on average, the world's paupers are catching up to the world's princes. Their standards of living are increasing as they gain wealth, they gain access to health care, heated homes, newer clothes, and cleaner water. And again, international trade, combined with technology and increased productivity, is helping to drive down the prices of goods. Millions of people who could not afford refrigerators, cell phones, computers, air conditioners, cars, washing machines and televisions in previous decades are now eagerly snatching them up. Compare it to a simple historical example: the light bulb. A single regular lightbulb (not even a fancy energy-efficient one) can generate the equivalent of 34,000 candles. In the early nineteenth century, it would have taken the average worker a *full year* to buy that many candles.[45]

Are there still extremes of wealth and poverty in the world? Yes, every society has always had and will always have economic inequality. But inequality, when it comes to money, is not the primary problem to solve. Standards of living are what matter, and this makes poverty the real enemy, not inequality. Almost everyone is equal in communist North Korea, or poverty-stricken Tanzania—equally poor. Eliminating extremes of inequality should be one of the world's long-term plans—countries where incomes are more evenly distributed have been shown to often have longer lifespans and other social benefits, as well as psychological benefits.[46] But for now our urgent goal is to reduce poverty.

As an example of why standards of living are more important than wealth, let's look at Bill Gates. The home of Bill and Melinda Gates is worth $53 million, a drop in the bucket of his multi-billion-dollar worth. His home theater has its own popcorn machine. He has an artificial stream stocked with salmon and trout. He has his own trampoline room—but don't worry, it has a 20-foot ceiling.[47] So let's pretend Gates' neighbor is worth only $1 billion and has a $3 million home. Sadly, this guy has to microwave his own popcorn, and his private backyard stream is filled only with guppies. The Gates are dozens of times richer than their neighbor, but is his tragic no-trampoline-room quality of life drastically different from the Gates family? No. Neither family suffers from any material want. For all intents and purposes, these two neighbors have identical standards of living.

We need a certain amount of income to fulfill our basic human needs. Past this point, once we reach a safe spot in the middle class, more income fulfills our wants—things that are nice to have, not essential. Reaching another point pushes our wealth into the realm of extreme luxury. Our goal in reducing poverty is to help everyone on Earth get to the first rung on the ladder of development, in which their essential needs are met. If we can accomplish this, more and more people will advance—by their own effort—to the next rung on the ladder until they reach a comfortable middle-class lifestyle. In no scenario will everyone on Earth be as rich as Bill Gates.

For most of human history, the poor desired possessions such as a warm home, durable clothes, and good health. In developed countries, at least, a majority of the population already has those things. The developed world has achieved the goal of generations of poverty-stricken masses. Our standards to define poverty have drastically risen in the past century, and that's a great thing. There will always be those who own several summer homes, one in Hawaii, one in the Hamptons, and a cottage in the south of France. The goal is not to even out everyone's finances so that you and I each have three homes, too. (That's called communism, and it didn't work.) The goal is to make sure everyone has at least one home, and food, and safety, and their health—and we are slowly getting there. If some people have a lot more, that's fine, as long as everyone has their basic needs met, including the right to an education and good health care. If this means that Bill Gates can afford to own 41 cars instead of 28, who cares? As long as he didn't exploit anyone or break any laws to get there, good for him.

One reason that the media focuses on economic disparities is because we are all acutely aware of the lifestyles of the rich and famous. Through media advances like TV and the Internet, Bangladesh's poor might catch a glimpse of Paris Hilton's anorexic dog and lament that they will never be able to afford such an unnecessarily adorable accessory. Meanwhile, in the developed world, constant bombardment by celebrity drama taunts us into thinking we can all be in excellent shape, with voluminous hair, phosphorescent teeth, and above all, cooler stuff. It's easy to take the simple achievement of having food on the table for granted.

Another psychological factor comes into effect with regards to economic inequality. When we see an extremely rich person, cruising in her Hummer-limousine, our subconscious assumes that she is rich at the expense of someone else. This was a good conjecture in the past, when wealthy rulers and early capitalists often exploited the poor and got rich off of their labor. While this of course still happens, it is not inherently the case. This assumption of exploitation of the poor by the rich is based on the misconception that there is only a finite amount of money in the world: a single "pie" that we all get a tiny piece of. But fortunately, if a rich person gains a dollar, it doesn't mean that someone else is suddenly without a dollar. This is particularly important to understand when discussing capital—wealth in investments—where money itself can become abstract and hard to comprehend. Bill Gates does not have $50 billion in cash underneath his phoenix-feather-lined mattress. He has it in Microsoft stock, which goes up and down based on what investors think the company is worth. The economy is not a zero-sum game. In each transaction it is more likely than not that all parties gain. If this weren't true, why would anyone transact?

I don't want to come across as extolling a constraints-free market ideology as the be-all and end-all of world peace. We have to remember that free markets are not an end in themselves, but a means—to a prosperous, happy, healthy, free citizenry. Whenever a market drastically contradicts this end, it should be watched and potentially reigned in. Externalities—such as the environment, and health care, may need extra resources outside of the market system. The rising tide usually needs a little help in order to lift *all* boats. But as economist Gene Sperling explains, "We shouldn't replace a focus on growth regardless of equity with a focus on equity regardless of growth."[48] As with everything, a balance is best. Economic wealth already exists for many in the world. Economically at least, their lot does not need to be improved. Rather, the achievements of globalization need to be better dispersed, by bringing up the poorest of the poor to a healthy level. As we eliminate poverty, the problem of economic inequality will take care of itself.

Acronyms and Their Discontents

In a 2007 Pew Global Attitudes Project survey of 46 countries, large majorities everywhere said that international trade was a good thing.[49] But globalization still has many loud detractors. Extremes of wealth and poverty are one of their most common complaints. These inequalities are on the decline, but there are other fears associated with globalization. It is worthwhile for us to take a minute to explore a few of them.

The World Bank and the International Monetary Fund (IMF) were created at the end of World War II as part of an ambitious effort to refinance Europe's reconstruction and rehabilitation after the war. Along with the UN, they were part of the toolkit devised to prevent the world from slipping again into a depression or World War. To this purpose, the institutions were successful. The World Bank loans money to developing countries, and the IMF bails out countries that need financial assistance in times of crisis. Both help out only when recipients put certain strict policies in place. A third institution, the World Trade Organization (WTO), was founded much more recently as a forum in which countries can settle disputes over international trade. Countries the WTO determines to be in the right are allowed to impose tariffs against transgressing nations in order to punish misbehavers and encourage fair trade. These three intergovernmental organizations have helped shape the global economy and naturally draw a lot of heat when they make mistakes.

Countries successfully enter the global economy and create wealth for their citizens when they quickly adopt reforms, but this process still needs to be done carefully, at each country's own pace, using ideas customized for their own needs. The IMF's and World Bank's economic reform suggestions have often been too rigid, however. Their "Washington Consensus" assumes all countries can modernize the same way—superfast, using market reforms best suited for developed countries. In some cases, this shock of fiscal austerity can jump-start a country's economy, but in other cases it doesn't work nearly as well.

Once concerned citizens realized that these reform policies were not always having the desired effect, that they were in fact impoverishing developing countries further, the people began to voice their grievances. But the institutions consisted of high-level economists and diplomats who were not democratically elected. Left without a forum, many people protested, including liberals in the West who sympathized with the countries at risk. This first caught the world's attention (by surprise) in Seattle in 1999 in a globally broadcast protest against the WTO.

The protestors were correct: the IMF, WTO, and the World Bank were greatly in need of increased transparency, and no one in the developed world was listening. The protests successfully pushed issues that were being ignored onto the world stage—human rights, the environment, the world's poor, AIDS in Africa. But some of the protestors went too far in their beliefs. Some of them looked at the undemocratic institutions of the IMF, WTO, and the World Bank and interpreted their less successful policies to mean that all globalization is evil. They imagined that the world's wealthier governments were in cahoots with international corporations and in a bid to monopolize the world's wealth. While collusion and corruption are certainly rife in the world, and many corporate policies could stand improvement, poverty existed long before McDonald's, Nike, and Starbucks came along. It was worse, in fact. History has shown that there are no credible alternatives to a market-economy system, except perhaps at the micro-scale. Every other system that has tried to increase standards of living for large groups of people has failed.

Where does this leave our three intergovernmental organizations? For many reasons, including the protests for more inclusive policies, there has been a whiff of change. Transparency is increasing, and information is now being released on the WTO's Web site. But more reformation needs to be done. The WTO needs to let NGOs and other groups have a voice in its forums. The institutions should also be required to completely open their activities to the press.[50] These changes would be easier to make if the WTO were better funded. The World Bank is also changing. It is steering away from supporting vast construction projects, which are often controversial due to their environmental impacts. Instead, it is emphasizing community development and helping small businesses in the developing world.[51] The major economies of developed countries can still exploit their advantage in these organizations. But without these institutions, inequality would be worse. There would be fewer checks on the largest developed countries' power in the economic realm. New, emerging economies remain underrepresented in global institutions, but this is changing quickly. For example, in 2008, for the first time the regular meeting of the "G7"—the leaders of the world's largest economies—paled in comparison to the meeting of the "G20," which included many more emerging economies. The G20 was looked to for leadership and direction with dealing with the financial crisis—it was not merely a problem for the United States and European Union. "The old, rich-only G7 looks increasingly anachronistic," as the *Economist* described it. A year later, and the G7 was out as an economic force, and the G20 was in. Slowly the West is realizing that its policies and demands need to be more flexible. With fairer representation, increased transparency, and more accountability, these institutions could be much more effective catalysts in eliminating poverty and spurring development.[52]

The homogenization of culture in the form of Westernized entertainment, food, and information is yet another concern of globalization's detractors. But as we've discussed, despite fears of uniformity, globalization allows for more diversity and fosters the existence of niche markets alongside worldwide fads. Another concern is how development and rising incomes increase pollution. The only alternatives to this are to either deny the third world the quality of life enjoyed by those in the first world, reduce the quality of life in the first world to the standards typified in third world countries, or develop new sources of energy that produce less pollution. The latter choice is clearly the way to go, and we'll examine those technological developments in the chapter about the environment.

It's not just protestors who have fears and unanswered questions about globalization; many other Americans do as well. Their biggest concern is local jobs. If the United States allows labor from India and products from China, will this hurt American workers, many of whom are getting laid off? Yes and no. Certain industries are hard-hit by globalization—manufacturing, for example. But competition encourages us to improve our performance, and if China is better at manufacturing (i.e., if it can produce the same quality but more cheaply), they should do the manufacturing while the United States does something it is better at. This is the core of Adam Smith's capitalism. And free trade enables the United States to import the best the world has to offer:

inexpensive Chinese manufactured goods, Japanese cars, Swiss watches, Persian carpets, and Colombian coffee.

Of course, this is small comfort to the laid-off worker. Nevertheless, statistics show that outsourced jobs are only responsible for a small percentage of unemployment (increased technology and efficiency are responsible for a far greater percentage.) There's a limit to how many jobs can be exported, since the vast majority of jobs still require personal contact in close proximity to coworkers and customers. The United States maintains one of the world's lowest unemployment rates, and the number of Americans working for foreign firms is greater than the number of foreigners working for American companies. Still, the government can do more to soften the blow to those workers hit hardest by globalization, by providing support and training, and helping shift them to newer industries.[53]

It's also natural to think that as the world's economy becomes more integrated, it becomes more vulnerable because we assume that a small crisis can quickly spread and develop into a large one. This fear was proved correct when problems in the housing sector in the United States and Europe led to a global meltdown in 2008. But months later, we saw different economies recovering fast, independent of what was still going on in the recession's countries of origin. We have learned a lot since the last global depression, in the 1930s, and thanks to floating exchange rates and other economic advances, countries can better manage economic crises. Even Argentina's severe financial collapse of 2001 was mild enough that Argentina recovered relatively quickly. What is especially striking is that even after economic crises, countries don't turn their backs on globalization and go back to isolationist policies, not even Argentina.[54] With smarter international agreements, more cooperation, and better control of monetary policy, the global economy can become more stable than ever.

Another fear about globalization is that it might make individual governments obsolete. The global economy is seen as undemocratic—leaders of nations are democratically elected, but corporations and economists are not. As we discussed, people and NGOs do need more of a direct voice in economic policy-making. But, although the traditional concept of sovereignty is evolving to embrace a more global perspective, thinking that countries are becoming obsolete is a very premature assumption. Trade agreements, powerful global corporations, and international law place constraints on states. So countries may agree to give up a tiny bit of power in order to benefit from free trade. These constraints on a country's sovereignty are significant enough to help keep them from abusing their power, but they are not strong enough to seriously infringe on their rights. Martin Wolf writes, "International integration merely tends to make policy more transparent and government more predictable, both of which are desirable." So economic globalization, the spread of democracy, and the trend of transparency all waltz hand-in-hand toward an integrated peace. Also, as powerful as the IMF, World Bank, and WTO may be, ultimately each country has the option to either accept or reject their policies. If Mozambique or Fiji or Belize do not want to obey the rulings of the WTO, they are free to disregard those rulings, but they can expect to suffer trade consequences as a result. For the time being, nation-states are still the leading players on the international checkerboard.[55]

How Do We End Poverty?

Because nations are still the majority shareholders of world power, they have the biggest responsibility to follow through with their promises to eradicate poverty. More nations of the world are aligned on the same "side" than ever before in history—the side of market-driven economies, increased globalization, and peaceful diplomacy. Teamwork to undertake an ambitious project like the eradication of poverty is now well within our reach. For the first time, we have the ability and the wealth to end the world's most extreme poverty, and this means we have the responsibility and duty to do so. The developed world's wealth has skyrocketed in recent decades. We need to share our wealth—not just by giving it away, but also by building more of it and helping the developing world to build their own wealth, too. Connecting poor countries to the global economy is the key.

How do we bring developing countries in from the cold? Jeffrey Sachs argues that each country is an individual case that requires a specific diagnosis.

He reiterates that the IMF and the World Bank failed by treating all countries equally. He came up with a differential diagnosis checklist that's much like a doctor's checklist of questions intended to uncover all of a patient's symptoms. Sachs's list is impressively robust, including questions that cover everything from a nation's climate to its gender relations, tax administration, and disease.[56] Let's examine a few of the most important issues that are universal to almost every developing country. External help is always necessary for countries that are at the very bottom of the world's economic distribution. Assisting countries in specific areas helps them climb onto the first rung of the ladder of development and sustain the momentum to keep climbing it by themselves.

First of all, developing countries usually need better governance. The poorest countries are those whose governments do not enforce the rule of law (either because they can't or don't want to) and thus encourage corruption. Professor of Economics Gary M. Walton writes, "The daunting challenge for poor nations is to craft better political institutions and to promote the rule of law, rather than the more arbitrary rule of men."[57] Governments that create arbitrary laws often become corrupt in countries with weak political structure and inadequate systems of justice, condemning many third world nations, particularly in Africa, to decades of poverty.

Dictators are notorious for wasting millions of dollars on vanity projects such as huge statues of themselves. Virtually everyone who has access to television is familiar with images of the many statues of Saddam Hussein that were toppled during the invasion of Iraq in 2003. North Korea is peppered with enormous monuments of Kim Jong-il, but President Saparmurat Niyazov of Turkmenistan outdid them all by making sure he had some giant statues made of solid gold. "I'm personally against seeing my pictures and statues in the streets—but it's what the people want," President Niyazov modestly said.[58] President Niyazov, who died in December 2006, also opened an 88-acre theme park named after himself, and renamed the word for "bread" to the name of his late mother.[59]

The poorest countries in the world are failed states unable to participate in the global economic system. Connecting these countries to the rest of the world is essential for their development. A truly democratic system of governance, true transparency, and adherence to the rule of law are needed to modernize the world's worst kleptocratic states. At the minimum, the governments of poor countries need to provide security and establish protective laws so that people who enter into a business deal know that they have legal recourse if the other person doesn't hold up to their end of the bargain. Trust is ephemeral in countries with scant rule of law, and that does not bode well for their economies. Similarly, property rights are essential for the poor, who often cannot prove that they own a piece of land and don't even have the identification to prove who they are in order to borrow money or make any investments.

As long as some national governments remain corrupt and exploitative, or ineffectual and impotent, poverty in those states will remain. A cycle of progress is needed: improved democracy and rule of law can put better leaders in place in third world countries, which can then open up their countries to fair economic globalization and the diverse global culture. Or, vice versa: the cultural demand to join an increasingly global community—with improvements in technology, health and communication—will empower citizens to elect leaders who support democratic laws and ideals. All the secret trends toward peace reinforce one another. The goal is to put in place governments that are sincerely concerned for the welfare of their people. Then not only will they not block progress, they will actively encourage it.

While protectionism, capital controls, and tariffs are barriers to free trade and growth, a completely laissez-faire, markets-rule attitude is almost as unhelpful. The real trick is deciding what functions government and markets each do best. Even Adam Smith, the father of capitalism, described how the state has powerful responsibilities in defense, justice, infrastructure, and education. I would also add healthcare and the environment to that list. In these areas collective action and decision making are more effective than private-market forces.[60] The state can provide public goods that the market cannot provide by itself, fix market failures, and help those people who slip through the cracks and are hurt by market forces—the young, elderly, disabled, or unemployed. Martin Wolf describes a list of public goods, including security of property, impartial rule of law, sound money and monetary policy, infrastructure such as roads, research, and merit goods such as health and education. In addition, governments can make sure that competition stays within a certain range by breaking up monopolies if necessary and can regulate environmental issues.[61]

After governments take up their unique responsibility to improve the lot of their citizens, businesses have an important role to play in spreading globalization to the world's poor. Free trade is the core of globalization, and third world countries need access to markets to sell their goods and services. Exports of their products translate into the import of cash that can be used for development projects and reinvestment in businesses.[62] Perhaps one of the best aspects of free trade is foreign direct investment (FDI) in poor countries' economies, which is growing very rapidly. FDI refers to rich countries' investing in building new businesses in a third world country, such as opening a factory, or financially investing in existing third world companies. FDI often helps to generate additional economic incentives; as investors choose a new country to invest in, that country begins to look more stable and tempting to other investors. As the country gains credibility, it continues to attract even more investors.

Global corporations are increasingly stepping into the developing world. This brings us to another complaint of globalization's detractors: corporate exploitation of workers in the third world. We have probably all seen reports about sweatshop labor in developing nations such as Bangladesh, China, Indonesia, and the Philippines. While the current situation has a great deal of room for improvement, it is not nearly as bad as the alternative.

When a multinational corporation opens a factory in the developing world, its wages and working standards are terribly low. This is why the corporation sets up shop there, after all—to save money on labor. But often the wages are low only by Western standards. These countries are not filled with pastoral towns out of Norman Rockwell paintings, an idyllic Eden shattered by Reebok and the Gap. They are traps of poverty and hunger that their citizens are desperate to escape. Nicholas Kristoff, warning against the United States over-tightening labor standards in trade agreements, reports in *The New York Times*:

> But while it shocks Americans to hear it, the central challenge in the poorest countries is not that sweatshops exploit too many people, but that they don't exploit enough.

> Talk to these families in the dump [literally, the vast fetid garbage dump in Phnom Penh, Cambodia] and a job in a sweatshop is a cherished dream ... "I'd love to get a job in a factory," said Pim Srey Rath, a 19-year-old woman scavenging for plastic. "At least that work is in the shade. Here is where it's hot." Another woman, Vath Sam Oeun, hopes her 10-year-old boy, scavenging beside her, grows up to get a factory job, partly because she has seen other children run over by garbage trucks. Her boy has never been to a doctor or dentist, and last bathed when he was two, so a sweatshop job by comparison would be far more pleasant and less dangerous. ... When I defend sweatshops, people always ask me: But would you want to work in a sweatshop? No, of course not. But I would want even less to pull a rickshaw.[63]

Foreign corporations entering developing countries can thus be steps toward development. New jobs created by global corporations are often the best hope the poor have to climb out of poverty. Factory workers eventually become skilled enough to demand better wages, at which point they can organize and even start their own businesses. Corporations, having kick-started that country's economy, can then move onto the next developing country. Meanwhile, the slightly-developed country that the corporation just abandoned can now offer improved services to attract new industries. In this way, each country grows its economy step-by-step. Though acting out of self-interest, it's possible for companies to slowly increase standards of living wherever they go.

Don't get me wrong, obviously there is a profit motive for corporations to exploit third world workers, and we know this kind of exploitation happens. Luckily, even the companies that wish to do so are increasingly discouraged by the potential impact it would have on their public image if they were to be found out. This is how boycotts prove useful—not just in stopping one company's practices, but as a deterrent to abuse for others. Ultimately, consumers are responsible for knowing where their products come from and under what conditions they were made. Again, transparency is the answer. With careful monitoring and citizen reporting, we can make sure global corporations stay on the correct side of the line between exploitation and economic development. That millions of people are now easily outraged by exploitation is in itself another positive sign of our advancing global ethic.

Companies are increasingly seeing poor countries not just as sources of labor, but also as sources of sales. More and more corporations are realizing that public service does not have to mean sacrificing profits. By seeing the world's poor as a new customer base, companies are finding new ways to bring products to a wider range of people, while benefiting from economy of scale. Savvy corporations can parlay this initiative into excellent public relations campaigns and also satisfy their investors while helping the world's poor gain access to inexpensive medicine, clothes, mobile phones, and educational supplies. To the poor, those purchases are investments that can help them climb out of impoverishment.

As developing countries embrace the global economy, they face competition from their neighbors for labor, development, and investment. This competitive pressure inspires them to keep improving their policies, further speeding their economic growth. As citizens become wealthy enough to own TVs and vacations abroad, they see the wealth around the world and place even more pressure on their governments to democratize and focus on global economic access.

Progress on the Millennium Goals

Many of Sachs's ideas for reducing poverty intentionally coincide with the UN's Millennium Development Goals. These eight quantifiable goals, agreed upon by 147 world leaders who met in New York in 2000, span the entire range of human needs, encompassing every arena in which the world desperately needs to improve. These goals, set for 2015, are:

1. Eradicate extreme poverty and hunger

2. Achieve universal primary education

3. Promote gender equality and empower women

4. Reduce child mortality

5. Improve maternal health

6. Combat HIV/AIDS, malaria, and other diseases

7. Ensure environmental sustainability

8. Develop a global partnership for development[64]

The eighth step, to develop a global partnership for development, was included to make sure that everyone was in support of the goals. Each of the other seven goals has very specific targets—numbers to meet in each region. We are only examining the first goal throughout this chapter, but the other goals all intertwine and contribute to the global agenda to end poverty.

Sachs breaks down five areas to best channel investments that will work toward all the Millennium Development Goals. These are the areas where the resources of governments, NGOs, and individuals would best pay off:

1. Agricultural aid would help the poor afford fertilizer and improved seeds, which in turn would increase food yields.

2. Basic health investments such as a small clinic for every village, mosquito nets to prevent the spread of malaria, and skilled birth attendants would ensure the overall health and longevity of a country's citizens.

3. Education, especially that of girls, provides the best investment in a community since women typically invest in their families. Meals offered in schools are yet another wise investment, as they are quite effective at

guaranteeing attendance. Funding vocational training also helps sustainable development take root.

4. Technology is essential to help grow a village's economy in countless ways and accelerate sustainable development. This includes providing electricity to villages so that they have pumps for safe well water, refrigeration, and lights so that students can study at night; communication services such as mobile phones and access to the Internet; and transportation such as access to trucks.

5. Finally, safe drinking water and sanitation are desperately needed and make good health investments.[65]

For some ineffable reason, and despite their relative obscurity in America, the Millennium Goals have stuck on the world's radar, when other frequent milestones and declarations often have not. Consequently, governments around the world are striving to meet their 2015 goals. They're making progress. For example, by 2008, 24 of the 71 countries reporting about cutting their poverty in half are on track. 90 countries are expected to reach their goals of reducing child mortality. Bangladesh, to cite a specific example, has been pushing to meet the goals and has made surprising strides in gender equality. It achieved gender parity in school attendance in 2005. Literacy rates among young women increased from 38 percent in 1991 to more than 60 percent in 2001. And women now have an average of three children, compared with seven in 1970.[66]

Foreign aid in these areas is essential for helping the world's poorest citizens. Through trial and error, we are learning how to channel aid effectively. For example, MIT's Poverty Action Lab works with the World Bank, using tools like random testing and double-blind trials to determine what development projects work best. And as the governments of developing countries improve, they can help distribute aid more efficiently, with less corruption. But the world's rich countries still have to drastically increase their aid. As Easterbrook writes in *The Progress Paradox*, when the United States was rebuilding Europe after World War II, 15 percent of the federal budget went to foreign aid. When polled today, most Americans *think* 15 percent goes to foreign aid, and they want that reduced to between one and five percent. But in reality, the United States now devotes less than 0.5 percent of federal spending to foreign aid.[67]

Luckily, despite this dearth of foreign aid, private donations to charities in the United States keep growing. Donations increased after Bill Gates started working with his foundation, inspiring other wealthy Americans to donate more to charity—most notably, Warren Buffet, who is donating most of his fortune to the Gates Foundation. Foreign aid and private donations play an important role in helping to reduce poverty, but to be most effective, their goal should always be to work toward sustainable development.

One of the best ways to enable the poor to create their own wealth is through microfinance. A catchall term, microfinance describes loans (microcredit), investments, and banking with very small sums. The world's poor rarely have access to fair banking, nor do their circumstances allow them to acquire credit ratings. So, a microfinance firm might step in and lend someone—more often women, who have been shown to spend the money more wisely—the equivalent of, say, $100. While this may be a small sum for the banks to temporarily part with, that $15 is worth a lot in impoverished countries. The recipient can invest in some cloth to make handmade clothes to sell, or she can buy extra livestock—to start her own small business. She might soon be able to expand her business by buying a cart for the market, or a loom, or a better oven. Due to its interest rates (high by our standards, low by others) and to the vast number of people microfinance is serving, it is starting to turn a profit. To the Western banks providing this service, the profit margin provides a good incentive to participate. Due to the opportunities microfinance creates, "Financial services for the rich and poor are becoming increasingly alike," according to the *Economist*.[68] Microfinance is making the headlines; in fact, the 2006 Nobel Peace Prize recipients were recognized for their pioneering work in the microcredit field. There are now over 130 million borrowers worldwide.[69]

Technology has a part to play in working toward the Millennium Development Goals as well. LifeStraw is a product designed to get clean drinking water to the millions of people who lack access. The small blue tube has a sophisticated set of filters that turn any surface water potable. It has been proven effective against typhoid, cholera, dysentery, and other diseases.[70]

Technology is also being used to foster education, another Millennium Development Goal. One Laptop Per Child is a project that hopes to deliver millions of cheap computers to kids throughout the developing world, funded by donors as well as governments. "Cheap" is an understatement for the laptops; it took years but they've developed a robust machine that costs only $188 to manufacture, and the cost keeps coming down (It's expected to drop to as low as $75 in 2010.) Some of the small but stylish laptop's features include: a screen that is readable even in bright sunlight; a solar-powered battery; a digital camera and a video camera for videoconferencing; easy transformation into an e-book reader; shock absorption for accidents; and Wi-Fi connectivity that can share its connection to other laptops within a 1/3-mile radius, creating a chain of connectivity. The computers come loaded with collaborative, educational software. Private donors can donate $200 at laptop.org to buy a laptop for a child. The Uruguayan government has been the first to distribute the laptops to all of its schoolchildren countrywide.[71]

Rich Countries Need to Do Their Part

The developed world continues to find new ways to help poorer countries build wealth. Developing countries often have many self-inflicted problems caused by poor governance. But those who oppose globalization point out that American and European policies still harm developing countries, too. Unfortunately, they are correct—trade barriers, third world debt, and protectionism are just a few factors that continue to stifle the growth of developing countries.

Trade barriers put into place to protect local industries end up hurting developing countries in the long run. North America and Europe still have many trade restrictions against poor countries that dash those countries' hopes of competing against Western products. Agriculture is one area where developed countries impose the most damaging restrictions against the developing world. The United States, the European Union, and other rich countries subsidize their farmers with billions of dollars of taxpayer money. (Keep in mind that this is often not small private farmers, but rather huge agricultural conglomerates.)

As a direct result of these government subsidies, food from third world nations can't compete in other markets. As poor countries also put up restrictions against their poorer neighbors, the cycle of poverty continues. One study deduced that the world's least-developed countries face tariffs four or five times higher than rich economies, which is counterintuitive, to say the least.[72]

Foreign direct investment in developing countries, while growing, still remains limited; poor countries invest in developed countries more than developed countries invest in developing markets. Similarly, third world debt is another contentious issue, although progress is being made. The external debt of poor countries, measured as a percentage of developing countries' exports of goods and services, dropped from 150 percent in 1996 to about 86 percent in 2005. That's more than a 40 percent drop in less than a decade.[73]

Debt bequeathed by corrupt and illegitimate governments is perhaps the worst kind of debt. A military regime, for example, might borrow millions of dollars from the United States ostensibly to help its people and instead use the money to finance its armies or build lush palaces. Years later, even if the people have replaced their dictator with more fair-minded leaders, the country still owes the United States millions of dollars. By any measure, this is not fair. Fledgling democracies are then stuck sending their tax revenues to the developed countries rather than using it to feed or educate their people. U2 frontman Bono has been instrumental in lobbying developed countries to simply write off such debt, which is reasonable since it will most likely never be paid back anyway. These debt write-offs are often more significant sums than actual foreign aid from rich nations. The United Arab Emirates, for example, just wrote off $7 billion owed to it by Iraq, which had been accrued under Saddam Hussein's reign. Sometimes creditors can attach conditions to the write-off, such as Germany did with Indonesia: Germany wrote off $70 million in debt and Indonesia promised to invest half the equivalent in health programs for its citizens. To help prevent the need to initiate additional debt write-offs, Martin Wolf suggests putting a global institution in place to evaluate, in advance, whether or not a regime is legitimate.[74]

While the Western world can recommend reforms to the developing world, we have to be careful not to be hypocritical. Capitalism is not perfect, and the

West needs to iron out its own kinks even as it promotes growth in the third world. The *Economist* writes, "At the heart of capitalism's troubles lies executive pay," referring to the bonuses, stock options, retirement packages, and other perks of many top American executives.[75] For example, 44 percent of American CEOs have contracts in which they will receive severance even if they're fired because of embezzlement. Great incentivizer! Similarly, corruption in the West, while not as common as in developing countries, often involves much larger sums of money in each individual case.[76] Recent blatant examples in the West include scandals involving large-scale corruption in companies such as Enron, Tyco, Global Crossing, Arthur Andersen, and others.

Minimizing or even eliminating world trade in hopes of saving a nation's home industries is another danger looming in first world countries. Protectionism will always be a tempting strategy for politicians—short-term trade barriers can save a few jobs and win the support of voters—but this only hurts the public in the long run. Experienced elected representatives must not give in to the temptation. Rather, they should remember the benefits that free trade and globalization bring both to the world's poor and, eventually, their constituents at home through lower prices. Governments can best help those hurt domestically by globalization through education that fosters dynamic job skills, expanded health insurance, and training and aid during unemployment.[77] The influence of corporations on government officials, though often detrimental and obviously undemocratic, can help to temper protectionist ideas. No transnational corporation wants to see its global market reduced to that of a single country.

Developed countries would also do well to welcome immigrant workers, and here's why. Yet another piece of good news in the last decade is the surprising reduction in world population, despite the common fears of overpopulation. This fear was first put forth by Thomas Malthus, an eighteenth-century British economist. Among his cheery writings we find, "The power of population is so superior to the power of the earth to produce subsistence for man, that premature death must in some shape or other visit the human race. ... sickly seasons, epidemics, pestilence, and plague advance in terrific array, ... gigantic inevitable famine stalks in the rear, and with one mighty blow levels the population with the food of the world."[78]

Our planetary population is now 6.5 billion. Many countries in Asia and Africa are overcrowded, and their populations continue to grow, placing a burden on scarce resources. In the 1970s and '80s it was widely understood that overpopulation would cause global famine and countless other disasters, as put forth by new theorists we can describe as "neo-Malthusians." But as it turns out, Malthus was wrong. This catastrophe never happened, nor is any large-scale overpopulation doom-and-gloom likely to take place in the future. As a report in the *Atlantic Monthly* described, "Fertility has declined dramatically, even in poor countries, as a result of economic changes and the more widespread use of contraception . . . the United Nations' projection for world population sees the total achieving near stability after 2200."[79] In fact, the global average fertility rate worldwide has dropped from an average 4.8 children to 2.6 in only 25 years. In other words, our growth rate is slowing, as Figure 14 shows.[80]

FIGURE 14: WORLD POPULATION ANNUAL GROWTH RATE, 1965–2005

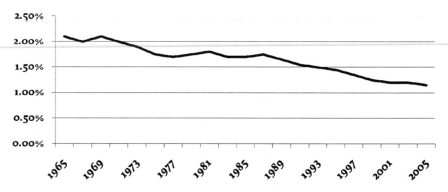

But isn't overpopulation still the reason for such poverty and famine in Africa and other places? Rapid population growth is problematic, but regions in the United States and Europe have much higher population densities than many African countries. Here's a handy way to visualize population from economist Thomas Sowell: divide the state of Texas into lots of 5,000 square feet, with a house on each lot. Put a family of four in each house and you've got the entire world's population. Now, I've been to Texas, and it's a big state, but it's easy to see there is a whole lot of land in the world left over in that scenario.[81]

Rather than overpopulation, it is more often government mismanagement and kleptocracy that cause famine—look at the dictatorships of North Korea and Zimbabwe, for example.[82] Thanks to the green revolution and other technology, it's possible to generate enough food for everyone. While overpopulation in particular countries is a real issue that tends to exacerbate other problems, it is an issue that will eventually resolve itself as economic development occurs. To help out, first world countries could encourage immigration, since many developed countries—in particular Japan, Russia, and Western Europe—are experiencing a decline in population due to their low birth rates. This means they will end up with a lot of elderly citizens and few workers to support them. The United States takes in far more immigrants every year than any other country, and it hasn't hurt our economic growth; if anything, it helps growth. America's rich history is dependent on immigrants, each generation of which have contributed to the diverse cultural and economic success of the country. In addition, immigrants develop useful skills, make comparatively large sums of money, and then send some of it back to their relatives in the mother country. Everybody wins. Developing countries have too many people who need jobs, and developed countries need more workers, so as long as protectionist barriers continue to drop, the world's population distribution could balance out dramatically.

What We Need to Do

When we examined the history of the European Union, we saw their success in improving the democracies and societies of prospective members. They dangle the carrot of membership, and developing countries strive to meet the standards of reform. This dynamic is partly responsible for the climb from poverty that Eastern Europe experienced. Motivated by the European Union, many Eastern European nations have improved their economic policies. If a similar tactic could be used globally, prosperous countries could spread their influence into neighboring regions using positive incentives. For example, what if the European Union enticed Belarus, and Vietnam's success encouraged similar results in Cambodia, and Australia reached out to Indonesia, and South Africa influenced its more anarchic neighbors? Not only would the new countries become more prosperous, but also the developed countries would see their border security improve and share in the economic benefits. Illegal trafficking, terrorism, and pollution could be brought under better control. This is already happening in many places, and such change represents a drastic shift from a history of distrust and competition between neighboring nations.

Cooperation is key to solving the problem of extreme poverty. The ties of trade and economics act secretly and subtly to pull the world tightly together and promote peace. The economic push toward peace does not require a great deal of altruism, just self-interest tempered with some laws and guidelines— and lots of cooperation. Every state and non-state actor is going to have to work together to solve the world's poverty problem once and for all. In addressing the collaboration that needs to take place to eliminate poverty, the publisher of *Forbes*, Rich Karlgaard, states, "Government has the authority, NGOs the special expertise, charities and churches the ground troops and distribution channels, and business the money and tools."[63]

These organizations, some of which have been working for decades to alleviate poverty, are increasingly realizing the key role that health has to play in the equation. We've already looked at the successes of the Gates Foundation, for example. Medical technology helps the third world develop and gives them the strength to build their economies. Health is the realm in which it is easiest to both measure our results and clearly see our successes. And as we'll see next, there have been many, many successes.

10

HEALTH

Finding the Fountain of Youth

Four categories of technological innovation continually push human history: war, health, energy, and communication. As Jonathan Schell points out, science has been a "sleepless dynamo of historical change, spilling fresh energy decade after decade into the modern world." Science also tends to soften local distinctions as inventions eventually make their way to every region of the world.[1] In this way science becomes a unifying force, helping to minimize inequality, and like the other trends we've examined, it both informs and benefits from humanity's new global perspective. All four of these areas of technology secretly add impetus to the movement toward peace. We examined the vast strides that communication technology has made in empowering the world's people. We also looked at the technology of war and saw how it advanced so far as to nullify itself: nuclear weapons are too powerful and dangerous to ever be used. Now let's think about another area of technology that motivates change—our health.

THE GREEN REVOLUTION: PART OF A BALANCED BREAKFAST!

My former boss was really proud of eating mostly organic food, and his wife and two children are vegetarians. He extolled the virtues of organic vegetables to me many times. There are some good reasons to eat organic food—livestock are often treated more humanely, and organic farmers do not use pesticides or artificial fertilizers. But my boss didn't emphasize those reasons; he only mentioned the health benefits. He lamented the current diet of most Americans—filled with saturated fats, trans fats, high-fructose corn syrup, and tons of unpronounceable additives. He complained about junk food and fast food and railed about how the Western diet is making our population fatter and unhealthy, increasing the risk for diabetes, heart problems, and a slew of weight-related medical conditions. He wished he could live in the past when people lived off the land, growing their own food—pure, organic food provided by nature.

My former boss was right about the unhealthy food we consume in the West. Obviously people who eat a diet of fish and lima beans live longer than those of us camped out at Taco Bell, all other things being equal. But his idyllic dream of the past failed to account for the modern-day benefits of technology. People in previous centuries did grow their own food—when they could. Much of the time, they starved or were severely malnourished. And even with a plentiful harvest of corn and a full nest of rabbits to stew every night, how many nights in a row can you eat corn and rabbit stew? If I were faced with a choice between a world of severe malnutrition that kills you when you're 40, and a world with optional obesity that kills you when you're 70, I would gladly take the latter.

Much of our fast food is terribly unhealthy for us when compared with other healthy alternatives available today. But when compared to food from centuries past, Big Macs are like Flintstones Vitamins, just without the molded dino shapes. To no avail, I asked my boss, "If people in the past ate such healthy, organic food, why are we so much healthier than they were?" Our life expectancy keeps going up and up and up. Countries such as Japan, whose citizens generally have a healthier diet than their American counterparts, do have longer life expectancies, but only by a few years. The fact is that the world's obesity problem is real and needs attention, but compared to humanity's eons-long quest for sufficient food, it's not a bad problem to have. Our ancestors would be astonished—maybe even insulted—that an obesity epidemic could even be possible.

Improvements in medical technology are increasing life expectancy and quality of life globally, and it started with agriculture. Less than a century ago, agricultural science started to advance in leaps and bounds. First, pivotal advances in the chemical processes to make nitrogen-based fertilizers helped to boost agricultural yield in developed countries. Second, the third world underwent a green revolution—technological advances that helped to increase agricultural production in many countries that were previously unable to feed their populations. This was easily "one of the most important triumphs of targeted science in the past century," as economist Jeffrey Sachs described it. Starting in 1944, the Rockefeller Foundation took the initiative to breed high-yield strains of staple crops in Mexico. It was soon joined by other foundations as well as government efforts. The technology spread to India, a country that no one thought would ever feed its massive population but which now experiences surpluses. The new developments kept spreading, to other parts of South Asia, East Asia, and the Americas. As a result, the average person in the developing world now consumes 25 percent more calories a day than people did before the green revolution.[2] Amazingly, while the world's population increased by over 150 percent from 1950 to 2002, the real price of food commodities dropped 75 percent. In addition, due to increased crop yield many countries are using less cropland— an environmental boon.[3] Today, many NGOs and charities continue to focus on health and nutrition, and the UN works for health with technological improvements in water, sanitation, nutrition, and other areas, as well as with programs like food-for-work and food programs for children.

And so the agricultural revolution marches on. The science sometimes advances in bizarre and amazing ways. For example, scientists are even developing a way to grow meat in labs. This is not fake meat, but real meat grown from cultures of animal muscle tissue. It would be indistinguishable from the meat we eat today, but no animals would be killed to produce it. If successful, this method of meat production would be a victory for anyone opposed to slaughtering animals and for those who abhor the conditions found on factory farms today.[4]

Less strange than the meat-growing concept are genetically-modified (GM) foods. Though becoming increasingly accepted, many countries, particularly in Europe and Africa, are still skeptical of GM crops. They feel these products have unknown dangers, such as biodiversity reduction if they spread out of control. But GM crops are a logical next step in the green revolution. They hold a key component to the continuing issue of feeding the earth's masses. The Food and Agriculture Organization estimates that to keep up with population growth, we need a 70 percent increase in world food production by 2050. The easiest way to reach that is for farmers in the developing world to increase their yields. GM crops can be modified to be pest-resistant, larger, healthier, and more nutritious. If crop yield increases, even less land would be needed for agriculture, freeing up more natural environments. GM food has only been commercially available for a decade, but the business is booming: the area of GM-cultivated land increased by 12 percent in 2007, to 114 million hectares globally. While careful research and caution is always needed, where GM crops have been introduced, so far they have been successful.[5]

Genetically-modified crops also form an important part of the solution to the fluctuating food prices we've seen since 2007. As the *Guardian* reports, "Prices for wheat, corn, soybeans and rice have surged to record highs in recent months amid disappointing global harvests, growing demand for biofuels and rising appetites for better diets." That demand for a more robust diet is a side effect of the increasing fortunes of the developing world, particularly China and India. The increased prices led to hoarding and even riots in places like Haiti, Bangladesh and Egypt. But, for the most part, the laws of economics prevailed—high prices are good for farmers and encourage investment, leading back to a higher supply—and prices have returned to reasonable levels. But without continuing breakthroughs in agriculture, the world will remain perilously close to sustainable levels of food and prices will continue to fluctuate. A cornucopia of suggested solutions is on the table, such as reducing our use of biofuels (which can cause more environmental harm than good), minimizing portions in American restaurants, buying seasonal foods locally so they do not have to be transported long distances, encouraging vegetarianism (meat takes more resources to produce), and producing a new generation of GM crops that are drought-resistant in addition to pest-resistant. Though the world remains susceptible to food crises, the long-term trend of increased agricultural yields still seems likely.[6]

One of the major side effects of agricultural efficiency is increased urbanization. For most of history, everyone farmed, but today most countries have such advanced economies that they need only five percent of their workforce engaged in agricultural production.[7] As fewer people are needed on farms, more of the population can pursue other non-farm jobs, which are often more effective when clustered together—hence the migration of workers to cities. As time progresses, this migration snowballs the diversification, to industrial production and science, and then education and health services, and then art and writing, and then entertainment, and then dry cleaning, dog walking, landscaping, selling shirts, giving massages, designing Web sites, auditing, truck driving, marketing, consulting, and whatever you do. By specializing in so many different jobs, humanity as a whole gets better at everything. We can each find something better-suited to our particular talents and capacities, and often it is less physically grueling than farm work. We sometimes lament the loss of an idyllic farm past, but the developed world today is the first time in history that large groups of people have had the freedom to say, "I don't like my job. I think I'll look for a new one." (And if you like being a farmer, you can still choose to be one.) Even a few decades ago, it was assumed that you might not enjoy your profession. Today, we feel entitled to some happiness and fulfillment in our work, and we are willing to search for it. And increased urbanization (in 2008, for the first time, the majority of people on Earth lived in cities) leads to many gains in efficiency for businesses, the arts, and individuals.

So advancements in the science of agriculture have helped not only the world's nutrition and health, but also allowed humanity to devote more time to other endeavors. The various scientific fields that have contributed to humanity's overall health have been among the most successful. Worldwide improvement in health is one of the areas in which the movement toward peace is most evident and easily measurable. But even more good news than you might expect still remains hidden amidst a barrage of cancer scares, fad diets, and obesity statistics. We will look at several areas of improving health, but the overall indicator is life expectancy.

THE PRINCE AND THE PAUPER:
EQUALLY HEALTHY

At the beginning of the book, we looked at life expectancy in Genghis Khan's time, an average of 25 years or so. It took thousands of years for the average life expectancy to rise from 25 (or less; Britain hit an average of 17 years in the plague-ridden fourteenth century) to around 30 years in the mid-eighteenth century. By 1800, Britain led the world with a life span of ... only 36 years.[8] Today we're blessed with a worldwide average life expectancy of 68 years; 77 years if you look at only rich countries.[9] This factors in people who die from accidental or health-related deaths such as car accidents, malaria, AIDS, smoking, infant mortality, gang wars, you name it. Since life expectancy keeps going up, we can generalize that we are doing better in all those areas. But that's not necessarily true, so we need to dig a little deeper if we want to sniff out some more interesting trends. So let's get more specific.

Figures 15 and 16 show three different levels of life expectancy. The black areas represent nations with an average life expectancy of more than 70 years, the gray areas represent expectancy between 55 to 70 years, and the white areas represent less than 55 years. Upon first glance, the maps illustrate the horrible injustice of a world in which the citizens of rich countries live to be over 70 years of age, but sub-Saharan Africans die decades earlier. But when we compare the two maps together, there is overwhelming good news. The life expectancies of South America, China, Southeast Asia, and the Middle East have all tipped over above 70 years. And while the only countries that have gotten worse are in the very southern tip of Africa, Northern Africa has improved. Also, while several nations outside Africa had very low life expectancies in 1990, the only two that remain low in 2005 are Afghanistan and Haiti. By 2005, of all the countries in the world, only five have life expectancies below 40 years of age: the Central African Republic, Zambia, Zimbabwe, Lesotho, and Botswana—about 31 million people total, or less than one percent of the world.[10]

It's worth remembering that every region on Earth had an average life expectancy well under 40 just a few hundred years ago. That means even today's sub-Saharan Africans are living longer on average than everyone did throughout most of human history. The world's improvement is clear and remarkable.

FIGURE 15: AVERAGE LIFE EXPECTANCY PER COUNTRY, 1990

FIGURE 16: AVERAGE LIFE EXPECTANCY PER COUNTRY, 2005

FIGURE 17: LIFE EXPECTANCY AT BIRTH: BRITAIN, 1875–2000

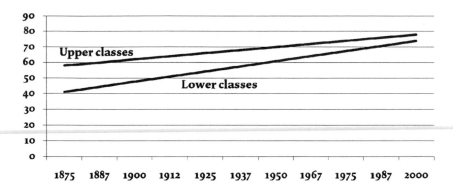

FIGURE 18: GLOBAL INFANT MORTALITY RATES, 1950–2005

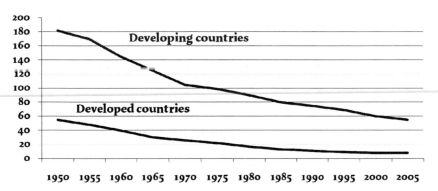

Figure 17 offers further enlightening information. One hundred and thirty years ago, there was a 17-year gap in life expectancy between the poor and the rich in Britain. Today there is less than a four-year gap. (Britain is an ideal country to examine because it has kept really good records for centuries.) As Glenn Reynolds, author of *An Army of Davids*, explains, "Aristocrats always had much longer and healthier lives than the common folks . . . [but] there's no longer such a huge discrepancy among classes."[11] Figure 17 can help us visualize the trend of converging classes. As we discussed about poverty, this is more evidence of the poor catching up to the rich—not in terms of how many cars they have or how much bling they flash, but in terms of basic conditions such as health. The poor today live longer and are much better off than the elite were 100 years earlier. There is also no longer any difference in height or other obvious physical traits between the rich and the poor.

Figure 18 shows a similar convergence in infant mortality rates. Infant mortality measures the number of babies who die within their first year of life, a number expressed per 1,000 births. Before the year 1750 or so, more than 20 percent of babies worldwide died before their first birthday (200 or more per 1,000). Then Europe started to advance in health. There is still a significant gap between the rates of infant mortality for industrial countries and developing countries, as shown in Figure 18. The rate for industrial countries has hit an impressively low number and is unlikely to decline further without some drastic medical breakthrough. As another example of disparity, the infant mortality rate in the United States is 6.4 infants per 1,000 births, but specifically among African Americans it is 13.8—still a low number, but almost double the U.S. average. Nevertheless, in every area of the world and in every ethnic group, the infant mortality rates continue to decline. In a few decades they will most likely converge at a rate of 10 infants per 1,000 births, if not fewer. Iceland holds the current record, with only 3 infants dying for every 1,000 born—a 99.7 percent survival rate.[12] In absolute numbers, less than half as many children die before their fifth birthday worldwide as did in 1960—and this is with double the world's population. Bill Gates, speaking with the expertise and optimism flowing from his foundation, calls this humanity's greatest achievement of the past five decades, and has high hopes that the number can be cut in half again in 20 years.[13]

While we're busy improving medical technology to save people from dying, fewer children are being born. Even with reduced infant mortality, modern contraception has brought the world average fertility from five children per woman in 1950 to 2.6 children in 2000.[14] This reduction in population growth is a much needed pressure valve that helps to diffuse overpopulation and dwindling resources in certain areas. Giving birth to fewer children allows families to invest more in each child, increasing their chances to live, receive an education, and achieve success. Families can give their children more food, more clothing, and more money to get started on their own once they leave the nest.

Today's parents are devoting more time to their children, too, despite the common perception of today's frazzled parents versus the relaxed 1950s nuclear family. American fathers today are spending more time with their children than ever before, since many child-rearing duties are no longer considered solely "women's work." Though more frequently employed than in the past, American mothers spend much less time on housekeeping (thanks to better technology and lower dusting standards) and shift that available free time to their children. Couples are not just having fewer children, they're also waiting longer before having them, which makes them better prepared to be parents. All of the increased attention that is being given to the children helps to create children who feel loved, are happy, and are psychologically stable.[15]

Healthier children help raise the average life expectancy as well. With all of these factors increasing our life spans, it brings up the question: We may be living longer, but is it a good life? People with poor health living in previous centuries probably wouldn't have wanted to live longer if that only meant it would extend the amount of time they spent enduring pain and feebleness. But happily, those of us who live in developed countries are increasingly healthier overall. As the *New York Times* put it, "Human bodies are simply not breaking down the way they did before." Many of us are healthier throughout our lives, all the way up to the final years, in which our quality of life is much better than it was in previous generations. So the age at which we start to become "old" is rising, too. Chronic ailments like heart disease and arthritis now occur decades later in life than they used to, and they are often much less severe when they do occur.[16] And today older folks enjoy more activities than ever before. Gregg Easterbrook explains, "The notion of the 'healthy old'—people in their seventies and even eighties who are in sound health, live independently, travel often, even engage in sports—has gone from pipe dream to standard expectation." If you're a youngster reading this, take comfort in a recent comprehensive survey on aging, which shows that most people 65 and older say they didn't experience the health declines typically associated with aging to the degree that young people anticipate.[17] Longer life spans give us more time to accumulate knowledge and dig deeper into our fields of specialization; likewise, they also give us more free time to branch out into diverse interests.

Many scientists and doctors believe that our health improvements stem not just from better medical technology, but from better nutrition and health early in life—as early as the womb. If this assessment is true, we are in for some healthy surprises as America's first generation exposed to childhood vaccines and antibiotics now enters retirement age. Good health often has a snowball effect: less cardiovascular disease, for example, often means less dementia later in life. Escaping childhood diseases may mean a reduced risk of contracting cancer decades later. Today even our jobs are much healthier—would you rather get cramped muscles from digging in a mine or from using a computer mouse? People in previous centuries often literally worked themselves to death. They had no choice but to keep working until their bodies refused to go on.[18]

Today the average citizen of an industrialized country stands up to five inches taller than his ancestors a few centuries past.[19] This is why when you're visiting museums the little Egyptian sarcophaguses and European suits of armor seem so tiny. People are getting better looking too, with better skin care, hair care, and full sets of teeth. (Few people had all their teeth in the past. Another thing we take for granted.) We saw earlier that even our IQs are slowly increasing year after year. Over a surprisingly short period of time—only four or so generations—large sections of humanity have changed from sickly looking weaklings to a group so tall and robust as to rival Hercules, so beautiful as to rival Adonis or Aphrodite, and so smart as to rival Athena. Throwing modesty out the window, if our ancient ancestors could see us now, they might mistake us for their gods.

Eating More, But Smoking Less

Problem is, we might be more easily mistaken for Buddha than Apollo. The primary negative news about health in developed countries is the rising incidence of obesity—and the United States is among the fattest. This is one reason why our life expectancy still lags behind some countries, such as Japan and parts of Europe. Yet life expectancy continues to improve, so the effects must not be as negative as we suspect. A counter-trend is also developing: the rise of low-fat foods and diets. Though many diets are dubious at best, the underlying desire to lose weight is so overwhelming that it has created a vast weight-loss industry in just a few decades. They now make low-fat Doritos and diet Mountain Dew, so you know the drive to lose weight has infiltrated every food sector. However, obesity is still seen as a personal issue, not as a social issue or a matter of public health. If it shifts in that direction, we have a good chance of licking the problem. We've tackled worse health issues in the past. A combination of social pressure, increased health information for better consumer choices, and government regulations can help slim down Americans. Programs targeting childhood obesity are particularly important, and creative solutions have been increasingly implemented by many schools. Plans are also moving along to require calorie counts on display at restaurants nationwide, something that I've noticed is helpful since I've seen it firsthand for the past few years in New York City.[20] Perhaps change will come after we realize the impact of obesity on society's overall health care costs affects all of us. This ties into the overall issue of reforming America's health care system.

This general pattern—new regulations, better information and social pressure—is what happened to smoking. An astonishing 1.1 billion people smoke today, and smoking contributes to almost five million deaths a year, whether through cardiovascular disease, lung disease, or throat and lung cancer. The World Health Organization estimates that 100 million people died in the twentieth century as a result of tobacco, making it the leading preventable cause of death. Smoking rates are growing in the developing world—85 percent of smokers are now in low- or middle-income countries. Yet this is partly because of new disposable income for many of the world's poor—as a result of their relatively recent emergence from extreme poverty. Luckily, anti-smoking efforts are starting to spread to the developing world. Michael Bloomberg, the billionaire mayor of New York, and the Bill and Melinda Gates Foundation recently announced a joint donation of $500 million to combat smoking in the developing world, particularly in five countries where most of the world's smokers now live: China, India, Indonesia, Russia, and Bangladesh. The New York Times reports:

The campaign will urge governments to sharply raise tobacco taxes, outlaw smoking in public places, outlaw advertising to children and free giveaways of cigarettes, start anti-
smoking advertising campaigns and offer their citizens nico-
tine patches or other help quitting. Third world health officials,
consumer groups, journalists, tax officers and others will
be brought to the United States for workshops on topics
like lobbying, public service advertising, catching cigarette
smugglers and running telephone hot lines for smokers
wanting to quit.[21]

As poor countries get a foot on the ladder of development, their governments will no doubt realize the health costs smoking imposes on their societies,
and they will follow the lead of the developed world.

That's because the popularity of smoking in the developed world is plum-
meting fast. The tactics listed above are working. Cigarette companies know
that Westerners have finally caught on to smoking's dangers, so they're now focusing marketing efforts on the developing world, to entice less savvy consumers whose governments have fewer regulations. The decline in smoking in the
developed world is so extreme that even with the increase in smoking in poorer
countries factored in, the worldwide decline can clearly be seen in Figure 19.[22]

FIGURE 19: ANNUAL WORLD CIGARETTE PRODUCTION
PER PERSON, 1950–2004

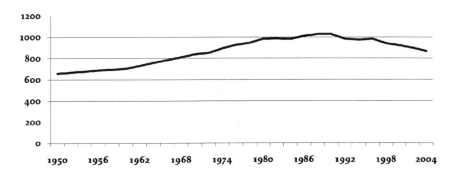

Smoking is increasingly being banned by businesses, restaurants, towns, states, and countries. In 2004, a controversial move in Ireland banned smoking in all bars and restaurants. In a few months, tobacco sales fell 16 percent. Norway, Italy, and Scotland have followed Ireland's example. Even the stereotypical image of the beret-clad smoking Frenchman isn't safe—France followed suit in 2007.[23] New York City banned smoking in public places, bars, and restaurants, with much controversy. I don't smoke, but I thought about the possible infringement of civil liberties: does the government have the right to tell you not to smoke? A growing number of citizens are saying, "Yes, it does." Society is turning against smoking, especially after getting a taste of the pleasures of a smoke-free environment. The bans are working: New York City reduced smoking among adults by 20 percent and among teenagers in public schools by 50 percent.[24]

New York City's ban on smoking in public places went into effect just a few months before I moved into the city, and after being used to smoky restaurants and bars in New Jersey, it was a revelation. No longer did I have to air out my jacket or replace my stinging contact lenses after leaving a smoke-filled restaurant. And when my throat hurt in the morning after hanging out with my friends, I knew it was only from yelling and not from a harmful dose of secondhand smoke. New Jersey soon followed suit and banned restaurant and bar smoking only two years later. I doubt it will be long before most of the country succumbs to the pressure of people seeking the right to breathe clean air. More than half of the states in the U.S. already have at least partial bans. Private trends are mimicking public ones: nearly three-quarters of American households now forbid anyone to smoke inside. This is a big jump from 43 percent only a decade earlier.[25] Together, all these trends are working: in 2007, the number of American adults who smoked dropped an entire percentage point, to 19.8 percent—the lowest number on record.[26]

A CRIME-FREE, ACCIDENT-FREE, SNIFFLE-FREE AMERICA

In the United States and Europe, most afflictions are in decline. The incidence rates for heart disease and strokes are 60 and 70 percent lower, respectively, than 1950 rates (adjusted for population). Since the 1990s, rates have also been falling for most cancers—even accounting for an increasingly aged population. According to Columbia University's Dr. Alfred Neugut, "There was a revolution in treatment between 1998 and 2000. And 'revolution' is a mild word. We went from having one drug to having six or seven."[27] Patient deaths due to anesthesia have deceased more than forty-fold in the past 20 years. AIDS-related deaths in the West are remarkably low, and even the rate of suicide is declining.[28]

In addition to the decline of illnesses, many alleged dangers in the West are secretly trending toward peace, despite everyday worries and media scares. Deaths by fire have declined 50 percent in 20 years, thanks to smoke alarms and other building safety measures. Fatal airplane crashes in the United States have declined 65 percent in the past decade, to *one for every 4.5 million departures*. Teen pregnancy is way down in America, which is mostly due to increased birth control, not abortions; the teen abortion rate has been dropping significantly too, as has the overall number of abortions. In fact, the percentage of teenagers having sex has actually decreased over the years, and teens are waiting longer before having sex, not that you'd know it from a panicky media. As reported by *The New York Times*:

> "There's no doubt that the public perception is that things are getting worse, and that kids are having sex younger and much wilder than they ever were," said Kathleen A. Bogle, an assistant professor of sociology and criminal justice at La Salle University. "But when you look at the data, that's not the case. ... I give presentations nationwide where I'm showing people that the virginity rate in college is higher than you think and the number of partners is lower than you think and hooking up more often than not does not mean intercourse," Dr. Bogle said. "But so many people think we're morally in trouble, in a downward spiral and teens are out of control. It's very difficult to convince people otherwise."

The rates of teens dropping out of high school, smoking, and drinking have also been declining for a decade.[29] For example, the percentage of 12th-grade

294 | T H E   S E C R E T   P E A C E

boys who reported binge drinking (having five or more alcoholic beverages in a row in the past two weeks) dropped from 52 percent in 1980 to 29 percent in 2007; girls' rates during that time dropped from 30 percent to 22 percent.[30]

Younger kids, too, are doing much better than many people's vivid imaginations assume. An extensive 1999 Justice Department report acknowledged only 115 abductions by strangers in the U.S. that year. In those cases, young children and infants were far less likely to be abducted than were teenagers. Likewise, a 2009 task force created by 49 state attorneys general concluded that there is no significant danger of children being sexually solicited online, despite common perception. And new social networking sites such as MySpace and Facebook have not increased the level of danger at all. The 278-page report was based on scientific data on online sexual predators, and meetings between dozens of academics, experts in child safety and executives of 30 companies.[31]

Another good trend: methamphetamine use in the U.S. has dropped significantly in the past few years; the proportion of 18-year-olds using the drug in the past year dropped by two-thirds since 1999, thanks mainly to education efforts. This success surprisingly curtailed a well-publicized growing crisis with crystal meth in rural America. Other countries are having success fighting drug abuse, as well. In 2001, Portugal controversially decriminalized drugs, and to everyone's surprise, it has been a big success. What this means is that if you are caught with drugs of any kind, you can't be arrested, but are instead recommended to a commission of psychiatrists and social workers that work with you to help you kick your habit. Officials believe that more addicts are seeking treatment now, thanks to assuaging their fears of prosecution. Portugal now has some of the lowest drug rates in Europe.[32]

Good statistics abound on nearly every social issue. The number of chronically homeless people in the U.S. dropped 30 percent in just two years, from 2005 to 2007, thanks to a new government "housing first" strategy.[33] Traffic accidents—the leading cause of death among young adults—are dropping, too. Around 42,000 Americans died in crashes in 2002, compared to 52,000 in 1970, even though the population density and number of cars rose dramatically. Workplace fatalities are down, too. Safer technology helps prevent accidents, and our healthcare advances allow more accidents victims to pull through.[34]

To top it all off, the human race is even getting more beautiful. In a valiant effort to verify our superficiality, researchers discovered that women rated as "attractive" tended to have 16 percent more children than everyone else, and more girls than boys. This adds up fairly quickly. (Handsome men, however, showed no difference, thus proving that no one really cares what men look like, and that we should just go ahead and wear sweatpants into the office every day.)[35]

With all this good news, what are the downsides? The first is increased obesity rates, which we discussed. The second major downward trend is the increasing cost of health care. This is a direct result of our success in increasing life expectancy. As our populations age, there are more medical costs and fewer people to pay for them. In the rich world in 1980, there were 20 people of retirement age for every 100 people of working age. So workers feed money into public programs such as Medicare and everyone's happy. But that 20 percent ratio is now 25 percent, and by 2050 it might be 45 percent. Japan, one of the most rapidly aging countries, might hit a 70 percent ratio, meaning there would be 70 older people for every 100 workers. Our current programs are financially unsustainable.[36]

So what can we do? Three partial solutions come to mind. First, raise the retirement age. This resting period was never meant to be applied to decades of our lives, but only a few final years. (Life expectancy in 1935, when American Social Security was created, was 62; now it's around 78.) Working longer attacks the problem doubly: one, fewer people are drawing money from the system, and by working they're simultaneously contributing as well. Secondly, along those lines, our concept of "employed" needs a little more flexibility. There should be better ways to phase out employment, to work part-time, and to easily retrain and try out new careers and interests. Countries also need to put anti-age-discrimination laws in place, such as in the U.S. and EU. Lastly, encourage immigration. This is a perfect solution: richer countries have aging populations and will soon need many jobs filled, while developing countries have surplus workers and many young people desperate for jobs and money. It won't be politically popular, but it will become increasingly necessary.[37]

Our increasing health care costs, in America and in other countries with quickly-aging populations, is certainly the downside to all of the positive health news. But yes, there are some glass-half-full ways to look at even this thorny issue. First, our healthcare standards are much higher than they were several generations ago. Most people in the past just lived with their aches and pains. Today, we will stop at nothing to root out the cause of any skin blemish, muscle ache, sore throat, or case of the sniffles. We've done such a good job of eliminating pain and death that we place a much higher value on each life and will work hard to make it perfect. Second, our current technology is much more advanced and, thus, expensive. But it gives us good results. Third, we now fight tooth and nail to save the lives of many people who would have been accepted as lost causes in the past. Victims of severe accidents, those injured at war, those who are missing limbs, children with birth defects, the very old, and the very young are now all within our means to help. My best friend's nephew was born three months premature and weighed less than two-and-a-half pounds at birth. He didn't leave the hospital for months, and his parents had to watch through the hospital room's window as he lay hooked up to countless machines. Years later, he is a healthy young boy and has a baby brother, too. A fourth reason why increased health care costs are not as bad as we think is more subjective: our society is much wealthier now, and isn't it better to spend our money on services and products that will help keep us healthy rather than say, SUVs, cigarettes, or lottery tickets? I believe most of the world's citizens in the past would have given their health higher priority and would have sacrificed more to be healthy had it been possible. Today we take for granted that we should be in tip-top shape all the time. Our great achievement is that today many people can be; now we need to work to include everyone on that list.

Nevertheless, the health care industry still needs a lot of work. As advanced as our treatments are, the industry still lags far behind others when it comes to information-sharing. But just as our other secret peace trends have been driven by the easier flow of information and democratized access to it, so is health care on the cusp of being transfigured by becoming more personalized, open, and accessible to all. The demand from empowered consumers who are living longer and paying more will soon lead to easy ways to access their own medical information. Today, that information is still shockingly difficult to both find and understand. As Internet guru and investor Esther Dyson explains, "The information now is stuck in a form where you can't compare [data] ... Imagine trying to lose weight if you didn't have a scale." She adds, "Now it gets rationed, but it's not clear how ... the system is impenetrable to the users." The system needs to become transparent so patients can comprehend costs and chances of treatments. Ideally, patients will "own" their own personal health data, instead of it belonging to hospitals or institutions. (I know someone whose physical therapy medical records were all destroyed after her physical therapist died. Turns out this was not only legal, but a commonly recommended procedure.)[38]

In addition, our health knowledge is changing from a one-way flow—doctors to patients—to a conversation everyone is participating in, by connecting online and both meeting in chat rooms and in face-to-face groups. The web site PatientsLikeMe, for example, lets members from around the world share advice and support about any given ailment, which is especially helpful with chronic illnesses or stigmatized conditions such as depression. Even doctors now have their own secure medical chat rooms.[39]

In order for our information to become accessible, it needs to be digitized, which is shockingly seldom done now. When this happens, it will revolutionize the speed and accuracy of treatments. Some developing world countries are surprisingly leapfrogging the West in this regard, especially by using mobile phones (known as mHealth.) For example, text messages were sent to millions of South Africans encouraging them to overcome stigmas and contact the national AIDS hotline, to great success. A study in Thailand showed drug compliance jumped to over 90 percent when patients got daily text reminders to take their pills. And health-care practitioners in Kenya can update patients' medical records on-site by using mobile technology. These innovations are encouraging, because developing countries face challenges we can barely imagine here in the developed world.[40]

IMPROVING HEALTH IN THE DEVELOPING WORLD

Not all countries have the luxury of worrying about the cost of top-notch health care and aging populations. Rather, they struggle with basic, mortal illnesses that the developed world has long eliminated from our plush lifestyles. Primary among these afflictions are Africa's three scourges of malaria, malnutrition, and AIDS. As I mentioned when we examined economics, global health is a critical factor in eliminating poverty. Several years ago aid agencies finally realized the importance of health as a first step toward development, and started to redirect greater funds toward global health. We are now starting to see the payoff.

The diseases ravaging the developing world are vastly different from the ones we are used to dealing with in the West, so most Americans are unfamiliar with the horrors of, say, malaria. After AIDS, malaria is the most deadly disease in Africa. It kills children in large numbers, encouraging families to overcompensate and have more children, putting additional pressure on resources. Unable to afford to educate all of their children, parents watch as their kids grow up without the education necessary to break out of poverty. Malaria used to be common in the Southern United States, Southern Europe, China, and South America, but now it's primarily a risk in Africa, India, Central America, and a few other equatorial locations. Malaria is easier to control in cooler countries because it is spread by Anopheles mosquitoes, which thrive in sub-Saharan Africa's warm weather. Despite the challenges, malaria can be controlled in Africa just as it is in other regions. Household spraying, insecticide-treated bed nets, and antimalarial medicines can be extremely effective in controlling it—if enough funding is available to scale up their implementation. Great progress has been made in distributing bed nets, and some areas that have put effective malaria control programs in place, such as southern Mozambique, have seen child mortality drop by as much as 90 percent. And if all goes well, GlaxoSmith-Kline is months away from approval of a vaccine that seems to cut the risk of infection in half. But it remains a sad irony that we have drugs available to cure most strains of malaria, but we lack the resources to distribute them to some places that need them the most.[41]

Like malaria, malnutrition is another tragedy less frequently encountered in the developed world. For the vast majority of human history, everyone was malnourished. Food production rarely rose above sustenance levels, and food choices were poor even when food was available. Today, less than 15 percent of the world suffers from chronic malnutrition, and many of us are overweight.[42]

Obesity also claims many lives, but compared to the blight of malnutrition, that problem is much more digestible.

For the starving masses—again, mostly in Africa, but also in India and throughout the developing world—new technology and medical advances are winning the battle against malnutrition. Today, for the first time in human history, over half of the world's population has water piped into its homes. Eighty-three percent of the world has access to clean water, which is remarkable; the number was 77 percent in 1990.[43] And nutritional science is advancing as well. For example, take Plumpy'nut—an adorably-named, peanut-based goopy food that is helping greatly to reduce malnutrition. To restore her health, a starving child can subsist on a four-week course of Plumpy'nut for just $20, a tenth of the cost of the usual treatment available. Furthermore, she can eat it at home instead of having to travel to a distant, crowded hospital. Plumpy'nut has the consistency of mashed potatoes, so even infants can suck it out of the packet themselves. Plumpy'nut has already been used to great success in Darfur and Niger.[44]

Of Africa's three great health obstacles, AIDS gets much more press than malaria or malnutrition. It is estimated that 1,800 children a day become infected with HIV, mostly newborns. Over 30 million people worldwide are living with the disease, making it a pandemic, and some African countries' populations are completely devastated. In South Africa, for example, 18 percent of the population is HIV-positive. Amidst this dire news, however, glimmers of hope can be seen. Astonishingly, the annual number of AIDS deaths has fallen by half, from 3.9 million in 2001 to 2.1 million just six years later. AIDS is conquerable, and an end to the disease is within sight.[45]

A recent UN report found that the spread of AIDS worldwide is slowing. The rate of new HIV infections peaked in 1998 and has been falling ever since then. The world is finally learning how to both treat and prevent the disease, and people are changing their behavior to avoid infection. Since we have now had several decades of living with AIDS, we can objectively review the results of international policies. Several countries, such as Cambodia, have been successful in curbing AIDS through a concerted educational effort via the media and schools. In Kenya and Zimbabwe, fewer teenagers are having sex, and condom use has increased, slowing the spread of the disease among 15 to 24-year-olds.

Some countries, such as Thailand, have seen success by targeting prostitutes with condom education. Other governments have used public ad campaigns to spread facts about AIDS; in many developing countries, myths persist about how the disease is contracted. In most countries, blood for transfusions is finally being screened for the disease. In southern India, where large numbers of the population are afflicted, the prevalence of HIV is slowing, too. China denied the existence of any cases of AIDS for decades, but it has finally admitted its problem and is concentrating on solving it. The Chinese government is sending volunteers into rural villages to spread information, and it is also broadcasting a series of TV documentaries about AIDS. And as for South Africa, with the world's largest HIV-positive population, the number of new HIV infections has started dropping significantly as teens are increasingly using condoms.[46]

After ignoring the disease for so long, the developed world is at last devoting necessary funds to the AIDS crisis. The trick is to use the funds wisely. The Copenhagen Consensus found that combating AIDS and malaria has the best return of any aid investment. Developed countries, charities, and NGOs are now allocating vast resources to fighting both diseases. Research devoted to the treatment of AIDS and malaria has been extraordinarily successful. Thanks to ARVs, anti-retroviral drugs that block HIV's effects on the immune system, AIDS is no longer a death sentence for many people. In fact, a Yale study in western Kenya showed a 20 percent increase in labor-force participation and a 35 percent increase in hours worked among AIDS patients within six months of starting treatment with ARVs. The greatest difficulty is supplying the expensive drugs to the masses. But progress has been made, with GlaxoSmithKline, a British pharmaceutical company, recently waiving its patent restrictions. This allows generic drug manufacturers in India to supply the drugs very cheaply. This is thanks to a coalition of activists led by Bill Clinton, and helped by $15 billion in new funds made available by the Bush administration. Astonishingly, while in 2002 only 1 percent of Africans who needed the drugs had them, in 2007 28 percent—or 1.34 million people—were able to receive treatment, and the number is growing.[47] Likewise, more than half of all HIV-positive pregnant women are now receiving drugs that help prevent transmitting the disease to their newborns, compared to one in 10 in 2004.[48]

Research has now shifted to discovering preventative measures. Surprisingly, circumcision was recently discovered to potentially reduce risks of contracting HIV by up to 60 percent—which could save three million lives in Africa alone over the next 20 years.[49] And the Gates Foundation and scientists worldwide are desperately searching for a vaccine. Gene therapy has had some tentative lab success with inserting HIV-resistant genes into people, which then duplicate other resistant genes, in effect causing the body to "vaccinate" itself. A combination of two vaccines tested in Thailand was recently proven to cut the risk of infection by a breakthrough 31 percent.[50] There are also preventative pills being developed, which would be taken regularly like a birth-control pill, and anti-microbial gel that can be applied by women before sex to reduce the chance of contracting HIV by as much as 80 percent.[51]

Much progress has also been made in battling other diseases that plague the developing world. In 1974, only five percent of children in developing countries were immunized against polio, tetanus, measles, whooping cough, diphtheria, and tuberculosis. Today, that number is 80 percent, which is why you probably don't know of anyone who has recently died of whooping cough. The vaccine industry is experiencing a rebirth thanks to new demand and new technology. They are working hard to develop vaccines that don't require needles or refrigeration. Mapping the human genome vastly increased the number of targets available for researchers; vaccines for meningitis-B and a virus that causes cervical cancer are both brand new.[52] The annual number of people who die of measles worldwide dropped by 60 percent between 1999 and 2005, beating a UN goal. Measles deaths in Africa are down more than 90 percent in only seven years.[53] Even malaria has promising vaccine news: a new trial vaccine has been shown to reduce the infection rate by 65 percent.[54] Polio is on the cusp of being eradicated; in 1988 polio existed in 125 countries and killed 350,000, while today it is found in only four countries (Nigeria, India, Pakistan and Afghanistan), with a worldwide total of only 784 cases a year.[55]

Even more impressive than the worldwide decrease in polio is the complete eradication of smallpox, which is one of our greatest health achievements. Smallpox killed millions of people throughout the millennia, but it was systematically hunted down by the World Health Organization, resulting in a smallpox-free world by 1980. The elimination of smallpox has saved an estimat-ed $1 billion a year in vaccinations and treatment worldwide.[56] As Easterbrook writes, "We worry about smallpox falling into the hands of terrorists, but for-get that fifty years ago it was rampant in poor nations ... [and] river blindness, once a scourge of Africa, has been nearly eradicated."[57]

Buoyed by these successes, the international scientific community can now muster an impressive response to new diseases such as avian bird flu and swine flu (a positive direct result of media hyper-attention on an issue.) New technology is helping too—data from websites like Google and Twitter can be used to instantly track the spread of the flu, since people experiencing symp-toms tend to search and talk about it. As another example, genetically sequenc-ing HIV (an essential step to understanding the virus) initially took five years, but technology has advanced to the point where sequencing a new virus now takes only a day or two.[58] The ability to quickly improve technology, coordinate efforts worldwide, and act quickly to stop the spread of disease is an important development in health. But it's only the tip of the iceberg of what is going to be possible in a few short years.

SCIENCE MARCHES ON: GENETICS, NANOTECH & MORE

Here's a riveting bit of U.S. Presidential trivia, written by Richard Lederer, which serves as a gripping reminder of how far we've come with our medical know-how:

> After James Garfield was shot by Charles Guiteau, he spent 80 days on his deathbed while a team of doctors probed him with unwashed hands and unsanitary medical instru-ments. They tried to find the bullet with a metal detector in-vented by Alexander Graham Bell—but the device failed be-cause Garfield was placed on a bed with metal springs, and

no one thought to move him. To escape the Washington heat, Garfield was moved to a seaside cottage in New Jersey early in September. There he died on Sept. 19, 1881, succumbing to death by doctors.

An even more absurd example: when Lincoln lay dying after being shot, his physician applied some "mummy paint" to the wounds. Yes, this was actual Egyptian mummy parts ground to a powder, believed at the time to be a practically universal remedy.[59] Can you imagine if modern medicine had been at hand instead? Who knows, maybe Lincoln could have served out his term in office. It's sobering to realize that none of these examples are from our distant caveman past, but rather just five or six generations ago. What makes it even worse is that those were the most highly-esteemed doctors and state-of-the-art medical technology of the time, since they were for the President!

The twentieth century brought the world innumerable new health technologies, which are useful to reflect upon to remind ourselves of just how lucky we are. In addition to the development of vaccines and the progress made against disease, we also have prosthetics such as artificial joints and limbs, pacemakers, and hearing aids; a revolution in pharmaceuticals like anti-inflammatory drugs, antidepressants, and birth-control pills, and incredibly adroit heart surgeries and organ transplants.

What about the future? All industries related to the study of the human body are booming—genetics, healthcare, pharmaceuticals. Medical discoveries are emerging faster than in most other scientific fields. As life expectancies keep going up, new medical breakthroughs offer the promise that humans can someday live to be 120 years old and beyond. Stem cell research holds the potential for nerve regeneration—actually, regeneration of just about any part of the body. Several breakthroughs happened with stem cell research in 2007. Incredibly, cells can now be generated from other cells in the body that look and act like embryonic stem cells without the need for embryos or eggs, eliminating much of the controversy from this line of research. Soon we should be able to grow complex organs from stem cells, and eventually, from our own stem cells.[60] It's easy to imagine pretty radical changes in the next few years—for one, spinal cord paralysis could be reversed, which is what the actor Christopher Reeve so heroically struggled to achieve. Going even smaller, nanotechnology holds the possibility to construct microscopic medical instruments that can go anywhere in the human body and rearrange any misbehaving molecules. Prosthetic limb technology has drastically advanced in the past few years, and the burgeoning field of "neuroprosthetics" might bear fruit very soon, allowing amputees to control artificial limbs with their normal mental impulses. Believe it or not, even artificial blood is being worked on by researchers. And a new field called pharmacogenomics seeks to tailor drugs for each person's unique physiology.[61] This approach might provide a solution to the increasing resistance of bacteria to traditional antibiotics.

At the cutting edge of health advancements is the realm of genetics, which has the potential not only to conquer all of humanity's health ailments but also to improve our quality of life. Since the 2003 success of the Human Genome Project, in which government and industry worked together to map out the entire sequence of human genes, the field of human genetics has moved along at a frantic pace. DNA testing is now an invaluable part of law enforcement. Genetic testing for disease helps parents weigh the options of bearing children with fatal genetic disorders. Cloning is a new genetic field that might allow us to clone our own replaceable organs, breed healthier livestock, and save endangered species.[62]

Undoubtedly, many of these new developments will be making news by the time you read this. In fact, in all of our discussions of technology I'm steering clear of dwelling on the most cutting-edge ideas. Any field could have a radical breakthrough—nanotechnology, space exploration, cloning, cold fusion. These scientific changes always knock humanity for a loop. We cannot predict precisely what they will be, but it's very unlikely that any new developments would derail the inevitable movement toward peace if we control them cautiously, democratically, and ethically. Each new technology creates ethical problems that necessitate an active and informed public. Genetically engineered crops are a nutritional godsend, but are they eliminating the broad diversity of natural crops? Is cloning human beings ethical? While the developing world is busy catching up to benefits currently available in the

West, are the rich world's rapid-fire advances in health care going to leave some developing countries behind?

Democratizing the decision-making processes by making information more publicly available, transparent, and easy to understand will be essential to addressing these questions. In addition, my hope is that the thought paradigm and global ethic we examined in earlier chapters are advancing fast enough to allow a mature humanity to tackle such issues. Carl Sagan once pointed out that "the most open and vigorous debate is often the only protection against the most perilous misuse of technology."[63] It's the misuse of technology that brings us now to examine the state of our environment.

11

ENVIRONMENT

Harnessing New Energy

If you're reading this book, you have most likely been blessed with an education and the leisure time to read books recreationally. I'm lucky enough to live within walking distance of Barnes & Noble (six of them— I live in Manhattan) so I can pick up books whenever I get a craving. Or, I can order them online, and sit in my Cookie Monster slippers while a team of people across America work to ship the book to me in a few days. If it's summer, I get to sit in an air-conditioned room and sip bottled water still cold from the refrigerator. If I drink too much, I need only shuffle a good 20 feet to take advantage of the indoor plumbing.

I am incredibly grateful that I was born in the United States in this day and age. Fifty years ago only a few people would have been able to enjoy the benefits that many of us take for granted today: bookstores may have been common in New York and other major cities, but megastores had not yet spread across the country, and online ordering was decades away. Air conditioning wasn't yet commercially available for the average family. A hundred years ago, both cars and refrigeration were rare, and the average person worked many more hours, so time for recreational reading was unusual unless you were well-off. Going back several hundred years, even the filthy rich couldn't have imagined the lifestyle that many of us take for granted today.

Our world is filled with a vast array of incredible inventions. Today, most families in the United States have more than one car, and they're a lot safer and creates less pollution than cars a few decades earlier did. The average American living space today has 3.3 rooms for every 2.6 people, a century ago it was common for a family of eight to share a single room. And while two generations ago 15 percent of American homes were heated, today the number is 95 percent.[1] Figure 20 shows the number of households that own certain products. The chart compares ownership of various appliances by all U.S. households in 1950 (represented by black bars) with ownership by households below the poverty line in 2001 (represented by white bars).[2]

FIGURE 20: OWNERSHIP BY ALL HOUSEHOLDS IN 1950 (BLACK BARS) VS. POOR HOUSEHOLDS IN 2001 (WHITE BARS)

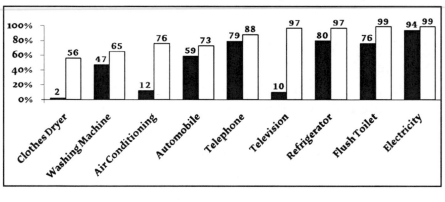

In 1950, almost no one had a clothes dryer, air conditioning, or a television. Items that the rich considered themselves lucky to have in 1950 have since become commonplace among even the poorest Americans. Clearly, America and the rest of the developed world have made incredible advancements in material goods. We are swimming with products from the essential to the superfluous—cars, huge homes, clothes, books, DVDs, iPods, elliptical machines, frozen dinners, and myriad other labor-saving conveniences and luxuries. Creating and using these products requires a great deal of energy. In addition, as globalization builds a new middle class in previously poor countries, new consumers want their deserved rewards—computers and toasters and even those little round robot vacuums. As a result, world energy consumption has been rapidly rising, and producing that energy is destroying the planet.

Worldwide, millions of cars and factories are spewing pollution, which is increasing dramatically every year. Due in part to environmental degradation, weather-related disasters are escalating every year, especially hurricanes. We need no better example than Hurricane Katrina, one of the deadliest natural disasters in U.S. history, to drive that point home. Our irresponsible stewardship of the environment has also severely damaged coral reefs, depleted the fish in our oceans, reduced wetlands, endangered or extinguished formerly thriving plant and animal species, caused deforestation in the Amazon and elsewhere, and led to droughts in Africa. This is not to mention the looming threat of global warming, the consequences of which are nothing if not unpredictable.

Our heavy reliance on fossil fuels and our poor stewardship of the environment have combined to form one of the most prominent negative trends today. We've seen so many trends point toward a secret peace, but the environment continues to be degraded, desiccated, and devastated. How could there possibly be any good news hidden in that?

BUT WE ARE LEARNING FROM OUR MISTAKES

In the mid-1980s, the world saw the first evidence of a hole in the ozone layer of the atmosphere and wisely panicked. The ozone layer is part of the upper atmosphere, and its oxygen blocks the sun's ultraviolet rays. The same ultraviolet rays that pale people like me try to protect themselves from on the beach would do much more damage if the stratosphere didn't have any ozone. Depletion of the ozone layer was first detected in 1974, but the discovery of the Antarctic hole in the mid-1980s really grabbed people's attention. Most readers can probably remember the phenomenal amount of attention the press devoted to the issue. The world gaped in horror at one of the most intimidating and insoluble problems it had ever faced. And guess what? We solved it. Scientists worked feverishly and soon traced the depletion to chlorofluorocarbons (CFCs), common chemicals used for refrigeration, aerosol spray propellants, and cleaning solvents. Governments around the world quickly adopted an agreement to limit the pollutants. Eventually, 184 countries—nearly every nation in the world—became signatories to the Montreal Protocol, which prohibits the release of CFCs. By acting quickly and cooperating internationally, CFC use had dropped 96 percent by 2005, and the world halted the spread of ozone depletion, which peaked and is stabilizing. It will still take four or five decades for the Antarctic hole to close up, but it's on its way.[3]

When the developed world started tackling the ozone problem in the 1980s, it also realized there were other problems that required joint participation. Acid rain was damaging crops and trees, eroding buildings, and tainting drinking water. So in addition to reducing harmful CFCs, countries worked together to reduce their output of sulfur dioxide, and sure enough, those countries are seeing their acid rain problem evaporate. Acid rain remains a problem in China and Eastern Europe, but the United Kingdom, for example, has had its rain acidity reduced by half in 15 years.[4]

When two of the earth's largest problems can be handled effectively, it suggests that nearly anything is possible. Certainly, there is much more good news. In developed countries—especially the European nations, Canada, the United States, and Japan—environmental conditions have been improving for the past three decades. This is a direct result of effective government regulation. Only one-third of American lakes and rivers were safe for swimming and fishing some 25 years ago; today, two-thirds are.[5] When polled, most Americans believe pollution is getting worse. But smog levels in the United States have been reduced by one-third since 1970—even as the number of cars has increased—thanks to the three-way catalytic converter and pollution-reducing initiatives. In 1990, 57 percent of the gasoline market worldwide was for leaded gas; by 2002 it had shrunk to less than 10 percent.[6]

Our beaches are cleaner, our skies are clearer, and industrialized countries have *more* trees now than they did a few decades ago. Take a look at Figure 21:

developing countries in Africa and South America are losing their forests, but industrialized countries in Europe and elsewhere are replanting at an impressive rate. China alone is adding about 4 million hectares of forest a year. When we hear the negative statistics about deforestation, we are usually focused on the final number. As terrible as the final numbers of deforestation are, we need to realize that there are also some positive trends. Forest area is expanding in 22 of the 50 countries with the most forest land. Replanting does not solve the problem completely; the loss of forest biodiversity is another important issue. But due to new policies and slowing development, many other countries are poised to reverse their tree depletion as well.[7]

FIGURE 21: CHANGE IN EXTENT OF FOREST, 2000–2005[8]

Region	Change in Area (thousand hectares)
South America	-21,256
Africa	-20,201
Oceania	-1,780
Central America/Caribbean	-1,158
North America	**-507**
Europe	**+3,303**
Asia	**+5,015**
World Total	-36,583

Many world cities have been revitalized environmentally. Chicago is an excellent case study, having planted 300,000 trees in the last two decades and created 72 new gardens and parks. Gregg Easterbrook explains in *The Progress Paradox*, "The Chicago River, described in the 1906 Upton Sinclair classic *The Jungle* as so loaded with filth that chickens actually were seen walking across it, and as recently as the 1970s still badly polluted, today hosts art festivals, boat tours, and dinner cruises." Researchers from the Harvard School of Public Health estimate that air pollution reduction efforts since the 1970s have been so successful that they have added five months to the nation's overall average life expectancy. Or take Mexico City, which by enacting tough environmental standards was able to reduce lead levels by 95 percent and carbon monoxide by 74 percent in the last 15 years.[9] Architects have come up with more energy-efficient buildings with solar panels to collect energy, cisterns to collect rainwater, and special glass that lets natural light in but minimizes heat loss in winter. This is an essential development since in America, buildings account for 65 percent of electricity consumption and 30 percent of greenhouse-gas emissions. On average, "green buildings" use some 30 percent less energy than conventional buildings, so their extra construction costs are quickly recouped.[10]

There is even good environmental news in one of the most dangerous places on Earth—the Demilitarized Zone. This stretch of land between North and South Korea is the most heavily fortified border in the world, rimmed with guns and armies and filled with land mines. And yet, as *The Week* reports, "precisely because so few people have ventured into the 150-mile-long, 2.5-mile-wide strip for half a century, it has become a wildlife haven." Hundreds of animal species make it their home—some endangered, and several no longer living in the rest of Korea. Studying the Demilitarized Zone can help us learn how to return land areas to their natural states.

In the four decades since the environmental movement began, most citizens of the developed world, and many in other countries, are well educated about the detrimental effects of pollution and its danger to the environment. In the United States, a majority of adults hold strong environmental beliefs: 87 percent believe we should have more respect and reverence for nature, 85 percent feel that global warming should be seen as a serious problem, 81 percent think it's important to set higher emissions standards for industry, and 79 percent agree that the government should spend more money on developing wind and solar power.[11] Environmental groups remain one of the most popular charity causes. Ecotourism is becoming more popular, too. Ecotourists try to have limited environmental impact wherever they visit, and the eye-opening experience of travel in lush landscapes often inspires them to work harder on global environmental issues. In 2004, the Nobel Peace Prize went to an environmental activist for the first time—Wangari Maathai, a Kenyan woman who leads the

Green Belt Movement, which empowers women and fights for environmental causes throughout Africa. And the second environmental Nobel Peace Prize went to Al Gore in 2007, along with the Intergovernmental Panel on Climate Change, for publicizing the potential dangers of global warming. While many environmentalists are in the liberal camp, conservative religious groups are becoming increasingly interested in environmental issues as well. It is essential to harness such public support to continue to curb pollution and brighten the future for our environment.

ENDING POLLUTION

Steps to save the earth can be divided into three areas: reducing pollution and our environmental impact, finding new energy sources, and decreasing our consumption of resources. Of these three areas, decreasing our consumption of resources seems the most implausible a solution. There are, of course, common token steps such as recycling and turning out lights when we leave a room. Many people are beginning to take bigger steps such as insulating homes and windows, buying more fuel-efficient or hybrid cars, composting organic waste instead of throwing it away, and using energy-saving light bulbs. But most of us do not feel pressure to give up our consumer lifestyle. And people in developing countries such as China are increasingly feeling entitled to the same technology and level of comfort that we enjoy in the Western world. Unfortunately, as Earth's poorer citizens finally gain the material goods they certainly deserve, the environment suffers as a result.

We are making significant progress in the other two areas, however: reducing pollution and harnessing new energy sources. Three groups have the ability to reduce pollution: government, business, and consumers. While all three groups are taking action, government regulation has been most successful so far. Most developed countries have implemented fuel-efficiency standards for their cars (though U.S. standards are still low—even lower than China's), and most have removed harmful lead from gasoline, banned CFCs, and set environmental standards for industry, which otherwise would have little incentive to reduce pollution. In 2002 toxic emissions by U.S. industries had declined by 51 percent in just 14 years.[12] New cars today emit less than two percent of the pollution per mile that cars made in 1970 emitted.[13] Even at this writing, new diesel fuel regulations are going into effect in the United States. Diesel engines will be much cleaner than before and will soon be phased into many more vehicles. As the *Economist* describes, "Hitherto diesel contained up to 500 parts per million (ppm) of sulphur, but the new rules limit sulphur to 15 ppm. ... Today's diesels are sturdy, smooth and up to 40% more fuel-efficient than petrol engines."[14]

On the world stage, multilateral environmental treaties have been multiplying. At first the treaties targeted specific issues such as wetland conservation. But now they are becoming broad frameworks that integrate many environmental issues, culminating thus far in the Kyoto Protocol, a pact addressing global warming. Kyoto lingered for a few years before going into effect; it needed countries that together totaled at least 55 percent of the world's emissions to participate. The United States declined, but Russia stepped up to the plate, and the pact went into effect in 2005. The Kyoto global warming initiative calls on industrialized countries to rein in pollution from carbon dioxide and other gases emitted from the burning of fossil fuels. The UN, too, has an arm that leads environmental efforts. One of its biggest successes was cleaning up the Mediterranean Sea. It convinced adversaries such as Israel and Syria, and Turkey and Greece to work together, and now more than 50 percent of Mediterranean beaches that were once polluted are usable again.[15]

In the United States environmental battles are best waged at the state level. Nine Northeastern states have reached a tentative agreement to freeze power-plant emissions at present levels and then cut them back 10 percent by 2020.[16] California passed an impressive landmark plan to impose caps on its greenhouse-gas emissions. It calls on the state's major industries to reduce their emissions by 25 percent by 2020. Governor Schwarzenegger hopes the plan will serve as "an example for other states and nations to follow as the fight against climate change continues."[17] Many states have introduced measures to encourage the use of alternative energy sources. But government regulations, whether international or local, can only go so far without the cooperation of industry and consumers.

Businesses are often the hardest group to get on board the environmental bandwagon because they're naturally torn between the seemingly incongruent goals of protecting the environment and making a profit. But at least four key motivators do encourage change. The threat of government regulation inspires companies to make the jump preemptively; they would rather get a head start and change their damaging environmental practices themselves than have external rules imposed upon them. British Petroleum (BP), for example, preemptively reduced its emissions below Kyoto Protocol requirements. A second motivator for businesses to clean up their act is the worldwide reach of most large corporations. Since they're already obligated to apply the Kyoto regulations to their operations in Kyoto-signing countries, they might as well apply the same standards to operations in the United States, since enacting different policies in different places can be even more costly than absorbing the cost of reducing emissions everywhere. A third key motivator for businesses is corporate image. Consumers are increasingly demanding environmentally friendly products. Though environmental friendliness is still not the main selling point for most products, companies benefit from projecting a corporate image of environmental concern. Similarly, the fourth motivator for businesses to change their actions is consumer boycotts. Many communities have successfully brought about changes in unsound practices once they came together to boycott environmentally harmful products.[18] It's easy to see how consumer action could be a corporation's worst nightmare.

But with intensifying pressure to watch the bottom line and report record growth every year, or even every quarter, businesses are loathe to lay out an investment that will not necessarily pay off. Over time, environmental investments *will* pay off—possibly in unexpected ways. Businesses will certainly lose money if ocean levels rise, for example. This was evident in the wake of Hurricane Katrina, which devastated most of New Orleans. Ecologist Gretchen Daily explains that ecosystems need to be seen as a kind of capital. "If managed properly, they will provide a steady stream of benefits. These not only include obvious goods like food and timber but also life-supporting services such as water purification, flood control, stabilization of climate, and pollination of crops. Right now, we have unprecedented demand for such ecosystem services and a decreasing supply, which increases their economic value."[19]

There are several possible ways to enable businesses to make a profit without compromising the environment. The most realistic proposal might be for businesses to barter pollution rights, known as a cap-and-trade system. This effectively puts a cost on pollution, giving less-polluting factories a market advantage. The more efficient companies will have more pollution rights (because they make less pollution), which they could then sell to companies that are less effective at curbing their pollution. This proposal would essentially fine companies for creating pollution, while other companies would be rewarded for their efficiency. The government gets this process going by setting a cap on the total pollution (which tightens every year) and awarding pollution credits in the first place. Then it steps back somewhat, allowing the system to run on its own, giving companies the incentive either to change their practices for the better or cave in to market forces. The European Union already has a cap-and-trade system in place, and a U.S. bill to implement the system recently passed in the House.[20]

Many businesses are already "going green." To enhance their corporate image, some companies are becoming carbon-neutral; for example, HSBC Bank USA is the first big bank to do so. Carbon-neutral firms cut their carbon emissions as much as possible and then make up for any remaining pollution by paying to reduce emissions in other places.[21] More commonly, companies go green by improving their energy efficiency. Those that have done so, according to the Economist, "have found energy efficiency to be surprisingly good for profits."[22]

Some companies are bowing to increasing consumer demand for green products, but consumers' actions are not yet completely commensurate with their words. Consumers are still slow to show overwhelming support for the environment with their pocketbooks. We may support recycled products and energy-efficient goods, but so far, these concessions have been modest. The extra few thousand dollars it would cost to purchase a hybrid car, for example, is enough to thwart some of the best-intentioned conservationists. And we only care about certain products, not all of them: I often look for recycled printer paper, but I don't choose which books to buy based on the environmental friendliness of their pages. However, the fact that environmental issues have become a competition point for thousands of products is a wonderful sign.

It should be getting easier for consumers soon—web sites and organizations like Good Guide are starting to roll up the many diverse environmental impacts of a product into easy-to-understand ratings. What if that organic food wasn't grown with chemicals, but its packaging has terrible dye? But what if that dye is actually better than the amount of water used to make a competitor's product? What if some components of your computer are fair-trade and others made by children exposed to toxic chemicals? To do it one better, factor in polluting information from Scorecard.org, too. The site ranks the top polluters across locations and industries. Without help, the consumer can be buried under an avalanche of data trying to determine products' environmental footprints, but with help, the new access to information can be revolutionary.[23]

All environmental economic propositions revolve around charging the real price it costs to make something, which includes the cost to clean up the pollution made by the factory that made the product. (The economic term is *negative externality*, a bad side effect not factored into a product's cost.) Trees provide more value than we think because they clean the air by absorbing carbon from the atmosphere (a positive externality). Factoring the loss of carbon absorption into the cost of wood products by increasing prices accordingly would encourage consumers to seek out the most environmentally friendly products (like recycled paper), since they would become much cheaper. Take tap water, for example: my water is included in my rent. So, unless I am already concerned about conserving water for other reasons, what incentive do I have not to waste it? I could leave the shower on all day and not pay a cent for it. Most of us are already accustomed to turning lights off when we leave the house since it will affect our energy bills; other resources should be treated the same way.

Environmental groups have proposed changing the current highway toll system by adjusting tolls to factor in the time of day and pollution levels. With such systems someone driving during peak rush hour would be required to pay more money, since he's spending more time on the road, because of traffic. In other words, we currently have tolls for distance traveled, not time (and hence, pollution). This disincentive to drive might lead to the development of other options such as public transportation or telecommuting and would pass the costs of pollution on to those who pollute the most.[24] The extra money charged could be reinvested in new energy research.

An even more ambitious proposal for improving the environment is a carbon tax, which places a small tax on how much coal, oil, fuel, and natural gas consumers and industries use since all of these energy sources contribute to global warming. Individual countries are often reluctant to impose carbon taxes due to the fear of increased costs making their industries less competitive. (Hypothetically, if an American carbon tax forces a chemical plant to become less competitive than a more-polluting Chinese one, and it goes out of business, the global production slack is picked up by the Chinese anyway, creating an increase in net pollution.) But many studies have shown that the impact would probably be minimal, with only a few key industries at risk of contraction, and then only in the range of one to two percent.[25] The Scandinavian countries have had a carbon tax for years; many environmentalists are proposing a global carbon tax.

Even without being forced to adhere to environmentally sound practices, consumers can initiate their own conservation efforts. A big conservation push started in the 1970s, and the current generation of environmentalists have absorbed many of its lessons. For example, recent awareness about waste over the last few decades, in the form of recycling, reusing products, and manufacturing better packaging, is paying off. As the *Economist* reports:

> ... the pace at which the rich world churns out rubbish has been slowing. Between 1980 and 2000 the amount of waste produced by the OECD countries increased by an average of 2.5% a year. Between 2000 to 2005 the average growth rate slowed to 0.9% ... well behind the rate of economic growth (2.2%) ...[26]

The way we get rid of our garbage might soon be radically changed, too. Lots of new, high-tech disposal methods are being developed. One particularly interesting one is called "plasma gasification," and uses electricity to make plasma so powerful it can disintegrate *any* trash into its constituent molecules. We're talking about banana peels, aluminum cans, dirty diapers, and even chemical weapons. The only output from that process is a black glass that can be used for many different types of construction and a synthetic gas that could be converted into fuel. Even more of a miracle, it's self-sustaining: electricity gets it going, but then as long as you put in trash the plasma keeps on working.[27]

More down-to-earth technology is partially responsible for the trend to less trash. As the computer age dawned, many people predicted a "paperless office"—but instead, as information was disseminated more easily, printing was in much higher demand. But it's finally coming true. Since 2001, American office workers' paper use has been in steady decline. A new generation is entering the workforce, one more comfortable with storing information on their computers, and increasingly, on the Internet. High-end paper remains in demand, for specialty uses such as printing photographs. But using paper for mundane tasks such as forms and memos is increasingly antiquated.[28] Personally, in my office, my younger coworkers tease me as a "tree killer" on the rare occasions when I print something; they never do. Why risk losing a piece of paper when you can store something online, accessible to everyone and easily indexed and searchable? It's now commonplace to pay bills online, file taxes online, and use Google to find restaurants—piles of unused Yellow Pages books lie lonely in my apartment building lobby.

In the 1970s, gas shortages and skyrocketing gas prices inspired a nationwide energy-saving movement in the United States. Today, recent fluctuating gas prices have again finally made a dent in our automotive usage and the types of cars Americans buy. But energy is still so cheap for Americans that many of us don't give a second thought to leaving our computers on, our cell phones plugged in, or our PlayStations on "pause" for a week. This is another sign of how wealthy society has become, but it can be bad news for the environment. If we're going to be that profligate with our energy—and it looks pretty hard to convince us otherwise—our best bet is to make sure the energy starts conserving itself.

RENEWING ENERGY

Promising new energy ideas are popping up left and right, and lots of venture capitalists are banking on energy as the next big innovative economic boom sector. The total world investment in clean energy was estimated at $30 billion in 2004, $49 billion in 2005, and $63 billion in 2006.[29] Solar power, wind power, and hydrogen fuel cells are all booming industries, and hybrid cars are becoming common. Historically, this makes sense. If we look back at the history of energy, we see humankind harnessing a lineage of different energy sources, each more efficient and less polluting than its predecessors. Figure 22 describes U.S. energy sources, and it starts with 1850, when the United States derived almost all of its energy from wood. Then coal—which is much more energy efficient than burning wood—became predominant and peaked in use around 1920. Oil, for all of its pollution, is still cleaner and more efficient than coal. Oil use started in 1880 and peaked as a percentage of our total in 1960; since then, we have derived about 40 percent of our energy from oil. Natural gas is the cleanest fossil fuel; its percentage of use peaked around 1970 and has declined since. Nuclear power is cleaner than all of the energies used thus far—it currently accounts for approximately eight percent of all of our energy. Hydroelectric power has been around for a long time but has never served more than a small fraction of our energy needs. Finally, other renewable energy sources, which we will examine below, have been quickly growing in use so far in the twenty-first century. Overall, this gradual "decarbonization"—shifting in use from high-pollution, high-carbon forms of energy to more efficient ones—is a process every country naturally goes through, though at different times and at their own paces.[30]

Humankind is ready to keep moving forward and find cleaner energy sources. As French economist Jacques Attali explains, "The world successfully overcame the disappearance of farmlands in Flanders, of charcoal in England, of whale oil in the Atlantic, of coal throughout Europe. The invasion of cities by horse droppings, feared by everyone in the late nineteenth century, never materialized." We'll overcome our current energy problems, too.[31]

FIGURE 22: U.S. ENERGY SOURCES,
AS PERCENTAGE OF TOTAL: 1850–2005

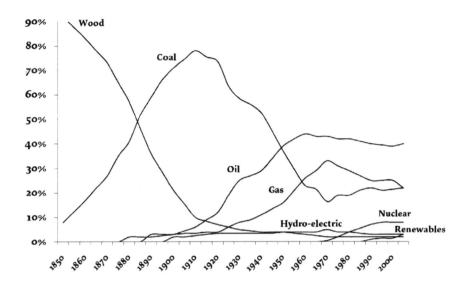

To further energize the search for viable alternatives, we must end our addiction to fossil fuels, particularly oil. The reason is not because we're running out of oil. This oft-cited idea is true—after all, there is a finite amount of oil in the earth, and many oil fields are being depleted. But when a field is used up, oil companies just move on to the next one. Over time, they have developed sophisticated means to extract oil from difficult places they could not access before, such as oil that is deep underwater or mixed with soil. Though U.S. oil reserves have peaked and might even be completely depleted in a few years, estimates of how much oil is left in the world remain high—possibly over a trillion barrels.[32] Oil companies and the world's governments know we will *eventually* run out of oil, but some current estimates place this event several decades away. Although, the cost to extract oil from the more difficult spots continues to go up, which means that oil will continue to get more expensive. And then there's the growing demand from rapidly industrializing countries like China, which is driving the price of oil up, too. This prohibitive cost will bring our use of oil to an end well before we actually run out.

While we may still have decades' worth of oil left, that doesn't mean that we can continue being irresponsible. For several reasons, we need to replace our dependence on oil with new energy sources and technology as soon as possible. As environmental author Dr. Indur M. Goklany put it, "The stone age didn't end because we ran out of stones, the iron age because we ran out of iron, or the bronze age because we ran out of bronze."[33] We have to curb our oil consumption in order to stop pollution and global warming, and we have to think ahead to identify the best energy alternatives to fuel the needs of future generations. But those aren't our only incentives to cut back on fossil fuel use. Basing the world economy on cheap oil grants those who control the oil disproportionate power. Some of the countries blessed with oil are responsible democracies—such as the United States, Canada, and Norway. But many of the oil-producing countries—such as Iran, Iraq, Saudi Arabia, Venezuela, and Russia—have strong authoritarian tendencies.

The Middle East (especially Saudi Arabia and Kuwait) ended up with the bulk of the world's oil, which is allowing those governments to remain authoritarian. When a country can get money from selling oil, it doesn't need to create alternate sources of income by developing other industries. Without the diversification of industry, a nation's citizens lack motivation to gain skills and education, or to pursue other fields, so unemployment rises, and the gap between the poor and the wealthy increases. With a lot of money flowing in, a ruler is very secure and can treat his populace however he wants, not to mention threatening any nations that depend on his oil. Flush with money, the government has no need to tax its citizens, and so doesn't feel obligated to answer to them democratically. The leaders of such countries tend to consolidate power and quash any sources of dissent. They may also blackmail the rest of the world with the threat of turning off the oil spigots. To put it succinctly, as the price of oil goes up, freedom goes down in oil-rich countries. This is what *New York Times* columnist Thomas L. Friedman, known for creating catchy nicknames, calls the "First Law of Petropolitics."[34] Lowering the demand for oil would force "oil-cratic" states such as Iran to embrace more democratic practices. It would also cut down on global conflict—ever since President Carter announced that the United States would do anything to protect its oil supply, several conflicts (including both of our journeys into Iraq) have had oil as at least a partial motivating factor.

The U.S. federal government recently announced the goal of obtaining three-quarters of the nation's automobile fuel from non-Middle Eastern sources by 2025.[35] Any talk of cutting down on oil use comes down to cars. Transportation consumes a great deal of the world's oil. With the rising fuel demands of China and other developing countries, worldwide car use is set to skyrocket. Unless we create more fuel-efficient vehicles or come up with practical alternative fuel sources, the current trend of oil consumption will continue. Thankfully, fuel efficiency is making progress in the right direction—and increasingly quickly. Hybrid cars are no longer a novelty, though they still only make up a small proportion of total car sales. The public is now familiar with the concept of a car running more efficiently by using both oil and electricity. The sales reports and projections in Figure 23, by JD Power & Associates, show the increasing popularity of the hybrid. The next generation of hybrids will probably be "plug-ins" (meaning you can charge them from a wall socket) such as the Chevrolet Volt, and with carmakers practically jumping all over each other to release the first mainstream all-electric car, we should see those by 2010, too.[36]

FIGURE 23: HYBRID CARS AS PERCENTAGE OF TOTAL U.S. VEHICLE SALES

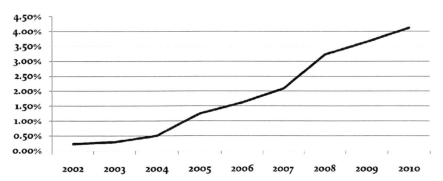

Many pundits thought it would never happen, but when gas prices surpassed $4 a gallon in 2008 (before the financial crisis lowered them again), U.S. car buyers finally began turning from SUVs to smaller, more fuel-efficient vehicles. In April 2008, four-cylinder engines surpassed six-cylinder models for the first time, and one in five vehicles purchased was a compact or subcompact car, a shift from one in eight a decade earlier. Even with gas prices having dropped since then, that trend seems unlikely to reverse, as people have realized the fickleness of the global market for oil. And China and India are ramping up production on tiny cars that get great mileage, with one model reportedly achieving 63 miles per gallon.[37] Meanwhile, carmakers are trying everything they can think of for an alternative energy source to power vehicles. A French company has come up with cars that run on compressed air, ingeniously called "air cars." (Believe it or not, Jules Verne actually came up with that idea in the 1860s.)[38] Compressed natural gas (CNG) is another environmentally friendly solution for automobile fuel, and some CNG cars are now in use.

Another option is biofuel, a form of alcohol made from plants. Ethanol (made from crops like corn) and biodiesel (made from plant oils), are more fuel-efficient and burn cleaner than gasoline, with fewer toxic byproducts. Corn-based ethanol production is growing fast in the American Midwest, thanks in large part to huge subsidies from the government. Unfortunately, corn is just about the worst source for ethanol. It has an energy balance of 1.3-to-1, meaning it only generates 30 percent more energy than it takes to produce it. Using corn also counterintuitively generates greenhouse gases as rainforests are cleared to make way for more crops. As American farmers plant corn to make biofuel, America is increasingly importing its soy and other crops, often from places that used to be forests or savannas. Recent studies show that if you take this into account, biofuels actually cause more greenhouse-gas emissions than regular fuels. A good way to picture this inefficiency is to realize that a person could be fed for a year on the corn it takes to create enough ethanol to fill the tank of an SUV just once. With that in mind, it's easy to see how this vicious cycle can contribute to spikes in worldwide food prices, as in 2008. If America can move away from using corn, other biofuel options abound: soybeans, prairie grasses, or sugar cane, which has an energy balance of 8-to-1. None of those are really mind-blowing, and imagining ethanol can be a quick solution to our energy problem is wishful thinking. But it remains one avenue of study, and scientists are also working to engineer man-made enzymes to make even better alcohol-based fuel molecules. Exxon recently announced funding $300 million for research into biofuels harnessed from engineering single-celled algae.[39]

California looks poised to put a law into effect that would force carmakers to reduce their vehicles' emissions 30 percent by 2016. If this happens, since 13 other states follow California standards, almost 40 percent of the U.S. car market would need improved vehicles. With carmakers forced to overhaul current technology to be cleaner in one state, the only feasible option would be for them to make all their cars that efficient. And with U.S. automakers newly penitent after requesting vast sums of bailout money from the government, they aren't fighting the proposed law as much as might be expected.[40]

Iceland has consistently proven itself to be a leader in using alternative energies. Ninety percent of the country's electricity comes from geothermal and hydroelectric power: turbines spinning from hot vents in the earth or from natural water sources.[41] Iceland opened the world's first filling station for hydrogen-powered cars in 2003 and launched a hydrogen bus program. Hydrogen cars emit pure water as their only exhaust. Iceland is hoping to become a hydrogen producer, exporting energy to mainland Europe. The Bush administration and U.S. industries bet on hydrogen vehicles as the new car technology that will eventually win out. However, this would mean not only reengineering cars, but also changing every gas station in the country—a daunting task. The process of extracting hydrogen is still dependent on fossil fuels, as well. Nonetheless, in the fall of 2006, BMW rolled out the first hydrogen car in serial production. The super-high-end 7-Series will be available for lease to select customers and will also feature a standard gas engine so as not to leave customers stranded if they're not near a hydrogen refilling station. As a bonus, a lot of these alternative-energy vehicles feature smoother acceleration and a much quieter engine.[42] Researchers are also developing cars that can drive themselves by interacting with sensors on other cars and on the road. With their improved efficiency, these cars would not only cut down on emissions but also reduce accidents and traffic fatalities.

It's not just cars that we have to worry about. Other fuel sources are being developed to meet the energy needs of our homes, businesses, factories, and towns. Energy production for these buildings actually accounts for more

326 | THE SECRET PEACE

greenhouse-gas emissions than cars do. New "eco-communities" are popping up around the world: towns and communities that are using high-tech methods to become more green. Places like Vauban in Germany and Dockside Green in Canada feature carshare services and houses designed to be low-energy. Masdar in Abu Dhabi will have gray-water canals cooling its no-cars-allowed streets. Special cities being developed in China collect filtered rainwater for bathing and burn biogas from human waste to generate electricity. Dunhuang, a Chinese oasis town deep in the Gobi Desert, is where one of the world's largest wind power projects is currently being built.[43]

Cities worldwide are joining the "complete streets" movement, to make sure streets are friendly to pedestrians and bicycles. For example, in New York, the streets in SoHo where I work are now covered in brand-new bright green bicycle lanes. And listen to this news reported by Leslie R. Brown, head of the Earth Policy Institute:

> One of the most remarkable modern urban transformations has occurred in Bogotá, Columbia, where Enrique Peñalosa served as mayor for three years. Under his leadership, the city banned the parking of cars on sidewalks, created or renovated 1,200 parks, introduced a highly successful bus-based rapid transit system, built hundreds of kilometers of bicycle paths and pedestrian streets, reduced rush-hour traffic by 40 percent, planted 100,000 trees and involved local citizens directly in the improvement of their neighborhoods. ... The success of Bogotá's bus rapid transit (BRT) system, TransMilenio, which uses special express lanes to move people quickly through the city, is being replicated not only in six other Columbian cities but elsewhere, too: Mexico City, São Paulo, Hanoi, Seoul, Taipei and Quito. In China, Beijing is one of 20 cities developing BRT systems.

Toronto is using a novel approach to be environmentally-sound: a kind of reverse geothermal power. They draw cold water from deep in Lake Ontario through huge pipes to power the city's air conditioning and provide drinking water. Stockholm and other cities are following suit. These city-level initiatives are increasingly important as the world's population becomes increasingly urban. On an even larger scale, countries such as Norway and Costa Rica have set specific goals to become carbon-neutral countries. Costa Rica is shooting for as early as 2021.[44]

Since its creation, nuclear energy has seen its ups and downs as a key player in generating electricity—and much of the world is on another nuclear energy "up." There are over 400 nuclear plants in the world now, and some countries such as France, South Korea, and India are eagerly building more. While much of the world's oil is located underneath dangerous regimes, the uranium needed for nuclear power is found in friendlier places, such as Australia and Canada. Nuclear plants do not emit any greenhouse gases, but they do generate radioactive waste. Its handling and disposal costs need to be factored into the cost of nuclear power. But by some estimates, the vast majority of nuclear waste could be recycled and blended back into fresh fuel. As environmental pioneer Stewart Brand points out, "Coal and carbon-loading the atmosphere are much bigger problems for the future than nuclear waste, which is a relatively minor risk." (And ironically, burning coal liberates trace amounts of uranium into the atmosphere anyway.)[45]

As for the safety of nuclear power, despite the stigma of Three Mile Island, do you know how many people have died in the U.S. due to radiation exposure from nuclear plants? None. The worst nuclear accident in the country, and no one was hurt. The meltdown at Chernobyl, on the other hand, was awful, but it was the product of a lax Soviet safety culture and backwards, unstable technology—picture a Russian Homer Simpson asleep on the job. That doesn't fly today. New technologies continue to make nuclear energy more and more safe. The chance of a meltdown or leak is minimal, although we do have the threat of terrorism to deal with. A nuclear power plant is a tempting target for a hijacked airplane or missile. The obvious solution to terrorist threats is to simply build the plants away from populated areas—though not too far away, since it costs money to move the electricity once it is generated. With plenty of precautions, the potentially dangerous downside to nuclear power is minimal compared to the potential consequences of global warming.[46]

Wind power is another promising energy source. In 2007, global wind power capacity jumped 27 percent, an astonishing rate of growth. Wind turbines in the United States, spurred on by tax incentives, now have enough capacity to power 4.5 million households, and capacity jumped by 45 percent in 2007 alone. Several Midwestern states are planning to make greater use of wind power, due to their consistently windy plains. China has been nearly doubling its capacity every year for the past four years, and other heavy investors in wind technology include Portugal, Italy, and the United Kingdom. Germany already gets seven percent of its electricity from wind power, Spain 10 percent, and Denmark a whopping 20 percent.[47]

FIGURE 24: WORLD WIND ENERGY GENERATING CAPACITY,
IN MEGAWATTS: 1980–2007

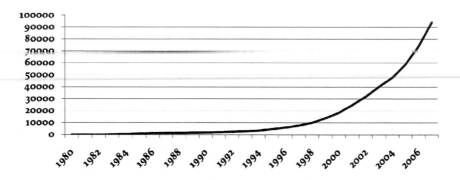

Wind power is growing fast as a viable source of energy, but solar power overtakes it as the world's fastest-growing energy source.[48] The worldwide generating capacity of photovoltaic [solar cell] production parallels that of wind power—it started in the mid-1990s and then shot up astronomically. In 2007, for example, global production of solar cells increased 51 percent. Solar collectors now provide hot water to about 40 million households worldwide. Spain, in an incredible initiative, passed a building code that includes a solar heating obligation for all new and renovated buildings in the country.[49] The engineering problems in making solar power more efficient are similar to those we overcame with computer technology, which long ago hit a tipping point that led to a continuing series of lightning-fast innovations. Nano-engineered materials being developed today might be the solar tipping point, making solar panels lighter, cheaper, and far more efficient at converting sunlight into electricity. Other ideas, currently being researched, include building in the Sahara enough solar power stations (and high-voltage cables) to power all of Europe. Solar power is on track to become cost-competitive with the retail price of electricity in just a few short years. The sun, through inefficient millennia-long chains of events, already provides *all* of our power, so why not get it directly?[50]

When a seed takes root, it draws its strength from its stored energy, but that energy is quickly exhausted. The seed must break through the earth and make at least one leaf to start the photosynthetic process of drawing power from the sun. Once the energy-making process has begun, the hard part is over. The sun can now bestow its infinite energy, helping the plant to grow more leaves and thus take advantage of more sunlight in a self-sustaining, self-building system. Fossil fuels are like the underground seed power that humanity had to use to develop the basic technology to start the Industrial Revolution and eventually lead us to renewable energies. Like the seed, we might exhaust our supply of fossil fuels just in time to get renewable energies. Once we fully grasp the benefits of renewable energy, not only will problems of pollution gradually dissipate, but we will find ourselves with more energy than we could ever use—even just by developing solar power alone. The sun produces enough energy in one second to meet Earth's energy needs for 500,000 years.[51] The challenge lies in finding practical and affordable ways to harness it.

None of these renewable energy technologies has yet turned out to be a "magic bullet," and wind and geothermal energy in particular seem unable to meet global needs. So, as the *Wall Street Journal* writes, in our age of energy interdependence, our goal should be promoting "energy diversity."[52] The most likely energy solution is the basket approach—a mixture of several renewable energy technologies. Thankfully, there are individuals and industries dedicated to developing each of them. For example, Sir Richard Branson, the British billionaire known for his Virgin brand, recently announced that all of the profits from his five airlines and his train company will be reinvested in developing alternative energy sources.[53] That is expected to reach an impressive

$3 billion over the next ten years, though it's a shame that many governments are not spending nearly that much. New developments in renewable energy have been steady and encouraging, yet they're still stuck on a small scale. But if history has taught us little else, we know the ability for small-scale initiatives to inspire change not only in industries, but also in global perspectives. While it may seem doubtful that anything short of a massive government push can dramatically increase the research and development budget of alternative energies in time to seriously help the environment, forward-thinking individuals, businesses, and the thousands of grassroots environmental groups throughout the world may prove to be the true leaders for saving our global environment.[54] Once the idea of renewable energy takes off, government could promote something on the scale of the Manhattan Project, the Marshall Plan, or NASA's space race. While each of those projects required massive government investment, they were successful much sooner than expected.

Besides spurring plans that consumers and private industry can then capitalize on, the government can do a lot of work to get its own house in order, too: the government is the largest energy-eater in any given country. I mentioned that my father volunteers as a dispute mediator, but his full-time job before retirement was for the State of New Jersey, consolidating energy contracts to save the state money by being energy-efficient. New Jersey has invested in many green technologies, not just because it is a liberal state that loves the environment, but also because it is more energy-efficient and less expensive to do so. Though California gets a great deal of media coverage for its environmental policies, by 2003 New Jersey's government drew 14 percent of its electricity from renewable resources such as wind and solar power—more than any other state.[55]

SECRETLY SAVING ENERGY

The alternative energy industry is booming, but one last way of improving our energy is often overlooked: energy productivity, which has increased about one percent a year for decades. Globally, "energy intensity"—the amount of energy needed to generate each dollar of output—is falling by 1.5 percent annually.

We're constantly improving our technology—light bulbs, cars, home appliances, industrial equipment—to meet higher energy-efficiency standards. Peter Stair notes, "If the world economy used energy today in the same way it did in 1970, it would require the energy equivalent of 11 additional Saudi Arabias—more than all the oil produced in the world. Thus 'saved energy' is arguably the world's leading energy source."[56]

One essential way to further save energy in America is by revamping our energy grid. A "smart grid" would allow more control, to even out peaks in demand and make sure no electricity is wasted. It could even allow homeowners to sell energy back to the grid, if they had solar panels.[57] There's also a new idea that might help drastically with individual conservation. It's hard to get people to reduce their own energy bills, but it's easy to get people to conform to what they perceive as social norms. So, by simply praising or condemning people on their energy bills ("This month you used 10 percent less energy than your neighbors! :) "), energy companies in California found that they could get their customers to reduce their energy bills drastically.[58]

Both LED (light-emitting diodes) and CFL (compact fluorescent lamps) lights are also potentially revolutionary. CFLs use 75 percent less energy to produce the same amount of light as a traditional incandescent light bulb, and can last 10 times longer. LEDs are even more efficient, but are still quite expensive. Between 2000 and 2007, CFL sales in the United States grew from 21 million units to 397 million, and now command a 20 percent share of the light bulb market. Eighty percent of households in Japan use CFLs, and Australia just enacted a plan to switch entirely to energy-efficient bulbs within a few years.[59] While it is costly here to replace all of our incandescent bulbs at once, developing countries can immediately begin using CFLs and LEDs in place of energy-hungry incandescent bulbs. LEDs are so efficient that they can even be powered by small solar cells instead of the huge electricity grid required for incandescent bulbs. About 20 percent of the world's electricity is used for lighting, but some estimates predict that LEDs could cut this in half by 2025.[60]

As we improve our technology, we can help the developing world leap forward to adopt improved energy solutions. This entails directly adopting a new technology and skipping over earlier, inferior versions. The best example of this phenomenon is the mobile phone. Africa and India have easily embraced mobile phones since they do not require the complex infrastructure needed for land lines. They skipped over regular phones and went straight to the new technology. Once technological discoveries are made, they can easily spread around the world. Different places do not have to reinvent them. As another example, it took 150 years for European life expectancy to increase from 40 years to 60. But thanks to better health technology, many developing countries were able to accomplish the same thing in only four decades—and that was with a far larger population.[61]

Other trends in the developing world help, too: for example, the growing exodus from rural settings into cities. While this transition is often problematic and overwhelming for developing countries in the short-term, in the long-term it reduces the world's carbon footprint. With more people in cities, public transportation is more common than gas-guzzling private transportation, energy needs to be shipped less to remote areas, and money is saved on heating as well. Our collective unconscious conjures up images of city smokestacks polluting and farmers relaxing with nature, but the opposite is increasingly true.[62]

By quickly adopting new technological developments, the developing world has gained an advantage over the Western world. Emerging economies can skip the worst of the Industrial Revolution, and with it skip the worst of pollution. We have much cleaner technology now, so our environment-saving goal should be to encourage these technological leaps around the world. China has the right idea—it is investing heavily in both wind and solar power and could become the world leader in both industries. The Chinese government has also set the remarkable goal of increasing its energy that comes from renewable sources to 16 percent by 2020.[63] The *Economist* reported on another "leapfrog" example: "By the time Chinese consumers started buying fridges in large numbers, refrigeration technology no longer depended on ozone-destroying CFCs."

The developing world is trying its best to conserve another resource, too: water. Some progress has been made. Ensuring everyone has access to clean water and sanitation is one of the Millennium Development Goals, and huge regions such as Latin America, the Caribbean, and East Asia and the Pacific are all on track to meet their targets. South Asia is on track for access to water but not yet sanitation. Scientists, governments, inventors, and private companies are all working hard on innovative solutions to the water problem—not just encouraging us to use less, but trying to make more. Viable ideas include large-scale desalination, "nano" desalination, drawing water from the air using special windmills, and converting wastewater through new sanitation plants. "Playpump," which enables deep extraction of water by using merry-go-rounds to power the pumps, expects to be providing water for 10 million people by 2010. Yes, seriously. There is a global water shortage, but plenty of smart people are working on it.[64]

GLOBAL WARMING

Saving energy and converting to renewable resources will save us money in the long run, take oil money away from despots, and reduce pollution—improving public health, enhancing the beauty of our skies and natural world, and making our cities and buildings cleaner. But another big reason to clean up our act is the elephant in the room we haven't discussed yet: the looming danger of global warming. In recent years, global temperatures have soared, and researchers are convinced that it is because of human activity—carbon dioxide emissions and other polluting greenhouse gases trapping sunlight in our atmosphere. After years of hearing denials, scientists have finally managed to convince governments, businesses, religious groups, corporations, and the public of the urgency of the global warming problem. Of course, there is overwhelming evidence: the Intergovernmental Panel on Climate Change reports that not only is the planet unequivocally warming, but that the majority of the change is due to human greenhouse-gas emissions. As USA Today declared on its front page, "The debate's over: Globe is warming." In recent years, record temperatures have been the norm—124°F in India and 117°F in Texas, for example. Repercussions of global warming may include rising sea levels, which have the potential to flood low-lying coastal areas (such as New Orleans, Venice, the Netherlands, and Bangladesh), and more severe weather patterns, such as droughts and hurricanes. Warmer temperatures also wreak havoc with crops and animal migrations.[65]

Since the threat of global warming has finally become lodged in the zeitgeist, what I'm about to say will be pretty heretical: Global warming is not a big deal. Don't get me wrong, the globe *is* warming, it *is* due to manmade actions, and once the problem is full-blown it *will* have some serious consequences. But how serious?

Freeman Dyson, one of the world's foremost physicists and a famously creative thinker, offers a unique viewpoint. He accepts the science of global warming but thinks the problem is blown out of proportion in the way it is discussed and reported. Essentially, the thinking is that yes, it is a problem ... but we have worse problems. So global warming, unfortunately, can't be a priority.[66] Here's a method to think about it:

First, it's important to remember that global warming is only a potential problem, it's not a full-blown problem yet.

Second, it might not turn out to be as drastic as we think. A new University of Wisconsin study indicates that since 2001, global temperatures have flatlined, not increased at the rapid pace that was predicted. This fluctuation does not disprove the basic science of global warming, but it does remind us that there are many factors in play in the earth's atmosphere that we just don't understand.[67]

Third, even if it is drastic, there's a chance it might be drastic in a good way. Some animals might adapt poorly, but others might flourish. Previously-harsh areas of the globe might become more habitable. Nothing says that saving the biosphere means preserving it exactly the way it is now, down to each spotted owl. Nature is ever-changing with or without us.

Fourth, even if it is drastic and bad, it might not be incredibly soon or sudden. The movie *The Day After Tomorrow* shows global warming creating a flash freeze over the earth and huge tidal waves destroying New York City, all in the span of a day. But Dennis Quaid and Jake Gyllenhal shouldn't have to rush to our rescue quite yet, as this seems patently preposterous.

Fifth, even if it is drastic, bad, and soon, we can find ways to deal with it. "Dealing with it" may sound trite, but humans (and plants and animals) have adapted to many environmental changes over the millennia. One dramatic way to deal would be "geo-engineering," a formerly-fringe suggestion that's gaining more legitimacy. It posits that since technology got us into this mess, technology can get us out: let's use planet-scale engineering to counteract climate change directly. One reasonable idea was pointed out by Steven Chu, America's energy secretary, who says that painting road surfaces and the roofs of buildings white would reflect tons of sunlight back into space, cooling the planet. Some ideas are much more unconventional: placing a giant sunshade in space, blasting droplets of seawater into the air to make clouds over the oceans, and even using the earth's own magnetic field to vent carbon dioxide into space. Freeman Dyson proposed creating forests of trees genetically-engineered to suck more carbon out of the air than normal. But the unknown consequences of these proposals make them highly controversial, and they are meant to be tried only as last resorts.[68]

Sixth, even if we can't deal with it before it happens or while it's happening, we might be able to reverse the effects later, after the fact—either with geo-engineering or just a natural reversal after we decarbonize our energy sources.

Seventh, and most importantly, even if we can't deal with it at all, we have plenty of worse problems right now. These problems are real, rather than potential; and more easily solvable, because we already have some experience toward solving them. After all, if the worst predictions about global warming come true, how many people might be affected? Millions? Hundreds of millions? Well, hundreds of millions of people are *already* dying worldwide—of disease, malnutrition, and poverty. Protecting the existing biosphere is a worthy goal, but it must take a back seat to addressing the evils of war, poverty, and inequality. These should demand our immediate attention.

This is not to say that global warming is not a serious threat worth fighting against, merely that we keep it in perspective when allocating resources to that battle. In addition, if we look at global warming as an air pollution problem, it has clear similarities to recent environmental successes, such as stopping ozone depletion, reversing acid rain, reducing smog, and reviving our rivers and shores. We should be confident in our ability to solve the global warming issue as well—with international cooperation, smart regulations, small economic sacrifices, personal conservation, and finding new energy sources. These efforts may be slow to bring about results, but we know they work.

MAKE MONEY, SAVE THE EARTH

Global warming, though a problem, doesn't need too much special attention. This is because with years of research under our belts, we now know a surefire way to help the environment: continue what we're doing. This may not be the fastest method, but the results are guaranteed. And it's a good thing they are, because in hundreds of years nothing has deterred humanity's steady march of using more material goods that use energy.

"Continue what we're doing" doesn't refer to stagnation. Rather, it means to keep advancing, which is society's natural course. If we do that, the environment will follow along. This concept is counterintuitive. It makes sense to assume that the environment is despoiled by our advanced technology, growing population, and the increasing number of objects we buy. This is why "back to basics" and "simplify" are environmental tagline hallmarks. But as John Tierney reports in the New York Times:

> The old wealth-is-bad IPAT theory may have made intuitive sense, but it didn't jibe with the data ... By the 1990s, researchers realized that graphs of environmental impact didn't produce a single upward-sloping line as countries got richer. The line more often rose, flattened out and then reversed so that it sloped downward, forming the shape of a dome or an inverted U.[69]

In other words, industrialization at first creates massive pollution, but when countries get wealthier they can afford cleaner water and air. As we saw in the chart earlier, they naturally transition to less carbon-intensive energies. Western countries seem to be at the top of the curve for carbon emissions—the amount of carbon emitted by the average American has remained fairly flat for decades now, and France's has even started to decline—and about to topple down into even less harmful environmental impact. As a bonus, countries industrializing now (such as China) have the benefit of newer technologies, meaning their industrialization stages are much less polluting than ours.

What this adds up to it that "the richer everyone gets, the greener the planet will be in the long run."[70]

I have little doubt that humanity can step up and solve its environmental issues; the only question is, in what time frame? If current trends continue, in a few decades the developed world will be conserving more, the developing world will be polluting less, and cleaner energy will be powering our cars and industry. Thankfully, many of the positive trends we have discussed up to this point—improvements in education, health, and global consciousness—all contribute to a growing awareness of our impact on the environment. *Foreign Policy* magazine found, in fact, that the more globally connected a country is—the more international treaties it belongs to, the more technology it has, the more cross-border traffic and tourism it has, and the more trade it has with other countries—the better its record will most likely be on environmental issues.[71]

The environment is the key arena in which global problems can bring humanity together, as we realize that environmental problems can only be solved through international cooperation. Perhaps environmental issues will hasten the process of peace as we are pushed into working together to solve problems of global concern. This could very well be the catalyst that inspires the next step of the world's unity. But there are many other actions we can take as well—starting right now. They range from small, mundane tasks to wildly ambitious undertakings. Many people around the world are already working on them, but they need our help, too. With everyone inspired to push peace forward, all the secret peace trends we've examined will accelerate exponentially, and then we can all breathe more easily.

Conclusion

Our Challenge and Responsibility

Genghis Khan was born into a family with no money or royal blood; he was an outcast on the barren steppes, trapped in slavery as a child. His inexplicable success through sheer will can be seen as an early trumpet heralding the rise of individual power to shape the world. Now we are reaching the culmination of many century-long trends, when each new piece of information humanity creates feeds into a cycle of progress. In the twentieth century, millions of people successfully traveled the path from rags to riches, and in the twenty-first, millions more are racing toward better lives. A planet of healthier, wealthier, smarter people now have the power to publish their thoughts online, to nonviolently topple unjust rulers, or conversely, to attack buildings with homemade bombs. We are all adjusting to the changing rules, grappling with ethical choices we're presented with for the first time. Luckily, new paradigms of thought are developing alongside this exciting potential. If we can harness this potential, humanity can grow past its painful adolescence and reach its full maturity. We may finally be ready to handle the responsibility of a united world.

The uplifting trends outlined here—the easy access to endless knowledge, the new tools for a media of the masses, the increased awareness of human rights, the advancement of women, the growth of nonviolent action, the democratization of power, the rise of the masses out of poverty, the advancements in health, and the newfound concern for the environment—zero in on a single point of convergence: the equality of all people. The hidden patterns leading toward peace in the world are preparing us all to become world citizens, unified in our commitment to peace and prosperity for all. We must accept unity in our diversity by embracing our differences rather than letting them divide us. Each person's intrinsic worth ensures that he or she can contribute to a global civilization in some way. Human imagination, ingenuity, and nobility know no bounds. Everyone has a vital role to play; each of us needs the opportunity and resources to build our own flourishing corner of society and then peacefully connect it to everyone else's.

My own little corner of the world is near the East Village in Manhattan. A few blocks from my humble-yet-unjustifiably-priced apartment are gleaming towers, national landmarks, screaming crowds toting shopping bags, art students in front of their easels, bustling businesspeople, tourists getting their caricatures drawn, and literally thousands of restaurants. I've seen celebrities sitting near me at diners, and men's heads spinning as stunning models sashay along the street. There are a dozen parks I can walk to, from the studiously bustling Bryant Park, with its birch trees and carousel, to the silent Stuyvesant. In December, I can see restaurants with their sidewalk trees wrapped in crystal white lights, even up to the thin branches. To put it simply, I am moved by the city's passion, which E. B. White described perfectly in 1948: "And whether it is a farmer arriving from Italy to set up a small grocery store in a slum, or a young girl arriving from a small town in Mississippi to escape the indignity of being observed by her neighbors, or a boy arriving from the Corn Belt with a manuscript in his suitcase and a pain in his heart, it makes no difference: each embraces New York with the intense excitement of first love, each absorbs New York with the fresh eyes of an adventurer, each generates heat and light to dwarf the Consolidated Edison Company."[1]

Late at night, on certain days in certain lights, I wander around my neighborhood and think about how hard it is to imagine a more ideal society. And yet ... over a century ago, Victorian London was the capital of the world and a paradise for the lucky and well-heeled few. They probably felt their city was perfect, too, and yet we look back at history and see streets of squalor, noisy horses, muddy roads strewn with effluent, dark coal-covered skies, starving children, and no electricity. We have advanced immeasurably since then. Nevertheless, I guarantee that in the early years of the twenty-second century my grandchildren, with their 120-year lifespans, will study our time period and gape aghast at the condition of our society. They'll see traffic jams of fossil-fueled vehicles, the homeless wallowing in the gutters of the city, clunky outdated technology, costly health care and overflowing tenements. If we play our cards right today, they'll be thankful that those experiences are long past.

Small efforts on our part, properly funneled, can have remarkable results in the long run. With a little extra effort, we can make all of our regular activities a bit more socially responsible. We can check that the charities we support are reliable (use Donorschoose.org, which allows very small contributions and lets you see directly who you're helping, or charities ranked favorably by *Forbes* magazine, for example). We can take low-impact vacations in developing countries, such as bicycling in Vietnam or floating down the Yangtze in China. We can vote with our wallets—researching products and supporting companies with ethical practices. The key to that is to also let corporations know *why* you are choosing (or not choosing) their products; try e-mailing them from their Web site or complaining in their most common forums, or Facebook, or Twitter. See if others share your thoughts. It might not get instant attention, but remember that it is somebody's job to read correspondence, so repeated ideas will get through.

Thinking about what you buy is a new kind of "ethical consumerism," and it's quickly accelerating. As *Time* reports, "Even amid the Great Recession of 2009, people have been trading in their SUVs for Priuses, buying record amounts of fair trade coffee and investing in socially responsible funds at higher rates than ever before. ... We are starting to put our money where our ideals are." People are supporting high-profile efforts like the (RED) campaign, which supports AIDS programs in Africa, and which has raised $135 million in only three years. Companies are competing to be greener and greener to capture the environmentally-concerned market. People are using fuel-efficient cars, and switching to energy-efficient light bulbs. Socially Responsible Investment (SRI) mutual funds now manage about 11 percent of all the money in U.S. financial markets.[2]

We can lobby our congressional representatives for increased foreign aid—a prosperous planet pays dividends to all of us. On an international scale, the industrialized nations have an obligation to advance the cause of world peace, a plan that would be simultaneously practical, morally righteous, and self-benefiting. The United States should take advantage of its current position as a world leader—in the areas of its military, economy, technology, even entertainment—to both humbly spread its ideals abroad and serve as an example by steadfastly clinging to them at home. The developing nations are ascending regardless of our input, so we need to take this chance to help them advance peacefully and ensure that they share our commitment to liberal market democracy.

America has stepped up to great challenges in the past: abolishing slavery, mobilizing for World War I and World War II, rebuilding Europe with the Marshall Plan, landing on the Moon. With a united effort, we can successfully reign in terrorism, rescue our environment, and spread democracy. With humility and generosity, we can reach out to the rest of the world's sovereignties to tackle extreme poverty and encourage development. Here are 10 causes, in no particular order, that we should encourage everyone to support, especially our governments.

1. Redirect much of our anti-terrorism resources to keeping a handle on the world's nuclear material, especially from Russia and Pakistan. Realize that some low-level terrorism will never be completely wiped out by military means, so work with law enforcement to instead contain it to certain levels.

2. Support introducing genetically-modified crops into developing countries, especially in Africa. Skeptics in Europe have already convinced some African countries that GM food is evil. It's not. (Though even if it was, it's better than starving.)

3. In America, rethink our disastrous war on drugs. It's not working. Legalizing and taxing marijuana and devoting that money to health programs would free up law enforcement resources to deal with more dangerous drugs. Or, at least rethink the prison system to be more rehabilitative in nature—the two issues are intertwined.

4. Invest in alternative energy, and don't be afraid to harness nuclear power. It's the single best option we have to curb greenhouse-gas emissions, at least until solar power advances dramatically. Above all, give up on corn-based ethanol, which actually hurts the environment.

5. Promote condom use, circumcision, and education programs to fight AIDS in sub-Saharan Africa.

6. Maintain support for UN peacekeeping missions. Compared to standard military action these have a high success rate in resolving conflicts, particularly if they arrive before a war breaks out, or after it is winding down (to make sure it doesn't flare up again).

7. Do everything in our power to push along the success of any of the U.N. Millennium Development Goals. We have until 2015, and are making some good progress, but more help is needed in many countries.

8. Stop exporting guns to violent, collapsing countries. This may sound simplistic, but it *is* a simple concept. The world ends up intervening in states that break down, or threaten their neighbors, or are unlawful enough that terrorists can hide out there. None of that violence is possible without guns. When anti-democratic military coups happen, it's not because the soldiers are good kickboxers. Civil wars do not break out with people slapping one another. Fewer guns in the world helps all these problems, not to mention lowers crime and reduces the chance of all-too-common gun accidents.

9. Put a global carbon tax in place, as the best way to account for a negative externality that we're not used to paying for. This is more efficient and straightforward than current cap-and-trade plans.

10. Help the Internet reach developing countries. It's looking more and more like this is best done with new, cheaper mobile phone technology.

Supporting any of those 10 projects will help move peace forward. But it's possible that even more success will come from *directly* impacting the secret peace. Remember the three forces that are driving the secret peace—spreading knowledge, democratizing power to the world's masses, and connecting with each other globally? It follows that directly working on them would have the most positive impact in the world, particularly the first, instigating force.

Spreading information then becomes our primary goal. Now, with the new tools at everyone's disposal, we don't really need to encourage people to generate more information—that's moving along quite well. We've got plenty of knowledge floating around. So the key area to focus on is to help people process it, harness it effectively, and steer clear of information overload. We're at a stage right now in which a vast amount of previously-unavailable data is surfacing, but it isn't yet available in an easily-digestible format. Many aspects of our lives have become mind-bogglingly complicated—our laws, our financial markets, our products and technology, our health care, our increasingly-specialized jobs and areas of research. Some things are even *intentionally* complicated—like insurance, automated phone support systems, and the fine print on your credit card policy.

As James Madison presciently said, "It will be of little avail to the people that the laws are made by men of their own choice if the laws be so voluminous that they cannot be read, or so incoherent that they cannot be understood."[3] On the part of the individual, this is where critical thinking comes in. But while it's everyone's responsibility to think for themselves, there's no reason why we can't make it easier. Do you look at the Nutrition Facts when you buy food products? They weren't always there. Posting calorie counts in restaurants, as they do here in New York, is the next logical step. The government doesn't need to over-regulate, but rather just make information available so citizens can make decisions for themselves.

The law and government itself are key areas to make comprehensible to everyone. As we examined when we looked at the democratizing effects of new technology, more and more governments are making data available, especially convenient geolocation information. And thanks to the Federal Funding and Accountability and Transparency Act of 2006, more states are making their budgets and spending records available to their citizens online. This again underlines the importance of transparency, which is equally important in business as well. For example, Gap has received high marks for its transparency in efforts to clean up its labor conditions worldwide, after admitting to violations years ago. HP has improved as well, applying similar transparency to its global supply chain. And Timberland shoes now come with labels that explain what materials and how much energy was used in their manufacture.[4]

As we saw when we looked at the environment, web sites like Good Guide aim for the same goal on a much wider scale. A single bottle of Mountain Dew, or ream of printer paper, or cell phone, has tons of components and packaging and employees and transport, all of which impact the world in ways we cannot possibly digest unless the data is summarized and easily scannable. We need ways to judge products on several factors—such as safety, environmental impact, labor, customer satisfaction, and resource usage—and describe them with simple numbers and charts. This is essential for continuing the trend of ethical consumerism, and making it more effective.[5]

We need look no further than the world's current financial predicament to see the importance of having knowledge available about our actions. What was the subprime mortgage crisis if not people buying homes who didn't understand that they shouldn't, and people buying investments that were so layered no one knew where the money really was, or what the risks really were? As *Wired* senior writer Daniel Roth puts it, "The financial world doesn't need new regulations. It needs radical transparency. Make companies report results in easy to understand, easy to crunch numbers—and let investors do the rest." *Wired* goes on to make more suggestions:

> Today, public companies and financial institutions disclose their activities in endless documents stuffed with figures and stats. Instead, they should be forced to file using universal tags that make the data easy to explore ... By giving

everyone access to every piece of data—and making it easy to crunch—we can crowdsource regulation, creating a self-correcting financial system and unlocking new ways of measuring the market's health.[6]

Other areas of our lives should be made easier to understand as well. The tax code, for one. And health care—data about illnesses is now available online, as are support groups, but the real revolution will come once we all have complete access to our own records and can easily compare symptoms and track data. The expanding power of the Internet will be the enabler of all of these new ways to access knowledge. Companies and individuals are constantly looking for ways to make the 'Net more useful, innovative, and fun. Many startups, such as Twine, are exploring what's called the "semantic web," in which web site data items are tagged and organized clearly to make their content more easily understood by computers. By treating the entire web as a single giant database, search results can be organized much more cleanly, and it can be easier to find what you're looking for.[7]

An oft-overlooked method to make information more comprehensible is to make it engaging and enjoyable. Government, in particular, is inherently complex (and often boring), and so we need to make learning about it fun and compelling, to encourage participation. Another critical piece of making information digestible is good graphic design, and interactive charts, graphs, and maps. These are particularly helpful to engage younger learners. In order to keep up with our global shift in available information, schools need to better prepare kids who know how to find new information, utilize it, and contribute to it, rather than just memorize old information by rote. Instead of remembering all the "correct" or "approved" facts, of which there are now simply too many, children will need to be able to discern if something new is factual or not, when they come across it.[8]

What about our other two forces—empowering the masses and connecting with a global outlook? Making the information above available and easier to understand is the best way to do both of those, as well. But we need to make sure that new knowledge reaches all corners of the developing world, in the form of broadband Internet and mobile phones. Everyone needs the chance to participate equally in accessing and creating information.

Taking all that information and putting it to good use is the next step. Volunteering is an obvious idea. So is forming community groups. It's easy to find volunteer opportunities online, and use Meetup.com to easily create groups. Sites such as AllforGood.org draw together listings from traditional volunteer sites as well as Meetup and others.[9] It's up to us to go ahead and self-organize to tackle the world's problems. The days of waiting for government, or our leaders, or the markets to solve our problems are over. Although while our governments do still hold a lot of power, it's important to use the new tools available to engage our leaders more directly than ever before—from the local level to the international stage.

Be aware of the emerging attitude of global citizenship and embrace it. The planet is heading in that direction; better to be a leader now than to catch up later. Use the Internet to teach your children as much about other cultures as possible. Reach out and connect with people who share your interests worldwide. Start a world-altering conversation. The more people coordinating efforts, the better. Meet your neighbors and remind yourself how generally nice most of the people in the world are.

Continue to use critical thinking. This is another area where we need a clearer way of presenting information—in this case, the credentials of authors and sources. On the Internet, everyone can look the same, so readers need ways to easily see which information is trustworthy. Look for objective news sources, and sample a blend of different ones if you have time. Double-check things on sites like FactCheck.org. When you think about the state of the world, try to see through the nightly news and your office's water cooler talk to sense the wider trends buried in the pessimism. As John F. Kennedy once said, "The great enemy of truth is very often not the lie—deliberate, contrived, and dishonest—but the myth—persistent, persuasive, and unrealistic."[10] The idea of a world dominated by declining values, idiotic entertainment, kidnappers and terrorists lurking around every corner, and countries spiraling into chaos, is a difficult assumption to dispel. The quest to find the secret peace runs between the lines of the world's media, and we are each tasked with investigating it for ourselves—and then with sharing the news, helping to take the "secret" out of the secret peace.

Motivating ourselves to embark on such a grand mission is no easy task. In the first half of the twentieth century, a tsunami of pessimism enveloped the world. It emanated from a developing world thirsty for independence from colonialism and from industrialized countries rife with disillusionment after the disasters of world war, communism, and genocide. Cynicism is one of the strongest detractors to peace, but contrary to popular opinion, human nature struggles against it, rising up to promote the good nature of our everyday efforts to work and live. By the end of the twentieth century the malaise had begun to clear until much of the world was cautiously optimistic, even in some places irrationally exuberant.

This mood among Americans instantly crashed alongside the twin towers of the World Trade Center in September 2001. Since then, the failure to find Osama bin Laden, to bring security to Afghanistan, and to create peace in Iraq has understandably spread disillusionment and apathy across America. To top it off, the world economy up and collapsed—causing many people, including the news media, to lose all optimism. But these reasons make it even more important to spread the message of the secret peace. While there are certainly failures in the world, there are many more successes hidden behind the scenes. Immediately after the 2001 terrorist attacks, the world's citizens briefly united in a show of overwhelming solidarity and support. This uplifting message was largely forgotten in the years that followed, but reviving its spirit is our challenge in order to journey faster towards peace.

The optimism advocated here isn't fake or unrealistic. We shouldn't "put on a happy face" just to make ourselves feel better, while blissfully ignoring the problems around us. Rather, optimism about the state of the world is realism, as the hundreds of clues to the secret peace have proven. Indeed, it is extreme pessimism that is the aberration, the unrealistic belief system. What's amazing about optimism, too, is that it creates self-fulfilling positive feedback loops. Optimism begets optimism, and greater success. Appreciating our successes inspires us to do even more. (And optimism is healthier, too: a study of 100,000 women asked questions to determine their outlook on life. Eight years later, the optimists were less likely to have contracted various diseases and 14 percent more likely to be alive overall.)[11]

As the world's medical miracles heal our bodies and a new creative culture of information technology advances our minds, we as a people still need to polish our spirit. We need a global ethic to match the pace of global change: a commitment to guaranteed human rights, environmental stewardship, and nonviolence. This needs to be woven into a sense of global unity as we increasingly realize our common world citizenship. We can watch as that global ethic continues to slowly emerge, or we can help shape it and speed its acceptance. On this quest, we should harness the world's spirituality and help temper it with moderation—avoiding violence and fundamentalism and embracing tolerance, love, and service to humanity. Our goal must be to wed the world's belief systems and rich cultures with modernity and scientific thinking. In the long run, that accomplishment will do more to fight terrorism than any military action. A peaceful world is not one in which we catch all the terrorists; it's one in which people don't want to terrorize each other in the first place.

Now that the majority of people in the developed world live in a state of relative peace, with their minimum material needs met, it is time to shift the world's focus to the developing world, so they can advance without repeating our mistakes. The world's most dire problems are only solvable by a united globe. If developed nations come together to help emerging nations rise up, the problems of the developed world's melancholy and the developing world's poverty can both be solved in one stroke. Given a realistic and positive mission, the United States, Europe, Japan, and the other industrialized countries can revitalize their energy and commitment. With cooperation, good news can spur us on to achieve even more success. Incredibly, many of the best inventions, policies, and solutions to the world's problems already exist—only on a microscale. Scaling them up is necessary to spread the freedom, human rights, and wealth we enjoy to the rest of the earth.

Admittedly, many challenges remain. Yet each crisis is an opportunity to capture public attention about an issue, to learn from our mistakes, and to try new solutions. As problems are resolved, we increase our capacity to focus on remaining issues—some of which will linger for a long time. The goal is not to craft a world of uniform perfection but to eliminate the worst of the world's physical suffering so that humanity can focus on its spiritual growth, its creativity, its love and justice. No amount of work will eliminate all suffering in the world. But that does not mean we should sit back and do nothing, nor does it justify letting others succumb to the absolute depths of suffering. Nathaniel Hawthorne wrote, "The world owes all its onward impulses to men ill at ease."[12] We should keep being outraged by injustices that remain in the world. Discovering the positive trends of the world doesn't mean we can rest on our laurels. Instead, it should spur us to embrace more enthusiastically our responsibility to ensure that the world becomes more peaceful as quickly as possible—while always keeping in mind that peace is an ongoing initiative, an infinite frontier, not a single static end goal.

Within our lifetimes, the world will change faster than ever. Will the overall change be superb, or abysmal? While I do believe peace is inevitable, none of the details are. It's up to us to dictate the time and implementation of the approaching peace, and what happens on the way. None of the individual trends in this book are destined to happen in a specific way; civilization is just too complex for us to make precise predictions. But there are so many positive things happening on so many fronts that they can't all go wrong. The momentum is behind peace. The positive changes are winning so far, and it's likely that they will come out on top soon. There will be great leaps forward—and major setbacks. But there has been too much progress for the setbacks to last for long. To avoid or at least soften the bumps, we need the collective will to bring the advancements of peace into the world in a planned and organized way. Can humanity agree on how we want our peace? Or will we just stumble toward it in an ad hoc way?

If all the positive momentum we've examined continues, the world will certainly achieve a successful framework of peace, equality, and democracy. The question is, will it be too late? H. G. Wells saw the future as a "race between education and catastrophe," and indeed we are racing, hoping to outrun a devastating nuclear terrorist attack or environmental disaster.[13] A calamity of either kind could dramatically stall our positive direction. Working together quickly is necessary in order to avoid the horrible irony of losing the race after coming so far as a species. The news of the secret peace should remind us that humanity's hard work is paying off, that world unity is indeed within our reach if we keep up our efforts.

Will we achieve the destiny of peace prophesied by the world's religions, the perpetual peace envisioned by Philo, Kant, Hegel, Wilson, and Gandhi? If we agree it is possible, it can become a self-fulfilling prophecy. Gaining knowledge of the positive trend of world events and of our joint humanity inspires us to push the process of global unification forward. More than mild optimism, we need an "audacious faith in the future of mankind," as Martin Luther King, Jr. eloquently said. King's confidence in peace was never shaken despite the tremendous adversity he faced. He declared, "We are living in the creative turmoil of a genuine civilization struggling to be born. ... I still believe that we shall overcome."[14]

In ancient Greek mythology, Pandora was given a gift by Zeus—a *pithos*, a large sealed storage jar.[15] It was supposed to remain shut, but Pandora's curiosity got the better of her and she peered inside, releasing all of the horrors of the world—sickness, fear, poverty, crime, war, deceit, ignorance, hatred. Thousands of years ago, the Greeks looked at the terrors bedeviling humankind and believed the gods must have sent them as punishment. Today we look at the wars and crimes of the world and know we have only ourselves to blame. But we also have the knowledge, responsibility, and power to put them right. We must renew our determination to do so, because Pandora's myth doesn't end there. After the evils had escaped, Pandora looked in the box again and discovered one last item lingering inside: Hope. Setting that hope free is our long-awaited chance to wrestle humanity's sorrows back into Pandora's box and advance into a well-deserved world of peace. As Victor Hugo wrote, "There is nothing more powerful than an idea whose time has come."

ACKNOWLEDGEMENTS

A fter working on this book for more than three years, the list of people to whom I owe gratitude is daunting. But it starts first and foremost with my wife Rachel, whose patience and support continues to be superhuman. My parents, Rod & Janet, also cannot be thanked enough—in addition to their support during the writing process, and actual help reviewing the book, the idea of the secret peace is a direct result of the uplifting worldview they imparted to me. I want to thank Marc Vogtman for his essential brainstorming help (throughout our entire lives, come to think of it) and ability to consistently come up with challenging ideas. Likewise with the unflappable Lawrence Miller—and I should also thank Lawrence in print for becoming a rabbi just for my wedding.

Scott Heiferman and Esther Dyson were each kind enough to fit the book into their busy schedules and give me their support. I want to thank Pat McGraw for her solidarity, and Jason Eckert for his reliable professional insight. There is also my brain trust of reviewers, advice-givers, cover-voters, and supportive friends. This includes my sister Kate, the remarkable Barbara Walker, old friends Bob and Barb Harris, the inspirational Peter Murphy, the illustrious Spud Grammar, the nigh-indispensable Viviane Valvezan, sister Shira Moses, Rich "The Dagger" Sbarro, Milos Kivich,

Amanda Murphy, Jay Tyson, Will Howard, Rick Boenigk, Karina Jenny Louise van Schaardenburg, and Theresa & Damon Ogando. Viviane gets an additional shout-out for her help with names. My managers and all my teammates at Meetup HQ get props for their tolerance of my essentially holding two jobs at once, as does Jon Zack. The New York Independent Publishing Meetup Group was also a good resource. Thanks go to my helpful agent Neil Salkind, my rooftop photographer Robin Gentile, and my life saving indexer Naomi Linzer. Thanks to Andreas Ramos for his riveting quote, and to the Worldwatch Institute. There are countless others who have helped, too. If I've forgotten you, it's probably not intentional.

Every effort has been made to maintain accuracy in the book's information, to verify sources, and to cite them correctly. But as there are nearly a hundred books and a thousand endnotes following, I'm sure mistakes have been made. Sorry about that in advance. Please bring any bugs that you uncover to my attention, and corrections will be made for future editions.

As a last note, I do want to thank all the acquaintances with whom the book has popped up in conversations. Your feedback was helpful, even though gut responses were always evenly split between "Positive news? Yeah right, have you seen it out there? You're crazy" and, "Positive news? Yeah right, have you seen it out there? You're crazy. But we sure need it." Yes, I have seen it out there, I am crazy, and we sure do need it.

BIBLIOGRAPHY

Recommended reading

Anderson, Chris. *The Long Tail: Why the Future of Business is Selling Less of More*. New York: Hyperion, 2006.

Attali, Jacques. *A Brief History of the Future*. New York: Arcade Publishing, 2009.

Bahador, Babak and Ghanea, Nazila, ed. *Processes of the Lesser Peace*. Oaklands, UK: George Ronald, 2003.

Brockman, John, ed. *What Are You Optimistic About?*. New York: Harper Perennial, 2007.

Cortright, David. *Gandhi and Beyond*. Boulder: Paradigm Publishers, 2006.

Easterbrook, Gregg. *The Progress Paradox*. New York: Random House, 2004.

Florini, Ann. *The Coming Democracy*. Washington, DC: Brookings Institution Press, 2005.

Gandhi, Mohandas K. *Essential Writings*, John Dear, ed. Maryknoll, NY: Orbis Books, 2002.

Goklany, Indur M. *The Improving State of the World*. Washington, DC: Cato Institute, 2007.

Johnson, Steven. *Everything Bad is Good For You*. New York: Riverhead Books, 2006.

Kant, Immanuel. *Political Writings*. Cambridge, UK: Cambridge University Press, 1991.

Katirai, Foad. *Global Governance and the Lesser Peace*. Oxford: George Ronald, 2001.

Lappé, Frances Moore. *Getting a Grip*. Cambridge, MA: Small Planet Media, 2007.

Parekh, Bhikhu. *Gandhi: A Very Short Introduction*. Oxford: Oxford University Press, 2001.

Reynolds, Glenn. *An Army of Davids*. Nashville: Thomas Nelson, 2007.

Sachs, Jeffrey. *The End of Poverty*. New York: Penguin, 2006.

Sagan, Carl. *The Demon-Haunted World*. New York: Ballantine Books, 1997.

Schell, Jonathan. *The Unconquerable World*. New York: Holt Paperbacks, 2004.

Shirky, Clay. *Here Comes Everybody*. New York: Penguin, 2009.

Vital Signs 2006-2007. New York: W.W. Norton & Co., 2006.

Vital Signs 2007-2008. New York: W.W. Norton & Co., 2007.

Vital Signs 2009. New York: W.W. Norton & Co., 2009.

Wolf, Martin. *Why Globalization Works*. New Haven: Yale University Press, 2005.

Wright, Robert. *Nonzero: The Logic of Human Destiny*. New York: Vintage, 2001.

Other books cited

Alterman, Eric. *What Liberal Media?*. New York: Basic Books, 2003.

Ariely, Dan. *Predictably Irrational*. New York: Harper; Rev Exp edition, 2009.

Barber, Benjamin. *Jihad vs. McWorld*. New York: Ballantine Books, 1996.

Bauerlein, Mark. *The Dumbest Generation: How the Digital Age Stupefies Young Americans and Jeopardizes Our Future (Or, Don't Trust Anyone under 30.)* New York: Tarcher, 2009.

Berger, Peter L., ed. *The Desecularization of the World*. Washington DC: Wm. B. Eerdmans Publishing Company, 1999.

Blackburn, Simon. *Think*. Oxford, NY: Oxford University Press, 1999.

Buckingham, Jane with Tiffany Ward. *What's Next*. New York: Harpercollins, 2008.

Burtt, E.A., ed. *Teachings of the Compassionate Buddha*. New York: NAL Trade, 2000.

Curtis, Drew. *It's Not News, It's FARK*. New York: Gotham, 2008.

Dahl, Gregory C. *One World, One People*. Wilmette, IL: Bahá'í Publishing, 2007.

Epping, Randy Charles. *A Beginner's Guide to the World Economy*. New York: Vintage, 2001.

Fine, Allison, Micah L. Sifry, Andrew Rasiej, and Joshua Levy, ed. *Rebooting America*. Personal Democracy Press, 2008.

Friedman, Thomas L. *The Lexus and the Olive Tree*. New York: Farrar, Straus and Giroux, 2000.

Gandhi, Mohandas K. *Satyagraha in South-Africa*. Ahmedabad, India: Navajivan Publishing House, 2006.

Gelb, Michael. *How to Think Like Leonardo da Vinci*. New York: Dell, 2000.

Goldberg, Bernard. *Bias: A CBS Insider Exposes How the Media Distort the News*. Washington, DC: Perennial Library, 2003.

Gore, Al. *An Inconvenient Truth*. New York: Rodale Books, 2006.

Hallinan, Joseph T. *Why We Make Mistakes*. New York: Broadway, 2009.

Harford, Tim. *The Logic of Life*. New York: Random House Trade Paperbacks, 2009.

Hewitt, J. Joseph, Jonathan Wilkenfeld, and Ted Robert Gurr. *Peace and Conflict 2008*. Boulder: Paradigm Publishers, 2007.

The Holy Bible: New Revised Standard Version. New York: Oxford University Press, 1989.

Huddleston, John. *Standing Up for Humanity*. Wilmette, IL: Bahai Publishing Trust, 1999.

Kainz, Howard P. *An Introduction to Hegel: The Stages of Modern Philosophy*. Athens, Ohio: Ohio University Press, 1996.

Kelleher, Ann and Laura Klein. *Global Perspectives: A Handbook for Understanding Global Issues*. Upper Saddle River, NJ: Prentice Hall, 2008.

Kennedy, Paul. *The Parliament of Man*. New York: Vintage, 2007.

Keown, Damien. *Buddhism: A Very Short Introduction*. Oxford: Oxford University Press, 2000.

Kick, Russ, ed. *You Are Being Lied To*. New York: The Disinformation Company, 2001.

Kim, Chul R., ed. *Design for the Other 90%*. New York: Cooper-Hewitt, National Design Museum, Smithsonian Institution, 2007.

Kimball, Charles. *When Religion Becomes Evil*. New York: HarperOne, 2008.

Korten, David C. *The Great Turning: From Empire to Earth Community*. San Francisco: Berrett-Koehler Publishers, 2007.

Landsburg, Steven E. *More Sex is Safer Sex: The Unconventional Wisdom of Economics*. New York: Free Press, 2008.

Langewiesche, William. *The Atomic Bazaar*. New York: Farrar, Straus and Giroux, 2008.

Mansfield, Harvey C. *A Student's Guide to Political Philosophy*. Wilmington, DE: Intercollegiate Studies Institute, 2001.

McClellan III, James E. and Harold Dorn. *Science and Technology in World History*. Baltimore: The Johns Hopkins University Press, 2006.

Momen, Moojan. *Hinduism and the Bahá'í Faith*. Oaklands, UK: George Ronald, 1990.

Nagler, Michael N. *Is There No Other Way?*. Berkeley, CA: Berkeley Hills Books, 2001.

Nesbitt, Eleanor. *Sikhism: A Very Short Introduction*. Oxford: Oxford University Press, 2005.

New York Times Correspondents. *How Race is Lived in America*. New York: Times Books, 2002.

Noveck, Beth Simone. *WikiGovernment*. Washington, DC: Brookings Institution Press, 2009.

Oldstone-Moore, Jennifer. *Confucianism*. New York: Oxford University Press, 2002.

Oldstone-Moore, Jennifer. *Taoism*. New York: Oxford University Press, 2003.

Pinder, John. *The European Union: A Very Short Introduction*. Oxford: Oxford University Press, 2008.

Pink, Daniel H. *Free Agent Nation*. New York: Business Plus, 2002.

Postman, Neil. *Technopoly*. New York: Vintage, 1993.

Priwer, Shana and Cynthia Phillips. *101 Things You Didn't Know About da Vinci*. Avon, MA: Adams Media, 2005.

Prothero, Stephen. *Religious Literacy*. New York: HarperOne, 2008.

Putnam, Robert D. *Bowling Alone*. New York: Simon & Schuster, 2001.

Rampton, Sheldon, and John Stauber. *Trust Us, We're Experts*. New York: Tarcher, 2002.

Rauchway, Eric. *The Great Depression and the New Deal*. Oxford: Oxford University Press, 2008.

Ruthven, Malise. *Islam: A Very Short Introduction*. Oxford: Oxford University Press, 2000.

Samuelson, Robert J. *Untruth: Why the Conventional Wisdom is (Almost Always) Wrong*. New York: AtRandom, 2001.

Sardar, Ziauddin and Merryl Wyn Davies. *The No-Nonsense Guide to Islam*. Oxford: New Internationalist, 2007.

Schacter, Daniel L. *The Seven Sins of Memory: How the Mind Forgets and Remembers*. New York: Mariner Books, 2002.

Scholl, Steven, ed. *The Peace Bible*. Chicago: Kalimat Pr, 2002.

Sémelin, Jacques. *Nonviolence Explained to My Children*. New York: Da Capo Press, 2003.

Singer, Peter. *Hegel: A Very Short Introduction*. Oxford: Oxford University Press, 2001.

Solomon, Norman. *Judaism: A Very Short Introduction*. Oxford: Oxford University Press, 2000.

Stendardo, Luigi. *Leo Tolstoy and the Bahá'í Faith*. Oaklands, UK: George Ronald, 1985.

Stephenson, Neal. *Snow Crash*. New York: Spectra, 2000.

Stiglitz, Joseph E. *Globalization and Its Discontents*. New York: W.W. Norton & Co., 2003.

Stossel, John. *Myths, Lies, and Downright Stupidity*. New York: Hyperion, 2006.

Strathern, Paul. *Marx in 90 Minutes*. Chicago: Ivan R. Dee, 2001.

Strauss, Steven D. *World Conflicts*. Indianapolis: Alpha, 2006.

Surowiecki, James. *The Wisdom of Crowds*. New York: Anchor, 2005.

Tuleja, Tad. *Fabulous Fallacies*. New York: Galahad Books, 1999.

Weatherford, Jack. *Genghis Khan and the Making of the Modern World*. New York: Three Rivers Press, 2005.

Wells, H. G. *The Shape of Things to Come*. London: Penguin Classics, 2006.

White, E.B. *Here is New York*. New York: Little Bookroom, 2000.

Wilkinson, Paul. *A Very Short Introduction to International Relations*. Oxford: Oxford University Press, 2007.

The World Bank. *The Little Data Book 07*. Washington, DC, 2007.

The World Bank. *Atlas of Global Development*. Glasgow: Collins, 2007.

Zaid, Gabriel. *So Many Books*. Philadelphia: Paul Dry Books, 2003.

Zinn, Howard. *The Power of Nonviolence: Writings by Advocates of Peace*. Boston: Beacon Press, 2002.

ENDNOTES

p. xiii

- John Lennon, archival footage in *The U.S. vs. John Lennon*, David Leaf and John Scheinfeld, directors. Lionsgate, 2006.

Introduction

1. Jack Weatherford, *Genghis Khan and the Making of the Modern World*, pp. xxi–xxiii.

2. *Ibid.*, pp. xvi–xix.

3. *Wikipedia*, s.v. "Genghis Khan," http://en.wikipedia.org/wiki/Genghis_Khan (updated June 24, 2006).

4. Tom Robinson, "About Me," www.trrobinson.com.

5. Mark Henderson, "How I Am Related to Genghis Khan," *The London Times*, http://www.timesonline.co.uk/0,,1-10889-220248-10889,00.html, May 30, 2006.

6. *Index Mundi*, s.v. "Life Expectancy," http://www.indexmundi.com/world/life_expectancy_at_birth.html, (updated September 2007).

7. Gary Walton, "A Brief History of Human Progress," http://fte.org/capitalism/introduction.

8. *Index Mundi*, s.v. "World Literacy," http://www.indexmundi.com/world/literacy.html, (updated April 17, 2007).

9. Noah Bierman, "DNA Ties UM Prof to Genghis Khan," *The Miami Herald*, http://www.miami.com/mld/miamiherald/news/14730611.htm, June 3, 2006.

10. Francis Fukuyama, "The End of History?" *The National Interest*, Summer 1989.

11. Gregg Easterbrook, *The Progress Paradox*, p. xv.

12. David Brooks, "Why the Poor Are Not Getting Poorer," *The New York Times*, as reprinted in *The Week*, December 10, 2004.

13. "Women Leaders," *The New York Times*, February 25, 2005; Instraw: United

Nations International Research and Training Institute for the Advancement of Women, "Women in Decision-Making," www.un-instraw.org; "Women take charge," *The Week*, April 25, 2008, p. 10; "Women in parliament," *The Economist*, April 4, 2009, p. 101; Claudia Goldin, Lawrence F. Katz, and Ilyana Kuziemko, "Précis: The Reversal of the College Gender Gap," *Monthly Labor Review Online* 129, no. 5 (May 2006); Tamar Lewin, "At Colleges, Women Are Leaving Men in the Dust," *The New York Times*, http://www.nytimes.com/2006/07/09/education/09college.html, July 9, 2006.

14. Jonathan Schell, *The Unconquerable World*, pp. 64–65.

15. UNESCO, www.uis.unesco.org/en/stats/statistics/literacy2000.htm.

16. Gary Walton, "A Brief History of Human Progress," http://fte.org/capitalism/introduction/03.php.

17. "Burgeoning bourgeoisie," *The Economist*, A special report on the new middle classes, February 14, 2009, p. 6.

Chapter 1: Hope

1. David Leonhardt and Majorie Connelly, "81% in Poll Say Nation is Headed on the Wrong Track," *The New York Times*, http://www.nytimes.com/2008/04/04/us/04poll.html, April 4, 2008.

2. "Elephant Dies at Los Angeles Zoo," *CNN*, June 11, 2006, http://www.cnn.com/US.

3. "Hamas Fires Rockets into Israel, Ending 16-month Truce," *The New York Times*, June 11, 2006, http://www.nytimes.com.

4. *New Orleans Times-Picayune*, as reprinted in *The Week*, "Noted," September 30, 2005.

5. Bernard Goldberg, *Bias: A CBS Insider Exposes How the Media Distort the News*, pp. 1-14.

6. Eric Alterman, *What Liberal Media?* pp. 3, 5-13.

7. Robert J. Samuelson, *Untruth: Why the Conventional Wisdom is (Almost Always) Wrong*, p. 194; *Wikipedia*, s.v. "Truthiness," http://en.wikipedia.org/wiki/Truthiness, (updated November 3, 2007).

8. Tad Tuleja, *Fabulous Fallacies*, pp. 2, 5.

9. Drew Curtis, *It's Not News, It's FARK*, pp. 86-89. New York: Gotham Books, 2007.

10. Nick Mamatas, "Go Out and Kill People Because This Article Tells You To," *You Are Being Lied To*, ed. Russ Kick, pp. 215–216.

11. Daniel L. Schacter, *The Seven Sins of Memory: How the Mind Forgets and Remembers*, pp. 4-5.

12. Gregg Easterbrook, "Life is good, so why do we feel so bad?," *The Wall Street Journal*, as quoted in *The Week*, June 27, 2008; "Study: World Gets Happier," *LiveScience*, http://www.livescience.com/health/080630-world-happiness.html, June 30, 2008.

13. *Wikipedia*, s.v. "Ben Hecht," http://en.wikipedia.org/wiki/Ben_Hecht (updated October 16, 2007).

14. *Snopes*, s.v. "Inboxer Rebellion: Missing Persons: Penny Brown," http://www. snopes.com/inboxer/missing/penny.asp (updated September 25, 2005). Thanks to Marc Vogtman for help with this topic.

15. *Snopes*, s.v. "The Seven Year Glitch," http://www.snopes.com/oldwives/chewgum. asp, (updated January 2, 2005); *Snopes*, s.v. "Hour Missed Brooks," http://www. snopes.com/oldwives/hourwait.asp, (updated January 3, 2005).

16. David Finkelhor, Heather Hammer, and Andrea J. Sedlak, "Nonfamily Abducted Children: National Estimates and Characteristics," Office of Juvenile Justice and Delinquency Prevention, U.S. Department of Justice, October 2002, http://www. ncjrs.gov/pdffiles1/ojjdp/196467.pdf; Brad Stone, "Report Calls Online Threats to Children Overblown," *The New York Times*, January 14, 2009.

17. Carl Sagan, *The Demon-Haunted World*, p. 413.

18. *ThinkExist*, s.v. "Joseph Goebbels quotes," http://en.thinkexist.com/quotes/ joseph_goebbels/.

19. Ilan Greenberg, "When a Kleptocratic, Megalomaniacal Dictator Goes Bad," *The New York Times*, http://www.nytimes.com/2003/01/05/magazine/05TURKMENISTAN. html, January 5, 2003.

20. Sheldon Rampton, and John Stauber, *Trust Us, We're Experts*, pp. 16–17.

21. Robert Wright, *Nonzero: The Logic of Human Destiny*, pp. 5-7, 340-342.

22. Sheldon Rampton and John Stauber, *Trust Us, We're Experts*, p. 17.

23. "Are Consumers Daft?" *The Economist*, August 4, 2007.

24. Carl Sagan, *The Demon-Haunted World*, pp. 73–76.

25. *Snopes*, s.v. "Halloween Poisonings," http://www.snopes.com/horrors/poison/ halloween.asp, (updated October 27, 2005).

26. For additional information on Ecto Cooler, refer to: http://www.x-entertainment. com/articles/0822/.

27. Quoted in Burtt, E.A., editor, *Teachings of the Compassionate Buddha*, pp. 49–50.

28. Carl Sagan, *The Demon-Haunted World*, p. 210.

29. *Thomas Jefferson on Politics & Government*, http://etext.virginia.edu/jefferson/ quotations/jeff1350.htm.

30. Charles Kimball, *When Religion Becomes Evil*, p. 189.

31. Drake Bennett, "Beyond the bread lines," *The Boston Globe*, as reprinted in *The Week*, December 5, 2008, p. 48; Eric Rauchway, *The Great Depression and the New Deal*, p. 1.

32. "Extremist nightmares," *The Economist*, March 7, 2009, p. 62; "What if ?," *The Economist*, September 12, 2009, p. 86.

33. Eric Rauchway, *The Great Depression and the New Deal*, pp. 24-26, 31-32.

34. Drake Bennett, "Beyond the bread lines," *The Boston Globe*, as reprinted in *The Week*, December 5, 2008, p. 48.

35. "Not just straw men," *The Economist*, June 20, 2009, p. 63.

36. "Why recessions happen," *The Week*, November 28, 2008, p. 12; "Diagnosing

depression," *The Economist*, January 3, 2009, p. 57.

37. "What does the stock rally tell us?," *The Week*, August 7, 2009; "Mounting evidence of a recovery," *The Week*, August 14, 2009, p. 40; "A long way to go," *The Economist*, July 25, 2009, p. 12.

38. "Surviving the slump," *The Economist: A special report on business in America*, May 30, 2009, p. 4; "Creative destruction," *The Economist: A special report on business in America*, May 30, 2009, p. 9; "The coming recovery," *The Economist: A special report on business in America*, May 30, 2009, p. 17.

39. Nicholas Dawidoff, "The Civil Heretic," *The New York Times Magazine*, http://www.nytimes.com/2009/03/29/magazine/29Dyson t.html, March 25, 2009.

Chapter 2: History

1. Moojan Momen, *Hinduism and the Bahá'í Faith*, pp. 33–37; *Wikipedia*, s.v. "Kali Yuga," http://en.wikipedia.org/wiki/Kali_yuga (updated September 19, 2007); *Wikipedia*, s.v. "Kalki," http://en.wikipedia.org/wiki/Kalki_avatar (updated September 21, 2007).

2. Jennifer Oldstone-Moore, *Taoism*, pp. 58–59.

3. Eleanor Nesbitt, *Sikhism: A Very Short Introduction*, p. 27.

4. Damien Keown, *Buddhism: A Very Short Introduction*, pp. 30–32.

5. Jennifer Oldstone-Moore, *Confucianism*, pp. 60–61.

6. Isaiah 2:4, *The Holy Bible: New Revised Standard Version*. New York: Oxford University Press, 1989.

7. Shraga Simmons, "Jewish View of the Messiah," *About Judaism*, http://judaism.about.com/library/3_askrabbi_0/bl_simmons_messiah4.htm.

8. Norman Solomon, *Judaism: A Very Short Introduction*, p. 117.

9. *Wikipedia*, s.v. "Logos," http://en.wikipedia.org/wiki/Logos (updated September 2, 2009).

10. *Wikipedia*, s.v. "Summary of Christian Eschatological Differences," http://en.wikipedia.org/wiki/Summary_of_Christian_eschatological_differences (updated June 14, 2006).

11. Ziauddin Sardar and Merryl Wyn Davies, *The No-Nonsense Guide to Islam*, p. 32.

12. "The Twelve Imams," *Knowledge of Reality Magazine*, Issue 13, http://www.sol.com.au/kor/13_02.htm.

13. Malise Ruthven, *Islam: A Very Short Introduction*, pp. 49–50.

14. Peter Singer, *Hegel: A Very Short Introduction*, pp. 14–31.

15. *Wikipedia*, s.v. "Georg Wilhelm Friedrich Hegel," http://en.wikipedia.org/wiki/Hegel (updated June 16, 2006).

16. Harvey C. Mansfield, *A Student's Guide to Political Philosophy*, p. 51.

17. Peter Singer, *A Very Short Introduction to Hegel*, pp. 31, 93; Howard P. Kainz, *An Introduction to Hegel: The Stages of Modern Philosophy*, pp. viii–xi.

18. John Huddleston, *Standing Up for Humanity*, pp. 72–82.; Paul Strathern, *Marx in 90 Minutes*, p. 16, 29-34.

19. Immanuel Kant, "Idea for a Universal History" and "Perpetual Peace" in *Political Writings*, pp. 50–51, 94, 102–108.

20. Neil Postman, *Technopoly*, p. 20.

21. *Wikipedia*, s.v. "Evolution," http://en.wikipedia.org/wiki/Evolution (updated June 23, 2006).

22. Robert Wright, *Nonzero: The Logic of Human Destiny*, p. 3-4; *Wikipedia*, s.v. "Pierre Teilhard de Chardin," http://en.wikipedia.org/wiki/Teilhard (updated September 20, 2007); *Wikipedia*, s.v. "Orthogenesis," http://en.wikipedia.org/wiki/Orthogenesis (updated September 14, 2007); *Wikipedia*, s.v. "Omega point," http://en.wikipedia.org/wiki/Omega_point (updated September 27, 2007).

23. Robert Wright, *Nonzero: The Logic of Human Destiny*, p.6-10.

Chapter 3: Thought

1. *Wikipedia*, s.v. "Wombat," http://en.wikipedia.org/wiki/Wombat, (updated November 11, 2006)

2. John Chambers, "Guts and Glory," *Forbes*, p. 164, May 7, 2007.

3. Steven E. Landsburg, *More Sex is Safer Sex*, p. 25.

4. Steven E. Landsburg, *More Sex is Safer Sex*, pp. 26, 31; Thomas E. Lovejoy and Mitchell Joachim, "The Salon Conversation," *SEED*, June 2009, p. 44.

5. Jill Lepore, "Our Own Devices", *The New Yorker*, May 12, 2008.

6. Kevin Kelly, "We Will Embrace the Reality of Progress," in *What Are You Optimistic About?*, ed. John Brockman, p. 156.

7. "Canon by Funtwo," *YouTube*, http://www.youtube.com/watch?v=A5Sl8sZuT-U.

8. *Wikipedia*, s.v. "Meme," http://en.wikipedia.org/wiki/MEME, (updated September 4, 2006).

9. Arthur Schopenhauer, quoted in *New York*, quoted in *The Week*, p. 17, June 13, 2008.

10. James Surowiecki, "The Open Secret of Success," *The New Yorker*, May 12, 2008, p. 48.

11. *Ibid.*, p. 48.

12. Luigi Stendardo, *Leo Tolstoy and the Bahá'í Faith*, pp. 15, 30, 42, 48.

13. Zach Dundas, "Reading the Future," *GOOD*, p. 24, Nov/Dec 2007.

14. "Electronics: Amazon upgrades the Kindle," *The Week*, February 20, 2009; "It wasn't all bad," *The Week*, May 1, 2009.

15. "Noted," *The Week*, April 17, 2009, p. 16; *Wikipedia*, s.v. "Zettabyte," http://en.wikipedia.org/wiki/ Zettabyte, (updated August 15, 2009); Ian Jukes, NECC session, http://web.mac.com/iajukes/iWeb/thecommittedsardine/Handouts_files/fgtgtg.pdf.

16. Julia Kirby and Thomas A. Stewart, "The Institutional Yes," *Harvard Business Review*, October 2007, p. 75.

17. *Wikipedia*, s.v. "English language," http://en.wikipedia.org/wiki/ English_language#Number_of_words_in_English, (updated August 18, 2009); Danny Sullivan, "Searches Per Day," *SearchEngineWatch*, http://searchenginewatch.com/2156461, April 20, 2006; "Google Searches per Day at 304 Million in June 2009," *USASEOPROS Blog*, http://blog.usaseopros.com/2009/08/05/google-searches-per-day-at-304-million-in-june-2009/, accessed August 20, 2009; Chris Anderson, *The Long Tail*, pp. 137-38.

18. Carl Sagan, *The Demon-Haunted World*, p. 362.

19. Robert D. Putnam, *Bowling Alone*, p. 186.

20. UNESCO, www.uis.unesco.org/en/stats/statistics/literacy2000.htm; "Charting a More Livable World For All," *The Interdependent*, Fall 2008, p. 20.

21. "Not all bad news," *The Economist*, July 26, 2008.

22. "Lexington: the underworked American," *The Economist*, June 13, 2009, p. 40.

23. Steven Johnson, *Everything Bad is Good For You*, pp. 142-143; *Wikipedia*, s.v. "Flynn Effect," http://en.wikipedia.org/wiki/Flynn_effect, (updated October 25, 2009).

24. *Ibid.*, pp. 181–182.

25. *Ibid.*, p. 65.

26. *Ibid.*, p. 11.

27. Adam Rogers, "Geek Love," *The New York Times*, March 9, 2008.

28. "Tony Blair and The Simpsons," *The Economist*, April 17, 2003, http://www.economist.com/world/britain/displaystory.cfm?story_id=E1_TSNTNQD.

29. Steven Johnson, *Everything Bad is Good For You*, pp. 86-87.; also,read this *Science News Online* article by Erica Klarreich for a fascinating account of the sophistication of *The Simpsons* episode I mentioned: http://www.sciencenews.org/articles/20060610/bob8.asp.

30. Whitney Pastorek, "The Office: Working Overtime," *Entertainment Weekly*, October 5, 2007.

31. Steven Johnson, *Everything Bad is Good For You*, pp. 128–129.

32. *Ibid.*, pp. 159, 168.

33. *Ibid.*, p. 144.

34. Amy Goldwasser, "What's the matter with kids today?," *Salon.com*, http://www.salon.com/mwt/feature/2008/03/14/kids_and_internet, March 14, 2008; Sharon Begley and Jeneen Interlandi, "The Dumbest Generation? Don't Be Dumb.," *Newsweek*, June 2, 2008; A.J. Jacobs, "You (We) Are Not Stupid," *Esquire*, July 2008; "The kids

are alright," *The Economist*, November 15, 2008, p. 98; Clive Thompson, "The New Literacy," *Wired*, September 2009, p. 48; Mark Bauerlein, *The Dumbest Generation: How the Digital Age Stupefies Young Americans and Jeopardizes Our Future (Or, Don't Trust Anyone under 30.)*

35. "All on the mind," *The Economist*, May 24, 2008.

36. Jamais Cascio, "Get Smart," *The Atlantic*, July/August 2009, p. 94; Gabriel Zaid, So Many Books, p. 113; Howard Gardner, "Personalized Education," *Foreign Policy*, May/June 2009, p. 86.

37. Carl Sagan, *The Demon-Haunted World*, p. 355.

38. Massachusetts Institute of Technology, http://ocw.mit.edu/OcwWeb/web/about/history/index.htm; Apple News email, "iTunes U: one-stop learning for all"; Roger C. Schank, "The End of the Commoditization of Knowledge," in *What Are You Optimistic About?*, ed. John Brockman, p. 229.

39. *Wikipedia*, s.v. "Renaissance," http://en.wikipedia.org/wiki/Renaissance, (updated August 24, 2006).

40. Clay Shirky, "Reliance on Evidence," in *What Are You Optimistic About?*, ed. John Brockman, p. 32.

41. Michael Gelb, *How to Think Like Leonardo da Vinci*, pp. 43-45, 276.; Shana Priwer and Cynthia Phillips, *101 Things You Didn't Know About da Vinci*, pp. 125, 130-131, 149, 152, 216.

42. To give credit where credit is due, the Chinese invented the printing press centuries earlier, but it was designed differently and not used as often. The invention did not spread out of China or cause as many ripples in society as Gutenberg's invention did. *Wikipedia*, s.v. "Johannes Gutenberg," http://en.wikipedia.org/wiki/Johannes_Gutenberg, (updated August 25, 2006).

43. Stephen Prothero, *Religious Literacy*, p. 128.

44. Carl Sagan, *The Demon-Haunted World*, p. 425.

45. *Wikipedia*, s.v. "Petrarch," http://en.wikipedia.org/wiki/Petrarch, (updated August 23, 2006).

46. Simon Blackburn, *Think*, p. 20.

Chapter 4: Technology

1. Margaret Mead, as quoted on *The Quotations Page*, http://www.quotationspage.com/quote/33522.html.

2. "Internet Usage Statistics: The Internet Big Picture," *Internet World Stats*, http://www.internetworldstats.com/stats.htm, updated June 30, 2009; Zoë Chafe, "Internet and Cell Phone Use Soar," *Vital Signs 2006-2007*.

3. Kai Krause, "A New Contentism," in *What Are You Optimistic About?*, ed. John Brockman, p. 291.

4. "Raising Alabama," *The Economist*, July 18, 2009, p. 30.

5. David Kirkpatrick, "Making connections," *Fortune*, August 1, 2006, http://money.cnn.com/magazines/fortune/fortune_archive/2006/08/07/8382578/index.htm.

6. "Winning the War on Spam," *The Economist*, August 20, 2005.

7. Alyssa Danigelis and Jennifer Pollock, "The Irresistible Force," *Fast Company*, March 2006.

8. "Calling an End to Poverty," *The Economist*, July 9, 2005.

9. Zoë Chafe, "Internet and Cell Phone Use Soar," *Vital Signs 2006-2007*, p. 70; "Connecting the world," *The Economist*, September 25, 2009, www.economist.com/displayStory.cfm?story_id=14529802; "The bottom line," *The Wall Street Journal*, as quoted in *The Week*, p. 38, February 22, 2008; Dambisa Moyo, "Africa," *Foreign Policy*, May/June 2009, p. 90; "The meek shall inherit the web," *The Economist: Technology Quarterly*, September 6, 2008, p. 3; "The power of mobile money," *The Economist*, September 26, 2009, p. 13.

10. "Calling an End to Poverty," *The Economist*, July 9, 2005.

11. Zoë Chafe, "Internet and Cell Phone Use Soar," *Vital Signs 2006-2007*, p. 70.

12. Evan Ratliff, "Me Translate Pretty One Day," *Wired*, December 2006; "How to Build a Babel Fish," *The Economist*, June 10, 2006.

13. Rupert Murdoch, "Mixed Media," *Forbes*, pp. 138-142, May 7, 2007.

14. Chuck Klosterman, "What We Have Here Is a Failure to Communicate," *Esquire*, August 2005; "Not all bad news," *The Economist*, July 26, 2008.

15. "Who killed the newspaper?," *The Economist*, August 26, 2006.

16. Daniel W. Drezner and Henry Farrell, "Web of Influence," *Foreign Policy*, November/December 2004; Jeff Jarvis, "The Ethics of Openness," *Rebooting America*, p. 217.

17. "Who killed the newspaper?," *The Economist*, August 26, 2006.

18. "It's the Links, Stupid," *The Economist*, April 22, 2006.

19. Daniel W. Drezner and Henry Farrell, "Web of Influence," *Foreign Policy*, November/December 2004.

20. "User-generated science," *The Economist*, September 20, 2008, p. 99; Tim Harford, *The Logic of Life*, p. 164.

21. Mike Nizza and Patrick Witty, "In an Iranian Image, a Missile Too Many," *The New York Times*, http://thelede.blogs.nytimes.com/2008/07/10/in-an-iranian-image-a-missile-too-many/, July 10, 2008.

22. "Where Writers Fear No Censorship," Asharq al-Awsat, as reprinted in *The Week*, p. 16, November 10, 2006; Daniel W. Drezner and Henry Farrell, "Web of Influence," *Foreign Policy*, November/December 2004.

23. "Blog standard," *The Economist*, June 28, 2008.

24. "The fever under the surface," *The Economist: A special report on the Arab world*, July 25, 2009, p. 12; David Wolman, "Cairo Activists Use Facebook to Rattle Regime," *Wired*, November 2008, p. 213; Mona Eltahawy, "The Middle East's Generation Facebook," *World Policy Journal*, Fall 2008, pp. 76-77.

25. "Iran: The Twitter Revolution," *The Week*, July 3-10, 2009, p. 20.

26. "Mobiles, Protests and Pundits," *The Economist*, October 28, 2006.

27. Glenn Reynolds, *An Army of Davids*, p. 134.

28. Ann Florini, *The Coming Democracy*, p. 28, 30.

29. Katherine Viner, "Internet has changed foreign policy forever, says Gordon Brown," *The Guardian*, June 19, 2009, guardian.co.uk.

30. Matt Bai, "The Web Users' Campaign," *The New York Times Magazine*, December 9, 2007, p. 29; Beth Simone Noveck, *Wiki Government*, p. 15.

31. Tim O'Reilly, "Gov 2.0: It's All About the Platform," *Techcrunch*, September 4, 2009, http://www.techcrunch.com/2009/09/04/gov-20-its-all-about-the-platform; Kevin Kelly, "The New Socialism," *Wired*, May 22, 2009; Beth Simone Noveck, *Wiki Government*, pp. xv, 17-19, 25.

32. "The road to e-democracy," *The Economist: A special report on technology and government*, February 16, 2008, p. 18, "Track my tax dollars," *The Economist*, February 7, 2009, p. 28, Beth Simone Noveck, *Wiki Government*, pp. xii, xv; Tim O'Reilly, "Gov 2.0: It's All About the Platform," *Techcrunch*, September 4, 2009, http://www.techcrunch.com/2009/09/04/gov-20-its-all-about-the-platform; Fred Wilson, "Urban Architects," *A VC: Musings of a VC in NYC*, September 21, 2009, http://www.avc.com/a_vc/2009/09/urban-architects.html; Tim O'Reilly and Jennifer Pahlka, "The 'Web Squared' Era," *Forbes*, September 24, 2009, http://www.forbes.com/2009/09/23/web-squared-oreilly-technology-breakthroughs-web2pointo.html; Craig Newmark, "Checks and Balances Reinvigorated," *Rebooting America*, p. 140.

33. Beth Simone Noveck, *Wiki Government*, pp. xii, xv.

34. Michael Wesch, presentation at Personal Democracy Forum, New York City, June 30, 2009. Kevin Kelly, "The New Socialism," *Wired*, May 22, 2009.

35. Katherine Critchlow, "Internet," *FHM US*, p. 44, November 2006.

36. Neil Postman, *Technopoly*, pp. 18-20.

37. "Internet Privacy: Watch What You Search," *The Week*, p. 18, August 25, 2006.

38. "Not Losing Facebook in China," *The Economist*, p. 79, September 15, 2007.

39. "Adland's Test Tube," *The Economist*, December 16, 2006.

40. "Fabulous Fabrications," *The Economist*, March 26, 2005.

41. "Wag the Dog," *The Economist*, July 8, 2006.

42. "Among the Audience," *The Economist*, April 22, 2006.

43. Robert J. Samuelson, *Untruth: Why the Conventional Wisdom is (Almost Always) Wrong*, p. 219.

44. "Web 2.0," *Wired: Geekipedia*, p.58, September 2007.

45. "The Wiki Principle," *The Economist*, April 22, 2006.

46. Brad Stone and Steven Levy, "Who's Building the Next Web?" *Newsweek*, April 3, 2006.

47. "Living a Second Life," *The Economist*, September 30, 2006.

48. Steven Johnson, "How Twitter Will Change the Way We Live," *Time*, June 15, 2009, p. 28.

49. Steven Levy and Brad Stone, "The New Wisdom of the Web," *Newsweek*, April 3, 2006.

50. "A Perfect Market," *The Economist*, May 15, 2004; Jacques Attali, *A Brief History of the Future*, p. 262.

51. Kevin Maney, "The Rating Game," *The Atlantic*, July/August 2009, p. 38.

52. Julia Kirby and Thomas A. Stewart, "The Institutional Yes," *Harvard Business Review*, p.75, October 2007.

53. "Santa's Helpers," *The Economist*, May 15, 2004.

54. Connie Bruck, "Millions for Millions," *The New Yorker*, October 30, 2006; "An idea whose time has come," *The Economist: A special report on entrepreneurship*, March 14, 2009, p. 6.

55. "Virtual Fun," *The Economist*, May 15, 2004.

56. Connie Bruck, "Millions for Millions," *The New Yorker*, October 30, 2006.

57. All long tail information: "Profiting from Obscurity," *The Economist*, May 7, 2005; "Wag the Dog," *The Economist*, July 8, 2006.

58. Glenn Reynolds, *An Army of Davids*, p. 23.

59. Daniel H. Pink, *Free Agent Nation*.

60. "Freelancers of the World, Unite!" *The Economist*, November 11, 2006.

61. James Surowiecki, *The Wisdom of Crowds*, pp. xxiii-xx, 5-6, 212-215.

Chapter 5: Unity

1. Al Gore, *An Inconvenient Truth*, pp. 12–15.

2. Cornell Lab of Ornithology, "All About Birds: European Starling," http://www.birds.cornell.edu/AllAboutBirds/BirdGuide/European_Starling.html; American Museum of Natural History, "Dodo," http://www.amnh.org/exhibitions/expeditions/treasure_fossil/Treasures/Dodo/dodo.html?dinos.

3. Arthur Lyon Dahl, "The Environment and the Lesser Peace," in *Processes of the Lesser Peace*, ed. Babak Bahador and Nazila Ghanea, p. 86.

4. Foad Katirai, *Global Governance and the Lesser Peace*, p. 15.

5. Robert Wright, *Nonzero: The Logic of Human Destiny*, p. 193.

6. The Universal House of Justice, *The Promise of World Peace*, p. 13.

7. Robert Wright, *Nonzero: The Logic of Human Destiny*, p. ix.

8. Ann Florini, *The Coming Democracy*, p. 58.

9. Foad Katirai, *Global Governance and the Lesser Peace*, p. 60.

10. Foad Katirai, *Global Governance and the Lesser Peace*, p. 57; Clay Shirky, "Reliance on Evidence," in *What Are You Optimistic About?*, ed. John Brockman, p. 32; Scott D. Sampson, "A New, Environmentally Sustainable Worldview," in *What Are You Optimistic About?*, ed. John Brockman, p. 134.

11. Malcolm Gladwell, "In the Air," *The New Yorker*, May 12, 2008.

12. *Ibid.*

13. Clay Shirky, *Here Comes Everybody*, p. 249.

14. James Surowiecki, "America in the World," *Good*, Sep/Oct 2006.

15. Gregg Easterbrook, *The Progress Paradox*, p. 26.

16. "Talking Business," *The Economist*, September 2, 2006, p. 49.

17. Kai Krause, "A New Contentism," in *What Are You Optimistic About?*, ed. John Brockman, p. 291.

18. "Economic and financial indicators: Working Hours," *The Economist*, July 29, 2006, p. 88. For all their accusations of workaholism, Japanese workers log in fewer hours than Australians and New Zealanders (who log in the most), the United States, Spain, and Italy. All of those countries, as well as Canada, Portugal, Britain, Sweden, France, Germany, and Norway, have seen a drop in the average annual hours worked per person, from 1994 to 2005.

19. The chart is based on information gleaned from Gregg Easterbrook's *The Progress Paradox*, p. 28; also, *Wikipedia*, s.v. "Eight-hour day," http://en.wikipedia.org/wiki/Eight-hour_day, (updated September 15, 2006).

20. Christopher Shea, "We May Not Be So Overworked After All," *The Boston Globe*, as reprinted in *The Week*, p. 14, August 24, 2007; "180 Trillion Leisure Hours Lost to Work Last Year," *The Onion*, Volume 43 Issue 28, p.1, July 12, 2007.

21. "Editors' Note," *World Policy Journal*, Fall 2008, p. 2.

22. Daniel Radosh, "While My Guitar Gently Beeps," *The New York Times Magazine*, August 16, 2009, p. 35.

23. Seanchai and the Unity Squad do not have this marketing problem, since plenty of people like their music wherever they go, but they are a good example of a niche product. Information about this band can be found at: www.seanchai.com.

24. Chris Anderson, *The Long Tail: Why the Future of Business is Selling Less of More*, pp. 5-13, 168-69.

25. Seth Schiesel, "An Online Game, Made in U.S., Seizes the Globe," *The New York Times*, http://www.nytimes.com/2006/09/05/technology/05wow.html, September 5, 2006.

26. Author Neal Stephenson was one of the first visionaries to imagine an interactive online world such as World of Warcraft's. In 1992 he came up with a similar online world, with similar avatars, in his novel *Snow Crash*.

27. Robert J. Samuelson, *Untruth: Why the Conventional Wisdom is (Almost Always) Wrong*, pp. 11–14.

28. "Don't dare put me in a box," *The Economist*, November 10, 2007; Daniel Deudney and G. John Ikenberry, "The Myth of the Autocratic Revival," *Foreign Affairs*, January/February 2009, p. 90.

29. Robert Wright, *Nonzero: The Logic of Human Destiny*, p. 329.

30. Clay Shirky, *Here Comes Everybody*, p. 47.

31. *Ibid.*, pp. 17, 107, 295.

32. "A service nation," *The Economist*, April 11, 2009, p. 30; Frances Moore Lappé, *Getting a Grip*, p. 27; Grant Stoddard, "What We Get From Giving," *Men's Health*, July/August 2009, p. 108.

33. Hillary Mayell, "Angelina Jolie on Her UN Refugee Role," *National Geographic*, June 18, 2003, http://news.nationalgeographic.com/news/2003/06/0618_030618_angelinajolie.html.

34. Bill Saporito, "The Jeff Sachs Contradiction: Celebrity Economist," *Time*, March 14, 2005.

35. "Leaders: Missionary Zeal," *The Economist*, January 29, 2005, p. 10.

36. Jonathan Alter, "New Windows on the World," *Newsweek*, August 30, 1999.

37. Microsoft PressPass, "Microsoft Announces Plans for July 2008 Transition for Bill Gates," June 15, 2006, http://www.microsoft.com/presspass/press/2006/jun06/06-15CorpNewsPR.mspx.

38. Donald G. McNeil, Jr., and Rick Lyman, "Buffett's Billions Will Aid Fight Against Disease," *The New York Times*, http://www.nytimes.com/2006/06/27/us/27gates.html, June 27, 2006.

39. *Ibid.*

40. "Putting the World to Rights," *The Economist*, June 3, 2004.

41. Molly Aeck, "Global Public Policy Cooperation Grows," *Vital Signs 2005*, p. 106.

42. Angelina Crowley, "Celebrities Help in Darfur, Sudan," *Associated Content*, June 3, 2006, http://www.associatedcontent.com/article/35973/celebrities_help_in_darfur_sudan.html.

43. Daniel Wheatly, "Global Governance: Has a Paradigm Shift in World Government Theory Brought the Lesser Peace Closer?" in *Processes of the Lesser Peace*, ed. Babak Bahador and Nazila Ghanea, pp. 238–239.

44. Foad Katirai, *Global Governance and the Lesser Peace*, p. 61–62.

45. Steven Pinker, "The Decline of Violence," in *What Are You Optimistic About?*, ed. John Brockman, p. 3. *Wikipedia*, s.v. "Bethlam Royal Hospital," http://en.wikipedia.org/wiki/ Bethlam_Royal_Hospital (updated July 15, 2008).

46. Steven Pinker, "The Decline of Violence," in *What Are You Optimistic About?*, ed. John Brockman, pp. 3-4.

47. *Wikipedia*, s.v. "Universal Declaration of Human Rights," http://en.wikipedia.org/wiki/Universal_declaration_of_human_rights (updated September 9, 2006); The Universal Declaration of Human Rights, http://www.unhchr.ch/udhr/lang/eng.htm; Geoffrey Cowley, "Bill's Biggest Bet Yet," *Newsweek*, February 4, 2002; Paul Kennedy, The Parliament of Man, p. 182.

48. Immanuel Kant, "Perpetual Peace" in *Political Writings*, ed. Hans Reiss , pp. 107–108.

49. Howard Zinn, "Vietnam: The Moral Equation," reprinted in *The Power of Nonviolence: Writings by Advocates of Peace*, p. 138.

Chapter 6: Equality

1. "Profile: Liberia's 'Iron Lady,'" *BBC News*, http://news.bbc.co.uk/1/hi/world/africa/4395978.stm, November 23, 2005; Laura Bush, "Time 100: The People Who Shape Our World: Ellen Johnson-Sirleaf," *Time*, April 30, 2006; *Wikipedia*, s.v. "Ellen Johnson-Sirleaf," http://en.wikipedia.org/wiki/Ellen_Johnson-Sirleaf, (updated September 13, 2006); *Wikipedia*, s.v. "Charles Taylor," http://en.wikipedia.org/wiki/Charles_Taylor_%28Liberia%29, (updated September 13, 2006).

2. Tatiana Serafin, "The 100 Most Powerful Women: #17," *Forbes*, August 31, 2006; *Wikipedia*, s.v. "Michelle Bachelet," http://en.wikipedia.org/wiki/Michelle_Bachelet, (updated September 20, 2006).

3. Chana Schoenberger, "The 100 Most Powerful Women: #89," *Forbes*, August 31, 2006; *Wikipedia*, s.v. "Portia Simpson-Miller," http://en.wikipedia.org/wiki/Portia_Simpson_Miller, (updated September 19, 2006); "Portia Simpson Miller – Heart, soul and guts," *Jamaica Gleaner*, February 26, 2006.

4. Reihan Salam, "The Death of Macho," *Foreign Policy*, July/August 2009, p. 66.

5. *Worldwide Guide to Women in Leadership*, http://www.guide2womenleaders.com/Current-Women-Leaders.htm. Incidentally, I remembered the number of countries as 192. That number is oft-cited, since that is the number of UN member countries. But turns out one country never joined the UN—Vatican City.

6. *Ibid.* The chart includes female Presidents and female Prime/Premier Ministers.

7. "Women Leaders," *The New York Times*, February 25, 2005; Instraw: United Nations International Research and Training Institute for the Advancement of Women, "Women in Decision-Making," www.un-instraw.org; "Women take charge," *The Week*, April 25, 2008, p. 10; "Women in parliament," *The Economist*, April 4, 2009, p. 101; "First woman minister," *The Week*, February 27, 2009, p. 9.

8. "The 100 Most Powerful Women," *Forbes*, http://www.forbes.com/lists/2006/11/06women_The-100-Most-Powerful-Women_Rank.html, August 31, 2006.

9. "Noted," *The Week*, January 19, 2007, p. 16.

10. Fareed Zakaria, "First Ladies, in the Truest Sense," *Newsweek*, November 28, 2005; Austin Ejiet, "The shock of an honest president," *The Monitor* (Uganda), as reprinted in *The Week*, February 2, 2007.

11. Nicholas D. Kristof, "When Women Rule," *The New York Times*, http://www.nytimes.com/2008/02/10/opinion/10kristof.html, February 10, 2008.

12. "Leaders: The importance of sex," *The Economist*, April 15, 2006.

13. Valerie Hudson, "Good Riddance," *Foreign Policy*, July/August 2009, p. 71.

14. BBC News, as reported by *WorldCampaign.net*, December 11, 2002.

15. "Leaders: The importance of sex," *The Economist*, April 15, 2006.

16. Isobel Coleman, "The Payoff from Women's Rights," *Foreign Affairs*, May/June 2004.

17. *Ibid.*

18. Instraw: United Nations International Research and Training Institute for the Advancement of Women, "Women in Decision-Making," www.un-instraw.org.

19. Claudia Goldin, Lawrence F. Katz, and Ilyana Kuziemko, "Précis: The Reversal of the College Gender Gap," *Monthly Labor Review Online* 129, no. 5 (May 2006).; Tamar Lewin, "At Colleges, Women Are Leaving Men in the Dust," *The New York Times*, http://www.nytimes.com/2006/07/09/education/09college.html, July 9, 2006; Daren Fonda, "The Male Minority," *Time*, December 11, 2000; "Leaders: The Importance of Sex," *The Economist*, April 15, 2006; "Catching up to the boys," *The Week*, August 8, 2008, p. 22.

20. Institute for Women's Policy Research: Fact Sheet, http://www.iwpr.org/pdf/C350.pdf, (updated August 2005).

21. Sam Roberts, "For Young Earners in Big City, a Gap in Women's Favor," *The New York Times*, http://www.nytimes.com/2007/08/03/nyregion/03women.html, August 3, 2007.

22. Reihan Salam, "The Death of Macho," *Foreign Policy*, July/August 2009, p. 68.

23. Steve Chapman, "Don't blame the pay gap on sexism," *Chicago Tribune*, as reprinted in *The Week*, May 11, 2007, p. 14.

24. Gregg Easterbrook, The Progress Paradox, p. 57.

25. Rebecca Tuhus-Dubrow, "The business case for female leaders," *The Boston Globe*, as reprinted in *The Week*, May 15, 2009, p. 38.

26. "Helping Women Get to the Top," *The Economist*, July 23, 2005.

27. Gregg Easterbrook, *The Progress Paradox*, p. 194.

28. Stirling Kelso, Joseph Manez and Henry Yung, "The Future is Gaining on You," *Fast Company*, March 2006.

29. "Have You Stopped Beating Your Wife?" *The Economist*, April 16, 2005.

30. Gregg Easterbrook, *The Progress Paradox*, p. 38; Steve Chapman, "Is pornography a catalyst of sexual violence?," *Chicago Tribune*, as quoted in *The Week*, November 16, 2007.

31. Christopher Dickey and Faiza Ambah, "Another Kind of Warrior," *Newsweek*, May 3, 2004; "Out of the Shadows, into the World," *The Economist*, June 17, 2004.

32. "Out of the shadows, into the world," *The Economist*, June 17, 2004.

33. *Ibid.*

34. Magda El-Ghitany, "Assessing Arab Women's Lot," *Al-Ahram* (Egyptian), October 14–20, 2004.

35. "Out of the shadows, into the world," *The Economist*, June 17, 2004.

36. Magda El-Ghitany, "Assessing Arab Women's Lot," *Al-Ahram* (Egyptian), October 14–20, 2004.

37. "Interview with head of UNIFEM's Arab states office, Dr. Haifa Abu Ghazaleh," *Irin News*, http://www.irinnews.org/report.aspx?reportid=26178, (updated March 8, 2006).

38. *Ibid.*

39. "Most blacks say MLK's vision fulfilled, poll finds," *CNN.com*, January 19, 2009.

40. Steven D. Strauss, *World Conflicts*, p. 11.

41. Joel L. Swerdlow, "New Americans: Their Origins, Their Destinations," *National Geographic*, September 2001.

42. Stirling Kelso, Joseph Manez and Henry Yung, "The Future is Gaining on You," *Fast Company*, March 2006.

43. "Free to Succeed or Fail," *The Economist*, August 6, 2005; Sheryl Gay Stolberg and Marjorie Connelly, "Obama is Nudging Views on Race, a Survey Finds," *The New York Times*, April 28, 2009.

44. "Free to Succeed or Fail," *The Economist*, August 6, 2005.

45. Correspondents of the *New York Times*, *How Race is Lived in America*, pp. 367–368.

46. "Ready to Run the Movie Again?," *The Economist*, October 6, 2007, p.28.

47. "The Cosby Show," *The Economist*, July 10, 2004, p.30.

48. About $17,000 in 2001. Whereas in 1948, white women held an average salary of $8,000 and black women's salaries averaged only $4,000. Lynette Clemetson, "Color My World," *Newsweek*, March 3, 2003.

49. "Free to Succeed or Fail," *The Economist*, August 6, 2005.

50. Lynette Clemetson, "Color My World," *Newsweek*, March 3, 2003.

51. Gregg Easterbrook, *The Progress Paradox*, p. 11.

52. Nicholas D. Kristof, "Love and Race," *The New York Times*, December 7, 2002.

53. Correspondents of the *New York Times*, *How Race is Lived in America*, p. 388. In order to come up with the numbers in figure 4, I interpolated data from two separate polls. The 1978 and 1991 polls only provided the general opinions of Americans without taking race into account. This means that the responses attributed to whites on the chart for those years are probably a little high (since the 11 percent black population, which has a higher number, is averaged in). The 1958 poll, only asked of whites, is from "Free to Succeed or Fail," *The Economist*, August 6, 2005.

54. Nicholas D. Kristof, "Love and Race," *The New York Times*, December 7, 2002.

55. Lynette Clemetson, "Color My World," *Newsweek*, May 8, 2000.

56. Gregory Rodriguez, "Mongrel America," *The Atlantic Monthly*, January/February 2003; "The counting of America," *The Week*, July 24, 2009, p. 11.

57. Ruth La Ferla, "Generation EA: Ethnically Ambiguous," *The New York Times*, December 28, 2003.

58. Naomi Zack, "Race and Mixed Race", Temple University, http://www.temple.edu/tempress/titles/1004_reg.html, 2007; Yehudi O. Webster, "Twenty-one Arguments for Abolishing Racial Classification," *The Multiracial Activist*, http://multiracial.com/site/content/view/213/40/, June 1, 2000.

59. The NBC sitcom, *The Office*, did a spoof of office diversity programs, "Diversity Day," an episode which did its best to offend every group equally.

60. Both ads are from the *New York Times Magazine*, October 21, 2001.

61. Correspondents of the *New York Times*, *How Race is Lived in America*, p. 374.

62. "Helping Women Get to the Top," *The Economist*, July 23, 2005.

63. Joseph E. Stiglitz, *Globalization and its Discontents*, p. 241.

64. http://www.tolerance.org, (updated September 24, 2007).

65. http://www.kidsbridgemuseum.org. I built the site with Need2Know Inc.

66. B.A. Robinson, "Public Opinion Polls on Homosexuality," *Religious Tolerance*, http://www.religioustolerance.org/hom_poll2.htm, (updated July 23, 2007); "Out and proud parents," *The Economist*, June 30, 2007, p.42; David M. Herszenhorn, "House Approves Broad Protections for Gay Workers," *The New York Times*, http://www.nytimes.com/2007/11/08/washington/08emply.html, November 8, 2007.

67. Gregory Rodriguez, *Los Angeles Times*, quoted in "Gays are leaving their ghettos" *The Week*, November 16, 2007.

68. "Comrades-in-arms," *The Economist*, June 20, 2009, p. 43; "Vote of confidence," *The Week*, May 8, 2009, p. 8.

69. Cornell Law School: LII/Legal Information Institute, "Disability Law," http://www.law.cornell.edu/wex/index.php/Disability_law, (updated June 2, 2006).

70. Robert L. Metts, Ph.D., "Disability Issues, Trends and Recommendations for the World Bank," http://siteresources.worldbank.org/DISABILITY/Resources/Overview/ Disability_Issues_Trends_and_Recommendations_for_the_WB.pdf, (updated February, 2000).

71. Adam Sternbergh, "What Ever Happened to Growing Up?" *New York Magazine*, reprinted in *The Week*, April 21, 2006.

72. Glenn Gaslin, "The Disappearing Comic Book," *LA Times*, July 17, 2001.

73. Entertainment Software Association, "Top 10 Industry Facts," http://www.theesa.com/facts/top_10_facts.php, (updated September 2007).

74. Steven Johnson, *Everything Bad is Good For You*, p. 195.

75. "March of the Independents," *The New York Times*, http://www.nytimes.com/imagepages/2006/10/24/us/politics/24indie_graphic_sub.html, October 24, 2006; John P. Avlon, "The rise of the independent voter," *The Wall Street Journal*, as reprinted in *The Week*, October 31, 2008, p. 16.

76. Jonathan Chait, "The pipe dream known as bipartisanship," *Los Angeles Times*, as quoted in *The Week*, p. 16, October 5, 2007.

77. George H. Gallup, Alec Gallup, Frank Newport, Gallup Organization, *The Gallup Poll: Public Opinion 2004*, p.103. Roman & Littlefield.

78. Timothy Samuel Shah and Monica Duffy Toft, "Why God is Winning," *Foreign Policy*, July/August 2006.

79. Grace Davie, "Europe: The Exception that Proves the Rule?," in *The Desecularization of the World*, pp. 68-71. Peter L. Berger, editor, Ethics and Public Policy Center, 1999.

80. *AP News*, "More Americans say they have no religion," March 9, 2009, http://townhall.com/news/religion/2009/03/09/more_americans_say_they_have_no_religion; Barry A. Kosmin and Ariela Keysar, *American Religious Identification Survey*, Summary Report, March 2009, pp. 1,3,7.

81. "The God Slot," *The Economist*, September 16, 2006.

82. Elisabeth Bumiller, "Bush Urges Freedom of Worship in China," *The New York Times*, http://www.nytimes.com/2002/02/22/international/asia/22PREX.html, February 22, 2002.

83. Laurie Goodstein, "More Religion, but Not the Old-Time Kind," *The New York Times*, p. WK1, January 9, 2005.

84. Patricia J. Williams, "Begging to Disagree," *The Nation*, January 7/14, 2002.

85. Laurie Goodstein, "More Religion, but Not the Old-Time Kind," *The New York Times*, p. WK1, January 9, 2005.

86. "Review: The Evolution of God," *The Week*, June 26, 2009, p. 21.

87. Walter Russell Mead, "Born Again," *The Atlantic*, March 2008.

88. Nancy Haught, "Teaching Religion, Teaching Tolerance," *The Oregonian*, October 28, 2002.

89. Stephen Prothero, *Religious Literacy*, p. 115.

90. Charles Kimball, *When Religion Becomes Evil*, p. 204.

91. Jerry Adler, "In Search of the Spiritual," *Newsweek*, August 29/September 5, 2005; "Good week for: Infidels, heretics, and apostates," *The Week*, p. 8, July 4-11, 2008.

92. Charles Kimball, *When Religion Becomes Evil*, p. 199.

93. Jeffrey Huffines, "Bahá'í Proposals for the Reformation of World Order," *Processes of the Lesser Peace*, ed. Babak Bahador and Nazila Ghanea, p. 31.

94. Jerry Adler, "In Search of the Spiritual," *Newsweek*, August 29/September 5, 2005; Neela Banerjee, "Americans Change Faiths at Rising Rate, Report Finds," *The New York Times*, http://www.nytimes.com/2008/02/25/us/25cnd-religion.html, February 25, 2008.

95. Michelle Boorstein, "Americans with 'No Religion' Often Defy that Label," *Miami Herald*, http://www.miami.com/mld/miamiherald/living/religion/15496296.htm, September 12, 2006.

96. Jerry Adler, "In Search of the Spiritual," *Newsweek*, August 29/September 5, 2005.

97. David Van Biema, "The True Values of Islam: One God and One Nation," *Time*, p. 39, September 24, 2001.

98. "The Yoga Boom," *The Week*, October 3, 2003.

99. Jerry Adler, "In Search of the Spiritual," *Newsweek*, August 29/September 5, 2005.

100. Alan Wolfe, "And the Winner Is ...," *The Atlantic*, p. 56, March 2008.

101. *Ibid.*

102. Foad Katirai, *Global Governance and the Lesser Peace*, p. 121.

103. Charles Kimball, *When Religion Becomes Evil*, p. 199.

104. Bhikhu Parekh, *Gandhi: A Very Short Introduction*, pp. 1–8, 35–48.

105. Mohandas Gandhi, *Essential Writings*, ed. John Dear, p. 78.

106. Bhikhu Parekh, *Gandhi: A Very Short Introduction*, p. 42.

Chapter 7: Peace

1. Jean-Marie Guéhenno, "Giving Peace a Chance," *The Economist*: The World in 2005, 2004; "From Saigon to Kabul," *The Economist*, October 3, 2009, p. 55.

2. Gregg Easterbrook, *The Progress Paradox*, p. 72.

3. "Peace: No longer Just a Dream," *The Week*, p. 22, January 13, 2006.

4. "The hobbled hegemon," *The Economist*, June 30, 2007; John Horgan, "Does Peace Have a Chance?," *Slate*, August 4, 2009, http://www.slate.com/id/2224275.

5. Ann Florini, *The Coming Democracy*, p. 128.

6. Michael Renner, "Number of Refugees Declines," *Vital Signs 2005*, p. 67; Roray Carroll, "Human Rights: Refugees," *The Guardian*, June 18, 2004, quoted by World Campaign; United Nations High Commissioner for Refugees (UNHCR), *2005 Global Refugee Trends*, http://www.unhcr.org/statistics/STATISTICS/4486ceb12.pdf, (updated 2006).

7. Michael Renner, "Number of Violent Conflicts Drops," *Vital Signs 2006-2007*, p. 82; "The death of the military coup," *The Economist*, December 12, 2008; Joshua Keating, "The New Coups," *Foreign Policy*, May/June 2009, p. 28.

8. Babak Bahador, "The Establishment of the Lesser Peace," in *Processes of the Lesser Peace*, ed. Babak Bahador and Nazila Ghanea, p. 53.

9. Reuters, *East African Standard*, as quoted by World Campaign, July 15, 2004.

10. Jeffrey Huffines, "Bahá'í Proposals for the Reformation of World Order," in *Processes of the Lesser Peace*, ed. Babak Bahador and Nazila Ghanea, p. 9; *Wikipedia*, s.v. "Fourteen Points," http://en.wikipedia.org/wiki/Fourteen_Points, (updated October 5, 2006).

11. Danesh Sarooshi, "Collective Security as a Means of Ensuring Peace," *Processes of the Lesser Peace*, ed. Babak Bahador and Nazila Ghanea, p. 164.

12. Gregory C. Dahl, *One World, One People*, pp. 61-64.

13. Jonathan Schell, *The Unconquerable World*, p. 256.

14. Jeffrey Huffines, "Bahá'í Proposals for the Reformation of World Order," *Processes of the Lesser Peace*, ed. Babak Bahador and Nazila Ghanea, p. 31.

15. *Wikipedia*, s.v. "Hague Conventions (1899 and 1907)," http://en.wikipedia.org/wiki/Hague_Conventions_%281899_and_1907%29, (updated June 17, 2006).

16. Steven D. Strauss, *World Conflicts*, p. 291.

17. Immanuel Kant, "Idea for a Universal History" and "Perpetual Peace," *Political Writings*, ed. Hans Reiss, pp. 94–95.

18. *Wikipedia*, s.v. "Just War," http://en.wikipedia.org/wiki/Just_War, (updated October 4, 2006).

19. John Horgan, "War Will End," in *What Are You Optimistic About?*, ed. John Brockman, p. 7.

20. Benjamin Friedman, "Homeland Security," *Foreign Policy*, July/August 2005.

21. Fareed Zakaria, "The Only Thing We Have to Fear ...," *Newsweek*, June 2, 2008.

22. Jacob Weisberg, *Slate.com*, quoted in "Five Years Later: Why No Second Attack?" *The Week*, September 22, 2006.

23. "The growing, and mysterious, irrelevance of al-Qaeda," *The Economist*, January 24, 2009, p. 64; Benjamin Friedman, "Homeland Security," *Foreign Policy*, July/August 2005; "How they see us: Closing in on a crumbling al Qaida," *The Week*, p. 16, May 30, 2008..

24. "Suicide Bombing: A Shift in Muslim Attitudes," *The Week*, p. 16, August 10, 2007; Fareed Zakaria, "The Only Thing We Have to Fear ...," *Newsweek*, June 2, 2008.

25. Noah Feldman, "The End of the War on Terror," *Esquire*, October 2008.

26. J. Joseph Hewitt, Jonathan Wilkenfeld, and Ted Robert Gurr, *Peace and Conflict 2008*, p. 3.

27. "The evil that men do (review of *Blood and Rage: A Cultural History of Terrorism* by Michael Burleigh)," *The Economist*, March 8, 2008.

28. John Lewis Gaddis, "Ending Tyranny," *The American Interest*, Autumn 2008, p. 27; "Fighting force," *The Economist*, February 14, 2009.

29. "The struggle against al-Qaeda," *The Economist*, October 25, 2008.

30. David Cortright, *Gandhi and Beyond*, pp. 212–213; Eric Schmitt and Thom Shanker, "U.S. Adapts Cold-War Idea to Fight Terrorists," *The New York Times*, http://www.nytimes.com/2008/03/18/washington/18terror.html, March 18, 2008.

31. Benjamin Friedman, "Homeland Security," *Foreign Policy*, July/August 2005.

32. "Border Security Strengthened by Fingerprint Technology," Home Office: Press Releases, http://press.homeoffice.gov.uk/press-releases/fingerprint-tech-update, October 9, 2007; Harry de Quetteville, "Saudis Build 550-mile Fence to Shut Out Iraq," *Telegraph*, http://www.telegraph.co.uk/news/main.jhtml?xml=/news/2006/10/01/wirq01.xml, September 9, 2006; J. Joseph Hewitt, Jonathan Wilkenfeld, and Ted Robert Gurr, *Peace and Conflict 2008*, pp. 46-49.

33. Alissa J. Rubin, "Iraq Marks Withdrawal of U.S. Troops From Cities," *The New York Times*, July 1, 2009; "Is it turning the corner?," *The Economist*, June 14, 2008; Michael R. Gordon, "After Hard-Won Lessons, Army Doctrine Revised," *The New York Times*, http://www.nytimes.com/2008/02/08/washington/08strategy.html, February 8, 2008.

34. Walter Laqueur, "The Terrorism to Come," *Harper's Magazine*, November 2004.

35. David Cortright, *Gandhi and Beyond*, p. 5.

36. "For Jihadist, Read Anarchist," *The Economist*, August 20, 2005.

37. Gregg Easterbrook, *The Progress Paradox*, p. 295.

38. Walter Laqueur, "The Terrorism to Come," *Harper's Magazine*, November 2004.

39. James Fallows, *The Atlantic Monthly*, quoted in "Five Years Later: Why No Second Attack?" *The Week*, September 22, 2006.

40. Matt Armstrong, "America Should Hire Al-Qaeda's PR Agent," *GOOD*, p. 118, Nov/Dec 2007.

41. John H. Richardson, "Seth Jones," *Esquire*, December, 2008, p. 186.

42. Glenn L. Carle, "The myth of the global jihadist threat," *The Washington Post*, as quoted in *The Week*, p. 14, July 25, 2008.

43. "Noted," *The Week*, October 31, 2008.

44. Mohandas K. Gandhi, *Satyagraha in South-Africa*, pp. 68–71; Michael N. Nagler, *Is There No Other Way?*, p. 83.

45. David Cortright, *Gandhi and Beyond*, p. 61.

46. Mohandas Gandhi, *Essential Writings*, ed. John Dear, p. 83.

47. Martin Luther King, Jr., *Nobel Prize Acceptance Speech*, December 10, 1964.

48. Michael N. Nagler, *Is There No Other Way?*, p. 102.

49. Jonathan Schell, "Strange Mandate," *The Nation*, November 29, 2004.

50. Michael N. Nagler, *Is There No Other Way?*, p. 122; David Cortright, *Gandhi and Beyond*, p. 114.

51. David Cortright, *Gandhi and Beyond*, pp. 205-206.

52. *Ibid.*, p. 86.

53. John Tierney, "An Antiwar Demonstration that Does Not Take to the Streets," *The New York Times*, http://www.nytimes.com/2003/02/26/national/26CND-MARCH.html, February 26, 2003.

54. David Cortright, *Gandhi and Beyond*, p. 206; "Methods," *Nonviolence Works*, http://www.nonviolenceworks.net/NVWSite.htm/about.htm/Methods.htm (updated winter 2001–2002).

55. Bhikhu Parekh, *Gandhi: A Very Short Introduction*, p.76.

56. Jacques Sémelin, *Nonviolence Explained to My Children*, p. 43.

57. David Cortright, *Gandhi and Beyond*, p. 142.

58. Bhikhu Parekh, *Gandhi: A Very Short Introduction*, p. 67.

59. "A Rainbow of Revolutions," *The Economist*, January 21, 2006.

60. "They Shall Overcome – But Perhaps Not Always," *The Economist*, p. 51, August 4, 2007.

61. *Wikipedia*, s.v. "Non-violent Revolution," http://en.wikipedia.org/wiki/Non-violent_revolution, (updated October 12, 2006); *Wikipedia*, s.v. "Rose Revolution," http://en.wikipedia.org/wiki/Rose_Revolution, (updated October 21, 2006); *Wikipedia*, s.v. "Otpor!," http://en.wikipedia.org/wiki/Otpor, (updated August 28, 2006); *Wikipedia*, s.v. "Carnation Revolution," http://en.wikipedia.org/wiki/Carnation_Revolution, (updated April 7, 2006); *Wikipedia*, s.v. "Color Revolution," http://en.wikipedia.org/wiki/Color_Revolution, (updated April 7, 2006); "A rainbow of revolutions," *The Economist*, January 21, 2006; Peter Ackerman and Jack Duvall, *A Force More Powerful*, film documentary, 2000.

62. Steven Johnson, *Everything Bad is Good For You*, p. 192; "Serener streets," *The Economist*, August 29, 2009, p. 28.

63. David Von Drehle, "The Myth about Boys," *Time*, August 6, 2007.

64. Chris Mitchell, "The Killing of Murder," *New York*, January 14, 2008; "Serener streets," *The Economist*, August 29, 2009, p. 28.

65. Gregg Easterbrook, *The Progress Paradox*, p. 38; "It Wasn't All Bad," *The Week*, p. 2, March 30, 2007; Steve Chapman, "Is pornography a catalyst of sexual violence?," *Chicago Tribune*, as quoted in *The Week*, November 16, 2007.

66."Noted," *The Week*, p. 20, May 25, 2007.

67."Fewer Militia Groups," *The Week*, April 29, 2005; "Extremism in America: The Militia Movement," Anti-Defamation League, http://www.adl.org/learn/ext_us/ Militia_M.asp?xpicked=4&item=19, 2005.

68."America's Tragedy," *The Economist*, p. 11, April 21, 2007.

69. Jennifer Pollack, "Under the Radar," *Fast Company*, March 2006.

70."The discreet charms of the international go-between," *The Economist*, July 5, 2008.

71. "Spare the rod, say some," *The Economist*, May 31, 2008.

72. Hillary Batchelder, "Do-Gooder Games," *Time*, August 14, 2006.

73. Jordan Vidal, *The Guardian*, as reported by WorldCampaign.net, http://www.world-campaign.net/mesarch.cgi?v=1045257810, February 14, 2003.

74. *Brainy Quote*, s.v. "Dwight Eisenhower," http://www.brainyquote.com/quotes/ authors/d/dwight_d_eisenhower.html.

75. Michael N. Nagler, *Is There No Other Way?*, p. 70.

76. Michael Renner, "Mixed Progress on Reducing Nuclear Arsenals," *Vital Signs 2005*, p. 81; Associated Press, "Nations Gather to Review Nuclear Treaty," *The New York Times*, http://www.nytimes.com/aponline/international/AP-UN-Nuclear-Treaty. html, May 2, 2005.

77. Wendy Orent, "The big, bad bioterror scare," *Los Angeles Times*, as quoted in *The Week*, July 31, 2009, p. 14.

78."The Long, Long Half-life," *The Economist*, June 10, 2006.

79. Steve Chapman, "Why nuclear terrorism is so unlikely," *Chicago Tribune*, as quoted in *The Week*, February 22, 2008.

80. Benjamin Friedman, "Homeland Security," *Foreign Policy*, July/August 2005.

81. "The Threat of Nuclear Terrorism," *The Week*, p. 13, April 15, 2005.

82. "Still the Stuff of Nightmares," *The Economist*, June 18, 2005.

83."The Big Clean-out," *The Economist*, June 5, 2004; "Still the Stuff of Nightmares," *The Economist*, June 18, 2005; Fareed Zakaria, "Tackle the Nuclear Threat," *Newsweek*, June 21, 2004.

84. Gregg Easterbrook, *The Progress Paradox*, p. 70.

85."How to Stop the Spread of the Bomb," *The Economist*, April 30, 2005.

86. William J. Broad, "Hidden Travels of the Atomic Bomb," *The New York Times*, December 9, 2008.

87."U.S.: North Korea agrees to shut down nuke programs," *CNN*, http://edition.cnn.

com/2007/WORLD/asiapcf/09/02/koreas.nuclear.ap/index.html, September 2, 2007; "Korean Leaders Sign Peace Pledge," *CNN*, http://www.cnn.com/2007/world/asiapcf/10/04/Koreas.summit/index.html, October 5, 2007; "The world this week," *The Economist*, September 5, 2009, p. 9.

88. Jim Walsh, "Bombing or Booming?", *The Interdependent*, pp. 25-28, Winter 2006-2007.

89. William Langewiesche, "The Ultimate Form of Terrorism," *The Week*, pp. 40-41, June 1, 2007; William Langewiesche, *The Atomic Bazaar*, p. 179.

90. "The Long, Long Half-life," *The Economist*, June 10, 2006.

91. Jim Walsh, "Bombing or Booming?", *The Interdependent*, pp. 25-28, Winter 2006-2007.

92. Michael Renner, "Mixed Progress on Reducing Nuclear Arsenals," *Vital Signs 2005*, p. 80.

93. Associated Press, "Nations Gather to Review Nuclear Treaty," *The New York Times*, http://www.nytimes.com/aponline/international/AP-UN-Nuclear-Treaty.html, May 2, 2005; Clifford J. Levy and Peter Baker, "U.S.-Russia Nuclear Agreement is First Step in Broad Effort," *The New York Times*, July 7, 2009, http://www.nytimes.com/2009/07/07/world/europe/07prexy.html.

94. Both quotes from Robert S. McNamara, "Apocalypse Soon," *Foreign Policy*, May/June 2005.

95. Associated Press, "Nations Gather to Review Nuclear Treaty," *The New York Times*, http://www.nytimes.com/aponline/international/AP-UN-Nuclear-Treaty.html, May 2, 2005.

96. "What to do with a vision of zero," *The Economist*, November 15, 2008.

97. J. Peter Scoblic, "Nuclear Spring," *The New Republic*, April 23, 2008.

98. Jonathan Schell, *The Unconquerable World*, pp. 355–365.

99. Barack Obama, quoted on the cover of *The Economist*, April 11-17, 2009.

100. "Peace: No Longer Just a Dream," *The Week*, p. 22, January 13, 2006; Steven D. Strauss, *World Conflicts*, p. 288; Michael Renner, "Number of Violent Conflicts Drops," *Vital Signs 2006-2007*, p. 82; Michael Renner, "Peacekeeping Budgets and Personnel Soar to New Heights," *Vital Signs 2009*, p. 80.

101. Michael Renner, "Peacekeeping Expenditures Set New Record," *Vital Signs 2006-2007*, p. 86; Michael Renner, "Peacekeeping Budgets and Personnel Soar to New Heights," *Vital Signs 2009*, p. 80.

102. And that is a conservative estimate, based on congressional appropriations. *National Priorities Project*, http://nationalpriorities.org/index.php?option=com_wrapper&Itemid=182.

103. Michael Renner, "Peacekeeping expenditures Set New Record," *Vital Signs 2006-2007*, p. 86.

104. Jean-Marie Guéhenno, "Giving Peace a Chance," *The Economist: The World in 2005*, 2004.

105. "Blessed Are the Peacemakers," *The Economist*, September 9, 2006.

106. Marc Vogtman, "Peace Through Spirituality and Religion: A Literature Review on

the Role and Effectiveness of Religion in Peacebuilding," October 30, 2002; *Wikipedia*, s.v. "Truth and Reconciliation Commission," http://en.wikipedia.org/wiki/Truth_and_Reconciliation_Commission, (updated October 5, 2007).

107. Michael Renner, "Number of Violent Conflicts Drops," *Vital Signs 2006-2007*, p. 82.

108. The United Nations, "Major Achievements of the United Nations," http://www.un.org/aboutun/achieve.htm.

109. "Gently Does It," *The Economist*, p. 27, July 28, 2007; "A nation of jailbirds," *The Economist*, April 4, 2009, p. 40.

110. "A new deal," *The Economist*, p. 36, March 2, 2008.

111. All death penalty information: "Fewer Executions," *The Week*, November 10, 2006; "The Search for a Humane Execution," *The Week*, June 23, 2006; "A Doctor's Revolt," *The Economist*, July 22, 2006; Anna Quindlen, "The Failed Experiment," *Newsweek*, June 26, 2006; "Briefing: Numbers," *Time*, p. 26, May 14, 2007; "Cause for a Pause," *The Economist*, p.35, September 29, 2007; "Revenge Begins to Seem Less Sweet," *The Economist*, pp. 20-22, September 1, 2007; "Death penalty ban," *The Week*, December 28, 2007-January 11, 2008; "Saving lives and money," *The Economist*, March 14, 2009.

112. James Traub, "Wonderful World?" *New York Times Magazine*, March 19, 2006.

113. "War, Disease, Hunger," *Worldcampaign*, http://www.worldcampaign.net/mesarch.cgi?v=1188428439, August 29, 2007.

114. "Melting the Guns," *The Week*, p. 9, August 10, 2007.

115. William Saletan, "A Weapon that Hurts without Killing," *Slate.com*, as reprinted in *The Week*, p. 12, March 2, 2007.

116. "Briefing: Adding Insult to Injury," *The Week*, p. 13, March 23, 2007.

117. "Robot Wars," *The Economist Technology Quarterly*, p. 10, June 9, 2007.

118. Immanuel Kant, "Perpetual Peace," *Political Writings*, ed. Hans Reiss, pp. 93–130.

119. Danesh Sarooshi, "Collective Security as a Means of Ensuring Peace," *Processes of the Lesser Peace*, ed. Babak Bahador and Nazila Ghanea, pp. 162–175.

120. *Ibid.*, pp. 162–175.

121. Ivan Dimitrov, "Legacy of Landmines," *The Interdependent*, p. 35, Summer 2008.

122. Mary Speck, "Americans Want a Stronger UN," *UNA-USA*, http://www.un-ausa.org/site/apps/s/content.asp?c=fvKRI8MPJpF&b=369041&ct=3849999, May 15, 2007.

123. Gregory C. Dahl, *One World, One People*, p. 215.

Chapter 8: Democracy

1. Andreas Ramos, "A Personal Account of the Fall of the Berlin Wall: The 11th and 12th of November, 1989," http://www.andreas.com/berlin.html.

2. Samuel P. Huntington, "Will You Become Your Own Nation?" *Time*, May 22, 2000.

3. Benjamin Barber, *Jihad vs. McWorld*, p. 4.

4. Robert Wright, *Nonzero: The Logic of Human Destiny*, pp. 203–204.

5. For example, *Wikipedia*, s.v. "Sykes-Picot Agreement," http://en.wikipedia.org/wiki/Sykes-Picot_Agreement, (updated October 26, 2007).

6. "Peace in Our Time," *Foreign Policy*, p. 19, November/December 2002; "The World This Week," *The Economist*, p. 6, September 1, 2007; "A Gesture of Peace," *The Week*, p. 8, March 23, 2007; Mike Nizza, "Rolling Into History on the Rails of Korea," *The New York Times*, http://thelede.blogs.nytimes.com/2007/05/17/rolling-into-history-on-the-rails-of-korea/, May 17, 2007.

7. Jonathan Schell, *The Unconquerable World*, p. 301.

8. Marc Vogtman, "Case Studies for Modified Sovereignty," March 1, 2003.

9. Kevin Connolly, "A Benchmark for Improbability," *BBC News*, http://news.bbc.co.uk/1/hi/northern_ireland/6636371.stm, May 8, 2007; "Historic Return for NI Assembly," *BBC News*, http://news.bbc.co.uk/1/hi/northern_ireland/6634373.stm, May 8, 2007.

10. Rod Rastan, "An International Legal Order," *Processes of the Lesser Peace*, ed. Babak Bahador and Nazila Ghanea, pp. 207–208.

11. Robert Wright, *Nonzero: The Logic of Human Destiny*, p. 216.

12. Randy Charles Epping, *A Beginner's Guide to the World Economy*, pp. 111–114.

13. John Pinder, *The European Union: A Very Short Introduction*, p. 99.

14. "In Praise of Enlargement," *The Economist*, September 30, 2006; Paul Wilkinson, A Very Short Introduction to International Relations, p. 98.

15. "Britain," *The Economist*: The World in 2007, p. 83.

16. Frank Bruni, "In European Union Milestone, 10 Lands Sign Pacts to Join," *The New York Times*, April 16, 2003.

17. "Bulgaria, Romania to Join EU," *The Week*, p.6, October 6, 2006; "Vote of confidence," *The Week*, May 8, 2009, p. 8.

18. *Encyclopedia Britannica*, s.v. "African Union," http://www.britannica.com/eb/article-9003949/African-Union, (updated September 24, 2007.)

19. The African Union, "The Vision of the AU," http://www.africa-union.org/root/au/AboutAu/au_in_a_nutshell_en.htm.

20. *Wikipedia*, s.v. "Union of South American Nations," http://en.wikipedia.org/wiki/South_American_Community_of_Nations, (updated November 30, 2006).

21. "Club Med," *The Economist*, July 12, 2008; "France vs. Germany: Compromising on a Mediterranean Union," *The Week*, March 28, 2008; Surin Pitsuwan, "A new miracle for tigers and dragons," *The Economist*: The World in 2008, p. 66; "Southeast Asian common market?," *The Week*, December 26, 2008, p. 9.

22. Ann Florini, *The Coming Democracy*, p. 10.

23. Steven Scholl, ed., *The Peace Bible*, p. 106.

24. *Ibid.*, p. 108.

25. Paul Kennedy, *The Parliament of Man*, p. xv.

26. "An Awful Certainty," *The Economist*, p.89, May 12, 2007; Gregory C. Dahl, *One World, One People*, p. 332.

27. Robert Wright, *Nonzero: The Logic of Human Destiny*, p. 209.

28. Gregory C. Dahl, *One World, One People*, p. 265.

29. Immanuel Kant, "Perpetual Peace," *Political Writings*, ed. Hans Reiss, p. 102; Jeffrey Sachs, *The End of Poverty*, pp. 348–349.

30. Ann Florini, *The Coming Democracy*, p. 207.

31. Robert Wright, *Nonzero: The Logic of Human Destiny*, p. 211.

32. Jeffrey Sachs, *The End of Poverty*, p. 333.

33. Daniel Deudney and G. John Ikenberry, "The Myth of the Autocratic Revival," *Foreign Affairs*, January/February 2009, p. 77.

34. The United Nations, "Major Achievements of the United Nations," http://www.un.org/aboutun/achieve.htm.

35. John Pinder, *The European Union: A Very Short Introduction*, p. 8.

36. Foad Katirai, *Global Governance and the Lesser Peace*, pp. 30–31.

37. "Caught in the Middle," *The Economist*, July 15, 2006.

38. Steven Scholl, ed., *The Peace Bible*, p. 66.

39. Richard S. Williamson, "Transitional Justice: Dark Past to Liberal Future," *The InterDependent*, Fall 2006.

40. *Ibid.*

41. "Better Late Than Never," *The Economist*, p. 37, August 4, 2007.

42. Reuters, "New World War Crimes Court Opens; Bush Spurns Treaty," *The New York Times*, http://www.nytimes.com/reuters/international/international-un-court.html, April 11, 2002.

43. Matthew Heaphy, "The Evolution of Justice," *The Interdependent*, pp. 26-29, Spring 2007; "Sudan's leader is accused, but others can expect to follow," *The Economist*, July 19, 2008.

44. Angelina Jolie, "A year for accountability," *The Economist: The World in 2008*, p. 78.

45. "Double Whammy," *The Economist*, November 18, 2006.

46. "How the Mighty Are Falling," *The Economist*, p. 59, July 7, 2007; "More Suspects in its Sights," *The Economist*, p. 52, May 26, 2007.

47. *The Declaration of Independence*, http://www.ushistory.org/declaration/document/.

48. John Lewis Gaddis, "Ending Tyranny," *The American Interest*, Autumn 2008, p. 6.

49. *New York Times Magazine*, as quoted in *The Week*, July 28, 2006; Jonathan Schell, *The Unconquerable World*, p. 255; Indur M. Goklany, *The Improving State of the World*, pp. 47-48. Washington, D.C.: Cato Institute, 2007

50. Rachel L Swarns and Norimitsu Onishi, "Africa Creeps Along Path to Democracy," *The New York Times*, November 6, 2002.

51. Nancy Jacobs and Rolando Peñate, "Animated Atlas of African History 1879–2002," Brown University, http://www.brown.edu/Research/AAAH/map.htm.

52. *Wikipedia*, s.v. "Women's Suffrage," http://en.wikipedia.org/wiki/Women%E2%80%99s_suffrage, (updated November 28, 2006).

53. Hendrik Hertzberg, "The States We're In," *The New Yorker*, August 24, 2009, p. 20.

54. All elections information from David C. Korten, *The Great Turning: From Empire to Earth Community*, pp. 348–49.

55. Simon Robinson, "Postcard: Bhutan," *Time*, April 7, 2008; "Thy kingdom gone," *The Economist*, August 9, 2008; "Ending a cult of personality," *The Week*, May 16, 2008; "Start dialing, comrades," *The Week*, April 11, 2008; "Communism light," *The Week*, July 25, 2008; "Briefing: Cuba after Fidel," *The Week*, July 25, 2008; Howard W. French, "Despite Flaws, Rights in China Have Expanded," *The New York Times*, http://www.nytimes.com/2008/08/02/world/asia/02china.html, August 2, 2008.

56. Daniel Deudney and G. John Ikenberry, "The Myth of the Autocratic Revival," *Foreign Affairs*, January/February 2009, pp. 85-6.

57. Robin Mejia, "These Satellite Images Document an Atrocity," *The Washington Post*, June 10, 2007, W20.

58. Joseph E. Stiglitz, *Globalization and Its Discontents*, p. 229.

59. Ann Florini, *The Coming Democracy*, pp. 34, 85.

60. *Ibid.*, p. 32.

61. *Ibid.*, p. 34.

62. Clive Thompson, "The See-Through CEO," *Wired*, pp. 135-139, April 2007.

63. Samuel P. Huntington, "Will You Become Your Own Nation?" *Time*, May 22, 2000.

64. Ann Florini, *The Coming Democracy*, p. 114.

65. *Ibid.*, p. 202.

66. *Ibid.*, pp. 117, 168.

Chapter 9: Economics

1. "The odd couple: A special report on the Koreas," *The Economist*, September 27, 2008; Randy Charles Epping, *A Beginner's Guide to the World Economy*, p. 117; "Fatalism v fetishism," *The Economist*, June 13, 2009, p. 82.

2. "What war?" *The Economist*, November 18, 2006; "Good Morning at Last," *The Economist*, August 5, 2006; *Wikipedia*, s.v. "Doi Moi," http://en.wikipedia.org/wiki/Doi_moi, (updated December 1, 2006); Randy Charles Epping, *A Beginner's Guide to the World Economy*, p. 116.

3. Erik Assadourian, "Global Economy Grows Again," *Vital Signs 2006-2007*, pp. 52–53.

4. "The New Titans," *The Economist*, September 16, 2004; "Wrestling for influence,"

The Economist, July 5, 2008.

5. Francois Bourguigon and Christian Morrison, "Inequality Among World Citizens: 1820-1992," *The American Economic Review*, Vol. 92, No. 4, pp. 727-744, September 2002; Hilary French, "Progress Toward the MDGs is Mixed," *Vital Signs 2007-2008*, p.108.

6. Jeffrey Sachs, *The End of Poverty*, p. 29.

7. Jeffrey Sachs, "We Are the Generation That Can End Poverty," *Good*, Sep/Oct 2006.

8. "More or less equal?" *The Economist*, March 13, 2004.

9. "Liberty's Great Advance," *The Economist*, June 28, 2003; "Another Day, Another $1.08," *The Economist*, p. 90, April 28, 2007

10. "Vanity Fair Releases Unprecedented 20 Different Covers for Africa Issue Guest-edited by Bono," DATA: Debt AIDS Trade Africa, http://www.data.org/news/press_20070605.html, June 5, 2007; Robert LaFranco, "Money Makers," *Rolling Stone*, http://www.rollingstone.com/news/story/6959138/money_makers/2, February 10, 2005.

11. Jeffrey Sachs, *The End of Poverty*, p. 20.

12. Jacques Attali, *A Brief History of the Future*, p. 67.

13. Steven E. Landsburg, *More Sex Is Safer Sex*, pp. 27-29.

14. Richard N. Cooper, "Doubling Our World's Economy," *World Policy Journal*, Fall 2008, p. 42.

15. Martin Wolf, *Why Globalization Works*, p. 34.

16. Jeffrey Sachs, *The End of Poverty*, pp. 47–48.

17. Martin Wolf, *Why Globalization Works*, p. 144.

18. Ann Florini, *The Coming Democracy*, p. 157.

19. Joseph E. Stiglitz, *Globalization and Its Discontents*, p. 9.

20. *Wikipedia*, s.v. "CFA Franc," http://en.wikipedia.org/wiki/CFA_franc, (updated December 10, 2006); Charles Kupchan, "Strengthen Regional Cooperation," *Democracy: A Journal of Ideas*, p. 25, Fall 2007; "Central American union," *The Week*, December 19, 2008, p. 8; "Big ambitions, big question marks," *The Economist*, September 5, 2009, p. 52.

21. Randy Charles Epping, *A Beginner's Guide to the World Economy*, p. 103.

22. Martin Wolf, *Why Globalization Works*, pp. 119–120.

23. "Down on the Street," *The Economist*, November 25, 2006.

24. "Surprise!" *The Economist*, September 16, 2006.

25. Joseph E. Stiglitz, *Globalization and Its Discontents*, p. 248.

26. *Wikipedia*, s.v. "Mao Zedong," http://en.wikipedia.org/wiki/Mao_Zedong, (updated December 4, 2006).

27. Jeffrey Sachs, *The End of Poverty*, p. 155.

28. Martin Wolf, *Why Globalization Works*, p. 160; The Chinese Government's

Official Web Portal, http://english.gov.cn/2005-08/08/content_27315.htm. In 1990, the Chinese population was 1,143,330,000. In 1999, the Chinese population was 1,257,860,000; *Wikipedia*, s.v. "Property Law of the People's Republic of China," http://en.wikipedia.org/wiki/Property_Law_of_the_People%27s_Republic_of_China, (updated March 25, 2007.

29. "The New Titans," *The Economist*, September 16, 2006.

30. Martin Wolf, *Why Globalization Works*, p. 160.

31. "Finally, Some Good News," *The Interdependent*, p. 29, Winter 2006-2007.

32. "New Deal for poor," *The Week*, p.9, April 18, 2008; Somini Sengupta, "Crusader Sees Wealth as Cure for Caste Bias," *The New York Times*, August 30, 2008.

33. "Burgeoning bourgeoisie," *The Economist*, *A special report on the new middle classes*, February 14, 2009, p. 6.

34. Jim O'Neill, "The rising tide that could lift the West's boats," *Financial Times*, as quoted in *The Week*, July 25, 2008; "Adios to Poverty, Hola to Consumption," *The Economist*, pp. 21-23, August 18, 2007.

35. "Poverty in Africa," *The Economist*, November 24, 2007; Liam Halligan, "Clout of Africa," *British GQ*, November 2007; "Lion cubs?," *The Economist*, April 19, 2008; Dambisa Moyo, "Letters: What's Ailing Africa?," *Foreign Policy*, July/August 2009, p. 13; Alex Perry, "Africa, Business Destination," *Time*, March 23, 2009, p. 58; Charles Kenny, "Think Again: Africa's Crisis," *Foreign Policy*, July 31, 2009; Michelle Sieff, "Africa: Many Hills to Climb," *World Policy Journal*, Fall 2008, p. 185.

36. Jim O'Neill, "The rising tide that could lift the West's boats," *Financial Times*, as quoted in *The Week*, July 25, 2008; "Dancing in Step," *The Economist*, November 13, 2004.

37. "America Drops, Asia Shops," *The Economist*, October 21, 2006.

38. Martin Wolf, *Why Globalization Works*, p. 189.

39. *Ibid.*, p. 166.

40. Thomas L. Friedman, *The Lexus and the Olive Tree*, pp. 248–254.

41. Jeffrey Sachs, *The End of Poverty*, p. 349.

42. "Income Inequality," *The Economist*, November 1, 2008, p. 109; W. Michael Cox and Richard Alm, "You Are What You Spend," *The New York Times*, http://www.nytimes.com/2008/02/10/opinion/10cox.html, February 10, 2008; "Cheap and cheerful," *The Economist*, July 26, 2008; "The new (improved) Gilded Age," *The Economist*, December 22, 2007; "More or less equal?," *The Economist*, *A special report on the rich*, April 4, 2009, p. 11.

43. W. Michael Cox and Richard Alm, "You Are What You Spend," *The New York Times*, http://www.nytimes.com/2008/02/10/opinion/10cox.html, February 10, 2008; "Cheap and cheerful," *The Economist*, July 26, 2008; "The new (improved) Gilded Age," *The Economist*, December 22, 2007.

44. "The new (improved) Gilded Age," *The Economist*, December 22, 2007.

45. Moises Naim, "Our Inequality Anxiety," *Foreign Policy*, May/June 2006; "Catching Up," *The Economist*, August 23, 2003; W. Michael Cox and Richard Alm, "You

Are What You Spend," *The New York Times*, http://www.nytimes.com/2008/02/10/opinion/10cox.html, February 10, 2008; Tim Harford, *The Logic of Life*, p. 196.

46. "Always with us?," *The Economist*, February 28, 2009, p. 90.

47. Richard Folkers, "Xanadu 2.0," *U.S. News & World Report*, December 1, 1997.

48. Gene Sperling, "Rising-Tide Economics,"*Democracy: A Journal of Ideas*, p. 67, Fall 2007.

49. Brian Knowlton, "Globalization, According to the World, is a Good Thing. Sort Of.," *The New York Times*, http://www.nytimes.com/2007/10/05/world/05pew.html, October 5, 2007.

50. Martin Wolf, *Why Globalization Works*, p. 211.

51. Randy Charles Epping, *A Beginner's Guide to the World Economy*, p. 136.

52. Joseph E. Stiglitz, *Globalization and Its Discontents*, p. 227; "Goodbye G7, hello G20," *The Economist*, November 22, 2008, p. 89; Edmund L. Andrews, "Global Economic Forum to Expand Permanently," *The New York Times*, September 25, 2009, http://www.nytimes.com/2009/09/25/world/25summit.html.

53. "Smile, These Are Good Times. Truly," *The Economist*, March 13, 2004; Ernest R. May and Philip D. Zelikow, "An Open, Civilized World," *The American Interest*, Autumn 2008, p. 23.

54. Martin Wolf, *Why Globalization Works*, pp. 310–311.

55. *Ibid.*, p. 276.

56. Jeffrey Sachs, *The End of Poverty*, p. 84.

57. Gary Walton, "A Brief History of Human Progress," http://fte.org/capitalism/introduction/.

58. *Wikipedia*, s.v. "Saparmurat Niyazov," http://en.wikipedia.org/wiki/Saparmurat_Niyazov, (updated December 9, 2006).

59. "Good week for:" *The Week*, December 22, 2006.

60. Jeffrey Sachs, *The End of Poverty*, p. 348.

61. Martin Wolf, *Why Globalization Works*, pp. 61–64.

62. Randy Charles Epping, *A Beginner's Guide to the World Economy*, pp. 132–133.

63. Nicholas D. Kristoff, "Where Sweatshops Are a Dream," *The New York Times*, January 15, 2009.

64. Jeffrey Sachs, *The End of Poverty*, pp. 211–213.

65. *Ibid.*, pp. 233–234

66. "Charting a More Livable World for All," *The Interdependent*, Fall 2008, pp. 20-21; Farah Ameen, "Bangladesh and the MDGs: Success is Possible, Notwithstanding Natural Disasters," *The Interdependent*, Fall 2008, p. 24.

67. Tim Heffernan, "Esther Duflo, 36," *Esquire*, December 2008, p. 159; Gregg Easterbrook, *The Progress Paradox*, p. 305.

68. "Micro No More," *The Economist*, November 5, 2005.

69. Gary Gardner, "Microfinance Surging," *Vital Signs 2009*, p. 75.

70. Chul R. Kim, ed., *Design for the Other 90%*, p. 106.

71. John Markoff, "For $150, Third-World Laptop Stirs Big Debate," *The New York Times*, http://www.nytimes.com/2006/11/30/technology/30laptop.html, November 30, 2006; Steven Levy, "Give One, Get One," *Newsweek*, p. 72, October 1, 2007; "Teachers' Aids," *GOOD*, Jan/Feb 09, p.87; "Laptops for all," *The Economist*, October 3, 2009, p. 46.

72. Martin Wolf, *Why Globalization Works*, p. 213.

73. "External Debt," *The Economist*, November 6, 2004.

74. "Briefing: That's What Friends Are For," *Time*, July 21, 2008; Michael Kazatchkine, "Stopping the plagues," *The Economist*: The World in 2008, p. 75.

75. "Pigs, Pay and Power," *The Economist*, June 28, 2003.

76. "The 2006 Transparency International Corruption Perceptions Index," Transparency International, http://www.infoplease.com/ipa/A0781359.html, 2006; "The Bottom Line," *The Week*, p. 40, October 12, 2007.

77. "Rich Man, Poor Man," *The Economist*, p. 15, January 20, 2007.

78. James Surowiecki, "Better and Better," *Foreign Affairs*, p. 133, July/August 2007; *Wikipedia*, s.v. "Thomas Malthus," http://en.wikipedia.org/wiki/Malthus, (updated October 31, 2007).

79. Don Peck, "Population 2050," *The Atlantic Monthly*, pp. 40-41, October 2002.

80. Danielle Nierenberg, "Population Continues to Grow," *Vital Signs 2006-2007*, pp. 74–75; "Somewhere over the rainbow," *The Economist*, January 26, 2008.

81. Steven E. Landsburg, *More Sex is Safer Sex: The Unconventional Wisdom of Economics*, p. 37.

82. John Stossel, *Myths, Lies, and Downright Stupidity*, pp. 24-26.

83. Rich Karlgaard, "How to Truly Help the World's Poor," *Forbes*, quoted in *The Week*, September 29, 2006.

Chapter 10: Health

1. Jonathan Schell, *The Unconquerable World*, p. 33.

2. Jeffrey Sachs, *The End of Poverty*, pp. 42, 259–260.; *Wikipedia*, s.v. "Green Revolution," http://en.wikipedia.org/wiki/Green_Revolution, (updated October 11, 2007).

3. Indur M. Goklany, *The Improving State of the World*, pp. 21, 124. Washington, D.C.: Cato Institute, 2007.

4. "A Meaty Question," *The Economist*, September 23, 2006.

5. Indur M. Goklany, *The Improving State of the World*, pp. 237-287. Washington, D.C.: Cato Institute, 2007; "The next green revolution," *The Economist*, February 23, 2008; "Whatever happened to the food crisis?," *The Economist*, July 4, 2009, p. 58.

6. Christopher Doering, "World Hunger Afflicted Millions More in '07," *The Guardian*, http://www.guardian.co.uk/business/feedarticle/7640583, July 9, 2008; "The next green revolution," *The Economist*, February 23, 2008; "A bad habit they can't give up," *The Economist*, July 12, 2008; Homi Kharas, "*The Economist* debate: Rising food prices," *The Economist*, http://www.economist.com/debate/index.cfm?action=article&debate_id=10&story_id=11829062, July 29, 2008; "Whatever happened to the food crisis?," *The Economist*, July 4, 2009, p. 58.

7. Gary Walton, "A Brief History of Human Progress," http://fte.org/capitalism/introduction/.

8. Ann Kelleher and Laura Klein, *Global Perspectives: A Handbook for Understanding Global Issues*, p. 5; Gary Walton, "A Brief History of Human Progress," http://fte.org/capitalism/introduction/.

9. Index Mundi, "World life expectancy at birth", http://www.indexmundi.com/world/ life_expectancy_at_birth.html,(updated April 17, 2007); "A world of Methuselahs," *The Economist, A special report on ageing populations*, June 27, 2009, p. 7.

10. The World Bank, *The Little Data Book 07*. Washington DC: 2007.

11. Quote and table source: Glenn Reynolds, *An Army of Davids*, p. 175.

12. Lauren Sorkin, "Infant Mortality Rate Falls Again," *Vital Signs 2006-2007*, pp. 78–79 ; Gary Walton, "A Brief History of Human Progress," http://fte.org/capitalism/introduction/; Gregg Easterbrook, *The Progress Paradox*, p. 49.

13. "It Wasn't All Bad," *The Week*, p. 2, September 28, 2007; "So near, yet so far," *The Economist*, January 24, 2009, p. 66; "The first epistle of St Bill," *The Economist*, January 24, 2009, p. 73.

14. Jeffrey Sachs, *The End of Poverty*, pp. 263–264; "A slow-burning fuse," *The Economist, A special report on ageing populations*, June 27, 2009, p. 4.

15. Robert Pear, "Married and Single Parents Spending More Time with Children, Study Finds," *The New York Times*, http://www.nytimes.com/2006/10/17/us/17kids.html, October 20, 2006.

16. Gina Kolata, "So Big and Healthy Grandpa Wouldn't Even Know You," *The New York Times*, http://www.nytimes.com/2006/07/30/health/30age.html, August 4, 2006.

17. Gregg Easterbrook, *The Progress Paradox*, p. 48; "Old age begins ... when you're older," *The Week*, July 17, 2009, p. 22.

18. Gina Kolata, "So Big and Healthy Grandpa Wouldn't Even Know You," *The New York Times*, http://www.nytimes.com/2006/07/30/health/30age.html, August 4, 2006.

19. Gary Walton, "A Brief History of Human Progress," http://fte.org/capitalism/introduction/.

20. "The truth shall make you thin," *The Economist*, July 25, 2009, p. 30.

21. Donald G. McNeil, "Billionaires Back Antismoking Effort," *The New York Times*, http://www.nytimes.com/2008/07/24/health/24smoke.html, July 24, 2008; Erik Assadourian, "Cigarette Production Drops," *Vital Signs 2005*, p. 71; "How to save a billion lives," *The Economist*, February 9, 2008.

22. Erik Assadourian, "Cigarette Production Drops," *Vital Signs 2005*, p. 71; "How to save a billion lives," *The Economist*, February 9, 2008.

23. "France's smoking ban takes effect," *BBC News*, http://news.bbc.co.uk/1/hi/world/europe/6319649.stm, February 1, 2007.

24. "How to save a billion lives," *The Economist*, February 9, 2008.

25. Associated Press, as reprinted in "Noted", *The Week*, p. 20, June 8, 2007; "How to save a billion lives," *The Economist*, February 9, 2008.

26. "Noted," *The Week*, November 28, 2008, p. 18.

27. "A decline in cancer deaths," *The Week*, p. 22, February 2, 2007.

28. Joseph T. Hallinan, *Why We Make Mistakes*, p. 7; Gregg Easterbrook, *The Progress Paradox*, pp. 48–49.

29. Joseph T. Hallinan, *Why We Make Mistakes*, p. 193; "Noted," *The Week*, p.18, reprinted from *Los Angeles Times*, June 23, 2006; "The Year in Medicine," *Time*, December 4, 2006.; "The world this week," *The Economist*, January 19, 2008; Tara Parker-Pope, "The Myth of Rampant Teenage Promiscuity," *The New York Times*, January 27, 2009.

30. David Von Drehle, "The Myth about Boys," *Time*, August 6, 2007.

31. David Finkelhor, Heather Hammer, and Andrea J. Sedlak, "Nonfamily Abducted Children: National Estimates and Characteristics," Office of Juvenile Justice and Delinquency Prevention, U.S. Department of Justice, October 2002, http://www.ncjrs.gov/pdffiles1/ojjdp/196467.pdf; Brad Stone, "Report Calls Online Threats to Children Overblown," *The New York Times*, January 14, 2009.

32. "Speedy decline," *The Economist*, May 3, 2008; "Treating, not punishing," *The Economist*, August 29, 2009, p. 43.

33. "It wasn't all bad," *The Week*, August 8, 2008, p.4.

34. Gregg Easterbrook, *The Progress Paradox*, pp. 50–53.

35. "A planet full of Angelina Jolies," *The Week*, August 14, 2009, p. 22.

36. "Scrimp and save," *The Economist*, A *special report on ageing populations*, June 27, 2009, p. 9.

37. "Work till you drop," *The Economist*, A *special report on ageing populations*, June 27, 2009, p. 11; "Scrimp and save," *The Economist*, A *special report on ageing populations*, June 27, 2009, p. 9; "Into the unknown," *The Economist*, A *special report on ageing populations*, June 27, 2009, pp. 15-16.

38. Anita T. Shaffer, "Internet seen as Rx for health care," *The Trenton Times*, July 10, 2009, pp. A3-A4; "Health 2.0," *The Economist*, A *special report on health care and technology*, April 18, 2009, pp. 17-18.

39. "Health 2.0," *The Economist*, A *special report on health care and technology*, April 18, 2009, pp. 17-18.

40. "HIT or miss," *The Economist*, A *special report on health care and technology*, April 18, 2009, p. 4; "A doctor in your pocket," *The Economist*, A *special report on health care and technology*, April 18, 2009, pp. 11-12.

41. Jeffrey Sachs, *The End of Poverty*, pp.198–199; Michael Kazatchkine, "Stopping the plagues," *The Economist: The World in 2008*, p. 75; Lauren Aaronson, "Into the Unknown," *GOOD*, Jan/Feb 2009, p. 52.

42. 815 million people currently suffer from chronic malnutrition. The United Nations, "Major Achievements of the United Nations," http://www.un.org/aboutun/achieve.htm.

43. *Chicago Tribune*, as reported by WorldCampaign.net, August 26, 2004.

44. "The Wonders of Plumpy'nut," *The Economist*, November 3, 2005.

45. "Progress in AIDS response but still a long way from meeting global targets," UN Department of Public Information and UNAIDS press release, http://data.unaids.org/pub/PressRelease/2008/20080609_hlm_pr_en.pdf, June 9, 2008.

46. "Good in Parts," *The Economist*, November 25, 2006; "WHO's counting?," *The Economist*, November 24, 2007; "Promising news on AIDS," *The Week*, June 19, 2009.

47. Alex Shoumatoff, "The Lazarus Effect," *Vanity Fair*, pp. 156-161, July 2007; Michael Kazatchkine, "Stopping the plagues," *The Economist: The World in 2008*, p. 75; "All together now," *The Economist*, July 18, 2009, p. 60.

48. Joy Cook, "UN 2008 AIDS Report: One Step Forward, Two Giant Steps Back," *The Interdependent*, Summer 2008; Celia W. Dugger, "Global Rise in Detection and Treatment of AIDS," *The New York Times*, October 1, 2009, http://www.nytimes.com/2009/10/01/world/01aids.html.

49. Tina Rosenberg, "How to stop Africa's AIDS epidemic – now," *The New York Times*, as reprinted in *The Week*, January 26, 2007; Charles Hirshberg, "Should all males be circumcised?," *Men's Health*, March 2009, p. 92..

50. "The Fighter Within," *The Economist*, November 11, 2006; "Progress on an AIDS vaccine," *The Week*, October 9, 2009, p. 25.

51. All AIDS information: Maria Newman, "Spread of AIDS Is Slowing, UN Report Finds,"*The New York Times*, May 30, 2006; BBC News, as reported by WorldCampaign.net, December 5, 2002; Lauren Aaronson, "Into the Unknown," *GOOD*, Jan/Feb 2009, p. 52; "A new way to block HIV," *The Week*, March 20, 2009.

52. "Beyond the egg," *The Economist*, p. 65, March 10, 2007; Bill Gates, "Saving the World is Within Our Grasp," *Newsweek*, p. 76, October 1, 2007.

53. "Numbers," *Time*, p. 23, February 5, 2007; Jeffrey D. Sachs, "Common Wealth", *Time*, p. 39, March 24, 2008.

54. "Exterminate! Exterminate!" *The Economist*, p.109, October 20, 2007.

55. Jeffrey Sachs, *The End of Poverty*, p. 263; Tamara Najm, "Polio on the brink of eradication," *The Interdependent*, p. 8, Winter 2006-2007.

56. The United Nations, "Major Achievements of the United Nations," http://www.un.org/aboutun/achieve.htm.

57. Gregg Easterbrook, *The Progress Paradox*, p. 287.

58. Ray Kurzweil, "Optimism on the Continuum Between Confidence and Hope," in *What Are You Optimistic About?*, ed. John Brockman, p. 299; Anne Applebaum, *Washington Post*, as quoted in "Quote of the week," *The Week*, May 22,

2009, p. 12; Miguel Helft, "Google Uses Searches to Track Flu's Spread," *The New York Times*, http://www.nytimes.com/2008/11/12/technology/internet/12flu.html, November 12, 2008.

59. Richard Lederer, "To Kill a President," *Mensa Bulletin*, p. 40, April/May 2008; Dan Ariely, *Predictably Irrational*, p. 177.

60. Alice Park, "A Breakthrough on Stem Cells," *Time*, http://www.time.com/time/printout/0,8816,1687965,00.html, November 20, 2007; Juan Enriquez, "A New You," *Foreign Policy*, May/June 2009, p. 86.

61. James E. McClellan III and Harold Dorn, *Science and Technology in World History*, pp. 400–405; "The dawn of the bionic man," *The Week*, p. 11, June 13, 2008.

62. James E. McClellan III and Harold Dorn, *Science and Technology in World History*, pp. 400–405.

63. Carl Sagan, *The Demon-Haunted World*, p. 289.

Chapter 11: Environment

1. Gregg Easterbrook, *The Progress Paradox*, pp. 16–17, 19.

2. Table by Gary Walton, "A Brief History of Human Progress," http://fte.org/capitalism/introduction/.

3. Arthur Lyon Dahl, "The Environment and the Lesser Peace," in *Processes of the Lesser Peace*, ed. Babak Bahador and Nazila Ghanea, pp. 87–88; Alana Herro, "Ozone Layer Stabilizing but Not Recovered," *Vital Signs 2007-2008*, p. 46.

4. Michael Klesius, "The State of the Planet," *National Geographic*, September 2002.

5. Gregg Easterbrook, *The Progress Paradox*, p. 41.

6. *Ibid.*, p. 42; Gregg Easterbrook, "Green Day," *Democracy: A Journal of Ideas*, p. 113, Fall 2007; Indur M. Goklany, *The Improving State of the World*, pp. 149-150.

7. Gary Gardner, "Deforestation Continues," *Vital Signs 2006-2007*, p. 102; "It Wasn't All Bad," *The Week*, p. 2, November 24, 2006; The World Bank, *Atlas of Global Development*, pp. 113-115.

8. Gary Gardner, "Deforestation Continues," *Vital Signs 2006-2007*, p. 102.

9. George F. Will, "The Greening of Chicago," *Newsweek*, August 4, 2003; Gregg Easterbrook, *The Progress Paradox*, p. 42; "How air pollution really matters," *The Week*, p.22, February 6, 2009; "It wasn't all bad," *The Week*, p.2, January 23, 2009.

10. "The Rise of the Green Building," *The Economist*, December 4, 2004.

11. David C. Korten, *The Great Turning: From Empire to Earth Community*, p. 332.

12. Gregg Easterbrook, *The Progress Paradox*, p. 43.

13. *Ibid.*, p. 89.

14. "Second Coming," *The Economist*, October 28, 2006.

15. The United Nations, "Major Achievements of the United Nations," http://www.

un.org/aboutun/achieve.htm.

16. "Reducing Pollution," *The Week*, p. 6, September 9, 2006.

17. Associated Press, "California Unveils Anti-Global Warming Plan," *The New York Times*, September 1, 2006.

18. Josie Glausiusz, "A Green Who Understands the Power of Greenbacks," *Discover*, p. 15, September 2002.

19. *Ibid.*

20. Randy Charles Epping, *A Beginner's Guide to the World Economy*, p. 169; John M. Broder, "House Passes Bill to Address Threat of Climate Change," *The New York Times*, http://www.nytimes.com/2009/06/27/us/politics/27climate.html, June 27, 2009.

21. "Can Business Be Cool?" *The Economist*, June 10, 2006.

22. *Ibid.*

23. Bryan Walsh, "10 Ideas that are Changing the World, #10: Ecological Intelligence," *Time*, March 23, 2009; Frances Moore Lappé, *Getting a Grip*, p. 66.

24. Randy Charles Epping, *A Beginner's Guide to the World Economy*, pp. 169–170.

25. "Economics focus: Emissions suspicions," *The Economist*, June 21, 2008.

26. "Less is more," *The Economist*, *A Special Report on Waste*, p. 16, February 28, 2009.

27. Michael Behar, "The Prophet of Garbage," *Popular Science*, http://www.popsci.com/scitech/article/2007-03/prophet-garbage, March 1, 2007.

28. "Not dead, just resting," *The Economist*, p. 18, October 11, 2008.

29. "Green Dreams," *The Economist*, November 18, 2006.

30. Table from "Selling Hot Air," *The Economist*, September 9, 2006; John Tierney, "Use Energy, Get Rich and Save the Planet," *The New York Times*, April 21, 2009.

31. Jacques Attali, *A Brief History of the Future*, p.133.

32. "Oil Reserves," *The Economist*, July 17, 2004.

33. Indur M. Goklany, *The Improving State of the World*, p. 98. Washington, D.C.: Cato Institute, 2007.

34. Thomas L. Friedman, "The First Law of Petropolitics," *Foreign Policy*, pp. 29-36, May/June 2006.

35. Eli Kintisch, "Alternative Energy," *Discover*, January 2007.

36. Stirling Kelso, "The Age of Increment," *Fast Company*, March 2006; "The road ahead," *The Economist*, September 6, 2008; "Bright sparks," *The Economist*, January 17, 2009; Lindsay Brooke, "The Electric Auto Fleet Moves a Few Steps Close," *The New York Times*, http://www.nytimes.com/2009/01/12/automobiles/autoshow/12elect.html, January 12, 2009.

37. Bill Vlasic, "As Gas Costs Soar, Buyers Flock to Small Cars," *The New York Times*, http://www.nytimes.com/2008/05/02/business/02auto.html, May 2, 2008; Michael Renner, "Vehicle production Rises, But Few Cars are 'Green'," *Vital Signs 2009*, p. 43.

38. William Underhill, "Fill'er Up, But Not With Gas," *Newsweek*, December 16, 2002.

39. "Briefing: The Ethanol Craze," *The Week*, p. 14, October 5, 2007; "Ethanol, schmethanol," *The Economist*, p. 84, September 29, 2007; Elisabeth Rosenthal, "Biofuels Deemed a Greenhouse Threat," *The New York Times*, http://www.nytimes/com/2008/02/08/science/earth/08wbiofuels.html, February 8, 2008; Michael Grunwald, "The Clean Energy Scam," *Time*, April 7, 2008; "Craig's twist," *The Economist*, p. 78, July 18, 2009.

40. "Vermont takes on Detroit," *The Economist*, p. 44, September 22, 2007; "California's green light," *The Economist*, p.40, January 31, 2009.

41. *Environmental News Network*, as reported by WorldCampaign.net, April 29, 2003; Wayne Curtis, "In Hot Water," *The Atlantic Monthly*, December 2006.

42. *Environmental News Network*, as reported by WorldCampaign.net, April 29, 2003; Reuters, "BMW to Roll Out Hydrogen-powered 7 Series," *Yahoo! News*, http://news.yahoo.com/s/nm/20060912/bs_nm/autos_bmw_hydrogem_dc, September 13, 2006; Nicholas D. Kristof, "Our New Hydrogen Bomb," *The New York Times*, February 21, 2003.

43. Keith Bradsher, "Green Power Takes Root in the Chinese Desert," *The New York Times*, July 3, 2009, http://www.nytimes.com/2009/07/03/business/energy-environment/03renew.html.

44. "A Cool Concept," *The Economist: Technology Quarterly*, p. 4, June 9, 2007.; Frank Bures, "Green Acres," *Wired*, p. 46, February 2008; Lester R. Brown, "Making Megacities Livable," *The Interdependent*, Summer 2008, p. 31.

45. "The Ghostly Flickers of a New Dawn," *The Economist*, November 25, 2006; "Jolly green heretic," *The Economist: Technology Quarterly*, p. 33, September 8, 2007; Don Wall, Ph.D., "Debunking the Nuclear Power Threat," *Mensa Bulletin*, March 2008.

46. Don Wall, Ph.D., "Debunking the Nuclear Power Threat," *Mensa Bulletin*, March 2008.

47. Stirling Kelso, "The Age of Increment," *Fast Company*, March 2006.; Janet L. Sawin, "Wind Power Blowing Strong," *Vital Signs 2006-2007*, pp. 36–37 (Chart source also); "The Answer, My Friend?" *The Economist*, October 8, 2006; Janet L. Sawin, "Wind Power Still Soaring," *Vital Signs 2007-2008*, pp. 36–37; Janet L. Sawin, "Wind Power Continues Rapid Rise," *Vital Signs 2009*, pp. 32–33; "Sunlit Uplands," *The Economist: A special report on business and climate change*, p. 16, June 2, 2007; "Wind of change", *The Economist: Technology Quarterly*, p. 22, December 6, 2008.

48. Janet L. Sawin, "Wind Power Blowing Strong," *Vital Signs 2006-2007*, p. 36.

49. Janet L. Sawin, "Solar Industry Stays Hot," *Vital Signs 2006-2007*, p. 38; Janet L. Sawin, "Another Sunny Year for Solar Power," *Vital Signs 2009*, p. 38.

50. "For energy, here comes the sun," *The Week*, p. 22, March 7, 2008; "The start of something big?," *The Economist*, p. 83, July 11, 2009; Janet L. Sawin, "Another Sunny Year for Solar Power," *Vital Signs 2009*, p. 40.

51. "Transparency," *Good Magazine*, p. 33, Nov/Dec 2007.

52. Doug Wilson, "Why 'energy independence' is a distraction," *The Wall Street*

Journal, as reprinted in *The Week*, p. 12, May 11, 2007.

53. Andrew C. Revkin, "Branson Pledges Billions to Fight Global Warming," *The New York Times*, September 21, 2006.

54. Robert Thompson, "The Five-Minute Guide: Oil," *Esquire*, October 2005.

55. SAIC Report, "NJ Aggregated Green Power Purchasing," *EPA Case Studies*, November 2003; "The elusive negawatt," *The Economist*, May 10, 2008.

56. Peter Stair, "Energy Productivity Gains Slow," *Vital Signs 2006-2007*, p. 48.

57. "Face Value: The alternative choice," *The Economist*, p. 64, July 4, 2009

58. Bonnie Tsui, "Greening with Envy," *The Atlantic*, July/August 2009, p. 24; David Zax, "The Last Experiment," *SEED*, June 2009, p. 46.

59. "Endangered Light Bulbs," *The Week*, p. 9, March 2, 2007; Alice McKeown and Nathan Swire, "Strong Growth in Compact Fluorescent Bulbs Reduces Electricity Demand," *World Watch*, Jan/Feb 2009, p. 29.

60. "Behind the Bleeding Edge," *The Economist*, September 23, 2006; "A brilliant new approach," *The Economist*, p. 87, March 21, 2009.

61. "Behind the Bleeding Edge," *The Economist*, September 23, 2006; Gregg Easterbrook, *The Progress Paradox*, p. 286.

62. Nate Silver, "The Real America," *Esquire*, February 2009, p. 56.

63. Eli Kintisch, "Alternative Energy," *Discover*, January 2007.

64. "Charting a More Livable World for All," *The Interdependent*, Fall 2008, p. 21; Doug Cantor and Lamosca, "How to Fix the Future: Water," *Esquire*, December 2008, p. 154.

65. "Global Warming: It's Here . . ." Time, August 24, 1998; Dan Vergano, "The Debate's Over: Globe Is Warming," *USA Today*, p. 1A, June 13, 2005; *Wikipedia*, s.v. "Intergovernmental Panel on Climate Change," http://en.wikipedia.org/wiki/ Intergovernmental_Panel_on_Climate_Change   #IPCC_Fourth_Assessment_ Report:_Climate_Change_2007, (updated October 20, 2007).

66. Nicholas Dawidoff, "The Civil Heretic," *The New York Times Magazine*, http://www. nytimes.com/2009/03/29/magazine/29Dyson-t.html, March 25, 2009.

67. "Global warming: Has it stopped?," *The Week*, p. 18, March 20, 2009.

68. "Face Value: The alternative choice," *The Economist*, p. 64, July 4, 2009; "Plan B for Global Warming?", *The Economist: Technology Quarterly*, pp. 3-4, March 10, 2007; Graeme Wood, "Moving Heaven and Earth," *The Atlantic*, pp. 70-76, July/August 2009.

69. John Tierney, "Use Energy, Get Rich and Save the Planet," *The New York Times*, April 21, 2009.

70. *Ibid.*

71. "Globalization and the Environment," *Foreign Policy*, pp. 66, January/February 2003.

Conclusion

1. E.B. White, *Here is New York*, p. 26–27.

2. Richard Stengel, "The Responsibility Revolution," *Time*, September 21, 2009, p. 38.

3. Allison Fine, Micah L. Sifry, Andrew Rasiej, and Joshua Levy, editors, *Rebooting America*, p. 17.

4. "Track my tax dollars," *The Economist*, February 7, 2009, p. 28; Richard Stengel, "The Responsibility Revolution," *Time*, September 21, 2009, p. 40.

5. Bryan Walsh, "10 Ideas that are Changing the World, #10: Ecological Intelligence," *Time*, March 23, 2009.

6. Daniel Roth, "The Road Map for Recovery," *Wired*, March 2009, p. 81.

7. *Wikipedia*, s.v. "Semantic web," http://en.wikipedia.org/wiki/Semantic_web, (updated September 30, 2009); Erick Schonfeld, "Sneak Peek at T2, Twine's Semantic Search Engine," *TechCrunch*, September 18, 2009, http://www.techcrunch.com/2009/09/18/sneak-peek-at-t2-twines-semantic-search-engine.

8. Reveta Bowers, "On Schools and Education," *What's Next*, Jane Buckingham with Tiffany Ward, p. 23.

9. Jeremy Caplan, "New Ways to Make a Difference," *Time*, September 21, 2009, p. 64.

10. Quoted in Robert J. Samuelson, *Untruth: Why the Conventional Wisdom is (Almost Always) Wrong*, p. 79.

11. "Long live optimism," *The Week*, August 28-September 4, 2009, p. 23.

12. Nathaniel Hawthorne, as quoted on *Quoteworld*, http://www.quoteworld.org/quotes/6331, October 29, 2007.

13. H. G. Wells, *The Shape of Things to Come*, Biographical Note by Patrick Parrinder, p. xi.

14. Martin Luther King, Jr., *Nobel Prize Acceptance Speech*, December 10, 1964.

15. *Wikipedia*, s.v. "Pandora," http://en.wikipedia.org/wiki/Pandora, (updated December 12, 2006); Quote from Victor Hugo, *QuoteDB*, http://www.quotedb.com/quotes/147.

Back cover sources

1. **Nuclear weapons:** Michael Renner, "Mixed Progress on Reducing Nuclear Arsenals," *Vital Signs 2005*, p. 81.
2. **Life expectancy:** "A world of Methuselahs," *The Economist, A special report on ageing populations*, June 27, 2009, p. 7.
3. **Mobile phones:** "The power of mobile money," *The Economist*, September 26, 2009, p. 13.
4. **Literacy:** UNESCO, "Latest Illiteracy Figures," www.uis.unesco.org/en/stats/statistics/literacy2000.htm.
5. **IQ:** Steven Johnson, *Everything Bad is Good For You*, pp. 142-143; *Wikipedia*, s.v. "Flynn Effect," http://en.wikipedia.org/wiki/Flynn_effect, (updated October 25, 2009).
6. **Casualties of war:** John Horgan, "Does Peace Have a Chance?," *Slate*, August 4, 2009, www.slate.com/id/2224275.

INDEX

Page numbers with an f indicate a figure.
Page numbers with an n indicate an endnote.

Keep up with the good news at
www.secretpeace.com

Contact me at
jesse@jesserichards.com

CPSIA information can be obtained at www.ICGtesting.com

231162LV00009B/16/P

9 780984 369508